Finding God in the Gulag

Finding God in the Gulag

A History of Christianity in the Soviet Penal System

JEFFREY S. HARDY

OXFORD
UNIVERSITY PRESS

Oxford University Press is a department of the University of Oxford.
It furthers the University's objective of excellence in research, scholarship,
and education by publishing worldwide. Oxford is a registered trade mark of
Oxford University Press in the UK and in certain other countries.

Published in the United States of America by Oxford University Press
198 Madison Avenue, New York, NY 10016, United States of America.

© Oxford University Press 2024

All rights reserved. No part of this publication may be reproduced, stored in
a retrieval system, or transmitted, in any form or by any means, without the
prior permission in writing of Oxford University Press, or as expressly permitted
by law, by license or under terms agreed with the appropriate reprographics
rights organization. Inquiries concerning reproduction outside the scope of the
above should be sent to the Rights Department, Oxford University Press, at the
address above.

You must not circulate this work in any other form
and you must impose this same condition on any acquirer

Library of Congress Cataloging-in-Publication Data
Names: Hardy, Jeffrey S., 1978– author.
Title: Finding God in the Gulag: a history of Christianity in the Soviet penal system /
Jeffrey S. Hardy.
Description: New York, NY : Oxford University Press, [2024]
Identifiers: LCCN 2024020031 (print) | LCCN 2024020032 (ebook) |
ISBN 9780197751671 (hardback) | ISBN 9780197751695 (epub) | 9780197751701 (online)
Subjects: LCSH: Concentration camps—Soviet Union—History. |
Prisons—Soviet Union—History.
Classification: LCC HV8964.S65 H35 2024 (print) | LCC HV8964.S65 (ebook) |
DDC 365/.450947—dc23/eng/20240722
LC record available at https://lccn.loc.gov/2024020031
LC ebook record available at https://lccn.loc.gov/2024020032

DOI: 10.1093/9780197751701.001.0001

Printed by Sheridan Books, Inc., United States of America

Contents

Preface	vii
Acknowledgments	ix
Introduction	1
1. Separating Church and State in Bolshevik Prisons	14
2. The Spiritual Life of Solovki	39
3. The War against Religion in the Gulag	70
4. Belief and Disbelief from the Great Terror to Stalin's Death	92
5. Western Worshippers and Gulag Gangsters	120
6. Khrushchev's Reforms and the Camp for Sectarians	146
7. Religious Dissidents under Brezhnev	176
8. Christianity as a Re-educational Program	203
Epilogue	223
Notes	231
Bibliography	245
Index	255

Preface

My first exposure to the Soviet Gulag came in ninth grade. This was 1992, just after the collapse of the Soviet Union, and my English teacher assigned *One Day in the Life of Ivan Denisovich*, Alexander Solzhenitsyn's famous novella about Joseph Stalin's labor camps. Most other students found it difficult to understand, boring, or downright inappropriate. In fact, a few in our conservative suburban town in Orange County, California, were sufficiently offended by the swearing (or at least their parents were) that they complained to the school administration, which forced our teacher to apologize to the class—under notable duress—and replace the book. But I was riveted. The whole premise of the story—a seemingly horrible day in a repressive labor camp that is presented as a good one—captivated my young imagination, as did the colorful cast of characters that Solzhenitsyn paraded before his readers. Raised in a devout Christian household, I was particularly moved by the protagonist's interactions with a fictionalized religious inmate, Alyoshka the Baptist.

Alyoshka is the epitome of Christian devotion: prayerful, honest, hardworking, long-suffering, and eager to share his religious convictions with others. He turns a blind eye when other inmates break regulations and readily serves the other men in his labor brigade (even hiding their contraband goods). He keeps a Bible in a secret compartment in the barrack wall and reads passages out loud so that others may hear Jesus Christ's message of martyrdom: "Yet if any man suffer as a Christian, let him not be ashamed; but let him glorify God on this behalf." And in a final conversation just before the end of the story, Alyoshka admonishes the skeptical Ivan Denisovich to pray fervently for salvation. When Ivan protests that no amount of praying would reduce his sentence, Alyoshka quickly replies: "What d'you want your freedom for? What faith you have left will be choked in thorns. Rejoice that you are in prison. Here you can think of your soul."[1]

In the decades following this first exposure to the fascinating world of Soviet prison camps, my interest in the Gulag grew substantially. I learned Russian, visited Gulag sites in and around Magadan (sometimes referred to as the "capital of the Gulag" for its extensive Stalin-era camp complex),

viii PREFACE

spent countless hours in the former Soviet Union's libraries and government archives, and eventually wrote a book, *The Gulag after Stalin*, on how Nikita Khrushchev's regime transformed the Soviet penal system. During my research, I came across many accounts of Christians in the camps and ultimately decided that another book was needed to tell their story. A book about those who, like the semifictional Alyoshka the Baptist, prayed, communed with coreligionists, celebrated Easter, read the Bible, and shared their beliefs with others. A book about prisoners who converted to Christianity and those who lost their faith in God amid the terrible tragedy of the Gulag. A book also about guards and administrators who fought against or chose to ignore religious practice among their inmates.[2]

Finding God in the Gulag is that book. If it provides intellectual stimulation, satisfies a bit of historical curiosity, or helps you explore your own beliefs and values, then it will have succeeded in its intent. It has undoubtedly accomplished these things for me.

Acknowledgments

I received advice and assistance from numerous people and institutions while writing *Finding God in the Gulag*. The College of Family, Home, and Social Sciences and the Kennedy Center for International Studies at Brigham Young University provided generous research funding, as did the Oxford-based Keston Institute. Archivists at the Memorial Society in Moscow; the State Archive of the Russian Federation; the Keston Center for Religion, Politics and Society at Baylor University; and various other archives graciously shared their expertise. Members of the Carolina Russia Seminar and participants in several conference panels over the years asked penetrating questions about my research and provided valuable feedback on early chapter drafts. Steve Barnes, Judith Pallot, Alan Barenberg, Emily Johnson, Wilson Bell, and Tyler Kirk, among others, have been instrumental in shaping my thoughts about the Gulag and its inhabitants. A number of student research assistants—Nina Linchenko, Spencer Kelly, Amy Daniel, Danielle Leavitt-Quist, Zander White, Jacob Stebbing, Aaron Palmer, and Michael Green— helped with various aspects of this project. Joseph Stuart assisted in making final revisions to improve readability. Portions of chapter 2 were previously published in *Rethinking the Gulag: Identities, Sources, Legacies* (edited by Alan Barenberg and Emily D. Johnson, 2022), and I am grateful to Indiana University Press for permission to republish them here.[1]

Closer to home, I am grateful to my parents, Rachel and Arnold Hardy, for editing an early draft of a few chapters and always supporting my various pursuits. Most of all, I am thankful for my wife, Pam, and my children, Brianna, Jared, and Ashley. They are the primary source of inspiration and love in my life. This book could not have been written without them.

Introduction

In early 1923, a Baptist parish in the Russian city of Vyazma was forcibly closed by local authorities of the newly formed Union of Soviet Socialist Republics (USSR). This was six years after the Bolshevik Revolution of 1917 and two years after the conclusion of the Russian Civil War, which saw the Bolshevik "red" forces emerge victorious over several "white" armies. Vyazma leaders, guided by the ruling ideology of Marxism-Leninism, were attempting to diminish religious influence among the population while also turning this particular church building into a dormitory for factory workers. Several church leaders were arrested for protesting this small step on the path to Soviet-style socialism, and when parishioners descended on the local branch of the secret police to petition for their release, the deputy chief "with a smile remarked: 'let them sit for a while [in prison] in the name of Jesus Christ.'"[1]

Sit they did, as did countless other Christians imprisoned by Soviet authorities from 1917 until 1991. Some, like the Vyazma Baptists, were arrested for directly protesting the radical socialist regime's antireligious policies. Some were detained for their continued religious activism—leading congregations, conducting missionary work, organizing Sunday schools, or mobilizing young people into Christian societies. And some were arrested for a host of nonreligious reasons: political opposition to Soviet power, national or class identity, or "ordinary" crimes such as theft or assault. These Christians brought their beliefs and practices to the camps and prisons of the Soviet Gulag, which was designed, in theory, to re-educate criminals and ideological enemies and turn them into conscientious Soviet citizens. And although their experiences while imprisoned varied considerably, faith played an integral role in the lives of many Gulag inmates, both individually and collectively.

It may be surprising that religious practice could survive in the Gulag, which gained infamy for hard labor, violence, and death. Religion was

---

Finding God in the Gulag. Jeffrey S. Hardy, Oxford University Press. © Oxford University Press 2024.
DOI: 10.1093/9780197751701.003.0001

2 FINDING GOD IN THE GULAG

supposed to be extirpated from Soviet society, although Soviet leaders from Vladimir Lenin onward persistently wavered on how and how quickly this was to be done. The country's penal institutions presented a logical place where this could be first accomplished; after all, they were supposedly tightly controlled environments run by the Soviet secret police. But notable in many memoirs and letters written by religious and nonreligious prisoners alike is how they characterize the prisons and labor camps as liberating in some ways. Living communally with inmates from various national, intellectual, and religious traditions and no longer afraid of arrest, they used the experience of imprisonment to interact with and learn from each other. As the religious philosopher Dmitry Likhachev, imprisoned in the 1920s, remarked of his imprisonment, "Suffering, repression and terror were by no means the whole picture. Intellectual life did go on, to a degree, even in the awful conditions of the camps and the prisons, and that intellectual life was even extremely intense in some cases, when people accustomed to thought and wishing to think found themselves brought together."[2] Many other religious inmates shared this observation regarding the vibrancy of spiritual and intellectual life in the camp. They prayed, sang, read scripture, and endured punishment together, seeing their collective suffering as part of God's will. Institutional control over inmates, it turned out, was never fully accomplished by Soviet agencies of repression.

For Christian inmates, faith in God often provided both a moral compass and a reserve of inner strength. It offered a cohesive worldview that at once challenged and accepted Bolshevism as a sign of the "last days." Religious Gulag prisoners frequently affirmed the observation made by Holocaust survivor Viktor Frankl that people with meaning in life are best suited to survive the worst atrocities and emerge with their dignity intact. Yet the intense pressures of the Gulag meant many believers did not survive, and not all who did retained their faith. Camp officials often repressed religious practice, and exhaustion, starvation, and complex interpersonal relationships among inmates blurred the lines of moral behavior. The question of why God allowed such terrible suffering, especially by those who identified as his chosen people, never went away. Some found meaning, but little comfort, in their suffering. They wrestled with God as they wrestled their bodies to perform grueling labor in the bitter cold. Others found only hopelessness and despair. The religious history of the Gulag, in other words, defies easy explanations.[3]

INTRODUCTION   3

The Gulag and Pre-Gulag Penal System

This book stands at the intersection of the Gulag and the history of Christianity in the USSR. These are both enormous topics, and a few words of background for each are needed before proceeding further. The Russian Revolution of 1917 brought to power a radical regime bent on the wholesale transformation of Russia and, eventually, the world. Promising an end to the exploitative structures of autocracy and capitalism, Lenin and his fellow Bolsheviks proclaimed a new era of class warfare, economic socialism, and "true" democracy that would ultimately create a classless socialist society, one that was happier and more productive than its capitalist counterparts. Innovations in the economy, education, labor, culture, and seemingly every aspect of everyday life defined this quest to build socialism. In late 1922, the USSR was formed, boasting a federal state structure that implied a "brotherhood" of equal nations—Russia, Ukraine, Armenia, and so forth—striving toward socialism together. Soviet leaders also propagandized global revolution, particularly among European workers and the colonized peoples of Africa and Asia. While socialist revolutions in other parts of the globe for the most part failed to materialize, optimism in the future burned bright among the Bolshevik faithful.

Reality, however, fell far short of lofty expectations due to several problems. For one thing, no country had ever adopted Marxist socialism, and all the theoretical treatises of the preceding decades did little to prepare the Bolshevik regime for the challenges inherent in governing a vast and impoverished country brought to ruin by World War I. The Bolsheviks also had to confront the reality that they were not popular in their own country, a fact made painfully evident by a terrible civil war (1918–1921) that resulted in millions of deaths and massive economic destruction. A harsh famine then devastated the countryside in the early 1920s, with millions perishing from hunger and disease. These realities forced Lenin to make a strategic retreat from socialism; his New Economic Policy of the 1920s allowed capitalism to flourish alongside nascent socialist structures. But Lenin himself died in 1924 without a clear successor, setting off a vicious succession struggle ultimately won by Joseph Stalin. Altogether, this meant that the first decade of the Soviet experiment was marked more by confusion and contradiction than by progress toward a fundamentally new socioeconomic system. This confusion and contradiction are certainly evident in early policies concerning imprisonment.

4   FINDING GOD IN THE GULAG

When people think of imprisonment in the Soviet Union, they typically, and rightly so, think of the Gulag. *Gulag* is a Stalin-era acronym for the Main Administration of Camps, a division within the Soviet secret police apparatus that managed the country's prisons and labor camps. It functioned as the Soviet Union's penal system, to which people were sent both by Soviet courts and by extrajudicial bodies of the secret police. It was created by Stalin in 1929 and endured until the end of the Soviet Union, albeit with a changed name after Stalin's death in 1953. Tens of millions of people were sent to the Gulag over the course of its existence, and millions of them perished. It was a terrible institution of repression and death.

Already in 1917, twelve years before the Gulag's creation, the Soviet regime began imprisoning people according to ideas and institutions both inherited from the prerevolutionary period and found in Bolshevik ideology. By the late 1800s, the tsarist regime had earned international notoriety for its brutal practice of Siberian exile. Romanov monarchs sent hundreds of thousands of people, including Polish nationalists and socialists of various stripes, east of the Ural Mountains, where they met harsh living conditions and compulsory labor. Although reformers within the imperial administration proposed to end Siberian exile in the late 1800s, it remained a central part of the tsarist judicial system until 1917. At the same time, the Russian Empire sent increasing numbers of prisoners to European-style penitentiaries. Rather than simply exact retribution, these prisons were intended to convert criminals into law-abiding and productive citizens prepared to enter the workforce upon release. The results of such efforts in Russia and elsewhere were mixed at best, and contemporary critics and modern historians have long questioned the effectiveness and sincerity of the aim of rehabilitation.[4]

Notably, penitentiaries in Russia and the West used religion as part of their rehabilitation programs. Quakers and other politically active Christian reformers in the United Kingdom, the United States, and elsewhere lobbied for incarceration as the preferred method for punishing and reforming lawbreakers starting in the late 1700s and early 1800s. Due to their influence, penitentiaries were built with chapels at the fulcrum of radiating cell blocks, signifying the centrality of religion in state-sponsored punishment. Religious images and maxims hung on cell walls, regulations mandated Bible study and prayer, chaplains visited prisoners, and administrators expected inmates to repent of their sins against God and society. The penitentiary was thus developed not only as a place of punishment and civic rehabilitation; it was a place of atonement, where wayward souls could become converted to Christianity and the norms of Christian society.[5]

When the Bolsheviks seized power in October 1917, they inherited much of the tsarist judicial system and its places of confinement. The interim Provisional Government, which briefly ruled Russia following the abdication of Nicholas II in March 1917, had abolished Siberian exile, but its memory was still fresh. Tsarist prisons, meanwhile, remained in use by the new political regime, as did detention camps for enemy combatants captured during World War I. This meant that Lenin and his associates, many of whom had served time in prisons and Siberian exile, had multiple existing models for dealing with convicts and enemies of the regime. Ultimately, the Soviet penal system drew from all these institutions: prisons, camps, and exile.

Curiously, there was little in Marxist ideology that could readily contribute to a reimagined penal system. Karl Marx and his followers believed that crime would wither away in a socialist society as the conditions of capitalist exploitation were abolished and new generations of people received a proper education free from the vices of greed and selfishness. In the meantime, Bolsheviks relied heavily on the old regime's penal institutions and ideas, along with many of its employees. The Soviet penal system was not, in other words, strictly a product of Marxist ideology, even if Marxist ideology would help determine which features of exile, the penitentiary, and the camp would be adopted. Nor was the Gulag a preconceived plan devised by Lenin or Stalin before the revolution.[6]

During the late 1910s and into the 1920s, Soviet politicians, judicial officials, and criminologists fiercely debated how best to combat crime and divergent political ideas through, in Lenin's words, both "persuasion and coercion." At first, incarceration in prisons and concentration camps (a term the Bolsheviks used unabashedly in this era) aimed to isolate criminals, class enemies, and "white guardists" (those who fought against the Bolsheviks in the Russian Civil War of 1918–1921) from society. But even as the civil war was ongoing, the discussion of how to reform prisoners commenced. As secret police boss Felix Dzerzhinsky made clear in 1920, Soviet concentration camps existed to isolate criminals and "parasites"—upper-class individuals characterized as living off the labor of others—and to teach them how to "live by honest labor." Dzerzhinsky frankly acknowledged the difficulty of this task, as these people had been raised in a corrupt capitalist system, yet he insisted that it was necessary. For those who proved particularly intransigent, Dzerzhinsky proposed harsh prison regimens similar to those of

6 FINDING GOD IN THE GULAG

the tsarist era to force such inmates to prioritize survival and modify their behavior accordingly. Crucially, this included a hard labor requirement so that "their labor, their muscular labor, would not be wasted." Dzerzhinsky's comments make clear that from its earliest years, the Soviet regime was interested in both isolation and rehabilitation, but it was also intent on creating harsh living conditions and extracting hard labor from its prisoners. Labor was at the heart of Bolshevik ideology, with top officials loudly repeating the biblical maxim "He who does not work shall not eat." And so it is not surprising that work was mandated in early Soviet penal facilities as both a method of re-education and a means of punishment.[7]

Creating a consistent ideology for places of incarceration was complicated by the chaotic nature of the early Soviet state. Three separate government agencies in the 1920s operated penal facilities: the People's Commissariat of Internal Affairs, the People's Commissariat of Justice, and the secret police. Some penal officials were most concerned with creating financially self-supporting institutions based on inmate labor. Others emphasized "re-educating" inmates using labor, educational programs, cultural productions, communal living, and inmate self-governance to try to stimulate new patterns of thought and behavior. Psychological and sociological experiments were conducted on inmates as Soviet social scientists attempted to better understand the nature of crime and the best way to "correct" criminals. And prison bosses were instructed "to remove all kinds of torture, by no means allowing these methods of physical influence: shackles, handcuffs, the penalty isolator, strictly solitary confinement, deprivation of food or of meeting with visitors through the bars." Yet not all agreed with such leniency. The secret police in particular was more interested in creating harsh conditions to punish enemies of the regime and scaring people away from committing crimes. Ultimately, it was the labor camps of the secret police that served as the central model on which the Gulag would be built starting in 1930.[8]

So what defined the Gulag? What distinguished it, at least in part, from other penal institutions? First, although the Gulag featured some prisons with individual cells, most inmates served time in camp-type institutions that featured communal barracks, dining halls, and other gathering places. In the 1920s, these were often called concentration camps or camps of special significance, among other names, while from the 1930s onward, they were known as corrective-labor camps or corrective-labor colonies. This collectivist incarceration model was quite different from the penitentiary systems of the West and adhered to Bolshevik ideology, which emphasized the reformative power of the collective. It also squared with the persistent scarcity of resources in the USSR—camps were much cheaper to construct and maintain than penitentiaries, allowing investments to be made in factories, hydroelectric dams, and railroads instead. These camps' location in the remotest corners of the Soviet Union also set them apart from other prison systems. In this, they resembled the old system of Siberian exile, with prisoners transported hundreds or thousands of miles away from their homes.[9]

A second central feature of the Gulag was compulsory labor. All inmates were expected to work, and they performed a dizzying array of tasks: railroad construction, coal mining, timber felling, agriculture, power plant construction, furniture making, sewing, and so forth. According to Soviet penal ideology, labor benefited society, paid for the costs of imprisonment, and taught convicts how to live healthy, productive lives. But to inmates forced to work twelve or fourteen hours a day, often in harsh climatic conditions, compulsory labor felt much more like harsh retributive punishment than a life skills program. Thus, whereas many penal systems expect inmates to work in some capacity, the ruthless exploitation of Gulag prisoners as a source of labor power was exceptional.[10]

Indeed, hard labor in remote locations, particularly under Stalin, help explain the Gulag's third central feature: high rates of violence and mortality. While most penal systems are violent to some extent, the Gulag was excessively so. Prisoners rarely had enough to eat, endured harsh treatment by guards, were vulnerable to criminal gangs among the inmate population, were often denied proper medical treatment, and faced terrible living and working conditions. Under Stalin, millions of people died in the Gulag. And they perished not because they received a death sentence but because vindictiveness and neglect, informed by an unsparing ideological stance against perceived enemies, produced malnutrition, exhaustion, disease, and acts of outright physical violence. Millions more survived the Gulag but suffered injury, psychological trauma, and shortened life spans.[11]

The final and perhaps most important distinguishing feature of the Gulag concerned its inmates. This was a massive institution that under Stalin held between 1 million and 2.5 million people. More than 20 million people served time in the Gulag from the 1930s to the early 1950s. Moreover, the inmates were not just common criminals; the Soviets also imprisoned millions of people for ideological or political reasons. As a high-ranking member of the secret police expressed at a conference on June 11, 1918, "the

8   FINDING GOD IN THE GULAG

revolution has laid on us the struggle with its enemies, and we are obligated to beat them mercilessly." Bolsheviks imprisoned various "class enemies"— wealthy businessmen, members of the old nobility, rich peasants who hired other peasants to work for them—along with ideological opponents ranging from monarchists to anarchists as they struggled to retain power during the civil war of 1918–1921. And this established a precedent for decades to come. While "counterrevolutionary" prisoners never represented a majority of the Gulag population, Bolsheviks imprisoned millions for suspected disloyalty.[12]

Religion in the Russian Empire and the Soviet Union

Prominent among "counterrevolutionaries" imprisoned by the Soviet Union were clergymen and other devout religious believers. The Russian Empire, before its collapse, was a place of religious intensity and diversity. Russian Orthodoxy, an autonomous branch of Eastern Orthodoxy, was the official state religion dating back to Prince Vladimir's famous conversion in 988. Onion-domed temples, walled monasteries, and wooden parish churches, symbols of Orthodoxy's power and wealth, dotted the Russian heartland. Monasticism played a vital role in the empire's spiritual life, as did pilgrimages to sacred sites such as the Monastery of St. Sergius outside of Moscow. Church rituals (baptisms, the weekly liturgy, confession, prayer, making the sign of the cross, weddings, last rites) and Orthodox-infused legal codes (with prohibitions against blasphemy, marrying outside of the faith, or converting to a different religion) helped define daily life for tens of millions of people. And Russia's rulers relied on the doctrine of the "divine right of kings" that defined them as intermediaries between God and the Russian people. The double-headed eagle on the Russian Empire's state seal signified this seamless union of church and state.

Several critical developments in Russian Orthodoxy took place in the nineteenth century. First, as education became important for the middle class and peasantry, the church opened thousands of parish schools. Thus, most schoolchildren in Russia before the revolution learned at the hands of their local clergymen. Second, as elsewhere in Europe, industrialization and rising educational levels contributed to a decline in religious observance, although monasticism experienced a resurgence as many sought refuge from the callous world of industrial capitalism. Third, a religiously infused Russian nationalism became the empire's ruling ideology starting in the

INTRODUCTION   9

1830s. This translated into stronger efforts to convert non-Orthodox subjects to Orthodoxy as part of the broader program of Russification (turning non-Russians into Russians in terms of language, culture, and religion). This was, at best, an uneven process but one that demonstrates the continued importance of faith in the late empire. In the wake of the 1905 revolution, Nicholas II grudgingly granted freedom of religion to his subjects as part of a broader set of liberal reforms. But this hardly reduced the church's influence in imperial affairs, with Orthodoxy remaining a powerful institution and set of beliefs.[13]

As Nicholas II's concession to religious liberty implies, many people in the Russian Empire were not Orthodox. Millions of Russian subjects identified with breakaway sects from Orthodoxy—Old Believers, Dukhobors, Molokans, Khlysts, and Skoptsy prominent among them—and periodically suffered from religiously motivated state repression. Many of them in the nineteenth century fled Russia to the United States, Canada, and other countries where they could more freely practice their faith. Ukrainian Greek Catholics (also known as Uniates, considered by some a pejorative term), who followed Orthodox worship practices but officially aligned with the Catholic Church, were prominent in Ukraine, although many were subjected to forced conversion to Russian Orthodoxy in the nineteenth century. Imperial expansion into the Baltics (Estonia, Latvia, Lithuania), Poland, Finland, Georgia, and Armenia in the 1700s and 1800s brought large numbers of Catholic, Lutheran, Georgian Orthodox, and Armenian Orthodox believers into the empire. Mennonites from the Low Countries and Germany fled to Russia to escape persecution in their native lands in the late 1700s and early 1800s, but many then fled Russia in the late 1800s and early 1900s as Russification policies ended the special religious protections they had previously enjoyed. Finally, a few Christian groups—Baptists, Seventh-Day Adventists, and Jehovah's Witnesses among them—began to spread in the Russian Empire in the late 1800s and early 1900s through intensive proselytization.

The extent of this religious diversity is reflected in the 1897 census (the first and last comprehensive census taken in the Russian Empire). Considered generally reliable, it counted roughly 87 million Orthodox believers (69.3 percent of the total population), 11.5 million Catholics (9.1 percent), 3.5 million Lutherans (2.8 percent), 2.2 million Old Believers (1.8 percent), 1.2 million Armenia Orthodox believers (0.9 percent), and a few hundred thousand other Christians. At least on paper, this meant that various strands

10   FINDING GOD IN THE GULAG

of Christianity accounted for approximately 85 percent of the population when the Bolsheviks took power in 1917. The empire also had large numbers of non-Christian believers. Muslims numbered around 14 million (11 percent of the total population) in 1897. The partitions of Poland in the late 1700s brought the majority of Europe's Jews under Russian rule, and by 1900, they numbered some 5.2 million (4.3 percent of the Russian Empire). Beyond the Urals, Buddhism and shamanism contributed to the Russian Empire's diverse religious ecosystem.

As followers of Marx, Lenin and his fellow Bolsheviks opposed organized religion and religious beliefs generally, calling them no more than primitive superstitions. Marx famously identified religion as "the opiate of the masses," a pacifying weapon wielded by the bourgeoisie to exploit the working class. And Lenin echoed this sentiment, calling churches "instruments of bourgeois reaction that serve to defend exploitation and to befuddle the working class." It came as no surprise, therefore, that the Bolsheviks launched an attack on religious institutions and beliefs upon seizing power in 1917. New laws separated the Orthodox Church from state structures. The educational system was secularized. Priests, pastors, imams, rabbis, and other religious officials were imprisoned as early as 1918, and when Bolshevik officials announced an amnesty for prisoners in November 1918, the secret police insisted that "priests carrying out counterrevolutionary agitation" should not be released. The terrible famine of 1921–1922 brought a new wave of repression against the Russian Orthodox clergy, as many resisted confiscation of church valuables to help provide relief for those afflicted (arguing, with good reason, that the Bolsheviks had ulterior motives for appropriating icons, sacraments dishes, and gold-leafed cupolas). In the 1920s, the Bolsheviks organized antireligious societies, such as the League of Militant Atheists, and disseminated antireligious messages through posters, newspapers, magazines, school lessons, and political lectures. Indeed, staunch opposition to religion quickly became a defining and enduring feature of the Soviet Union.[14]

However, the fact that religion endured throughout the USSR's existence illustrates that this assault on religion never fully succeeded. The Soviet Union was a massive country where religious ideas and practices were historically ingrained in culture and society, and the Bolsheviks, especially at first, had limited state capacity to carry out their radical agenda. But there was more than just scarce resources holding back the Soviet assault. At times, Soviet leaders spoke and acted as if secularism—the complete separation of church and state—was the only aim of government policy and that atheism, agnosticism, and religious belief were matters of individual conscience. To understand this position, one must remember that the Soviet regime was steeped in the Enlightenment language of human rights and that it enshrined freedom of conscience and religious worship alongside other civil liberties in successive constitutions. From its inception, therefore, the conflicted Bolshevik regime sought to reconcile freedom of religion with the desire to stamp out religion in the quest to build socialism.[15]

This inherent contradiction—whether to pursue an aggressive program of atheism or only ensure state secularism—meant that Soviet authorities wrestled with a range of questions concerning religious belief and practice. For example, the state required each Christian parish to set up a "religious association" led by parishioners rather than clerics and subsume church property under its control. This policy, in theory, removed power from the church hierarchy and gave it to ordinary citizens. But many local Soviet officials, inclined to stamp out religion altogether, rejected applications to create such religious associations and simply shut down the parishes instead. Another example of this tension was the Living Church, organized by the secret police along with a handful of ideologically supportive clergymen, which tried to seize the reins of Orthodox spiritual authority in the USSR. Bolshevik authorities pressured Orthodox priests and bishops to join the Living Church, and they exiled or imprisoned some who refused. This attempt to splinter the Orthodox hierarchy largely failed, and the Living Church would ultimately be abolished, but in the meantime, it put the Soviet regime in the odd position of actively supporting religious belief and practice. Indeed, contradiction defined Soviet religious policy, with antireligious repression ebbing and flowing throughout the USSR's existence.[16]

Many religious leaders in Russia actively condemned the Bolsheviks' antireligious actions. Most prominently, the head of the Russian Orthodox Church, Patriarch Tikhon, adopted a fierce anti-Bolshevik stance, declaring that they were the devil's emissaries. In response, Soviet officials harassed Tikhon and placed him under house arrest in the Donskoy Monastery. After his death in 1925, his successor, Metropolitan Sergius, pursued a more conciliatory line toward Soviet power to save the Orthodox community from destruction. This approach, however, caused Tikhon's supporters to form several breakaway movements to avoid association with a church that recognized Soviet power as legitimate. Such tensions could likewise be found in the Soviet Union's other major religious denominations as they struggled

12   FINDING GOD IN THE GULAG

to adapt to the new reality of Soviet power. Catholics, Baptists, Muslims, Jews, and others faced waves of repression from Bolshevik authorities, along with attempts to splinter their leadership ranks. For many Christians in this era, the Bolsheviks represented Satan's kingdom on earth, part of the chaotic events leading to the second coming of Jesus Christ foretold in the apocalyptic Book of Revelation.[17]

Yet not everyone mourned the displacement of Orthodoxy as the state religion or the general attack on organized religion. In addition to non-Orthodox believers who had long resented the state backing of Orthodoxy and saw in the Bolshevik Revolution a chance to live a freer spiritual life, there is a long history in Russia of people who only went through the motions of religious devotion for cultural or familial reasons or because they resented the church's authority and practices. Ordinary Russians often despised corrupt priests who lived lavishly on villagers' labor, so, understandably, some people cheered when their priests were repressed by Bolshevik authorities. And many were happy to be able to live their lives free from social pressure to conform to a set of religious beliefs and practices. In the end, however, those who adamantly opposed Soviet power on religious grounds, those who tried to reconcile their faith with the new political reality, and those who cheered Soviet antireligious policies all found themselves liable to imprisonment. And in the Gulag, belief, worship, secularism, and atheism all coexisted and interacted, sometimes in unexpected ways.

Note on Sources

I have consulted a wide array of sources while writing this book. Some are documents created by Gulag authorities, including decrees, reports, instructions, and various pieces of propaganda. These are useful for illustrating the state's view of religion in the Gulag and its efforts to combat belief. Most sources, however, were produced by prisoners—both religious and nonreligious—including memoirs, letters, petitions, poems, and artifacts. These firsthand accounts help illuminate the inner spiritual lives and collective outer lives of religiously active inmates.

None of these sources was created without purpose or bias. Gulag authorities wrote within a Marxist ideological framework and often attacked or attempted to downplay religious life in their institutions. Meanwhile, memoirs suffer from memory problems inherent in the act of narrative construction. Many memoirs written by religious inmates, for instance, were designed to showcase the glory of God and expose the evil practices of the Soviet regime. Historians must therefore be on guard against hyperbole and the possibility of outright invention. For this reason, I have chosen to exclude some of the more sensational memoirs and other sources out of concern for their unreliability. But the available sources cannot all be rejected because of their inherent biases—all sources reflect a particular perspective. In fact, one of this book's aims is to show how authorities and inmates alike interpreted and represented religiosity in the Gulag, attributing spiritual or ideological meaning to both ordinary and extraordinary occurrences.

Throughout this book, I aim to follow the lead of other scholars of religion in taking spiritual phenomena seriously. As a historian, I cannot examine the veracity of reported miracles, visions, or spiritual sensations, but I do accept that Christians in the Gulag genuinely believed that they experienced such things. And because these things mattered to them, they matter to me as I narrate their stories. To be sure, religion can at once be deeply meaningful but also utilitarian, and I will explore this tension in the pages that follow. But religion is experienced not just as a social construction or psychological crutch; it is often experienced as "the real presence of the supernatural in relationship with humans." As a historian, I endeavor to present it as such.[18]

This book uses two systems for transliterating Russian. The endnotes and bibliography employ the precise Library of Congress system typically used by academic historians. For the main text, however, I use a modified system for improved readability. Diacritical marks signifying the soft and hard signs in Russian are omitted (Tver instead of Tver'), "y" is employed in place of "ii" and "yi" (Dmitry instead of Dmitrii), and an initial "y" is added to words beginning in "e" or "iu" (Yuvenaly instead of Iuvenalii). I also use standardized names for persons and place names where appropriate (Alexander instead of Aleksandr; Moscow instead of Moskva).

1

Separating Church and State in Bolshevik Prisons

The day started normally on Wednesday, September 7, 1921, at the Andronevsky Special-Purpose Camp in eastern Moscow. The inmates of this historic Russian Orthodox monastery (see figure 1.1), which the young Bolshevik regime had converted into a prison camp during the civil war, worked during the day and then prepared for lights out at ten p.m. At midnight, however, the commander was informed that a group of female inmates was singing. They were Catholic, and the following day was the Feast of the Nativity of Mary. The commander, upset at this disturbance, ordered a guard to make them stop and go to sleep, but "they did not obey, they continued to sing and started to dance." The guard then informed the two ringleaders that they would be taken to the penalty cell, but they just "started to laugh." When more guards were brought in to force the issue, the rest of the inmates insisted on being taken as well, "since all had taken part in the singing and dancing." After just thirty minutes in the penalty cell, the Catholic women were released, but in the morning, they refused to go to work, as did other inmates who sympathized with them. The assistant commander on duty negotiated with them and ultimately persuaded them to cease their protest and go to work in the afternoon. Nothing more is known of this incident, but one thing is clear: imprisoned Christians in the Soviet Union found ways to preserve a strong sense of communal religious identity. And this inspired even nonreligious prisoners to side with them against Soviet authorities.[1]

Vladimir Lenin's Bolsheviks began their assault on religion shortly after seizing power in 1917. They executed, exiled, and imprisoned an array of religious authorities and lay believers, and those who remained free were subject to the same second-class citizenship imposed on wealthy capitalists and former agents of the tsarist secret police. Counterintuitively, though, the 1918 constitution (and subsequent Soviet constitutions) guaranteed freedom of religion, even promising "shelter to all foreigners who seek refuge from political or religious persecution." Political activists (including among the

Finding God in the Gulag. Jeffrey S. Hardy, Oxford University Press. © Oxford University Press 2024.
DOI: 10.1093/9780197751701.003.0002

Figure 1.1 Andronikov Monastery, 1887. Wikimedia Commons.

Bolsheviks) and religious believers immediately noted this contradiction. As a petition from one group of evangelical Christians to Soviet authorities hopefully declared, "A complete amnesty is needed for everyone suffering for their religious convictions, whether imprisoned or in exile. . . . In other words, we need to truly provide for the freedom of conscience and religion in the U.S.S.R." In fact, lay believers sometimes secured their incarcerated leaders' release, appealing to the constitution's right to exercise their religious liberty. But others had their petitions denied, leaving their priests and pastors to languish behind bars.[2]

This chapter tells the story of Soviet policymakers, guards, and prisoners in the late 1910s and 1920s as the fledgling Soviet regime negotiated thorny questions of religion and repression. Built-in tensions between the conflicting values of coercion, persuasion, freedom of conscience, secularism, and atheism affected a variety of day-to-day concerns in the prisons and concentration camps of Soviet Russia. Early Soviet penal officials wrestled with questions of whether they could use religious buildings as places of confinement, whether religious inmates could claim exemptions from labor on sacred days, and whether inmates could attend worship services and otherwise

16 FINDING GOD IN THE GULAG

practice their religion while incarcerated. They also made early forays into the use of antireligious propaganda.

In order to illustrate these tensions, this chapter relies heavily on sources produced by the regime itself: orders, reports, questionnaires, and various forms of propaganda. These sources often betray a Marxist worldview and a desire to build a new socialist society, but they also reflect a high degree of uncertainty and improvisation. Many guards and administrators were holdovers from the tsarist regime and not ideologically aligned with the Bolsheviks. And with little established policy concerning the intersection of religion and incarceration, local penal officials in the early years of Soviet power were often left to make their own decisions. This resulted in a surprising variety of decentralized policies that produced a repressive antireligious environment for some inmates while others openly worshipped and communed with fellow believers.

From Monasteries to Prisons

Upon seizing power in late 1917, the Bolshevik regime inherited many prisons and camps from the Russian Empire, but these quickly proved insufficient. Repression against class enemies, political opponents, common criminals, and combatants in the civil war of 1918–1921 produced a dramatic rise in the number of inmates, and it became immediately apparent that more places of confinement were needed. Curiously, the Bolsheviks turned to holy sites of Christian worship to establish many of these new prisons and camps. While some churches, monasteries, and other religious buildings were destroyed in the general assault on religion in the early Soviet period, many more were confiscated and repurposed. Some became hospitals, factories, barracks, or museums, while others were converted into warehouses or grain silos. It helped in this era of scarcity that churches were often the largest and sturdiest buildings in a particular area. Thus, even as the Bolsheviks declared a complete separation of church and state, they relied heavily on places of worship for the well-constructed indoor spaces they provided.[3]

The hundreds of Orthodox monasteries and convents dotting the former Russian Empire were the most attractive religious buildings for penal officials. These typically had fortified defensive walls to separate their inhabitants from the outside world, and their internal architecture featured cells where the monks or nuns had lived. They also had various communal spaces—kitchens, dining halls, workshops, and chapels—that could be readily used or repurposed. Already supporting self-sufficient communities before the revolution, monasteries and convents were almost perfectly suited for use as penal facilities. In fact, some had been used as prisons before the revolution, with the monks or nuns serving as jailers in the complicated judicial system of prerevolutionary Russia.

Monasteries in both large cities and remote rural locations were converted into penal facilities in the late 1910s and early 1920s, yet not all were found to be of equal value. In the provincial city of Yaroslavl, for example, concentration camps were set up at the Spassky Monastery and the Kazansky Monastery. Polish prisoners of war were housed in the former during the civil war, while the latter held hundreds of White Army officers as of early 1921. According to an inspection report from that year, however, while the Kazansky Monastery was in good shape, the Spassky Monastery was "so dilapidated that there is no other option than to swiftly close it and transfer its prisoners to other quarters." Shortly thereafter, the Yaroslavl archival department assumed responsibility for the facility (poor archivists!), and its prisoners were moved into the old Yaroslavl Provincial Prison (which had functioned as a military supply depot during the civil war). One immediately gets the sense from such reports that Soviet authorities were anxious to transform society but struggled to know precisely how to accomplish this.[4]

Moscow, which replaced Petrograd (St. Petersburg) as the capital city in 1918, provides perhaps the best glimpse at how the Bolsheviks converted religious compounds into penal facilities. Twelve concentration camps operated in the city itself between 1918 and 1922, along with several others in the surrounding Moscow Province, and many of these were repurposed monasteries. The Ivanovsky Convent in the central Kitay-gorod neighborhood of Moscow became the Ivanovsky Camp in 1918, and as of November 17, 1921, it held 316 men and 41 women guarded by 33 staff. In 1926, this complex was converted into the Experimental-Penitentiary Department of the State Institute for Studying Criminals and Criminality and was used to conduct psychological and sociological experiments into inmate re-education. The Rozhdestvenny Convent was turned into a concentration camp on July 1, 1920, though it closed just a year and a half later. The Pokrovsky Monastery became a concentration camp in May 1921 and housed several hundred inmates—most of them condemned by Soviet courts—until its closure in October 1922.

18 FINDING GOD IN THE GULAG

A search for suitable facilities for prison camps in Moscow Province illustrates the attractiveness of monasteries as camps and the indecisiveness of the young Bolshevik regime. In the town of Zvenigorod, just west of Moscow, criminals and prisoners of war were initially housed in the Savino-Storozhevsky Monastery, but then Bolshevik authorities decided to turn it into a health resort for Moscow's workers. On May 3, 1920, the Main Administration of Places of Confinement reported on its resultant efforts to find a new place for the inmates. "Above all," it began, "it is necessary to find buildings with suitable conditions for becoming camps." To this effect, it asked various provincial officials for lists of buildings that offered good prospects and ultimately inspected two locations, both convents that provided sufficient space and economic opportunity. First, the Spaso-Vlakhernsky Convent near Dedenev could hold up to 350 inmates, was conveniently located close to a railroad station, and had sufficient arable land to employ prisoners. Second, the Pokrovsky Convent at Khotkovo could hold up to 600 inmates and provide opportunities for agricultural labor and other jobs. Two days after these inspections, the order was given to convert the Spaso-Vlakhernsky Convent, which held 246 nuns (two-thirds of whom were characterized as old and unable to labor), into the needed camp. The local church council that administered the convent was summoned and informed of the news, but it protested vigorously. An appeal was granted, and the convent was ultimately allowed to continue operating because it was dutifully fulfilling its labor assignment, manufacturing insignia for the Red Army. Though viewed by the Bolsheviks as "non-laboring elements," it was ultimately the nuns' labor that saved their convent from closure [5]

As a different location was now needed, a new search was initiated, and three convents were identified as possible locations for the needed camp: the "fully suitable" Golovinsky Convent, which could hold 400 inmates and had 27 acres of arable land; the "less convenient" Zosimovsky Convent, which also could hold 400 inmates (235 nuns currently residing) and had an equal amount of cultivated land; and the already-inspected Pokrovsky Convent at Khotkovo, whose 330 nuns were characterized as "not performing any kind of labor... existing as parasites." A monastery in Kolomensky District, meanwhile, was rejected for its insufficient arable land. Ultimately, the previously scouted Pokrovsky Convent was selected, and by September 16, 1920, it held 557 inmates. The documents on selecting a new prison camp site in Moscow Province testify to the penal authorities' intention to repurpose monasteries and convents as places of confinement. Close proximity to railroad lines and the security benefit of fortified walls were desirable traits, as was the ability to provide opportunities for inmates to labor. And given the acute lack of funding facing the early Soviet state, already-existing monasteries provided a perfect solution. They even gave the authorities a convenient pretext for closing places of superstition and "parasitism."[6]

Despite such apparent scrutiny, some monasteries in Moscow, like those at Yaroslavl, were found to be inappropriate for use as prison camps, though not until inmates already occupied their cells. Sometimes the buildings were in poor condition, but Soviet prison officials also chafed at the idea of holding prisoners in places of religious devotion. A few brief accounts of the Novospassky Monastery shed light on this dilemma (see figure 1.2). Dating from the late 1400s, this monastery became a Bolshevik concentration camp starting in September 1918 and held 300 to 400 prisoners until closing in 1923 (although later in the 1920s, it was used as a women's "house of correction"). Inmates labored in the same workshops formerly used by monks, engaged in sewing, laundry, painting, woodworking, locksmithing, and other tasks. One inspection report on this facility noted the juxtaposition between the sacred and secular worlds that collided in these monasteries-turned-prisons: "Filth, icons and church ornaments are in the cells, but there are no bunks in the penalty cell." The report's author manifests clear disgust with the necessity of using religious buildings as prisons, equating icons with filth. He also implicitly criticizes the camp's commander, who was not diligent in erasing the original purpose of the monastery's buildings. But if the Soviet inspector criticized this situation, some prisoners expressed relief. Alexandra Tolstaya, daughter of famed writer Leo Tolstoy and a staunch opponent of the Soviet regime, was incarcerated at the Novospassky Monastery and characterized it as exuding "a feeling of solemn peace and comfort, which is only found in monasteries." Rather than sparking in her a feeling of dread or presenting to her the symbols and values of the new ideological regime, the monastery-prison reminded her fondly of a childhood trip to the Trinity Monastery of St. Sergius, thus providing a sense of both familial and religious comfort.[7]

This sense of religious continuity was aided by the fact that the authorities permitted several monks to remain alongside the inmates at Novospassky, thus ensuring points of contact between prisoners and religious authorities. The monks, however, were not thrilled with this arrangement, complaining that "without heating and care, the historic building of the monastery is

Figure 1.2 Novospassky Monastery, 1911. P. G. Vasenko, *Boiare Romanovy i votsarenie Mikhaila* (Saint Petersburg: Gosudarstvennaia tipografiia, 1913), 20.

beginning to collapse, the paintings are cracking, [and] the frescoes are crumbling." Moreover, they lamented, the inmates were chopping down trees, desecrating graves, and otherwise destroying the monastic environment. The monks' pleas were ignored, however, and they were ultimately expelled from the premises.[8]

As they did with the Novospassky Monastery, the Soviets transformed the ancient Andronnikov Monastery into a concentration camp for women in 1919. The first commander made his distaste for using this facility clear: "Upon assuming my duties as commander of the camp, on August 20, 1919, the camp was a completely derelict monastery, with nothing but bare walls and bunks, the latrines were ruined and filthy, and there were no water pipes or lighting or sewage or tools." In his view, this was no proper place to re-educate inmates and turn them into good Soviet citizens. At least one inmate in her memoir agreed, albeit for different reasons:

> The monastic surroundings, although they were picturesque, produced a sad, oppressive feeling because all of the buildings were surrounded by the cemetery. It was very green and shady, but the sight of all these graves and

crosses didn't gladden the soul: wherever your eyes turned you saw crosses, which only served to remind us that we were carrying our own cross.

Whereas some prisoners like Tolstaya were inspired by their camp's religious surroundings, for others they prompted the perpetual question of why God allowed such suffering to take place. Not all found comfort in the Christian symbolism found in these monasteries-turned-camps.[9]

After the civil war ended in 1921, many monasteries-turned-prisons were converted to other uses. This happened for three reasons. First, as already noted, some penal officials were distinctly uncomfortable with the use of religious buildings as prison camps because they were viewed as incompatible with the ideological values of the new regime. Second, the end of the civil war led to a reduction in the prisoner population, so fewer prisons were needed. Finally, the Soviet regime established a large concentration camp on the remote Solovetsky Islands (which will be discussed in chapter 2), which allowed penal authorities to close numerous smaller facilities. Paradoxically, given the distaste many penal officials had for using religious buildings to isolate and re-educate prisoners, the Solovetsky camp was also located in a monastery. The early Soviet era was full of such contradictions.

Religious Worship in Places of Confinement

In addition to deciding where to house inmates, early Soviet penal authorities faced pressing questions about how religious prisoners should be treated. One question regarded labor and religious holidays, with some prisoners asking to be allowed to rest and worship on Good Friday or on the Jewish Sabbath. The existing archival record on this question is scant but consistent: no religious accommodations were made. The Catholic women in this chapter's opening anecdote were compelled to work on a church holiday. And a 1921 petition from devout Jews asking to exchange Saturday labor for Sunday labor was rejected with the following justification: "the petition . . . clearly rests on motives of a religious nature, which after the decree on the separation of church and state should not be taken into consideration." Ultimately, most inmates in this early period worked for six days and rested on Sunday, the Christian Sabbath, though this was presented by penal authorities simply as a customary rather than religious practice. Other days considered holy by religious inmates were mandated days of labor.[10]

22 FINDING GOD IN THE GULAG

More ambiguous than the question of labor was the debate about whether prisons and camps should allow religious worship services to take place. Before the revolution, prisons in the Russian Empire typically employed a chaplain who conducted worship services and communed with individual prisoners. This was a central feature of incarcerated life and was designed to help criminals become law-abiding and God-fearing citizens. This was sometimes resented by the inmates, but others found the Sunday liturgical services or personal visits by priests to be a welcome reprieve from the monotony of prison life, a chance for spiritual nourishment, and a way to form communal bonds with other prisoners. After the revolution, many inmates, particularly those repressed explicitly for their religious activity, desired these same benefits. But given the antagonistic attitude of the Bolsheviks toward religion and early decrees on the separation of church and state, it seemed far from certain that organized worship in places of confinement would be allowed.

The historical record on this question is incomplete but still fascinating, providing insight into how local and central authorities approached the matter of religious worship. On December 9, 1918, just more than a year after the Bolshevik Revolution, penal authorities in the provincial capital of Kostroma asked the People's Commissariat of Justice whether they should continue to employ an Orthodox priest who was paid to minister to and provide religious services for the city's inmates. After not receiving an answer, they followed up on January 2, 1919, asking three questions of their superiors in Moscow: "(1) If churches in places of confinement should be closed, (2) if church services in them should be allowed according to the desire of the prisoners, (3) for how long the financial maintenance of priests at places of confinement should be maintained." Again, they received no response, strongly suggesting that judicial officials in the new Bolshevik regime were unsure how to address these issues. The eradication of religion in Soviet prisons, it seems, was not high on the priority list as judicial authorities struggled to fulfill their mandate to transform the courts, police force, legal codes, and places of detention along Marxist-Leninist lines.[11]

By the summer of 1919, with civil war raging, the question of religious worship had still not been resolved, but it was finally being discussed. On July 18, 1919, the Central Penal Department of the People's Commissariat of Justice sent out a questionnaire to each province, asking local authorities to report on whether chapels in places of confinement "have . . . been eliminated, and if they still exist, then under what motives has the Penal

SEPARATING CHURCH AND STATE   23

Department [of the province] found it necessary to leave them in place and to whose use has church property gone." The response was also supposed to include "how often worship services are conducted, if they are attended by prisoners, and what percent of the total number [of inmates] they represent." It is notable that this first mention of inmate worship by central authorities in Moscow did not come in the form of an order to stamp out religious practice in places of confinement. Rather, nearly two years after the Bolshevik seizure of power, a series of fact-finding questions was the first impulse of the nascent regime.[12]

Local administrators responded to the Central Penal Department's questionnaire over the following weeks, and these reports reveal widespread confusion concerning religious worship in penal facilities. Authorities at Vitebsk replied that the two prison chapels had been closed, "and in their place schools and reading rooms have been opened, and all church property has been cataloged and transferred to local clergy." The penal department of Cherepovets reported that "all prison churches . . . were liquidated and their buildings were converted into libraries, and all church property was turned over to the Department of National Education." Penal officials at Tver, Kursk, Kaluga, Perm, Saratov, Severo-Dvinsk, Vologda, and Pskov responded similarly, telling of prison chapels shuttered and church property either confiscated for use by the state or else handed over to local ecclesiastical leaders. Others reported that religious services in some penal facilities had been canceled due to a lack of priests. At the Balakhninsky County Prison in Nizhegorod Province, for instance, services were rare because most of the priests in the county had been "conscripted into the Red Army." According to other reports, services were not held "because of the absence of petitions of prisoners."[13]

Such reports claiming a lack of inmate interest in worship services were exceptional, however, and perhaps prompted by local officials trying to please their superiors in Moscow. As reported by Nizhegorod officials and confirmed by several others, "there are many [inmates] who want to attend worship services." Many local authorities therefore continued to allow prison chapels to operate, although the frequency and attendance levels of the services varied widely. In Yaroslavl, for instance, "worship services are held on Sundays and holidays and are always attended by at least two-thirds of the prisoner contingent." In Vyatka, a few prison chapels had been closed, but others held services on holidays, with between 20 and 70 percent of inmates attending. Officials from Ryazan reported that their chapels were recently

24   FINDING GOD IN THE GULAG

closed but that before their closure, prisoners patronized their services on Sundays and holidays "in large numbers, no less than 100–150 per service." Prisons in Vladimir and Nizhegorod Provinces reported more than 90 percent attendance at services held monthly or on holidays, with inmates also singing in the church choir. Orlov Province had several operating prison chapels with attendance ranging from 50 percent to "almost all inmates." Considerable demand for worship services clearly existed, even if a few Bolshevik prison administrators pretended otherwise.[14]

One of the most interesting responses to the Central Penal Department's questionnaire came from Tula Province. Local penal authorities had not closed the prison's chapels "because direction on this matter has been awaited from the center. In almost all places of confinement in Tula Province, on Easter, due to the desire of prisoners, worship services have been conducted, and now there are petitions to perform the same in the future." "From my point of view," the head of the Tula Penal Department opined, "I think it would be proper to resolve this matter after the example of [revolutionary] France, where during the time of separation of church and state this matter was resolved by surveying prisoners, the majority of whom spoke out for the holding of worship services." Drawing on the historical example of the French Revolution, this local authority advocated on behalf of religious prisoners while also prodding his superiors in Moscow to clarify policy. The Central Penal Department respond to this suggestion shortly thereafter, explaining that the prison churches could remain open if their operation did not violate the Bolshevik decrees on the separation of church and state. Christian worship in Soviet prisons was thus given official approval, although the details of how this was supposed to happen remained murky.[15]

One possible explanation for this willingness to permit religious ceremonies is found in the class-based language employed by penal authorities to describe their inmates. As the head of Arkhangelsk's penal department reported, the prison chapel held services only on holidays, and "attendance of prisoners is around 50 percent, which is explained by the fact that they are primarily peasants." Similar reports came from officials in Kostroma and Syzran, with the latter explaining: "The prison chapel entrusted to me has not been closed because . . . the overwhelming majority of prisoners have been peasants, who petitioned the head of the prison about church services in the prison chapel for the twelve most important holidays and during Holy Week of the great fast." To penal officials, therefore, the primary consumers of religious services were peasants, typically considered uneducated and superstitious by Soviet authorities. Until the peasants could be educated appropriately, prison bosses seemed to reason, church services in prisons were an acceptable concession to the demands of the Soviet constitution.[16]

But it was not just inmates who were attending church services in the penal facilities of Soviet Russia. Included in the response from Syzran was the admission that "a petition [for church services] was also submitted by prison workers in light of the isolation of the prison from the city" and that "the labor of the priest and expenses for worship are paid by the offerings of workers and prisoners alike." The Nizhegorod penal department made a similar report, informing central authorities that guards, rather than inmates, were the primary patrons of the provincial prison's chapel. One of its county prisons likewise had a church frequented by both guards and inmates. This should not be surprising, given the large numbers of guards who had previously worked for the tsarist regime and who were accustomed to attending and paying for religious services at their place of employment. But it is still a stark reminder that the early years of Soviet power were full of carryover and contradiction.[17]

This issue of financing religious services was a central concern for the new Bolshevik regime because it related directly to the separation of church and state. The report from Gomel made clear that its prison chapels remained open because local authorities had not received instructions to close them and because inmates' offerings paid for them. In the response from Vladimir Province, officials took care to specify that a local factory owner financially supported the Kovrovskaya Prison's working chapel. In citing monetary contributions made by inmates, guards, and even members of the bourgeoisie, local penal authorities tried to demonstrate compliance with new laws concerning the separation of church and state. Allowing religious worship, they believed, would only be permissible if the state bore no responsibility for its funding. A message from the Central Penal Department to Syzran confirmed this when it clarified that prison chapels could remain open as long as prisoners supported them from their own funds and they were also used for re-educational activities during the week.[18]

A related issue the Central Penal Department tackled in 1919 concerned the legal ownership of chapels within prison complexes. According to legislation on the separation of church and state, all church property in Soviet Russia had to be transferred to newly created religious associations made up of lay parishioners rather than clerics. For prison chapels, which were not open to the public, this posed a problem, one addressed by letters sent

26 FINDING GOD IN THE GULAG

in late 1919 from justice officials in Tambov and Ryazan Provinces to the Central Penal Department. In response, the department clarified that guards or administrators had to form a religious association and then transfer the property to that association "because of the impossibility of transferring the use of church property to the prisoners themselves." Worship services could then be funded by contributions from inmates, guards, or outside citizens. This no doubt created sufficient inconvenience that many prison chapels soon closed.[19]

One potential alternative to permitting worship services in prison was to allow inmates to leave their place of confinement under armed escort to attend chapel. The Petrograd penal department sent a circular letter to its penal facilities on July 31, 1919, instructing that "convicted prisoners who have expressed a desire to receive religious comfort should be sent with appropriate escort to the nearest prayer house." In this manner, freedom of religion and the mandate of secularism in state institutions could both be maintained without the necessity of guards forming a religious association to maintain a house of worship inside the prison.[20] But Petrograd authorities were not confident in the correctness of this decision and sent the circular for review to the Central Penal Department. The response from Moscow, dated October 18, 1919, was unambiguously negative: "The Central Penal Department, finding that escorting prisoners to prayer houses increases the chances for them to escape, considers that the given order should be rescinded."[21]

Surviving documentation from 1918–1919 makes clear that inmate worship protocols were matters of improvisation and local initiative rather than predetermined policy. The Central Penal Department allowed local officials significant leeway to decide whether inmates could worship, how often they could worship, and if prison church property would be confiscated or simply transferred to a new religious association. Some local officials shut down religious worship immediately after the Bolshevik Revolution and received no instructions from Moscow to restore services. Others allowed religious worship to continue and received no instructions from Moscow to stop. Officials in Moscow insisted only, and somewhat belatedly, that if prison chapels were to remain open, they must be transferred to a religious association, be used as educational and cultural facilities, and require no financial support from the state. They also clamped down on allowing inmates to leave prison to attend worship services. This is ultimately how freedom of conscience was negotiated in the penal sphere during the first years of Soviet power.

One might think that such barriers would be sufficient to completely eradicate officially sanctioned worship services in Soviet penal facilities. But by 1921, as Vladimir Martsinkovsky discovered at Taganskaya Prison in Moscow, this issue was still very much unresolved. The Taganskaya Prison chapel had been converted to a theater when Martsinkovsky, a well-known professor and leader of the Orthodox Russian Student Christian Movement, arrived, and the cross on its apex was removed during his stay. But religious inmates drew portraits of saints on the walls to restore it, at least in part, to its original purpose. Worship was not allowed to be held in the chapel, likely due to the ownership issue discussed above, but Orthodox liturgical services were held regularly in the prison school because, according to Martsinkovsky, they were requested by a sufficient number of inmates. Pictures of Karl Marx and Leon Trotsky adorned the wall of this room, and the traditional iconostasis that separated the physical space into the earthly and the heavenly in Orthodox churches was lacking. Still, inmates lit candles, the imprisoned metropolitan Kirill and other church officials conducted the liturgy, and a choir of prisoners sang. "And what singing!" Martsinkovsky remarked, before adding: "Only suffering can so inspire such singing."[22]

Religious Life in the Early 1920s

Given the lack of clear direction from central penal authorities and the continued presence of officially sanctioned worship services, it is no surprise that religious life flourished in some Soviet prisons and concentration camps. Although inmate memoirs from this time period are scarce, they do provide sketches of religious life in early Soviet prisons. Sergey Fryazinov, incarcerated in a few Moscow prisons in 1921, found that there were many guards left over from prerevolutionary Russia who were not inclined to preach Bolshevik values to religious inmates, much less oppress them for their faith-based opposition to the new powerbrokers. The commander of the Sokolniki house of correction (better known as Matrosskaya Tishina) allowed priests to live together in two neighboring communal cells, where they prayed, fasted, and celebrated holidays together. Like other inmates, they manufactured suitcases in the workshop and then played chess and found other amusements in the evening. And soon the religious prisoners were all amnestied and released, with the commander cheerfully giving them his parting blessing.[23]

28 FINDING GOD IN THE GULAG

Martsinkovsky likewise found that officials did not actively suppress religious activity in Soviet prisons in 1921. One might imagine that a Bolshevik regime bent on repressing religion in places of confinement would isolate such a well-known religious activist or otherwise restrict his activities. But even while imprisoned by the secret police, Martsinkovsky read publicly from the Gospels in his large communal cell and called for his fellow prisoners to act and speak like Christians. The prison boss denied his request to preach in a different cell, but he preached to those inmates anyway on a day when their cell was being disinfected and all the inmates crowded into the other cell. Before each meal, he and his cellmates would sing "Our Father." And when his Bible was discovered during a search of his cell, the guard did not confiscate it, even as he mocked Martsinkovsky for his beliefs.[24]

Martsinkovsky also found that religious activity was quite vibrant at Moscow's Taganskaya Prison. True, after delivering a public lecture supposedly on beauty that was primarily about Christianity, he was prohibited from further public instruction, with a camp official explaining that the religious freedom guaranteed by the Soviet constitution did not apply in prison. Yet that prohibition only related to prison-sponsored educational activities; informal religious conversations, instruction, Bible study groups, and group prayers, all of which Martsinkovsky participated in, continued unhindered in the cells. With the guards' permission, Martsinkovsky visited cells occupied by Orthodox clerics and death row inmates, to whom he spiritually ministered. As he recalled, "No one from the administration bothered us." One cell in the prison even had an official-looking placard, printed by the prison press, hanging on the wall that said, quoting 1 Peter 5:7, "Cast all your care upon Him, for He careth for you."[25]

This noninterference in religious life continued during an Easter celebration in the prison that was described by Martsinkovsky as magnificent, with red candles, incense, and brilliant Easter vestments for imprisoned clerics sent from well-wishers. Large numbers of inmates attended the services, exchanged Easter greetings, and ate the traditional Easter bread (*kulich*) and Easter eggs provided by faithful visitors. Their cell block orderly that day in the spring of 1921, a prison official from before the revolution, was visibly sad that he could not be home or at church on Easter, so they invited him into their cell to celebrate. As Martsinkovsky expressed, "today there is no prison, no wardens, no bars, no secret policemen ... there are only people, brothers, all sinful and all loved by God." Thus, even the guards in the early Soviet era were at times involved in cultivating the spiritual life of the prisons.[26]

Like Martsinkovsky, the young Sergey Fudel, imprisoned in 1922 at Moscow's Butyrka Prison, quickly discovered that even as an overtly religious priest's son, he was permitted to keep religious literature (see figure 1.3). He spent many hours reading the Bible and contemplating the love of Christ and the duty of a Christian and was also pleasantly surprised that the guards allowed inmates to visit imprisoned clerics in other cells. He immediately requested to see Father Vladimir Bogdanov in the neighboring cell, who administered the Eucharist to him in full view of the waiting guard. Others likewise took advantage of this privilege, receiving communion and confessing their sins to Bogdanov. Fudel later helped arrange for the liturgy to be performed in his cell, complete with icons, candles, incense, altar furnishings, and singing. Such good treatment was perhaps not the norm for imprisoned Christians, but these accounts by Fryazinov, Martsinkovsky, and Fudel help illustrate the range of experiences that religious prisoners enjoyed.[27]

Antireligious Propaganda

Producing and distributing antireligious propaganda were a final significant issue at the intersection of penal and religious policy that confronted early Bolshevik officials. Due to the chaos of the civil war, as Lenin and his supporters barely clung to power, there was very little published material in places of confinement and little re-educational activity in general. Few attempts were made to persuade religious believers to abandon their faith. In the 1920s, however, penal officials initiated efforts to reform convicts into law-abiding and educated citizens imbued with the values of Marxism rather than Christianity or other religions. This mirrored a new shift in religious policy in 1923 that dramatically reduced the direct repression of religion, particularly in the countryside. To borrow Lenin's words, the goal was to use "persuasion" rather than "coercion" to create a socialist society free from the religious "remnants of the past."[28]

With this strategy in mind, Soviet penal authorities laid out their overarching re-educational goal in the 1924 Corrective-Labor Code. This called for prison staff to accustom prisoners "to the conditions of communal life by means of corrective labor" and exert "practical influence on prisoners and strengthening those character traits that will prevent them from committing future crimes." Part of this program called for "raising the intellectual level

Figure 1.3 Sergey Fudel in 1921, shortly before his arrest. Wikimedia Commons.

and civic development of prisoners by means of general educational and professional knowledge." And although it was not explicitly stated in the Corrective-Labor Code, penal officials made clear that this meant promoting atheism to Soviet inmates. Yet this antireligious work was supposed to be done delicately; as one article from a prison newspaper made clear, "the struggle with religion and its servants is not a simple matter and requires caution. . . . Inexperienced propagandists provoke the religiously inclined masses and bring more harm than the clergy (priests, mullahs, rabbis)."

SEPARATING CHURCH AND STATE   31

Antireligious propaganda was therefore supposed to be well reasoned and dispassionate, appealing to the common sense of Russia's largely illiterate workers and peasants.[29]

As part of the broader re-educational program, antireligious propaganda was supposed to be done in full collaboration with inmates themselves. This aligned with the Soviet idea of organizing inmates into collectives that would help each other on the "path to correction." To facilitate this, prison authorities often offered small rewards—extra rations, better work assignments, the potential for early release—to those who lent their supposedly authentic voices to re-educational efforts. And some inmates, anarchists and socialists of various stripes among them, needed little persuasion to engage in antireligious propaganda efforts; although repressed by the Bolsheviks, they shared an atheistic worldview and were often eager to "enlighten" the religious inmates who surrounded them.

Evidence of antireligious propaganda can be found in official reports starting in the early 1920s. For example, a report by the 1st Moscow Labor Colony in early 1922 detailed the cultural and educational activities held over the previous year for the re-education of its inmates, emphasizing vocational training, literacy classes, the library, political indoctrination, and soccer. Prominent among these efforts was a lecture series devoted to "raising the intelligence of the listeners, broadening their worldview, awakening interest in acquiring knowledge on their own, and destroying incorrect superstitious imaginations about the world and mankind." Most of the thirteen lectures in the series were dedicated to the Bolshevik Party and current economic policy. However, one lecture was titled "Soviet Power and the Church," and another discussed the earth's formation in scientific terms, no doubt an attempt to counter the creation account found in the book of Genesis. Such lectures reveal that prison officials wanted inmates to view religion as inherently repressive and antiscientific, something that Soviet citizens should want to remove from their lives.[30]

Similar re-educational programs were increasingly disseminated throughout the Soviet penal system. At the Rybinsk Correctional Home, political discussions were held on various themes, such as production, agriculture, education, and the Red Army, but also on "Religion, the Church, and Soviet Power." The Moscow Women's Correctional House reported a series of lectures on the natural history of humanity, including one on "mankind among the ranks of other animals." The Tomsk Correctional-Labor House reported three antireligious lectures in December 1923, including two on

32 FINDING GOD IN THE GULAG

Christmas: "The Origins of Religion and the Legend of the Birth of Christ," delivered by a local political leader, and "Christmas Then and Christmas Now," given by an inmate. It also planned two antireligious lectures to be delivered (out of six lectures total) in January 1924 on the subjects of "Religion and Science" and "Christ and Marx." The Lefortovo Isolator of Special Significance reported as part of its educational plan for late 1926 and early 1927 that it would likewise endeavor to provide inmates with similar lectures. "In some respects," the report makes clear, "there will be an antireligious bias."[31]

Taganskaya Prison officials, meanwhile, purged the prison library of religious literature, though there was some confusion on this point, as related by Martsinkovsky. Inmates one day received coffee grounds wrapped in pieces of paper that they quickly discovered were pages from the Bible. Martsinkovsky immediately protested, and the prison boss ultimately decided that workers could destroy all the religious books in the library except the Bible itself, as it was considered a "literary monument." He explained that these instructions had just been communicated to him by telephone from his superiors, who, it seems, wanted to reduce religious influence in the prison without unnecessarily upsetting devout believers. In turning the Bible into food wrappers, the local prison wardens had done precisely that.[32]

Early Soviet prisons and concentration camps did not just remove religious literature from their libraries, but they also acquired antireligious reading material, including books, pamphlets, and periodicals with titles such as *The Atheist, Revolution and the Church*, and *Science and Religion*. By the mid-1920s, the Main Administration of Places of Confinement was sending detailed instructions on setting up antireligious displays featuring such literature and organizing local "Friends of the Journal *The Atheist*" societies. The Yaroslavl Isolator of Special Significance organized one such group, with dozens of inmates regularly attending (considered "fully satisfactory" by the prison administration). The Penza Provincial Correctional Home also set up a "Circle of Atheists," which reported that its goal for the second quarter of 1926 was to "acquaint prisoners with scientific information about the origins of the earth, about the ridiculousness of answering this question from a religious point of view and about the meaning of religion from a class-based point of view, contrasting religion and science." In this way, inmates themselves were tasked with conducting the antireligious propaganda.[33]

SEPARATING CHURCH AND STATE   33

Penal facilities in the 1920s also produced their own newspapers and literary journals, which often featured antireligious articles written by camp administrators or inmates. *Awakening the Walls*, "the literary-artistic-scientific journal" produced by prisoners at the Tsaritsyn House of Correction, for instance, featured a significant amount of antireligious material in its inaugural issues of 1922. The very first contribution of issue 3, the poem "Red Easter," celebrated the anniversary of the October Revolution while taking direct aim at Christianity:

> Today is the holiday of holidays, the celebration of celebrations.
> Today is the Great Holiday.
> Today is our Easter, Red Easter.
> Today we joyfully celebrate, not the resurrection of Christ, but the
>   crucifixion of the old, thoroughly rotten and deformed world. . . .
> Today we celebrate the fifth anniversary of the renewal of the de-
>   crepit world in the cleansing fire of revolutionary creation.
> Today we can count up our victories and trophies—we sent the
>   hydra-like counterrevolutionary to the grave, we are overcoming
>   epidemics, hunger, and other calamities caused by wars, we are
>   renewing our plants, our factories, our educational institutions,
>   we are improving living conditions, we are putting the national
>   economy on its feet . . .
> Long live Red Easter!
> Long live Red October!

The Christian imagery used in this paean to Soviet power is unmistakable, with the revolution assuming many positive traits traditionally associated with Jesus Christ and the Christian gospel. With terms like "resurrection" and "cleansing fire," the revolution is presented as accomplishing the renewal of a sinful and unclean world. It has brought peace, healed the sick, fed the hungry, and caused people to express millenarian joy.[34]

Further stories in the 1922 issues of *Awakening the Walls* attacked religion in various ways. One discussed the origins of life on earth to debunk the creationist "fairy tale." Another explained the supposed pagan roots of Christianity, arguing that the symbol of the cross came from the ancient practice of rubbing two sticks together to produce fire, which the superstitious then worshiped. A third rehearsed how the tsarist regime had discriminated against religious minorities and used religion "to forever repress the people."

34 FINDING GOD IN THE GULAG

It then denied that the Bolshevik regime had mistreated the Orthodox clergy since taking power, calling rumors of torturing and killing priests "nonsense." At the same time, however, it acknowledged the regime's antireligious stance: "Communists understand that as long a person hasn't broken with religion, as long as he believes in all these devils and angels . . . he will never become a real master of his own life."[35]

A series of antireligious poems published in a Vyatka prison newspaper in 1923–1924 pursued similar themes. The first, "I Prayed," described how endless prayers went unanswered even while the prayer giver became aware of the social injustices around him. The poem concluded, "Suddenly, like thunder, I awoke and understood the papal deceit. And my heart cried out from pain, oh, why did I realize this so late!" A second poem lauded the closing of a local church, which was then turned into a club for learning. A third, "Two Godfathers," parodied the fate of two churchgoers incarcerated under the new Bolshevik regime. It concluded, "May they learn that there is no God, no matter how much you pray to him." Although poetic in form, the message was bluntly clear: God did not exist, religion was a tool of oppression, and socialism was the way to move humankind forward.[36]

A final series of articles that help illustrate the nature of antireligious propaganda in Soviet penal institutions in the 1920s appeared in *The Voice of the Prisoner*, the Penza Provincial Correctional Home's newspaper. This newspaper cheered on the fact that inmates from the peasant class are "slowly throwing off unneeded religious traditions and are standing on the path to a real approach to life's questions."[37] As evidence of this, the newspaper editor cited numerous inquiries about religion along with antireligious poems submitted by inmates that, although lacking in proper grammar and rhythm, demonstrated a sincere desire to adopt an atheistic worldview. One particularly long poem demonstrated this quite explicitly:

> I don't know much grammar,
> After all, they didn't teach us much,
> But still, friends, I can see,
> That God has been foisted on us.
>
> From our early years until we have gray hairs,
> The priests they do assure us,
> That there is an almighty potentate,
> To whom yes, you must be obedient.

SEPARATING CHURCH AND STATE · 35

. . .

> Now everything is clear to me,
> That the priests played us for fools,
> Living in darkness, friends, is awful,
> The priests eat us, like bedbugs!
>
> Now I am in the Atheist's club,
> I've been a member for a while,
> I don't need a stool in the corner,
> And I don't sing prayers to gods.

Another poem published a few months later bore a similar message in the same unartful style:

> We no longer need priests,
> We have tired of their deceit.
> We want to live freely, in friendship,
> Having chased away the shadows, the opiate,
> And we believe in god no longer,
> He doesn't exist and never did.
> We believe in science, in knowledge . . .

Nothing is known about the authors of these poems. They may have been written by penal officials and only presented as the work of inmates. But it is also plausible that these poems were written by inmates whose own suspicion of religion coincided with a desire to extract tangible benefits from the prison administration in exchange for their intellectual labor. In either case, the authors' straightforward message and lack of literary refinement were intended to provide a sort of authentic, common-sense appeal to their semiliterate audience of peasants.[38]

In addition to printing such professions of disbelief, the editors of *The Voice of the Prisoner* sought to shame religious prisoners who tried to maintain their religious convictions. In 1925, for instance, an article focused on an imprisoned priest who was "constantly disturbing us with his godly legends and his evidences of god." But other inmates reportedly harassed him so much that he finally stopped. A similar article appeared in 1926 concerning an imprisoned nun characterized as educated but still deceived: "Every day

36 FINDING GOD IN THE GULAG

she does her prayers and genuflections. . . . It seems to me that Vera still sincerely believes in ridiculous fairy tales about god, his angels, and the saints." Other inmates, meanwhile, were becoming educated and abandoning religion, thereby improving their lives. "She needs to do more reading, studying, thinking," the author concluded, "and then she herself will begin to see the whole absurdity, the whole foolishness of what she believed in." Such tales of actual prisoners no doubt lent an immediacy to the message, presenting stark examples of how the prison experience can be beneficial in destroying illusions about religion and how religious inmates deserve any harassment they suffer.[39]

A final example from *The Voice of the Prisoner*, ostensibly written by a former Orthodox clergyman incarcerated at the Penza Provincial Correctional Home, compared the goodness of God with the goodness of Soviet power. Partially reproduced here, it illustrates the sometimes clever way that antireligious propaganda was conducted in the 1920s in Soviet penal institutions:

How does our god punish? We sit in prison and now endure various punishments, but we also know various mercies that Soviet power gives us, such as amnesty, pardon, discharge, early release, and so forth. Shall we see who it is more profitable to believe in? In our god or in Soviet power? . . . We'll start with Adam. Adam and Eve committed sin. And so what? We are all sinful. God got very mad and called the policeman, Archangel Mikhail, with a sword, to kick them out of their apartment. This happened, you should know, without a trial and for just one apple. . . . For such a crime, which for us falls under article 180 of the criminal code, and for which you could get at most six months, heavenly father determines the following punishment: Adam, by the sweat of your brow will you eat your bread, and not only you: your children, grandchildren, great-grandchildren, the entire human race. See how merciful he is! Eve, in sorrow will you bear children, and not only you but your daughters and their daughters, the whole female race, for ever and ever. . . .

We, comrades, of course understand that there is no god and no gods, and that this is all the fabrications of priests in order to scare us and more firmly hold us in their hands. And if there are among us prisoners those who believe in god, they must understand that it is more profitable to hold not to god, but to Soviet power, which punishes less and grants mercy better than god.

This article presents a practical approach to belief and speaks directly to inmates' innate senses of justice and mercy. It poses a stark question: will religion or socialism provide a better life? One wonders how much this article resonated with Soviet inmates, many of whom no doubt felt their imprisonment by Soviet authorities was unjust. On the other hand, some must have begun to think that God, if he did exist, had abandoned them.[40]

The preceding examples illustrate the varied and ad hoc nature of antireligious propaganda in early Soviet prisons. Conducted by local officials and inmates themselves, it lacked direction from Moscow. One result of this decentralization in prison policy is that many "cultural-educational" reports from penal facilities bore no mention of antireligious lectures or activities. Likewise, many prison newspapers published virtually nothing on religion, focusing instead on labor, education, discipline, international affairs, and Marxist ideology. Even central penal officials in Moscow, engaged in a wide range of issues related to creating a "new" correctional system, sometimes ignored inmates' religious beliefs. A circular sent from the Central Penal Department on May 7, 1920, for instance, asked all provinces to answer 57 detailed questions about their places of confinement, such as how the inmates were separated; what types of labor they were engaged in; what measures of punishment were used; who monitored the legality of detainment; whether there was a school and, if so, how many inmates attended; and so forth. But nothing in the long list pertained directly to religious worship or propaganda. Similarly, in a lengthy 1928 Ministry of Internal Affairs document on methods of studying prisoners' individual characters in order to categorize and re-educate them, penal officials were instructed to determine each inmate's social status, level of education, behavior, psychological health, attitude toward re-education, and other concerns. But religion was not mentioned as something to watch for and correct. Religion simply was not a pressing issue for most prison officials.[41]

—————

This chapter has explored how Bolshevik officials used monasteries as prisons, debated whether religious worship by inmates would be allowed, and only slowly and unevenly employed antireligious propaganda in re-educational efforts. Improvisation and contradiction figured prominently in these questions, and this was the case for several reasons. First, specific policies concerning religious life in places of confinement had not been considered before the October Revolution and had to be decided in reaction to events on the ground. Moreover, in the midst of revolution and civil war, more pressing problems took precedence over such issues. Second, the tension between an atheistic ideology and the discourse of human rights was real, with some officials trying to ensure the constitutional guarantee of the freedom of religion even if they believed in the scientific atheism espoused by the Communist Party. Third, even when officials developed specific policies governing religion in prisons, officials had limited capacity to enforce decisions made in Moscow across the various penal institutions scattered throughout the largest country in the world. The fact that many prison employees had previously been employed by the tsarist regime and were Christian rather than Marxist in their worldview made this inconsistency in implementation even greater. Lastly, there was some awareness among Soviet leaders that pushing too hard against religion could backfire, even in the semicontrolled environment of prisons and concentration camps.

A final example illustrates the continued confusion at the intersection of religion and imprisonment in the early years of Soviet power. In 1923, the People's Commissariat of Justice and the People's Commissariat of Internal Affairs, after considerable internal debate, ordered that prisoners on their deathbeds were welcome to receive last rites from a priest upon their or their relatives' request. This ultimate act of religious penance and comfort was deemed not to violate the separation of church and state even if the presence of a priest pronouncing a blessing might strengthen the faith of other inmates. Despite the many repressive measures taken against religious authorities, institutions, and doctrine, the state permitted priests to enter prisons and perform a holy ordinance of Christian faith. Seen from this view, the Soviet state appears less repressive of religion than is often thought. And perhaps most surprisingly, as chapter 2 will demonstrate, these contradictions and the indecisiveness surrounding religion in places of incarceration existed for several more years in the secret police's showpiece concentration camp at Solovki.[42]

2

The Spiritual Life of Solovki

In 1924, two articles written by inmates for the Penza Provincial Correctional Home's newspaper, *Voice of the Prisoners*, provided humorous depictions of life in the prison "republic." Satire offered an escape from the pains of prison life, and inmates no doubt laughed at the stereotypes and amusing scenes recounted in these commentaries. Alongside the geography, work assignments, and food of the prison, heated religious discussions merited special mention in the articles. One of the authors in jest numbered precisely 13.5 percent of participants in these debates among the believers, 11.5 percent as unbelievers, and the remaining 75 percent in favor of "both sides." Moreover, the authors portrayed the imprisoned clergy as "not enjoying special honor, and some of them occupy positions in the republic that are not after their order," such as chef. Also of concern was the declining numbers of clergymen, though not through release. As the second article quipped, "The clergy recently has been reduced in number on account of many of them being sent to various resorts in Arkhangelsk and the Siberian tundra."[1]

This chapter investigates religious life at the most famous of these "resorts," the Solovetsky Camp of Forced Labor of Special Significance, commonly known as Solovki or SLON (the camp's bureaucratic acronym). Located on the Solovetsky Islands in the far northern White Sea, SLON was the most populous Soviet prison camp in the 1920s and the predecessor of the Gulag. Soviet propaganda celebrated SLON as an experiment in re-educating criminals, class enemies, and political prisoners; indeed, it served as a model institution for both domestic and international audiences. Notably, it was located in one of the most important monastery complexes in Russian Orthodoxy. But far from a "resort," as former inmate Boris Solonevich related, it had been transformed "from a place of prayer and peace" into "a concentration camp." Another memoirist called it "the kingdom of the unhappy." Or, as a priest's wife, appealing for clemency for her sick husband about to be transferred to Solovki, lamented, "Ahead is the dark of night and of the grave, there is no more light, no more life, everything is over."[2]

Finding God in the Gulag. Jeffrey S. Hardy, Oxford University Press. © Oxford University Press 2024.
DOI: 10.1093/9780197751701.003.0003

40   FINDING GOD IN THE GULAG

The plight of the imprisoned was indeed tragic—many died at Solovki or endured harsh physical and psychological agony. Yet the story of imprisoned Christians at Solovki is not just one of suffering. Many letters and memoirs tell of spiritual peace and, at times, joy. Such inmate-produced sources are not without their biases, of course; most authors of the materials used in this chapter were repressed due to their political or religious opposition to the Soviet regime, and that sense of righteous indignation toward the Bolshevik is always present in their surviving documents. Nonetheless, these sources provide an important counterpoint to the official documents and propaganda on which chapter 1 was largely based. In particular, they tell of a sizable group of Orthodox monks, priests, bishops, and higher-ranking clergymen who were able to forge a vibrant spiritual society at Solovki. Rather than be "re-educated" by labor and other correctional devices, Orthodox clerics for the most part maintained their religious devotion. They ministered, celebrated Easter, and took comfort in the knowledge that they suffered for their faith. However, a schism in the Orthodox Church in the late 1920s caused a divisive split in this imprisoned clerical community. Though a source of peace and joy, religion also brought conflict to camp society.

SLON and Its Inmates

As chapter 1 illustrated, the Soviet penal system of the 1920s was operated by multiple government agencies and featured a wide range of detention facilities and policies. Amid this uncertainty and contradiction, the Soviet secret police organized a massive experimental prison camp on a remote archipelago in the White Sea. This was the site of the Solovetsky Monastery, which dates to the mid-1400s. Monasticism had always played an important role in the spiritual life of Russian Orthodoxy, with both men and women choosing to separate themselves from society and devote their lives to the worship of God. But strict separation was not always possible. The Solovetsky Monastery, founded by a small group of monks seeking isolation from the world, quickly became an important center not just of religiosity but of trade and politics in the White Sea region. During the great schism in the Orthodox Church in the 1600s, it served as a prominent outpost for the renegade Old Believers, who opposed the patriarch's liturgical reforms and consequently faced swift repression by tsarist troops. Then, in the 1800s, during a period of monastic revival, Solovki became a significant site of pilgrimage, which helped it become the second-richest monastery in the Russian Empire, behind only the venerable Trinity Monastery near Moscow which enjoyed the direct patronage of Russia's political dynasties. Like several other monasteries in Russia, the Solovetsky Monastery was also a place of imprisonment, housing hundreds of political and religious prisoners starting in the 1500s. There were never more than fifty inmates at a time, however, and in 1883, the last two prisoners of the prerevolutionary period were removed.[3] (See figure 2.1.)

After the revolution and the civil war, Bolshevik forces in 1921 investigated (and looted) the Solovetsky Monastery and forcibly relocated most of the island's residents to the mainland the following year. Although Soviet officials found the central monastic complex worthy of preservation, a devastating fire of uncertain origins in 1923 destroyed all but its stone walls. The task of rebuilding the monastery ultimately fell to Soviet prisoners and the few monks who remained on the island. The secret police brought hundreds of prisoners to the islands in the summer of 1923 and on October 13, 1923, announced the creation of the Solovetsky Camp of Forced Labor of Special

Figure 2.1 A contemporary view of the Solovetsky Monastery, restored to appear as it did in the early twentieth century. Shutterstock.

42 FINDING GOD IN THE GULAG

Significance (SLON). SLON quickly became the Soviet Union's largest carceral facility, with more than ten thousand inmates by the late 1920s.[4]

According to official propaganda, SLON helped criminals and counterrevolutionaries atone for their crimes and become honest Soviet citizens through labor and various cultural and educational programs. As one report published for an international audience declared, "The principle that people are not sent to prison to be punished merely, but to be made useful members of society, is applied to the full in Solovki." Indeed, various cultural and educational programs were available, alongside a full complement of labor tasks. Yet reports, letters, and memoirs frequently tell a story of exhaustive rather than ennobling labor, violent guards, terrible living conditions, and the constant threat of violence from the hardened criminal element among the prisoners. Too often, it was a place of suffering and death rather than re-education and redemption.[5]

The prisoner population at Solovki was quite diverse due to wide-ranging Bolshevik repressive policies during and after the civil war. As inmate Anton Klinger remembered, "in the Solovetsky camp you could find representatives of any nationality, any religion, any profession. Russians and citizens of all countries in the world, Orthodox Christians, Protestants, Lutherans, Catholics and Jews, officers, civil servants, workers, students, peasants, teachers, doctors, writers, artists, lawyers, traders, tailors." Numerous inmates later recalled a three-way categorization of inmates at Solovki. "Political prisoners," consisting of various socialists and anarchists, were kept separate from the other inmates and for a brief time enjoyed privileged treatment. Few, if any, Christians belonged to this group. Next came "counterrevolutionaries," typically class enemies such as former aristocrats and White Army officers, many of whom were religious. Church officials were also included in this category. Common criminals, imprisoned for various nonpolitical crimes such as murder, theft, speculation, and counterfeiting, formed the third and largest contingent. Some lay believers were found among this group, though few remaining sources attest to their religious beliefs and practices.[6]

Determining the precise number of religious prisoners at SLON is challenging. On October 1, 1927, camp authorities reported 119 inmates with "clerical rank," but memoirists typically recalled higher numbers. During the 1920s, around eighty bishops and archbishops and some four hundred lower-ranking clerics of the Orthodox Church spent time at SLON, alongside unknown numbers of lay believers, with sentences typically ranging between two and four years. Dozens of Catholic priests were also sent to Solovki, as were small numbers of Protestant pastors, Jewish rabbis, and Muslim imams. Many relatives and parishioners petitioned for their release—one distraught mother wrote to appeal the sentence of her son, Ignaty Sadkovsky, an Orthodox bishop, claiming that "by his temper and character he cannot be a counterrevolutionary." But those sentenced to Solovki, including Sadkovsky, typically were not released before their sentences had expired. In addition to imprisoned believers, several dozen monks received permission to stay at the Solovetsky Monastery as "free workers" in specialized industries such as fishing, shoemaking, and carpentry. As Klinger recalled, these monks "look at their continued existence in the monastery-turned-prison as a continuation of their great achievement of serving God." Their presence meant that the monastic tradition continued at Solovki for at least a few more years, even as the camp grew in size and importance; at the end of the 1920s, however, they were finally expelled from the islands.[7]

From a Sacred to a Profaned Place

Upon arriving at the Solovetsky Islands, prisoners entered a sacred world full of tangible reminders of religious devotion. Religious architecture dominated the skyline, and roads, canals, and other improvements testified to hundreds of years of labor by Orthodox monks. Indeed, the monastery's status as a place of pilgrimage made it a desirable place of imprisonment for some inmates. As related by one prisoner who witnessed an old priest weeping just before his transfer to Solovki, "It turned out that he was crying for joy, since he was going to die not anywhere in the taiga, but on the land made holy by Zosima and Savvaty [the founders of the monastery]." Religious scholar Dmitry Likhachev likewise recounted that upon arrival at Solovki, "I took off my student cap, which I had kept, and crossed myself. . . . I perceived Solovki and its Kremlin not as a new prison but as a holy place." The sacred nature of these islands thus provided a comforting sense of spiritual familiarity that lessened the initial pains of imprisonment experienced by Orthodox Christians.[8]

However, Solovki was quickly transformed from a sacred to a profaned place. On July 21, 1923, the Bolshevik authorities over Arkhangelsk Province decreed that churches without historical value at Solovki should be converted into barracks. The Indian prisoner Said Kureishi described how the

44 FINDING GOD IN THE GULAG

crosses were taken off the temples in the main monastery complex, and the central cathedral featured the Soviet flag with the hammer and sickle at its apex. The bells in the Tsar's Chapel at Solovki no longer rang to call monks to worship but rang instead at five in the morning to wake the inmates for the day's labor. An anonymous political prisoner detailed this transformation in a 1924 letter: "The crosses were removed from the church steeples, the walls of the church were denuded, the ikons were painted over; in place of the saints—portraits of Lenin, Trotzky and Marx were drawn, and instead of texts from the Bible, the mottoes of the Russian Communist Party appeared. Instead of vespers the old bells now sound prison signals."[9]

This intentional desacralization was readily apparent to observant inmates. As described by archpriest Mikhail Polsky, monks still crewed the transport vessel used to carry people from the transit port of Kem to the Solovetsky Islands, but the Bolsheviks had changed its name from *Archangel Mikhail* to *Gleb Boky*, for a prominent secret police leader. As he approached the dock, Polsky saw that the hotel where pilgrims had traditionally stayed had a new placard hanging above its door: "SLON Headquarters." Still, Polsky considered Solovki to be a sacred space. As he noted in his memoir, "Sometimes a place in and of itself can have great meaning. . . . It holds within itself the traces of lives well lived." Lay believer Olga Vtorova-Yafa, who visited the monastery as a pilgrim before the revolution and who was then imprisoned there, provided a slightly different interpretation of this transformation. The once magnificent complex of cupolas and bright paint had changed, she observed, so that "now, not one cupola, not one cross, just a monotone gray colors the entire kremlin complex, reminding one of the abandoned ruins of a medieval fortress." For Vtorova-Yafa, this was profoundly sad, yet it made sense. She mused, "there is a kind of internal harmony between what people are enduring here and what these sad remnants of buildings are saying. The stones and the people here are both marked by suffering." Leaving the monastery unchanged would have created, to her mind, an even harsher juxtaposition between the sacred and the profaned.[10]

After arrival at Solovki, inmates were placed in quarantine to prevent the spread of disease and then sent to one of the camp's various divisions. Some prisoners received assignments at small monastic outposts spread throughout the several islands of the Solovetsky archipelago. Camp authorities turned Anzer Island's Golgotha Monastery into a camp hospital, retaining its religious name referencing the site of Christ's crucifixion. The tiny monastic outpost on Bolshoy Zayatsky Island became a "penalty isolator" for women, where those who disobeyed regulations were sent. The Spaso-Voznesensky Monastery, located on a hill near the northern end of the main island, soon functioned as a penalty isolator for men. However, most of Solovki's inmates lived in and around the main monastic complex. Surprisingly, given their status as "counterrevolutionaries," camp authorities permitted many imprisoned clergymen to live together, which provided an intimate sense of spiritual brotherhood. Clergymen were also allowed to wear their ecclesiastical garb, pay public deference to their spiritual superiors, and greet each other with the traditional threefold kiss. "In short," one memoirist noted of the Orthodox community at Solovki, "they did not in any way depart from the centuries-old traditions of their caste."[11]

Yet life at Solovki in many ways challenged the Christian faith of believing inmates. They suffered from proximity to guards and common criminals, who employed "terrible swearing," including profaning God and various saints. As the Baptist Aleksey Petrov recalled, camp administrators "cursed God and Christ, they cursed everything that is clean and holy. My heart and soul were so offended by this unbelievably filthy atmosphere, that I was terrified. How could a creation of our Creator arrive at such a condition?" According to Ivan Zaitsev and others, the Bolsheviks also turned the most sacred places in former temples, such as where the altar stood, "into the most unclean places in the barracks, including latrines, trash bins, cesspools, and so forth." Guards shot at icons, drew pornographic images on the frescoed faces of female saints, and knocked over crosses and gravestones. They seemed to take special pleasure in desecrating the relics of saints. The most famous example of this was the uncovering of the relics of Saint Zosima, one of the monastery's founders, during a farcical ceremony in the Transfiguration Cathedral. After removing Zosima's head from his body and dumping his bones on the floor, the commander taunted the clergy, asking them, "Is this your main saint? Here, have him." Former inmates noted many other incidents of intentional sacrilege designed to offend the sensibilities of incarcerated Christians.[12]

As at other penal institutions in the 1920s, SLON administrators organized antireligious lectures. These were typically delivered in the theater room of the central SLON complex on Saturdays, after the workday had finished, with a nonreligious political prisoner or camp administrator leading the discussion. Such events did not always go as planned, however. One lecture attended by Boris Sederkholm was titled "What is god and why is religion

46   FINDING GOD IN THE GULAG

needed?" Sederkholm was amused to watch a poorly educated guard repeat vague antireligious platitudes and the outlines of Darwinian evolution to an audience of largely university-trained inmates, including many clergymen. Finally, a Muslim friend from Central Asia sitting next to Sederkholm called out, "You dog! Swine! Idiot!" and then cursed the lecturer in a mix of different languages. Someone then switched off the lights, and the meeting ended in chaos.[13]

One unique part of SLON's antireligious efforts was a museum dedicated to the history of the islands. The museum was run by a former priest, Nikolai Vinogradov, who had become an atheist but was genuinely interested in preserving the monastery's heritage. He was assisted in his work by the defrocked monk Vaska Ivanov, a cruel man known among the prisoners as "the antireligious bug" for his small stature and his many antireligious lectures. The museum's central exhibit detailed the monastery's history and included relics of the monastery's founders, the Royal Doors of the central chapel's iconostasis, and various icons, crosses, books, and other religious artifacts. The nonreligious inmate Franz Olekhnovich, who worked as a guard at the museum for a time, recalled that SLON administrators would give the inmates tours "in a very antireligious spirit." But the museum also served a different purpose after hours, as Olekhnovich let an imprisoned Christian peasant from Tula into the exhibits to pray.[14]

The camp press played a significant role in the antireligious campaign at SLON. With religious imagery and architecture surrounding the inmates, the editors of the camp's newspaper, *New Solovki*, and the camp literary journal, *SLON*, felt a clear mandate to undermine religious belief. The 1925 poem "To a Monk," for instance, criticized religious deception and encouraged the monk to abandon belief and join the working class. A related article, called "Goodbye God," reported a (no doubt fictional) conversation between two guards, with one telling the other that the bourgeoisie invented God to oppress the poor and uneducated. The second guard protested, noting that the Bible said the bourgeoisie would go to hell and the poor people to heaven. But that, according to the first, was just a trick to keep the poor people docile and obedient. It was a way to justify robbing them. Another article on Easter described how the original holiday celebrated the onset of spring, but organized religion had then appropriated it. In dealing with the holiday, therefore, the author suggested that they should continue to observe Easter but only in its original seasonal spirit. This was especially important "here at Solovki, the citadel of ecclesiastical feudalism."[15]

Illustrations in *New Solovki* and *SLON* likewise carried antireligious messages. A July 1924 edition of *SLON*, for instance, features a satirical drawing, "Pilgrimage to Solovki . . . Then and Now." On top, four peasants search for spiritual enlightenment or healing against the background of the famous monastery complex. On the bottom are several well-dressed men and women with suitcases being led by Red Army soldiers to the labor camp. These class enemies of the new socialist regime were certainly not making a voluntary pilgrimage to Solovki, but the illustrator suggests that they, too, would receive light, knowledge, and healing at the monastery complex. Of course, it would be socialism and the value of labor that they would learn, but ironically, it is portrayed as a pilgrimage akin to those of prerevolutionary times.[16]

A second set of pictures from the April 5, 1925, edition of *New Solovki* illustrated directly what the Soviets were trying to accomplish. Labeled "The Solovki Citadel and Dock," the first drawing portrays 1923 and the second 1925 (see figure 2.2). The contrast is unmistakable. Whereas in the first picture, the walls and steeples of the monastery are on prominent display, in the second illustration, while present, they are set much further back and obscured by economic activity, including a new dock and steamships. The remnants of the old, religious way of life thus recede into the background under Soviet control. The accompanying poem, "Labor Has Conquered," drives home this point, telling the inmate reader that "we have come far, and will go farther still" from the backward traditions of the past.[17]

Persistent abuse of religious sensibilities, combined with the difficult living and working conditions at Solovki, had a detrimental psychological effect on many religious prisoners. The imprisoned Catholic cleric Leonid Fedorov in a letter to a friend expressed doubt that his life was pleasing to God. After receiving a letter of comfort and encouragement in response, his second letter mused that perhaps "the contribution of the Russian [Catholic] Church to the riches of the Catholic Church was that precisely through suffering rather than victory it will show its belonging to the Mystical Body of Christ." And part of that suffering, he concluded, was the spiritual anguish and doubt that he experienced. Such spiritual despair was not unique to Fedorov. Zaitsev recalled one group of clerics who traveled with him to Solovki, noting that the experience of incarceration had made them "extremely depressed." Mother Veronika, apparently a nun with some authority, found praying difficult while in the penalty isolator and despaired that "her spiritual state was in a very slavish dependence on her physical condition." In a more extreme

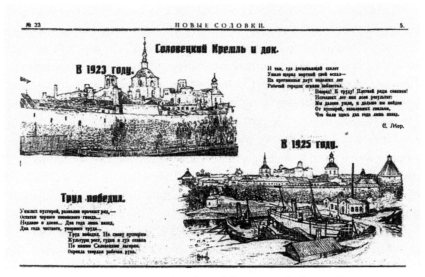

Figure 2.2 "The Solovki Citadel and Dock." *Novye Solovki*, April 5, 1925.

case, Nikolay Kiselev-Gromov, a SLON administrator, recalled an old priest who went mad in the penalty isolator after being beaten for taking offense at the blasphemous language used by guards during a search. One can only imagine how traumatic it must have been for these clergymen to see a sacred place be defiled and to be cursed and beaten for their belief in God.[18]

Labor and the Right to Worship

One aspect of incarceration that required adjustment and challenged clerical identity was the mandatory labor imposed by SLON authorities. The Solovetsky Camp was an explicit experiment in re-education through labor, so all inmates were required to work. According to inmate accounts, the clergy were given no special accommodations in the first few years of SLON's existence and typically performed "general work," which meant hard, physical labor cutting trees, building roads, or performing agricultural labor. While Orthodox monks traditionally performed physical labor as part of their daily monastic routine, priests and higher-ranking clergymen were unconditioned for such work. Zaitsev, for instance, recalled being tasked along with several clerics with carrying lumber from the sawmill to the monastic complex. Once on this path, he encountered Archbishop Yuvenaly, who had dropped his load and was crying. As Yuvenaly explained his predicament, "I'm just a little tired . . . and my legs hurt. . . . They don't believe me and say that I am simulating [injury] and swear at me with foul words. . . . But I am actually not well . . . I am not refusing to work. . . . I will work with patience . . . Jesus Christ commanded us to have patience. . . . He himself showed us an example of patience." The spiritual comfort of imitating Christ during great trial helped some clerics endure hard labor's physical demands, but the labor could, at times, be overwhelmingly difficult.[19]

Labor requirements for imprisoned clergy eased after the replacement of the camp's sadistic first commander, Aleksander Nogtev, with the more pragmatic Fedor Eikhmans in November 1925. By 1926, most Orthodox clerics had been removed from general work and given privileged jobs because they were, in the words of one inmate, "the most honest, the most accurate, the most good-natured, and the most conscientious workers of all the prisoners at Solovki." As political prisoner Gennady Andreev noticed, "wherever completely honest people were needed—at warehouses, supply depots, in the distribution of packages—the priests were employed." Photographs and even the Soviet propaganda film *Solovki* feature Orthodox priests in their clerical robes distributing mail or performing similar tasks. Archimandrite Feodosy worked as a supply depot guard and accountant, two light tasks that required a significant amount of trust. And in general, as Feodosy related, the clergy typically got along well with the administrators of the camp's labor department, which sometimes allowed them to get lay believers less physically taxing jobs as well.[20]

Like other prisoners, Christian inmates were often required to work even on holy days. As inmate Klinger described: "There are no Sabbaths or holidays. They make no exceptions even for the holiest of Christian days: Christmas and Easter." Yet some Christians tried to avoid such sacrilege, as they saw it. A Baptist inmate and his fellow believers, for instance, secured release from working on Sunday, promising to make up for the missed labor over the following days. But while they were resting that Sabbath day, a guard, unaware of the arrangement, berated them, declaring, "Get to work this instant, or else you'll all go to the punishment cell. You've stayed behind to cultivate your [religious] opiate; this is not home—this is a concentration camp, and here we will knock all of this opiate out of you!" Distraught at this turn of events, they quickly reported to work. A similar story of an Adventist inmate who performed extra labor on other days so that he would not have

50   FINDING GOD IN THE GULAG

to work on Saturday had a different ending. The arrangement was permitted for some time by his work supervisor, but then another supervisor replaced the first and threatened the Adventist with execution if he did not work on Saturday. The Adventist refused, saying, "I cannot, and if I need to die for my faith, then kill me." He was shot and killed on the spot. Securing time off for Sunday observance was thus possible in certain circumstances, but at any moment, this accommodation could be rescinded with sometimes lethal consequences.[21]

A few imprisoned Christians refused to work not just on Sundays but at all, viewing it as an unacceptable subjugation to God's enemies. Ivan Andreyevsky, a lay believer working as a camp doctor, recalled the arrival of around thirty nuns in 1929, who refused to answer even basic questions— name, place of birth, and so forth—posed by the guards. They were beaten, isolated, and starved for this, but nothing persuaded them to answer questions, much less perform their assigned labor. As the head of the sanitary department complained, "They are fanatical martyrs, they seem to seek out suffering. These are some kind of psychological masochists." Eventually, the camp administration, rather than executing the nuns or sending them to a penalty isolator, asked the inmate doctors to give them work releases on account of poor health to have an official explanation for why they were not working. When Andreyevsky explained this, however, the nuns insisted they were physically well and refused to be characterized as incapable of labor. Andreyevsky explained to them that many clergymen and monks at SLON worked, to which the women replied, "we do not condemn them . . . but we will not be forced to work for the power of the Antichrist." A week later, however, they agreed to sew blankets as long as they could remain together and sing psalms while they worked. But after a few weeks, they talked with a "fanatical" priest who convinced them they should abandon their labor on behalf of the Soviet regime. When camp administrators discovered this, they executed the priest and dispersed the nuns to various camp units so as to break their collective protest.[22]

As these nuns' experiences show, the nature of camp society produced stark moral quandaries for imprisoned Christians. Acting as informants for the administration was a constant pressure, even if most memoirs are silent on this issue. Other situations arose that tested the ability to judge ambiguous situations. Feodosy, while working as a night watchman, faced the question of whether to surreptitiously allow inmates to meet their imprisoned lovers outside the barracks. Ultimately, he chose not to prevent or report them,

THE SPIRITUAL LIFE OF SOLOVKI   51

preferring compassion and conscious rule breaking over Orthodox notions of obedience and sexual morality. At other times, he pilfered food from the supply depot to stave off hunger, even as other inmates went hungry. This produced feelings of guilt for the self-recognized sins of dishonesty and self-ishness, but Feodosy excused himself because of the intense pressures of physical survival.[23]

In another example related by Mechislav Leonardovich, who worked as a medical assistant in the camp hospital, one of the local secret policemen, Sokolov, ended up sick in the hospital for two weeks. As he started to recover, the female doctor, who despised him for his cruelty, asked him, "Perhaps, after this illness, you'll become better and stop killing people?" Sokolov responded that he was ready to kill many more enemies of Soviet power. At this, the doctor shot back, "Take care that God doesn't punish you. There are hundreds of widows and orphans in Russia who are asking God for your death, and you are thinking about new crimes." Sokolov then responded in-dignantly, "God? That's a bourgeois invention! What do I care about God? I will execute people all the same!" The doctor then screamed in anger, "I have a feeling that you won't succeed!" The next day, the doctor secretly poisoned Sokolov, and he died in the camp hospital. When Leonardovich confronted her, she quietly remarked, "It was going to happen to him eventu-ally. God is just." In the morally conflicted world of the Soviet concentration camp, even murder could be justified by religious belief.[24]

Given the repressive environment of the labor camp and the man-date to work on Sundays and holidays, one would expect religious wor-ship to be forbidden at SLON. In fact, camp policies concerning religious worship varied over the course of the 1920s, a result of continued improv-isation and confusion in Bolshevik policy. The first SLON commander, Nogtev, allowed Saturday night and Sunday religious worship by the local nonincarcerated monks at a small chapel in the main cemetery, a short distance south of the main monastery, but forbade imprisoned Orthodox clergymen from participating. Lay believers among the prisoners were tech-nically permitted to attend the monks' ceremonies but had to receive permis-sion first, which was rarely granted. Indeed, few even asked, because they knew that identifying as religious might result in a harder labor assignment and a reduced chance of obtaining early release. Meanwhile, those caught attending services without a pass were punished. The lay believer Zaitsev, for instance, possessed a pass that allowed him to move freely about the island due to his labor assignment, so he visited the cemetery church on the eve of

52 FINDING GOD IN THE GULAG

the Assumption of Mary. Later that night, a camp official instructed him that he needed a different pass to attend church and that this would not be forthcoming. The next day, he went to noon services anyway and was promptly sent to the penalty isolator at Sekirnaya Gora.[25]

When the more lenient Eikhmans replaced Nogtev as camp commander, he allowed the imprisoned Orthodox clergy to attend services at the cemetery chapel, a decision they greeted with joy. For the following three years, camp officials permitted daily liturgical services, complete with an inmate choir, after the working day was over. The propaganda film *Solovki* even featured clergymen walking to church, showing the Soviet public and foreign audiences that these remnants of the "old regime" were still allowed to practice their religion while other inmates played chess, read the newspaper, or danced (!) after work. Those attending church services were constantly reminded of their imprisonment, as a secret policeman stood guard outside, monitoring who was entering and exiting the building and listening for any anti-Soviet discussion. Even so, the services provided spiritual nourishment and provoked strong emotions. As Feodosy recalled of one service, "many wept, and I myself sobbed." Easter worship was particularly celebratory.[26]

Nonclerical inmates could only attend services sporadically from 1927 to 1929, but those who did often found themselves spiritually strengthened. An Orthodox lay believer recounted the 1929 Easter service held in the cemetery church to another inmate: "It was an unforgettable service.... It is difficult to speak of it with ordinary human words." Oleg Volkov recalled that in the evening after work, he would listen to the church bells and watch the procession of clergymen with their robes and staffs, "and one would never guess that they were all prisoners heading off to church." This spectacle intrigued Volkov sufficiently that he sometimes followed the procession to the chapel and listened to the elegant liturgy and the beautiful singing. In his words, "the worship services were solemn yet upbeat, grand even. And passionate. For all of us in the church saw it as a refuge besieged by enemies." And although he himself was not religious, he recalled getting a lump in his throat when the clergy, reading from the Bible, prayed for the sufferers, the laborers, the heavy-burdened, and the prisoners. Orthodox worship had a tangible spiritual impact on at least some lay believers and nonbelieving inmates, and in that sense, it is remarkable that SLON administrators, tasked with re-educating inmates according to Marxist values, permitted it. The cemetery church allowed for the persistence of a society and value system that were antithetical to Leninist socialism in a place where people were supposed to be converted to the latter. It gave strength, in other words, to those who desired to continue fighting against Bolshevik rule.[27]

Outside Orthodoxy, adherents of most other faiths were unable to openly conduct worship services at Solovki. The lone exceptions were imprisoned Catholics. From December 1925 to December 1928, the camp commander allowed Catholic prisoners to meet in a small chapel a few kilometers north of the central monastic complex. It was too small to hold all who desired to worship, but both men and women gathered to observe liturgical worship on Sundays and church holidays. Wafers and wine, emblems of the Eucharist, were sent from friends, and a prisoner made sacrament vessels. According to one account, the Catholic clergy tried to secure a building closer to the main monastery, but this was opposed by Orthodox clergy who had some sway with the camp administration. It is unclear if this is true or not, but there were some tensions at Solovki between the rival Christian faiths. Still, the operation of both Catholic and Orthodox chapels at Solovki demonstrates that even ten years after the Russian Revolution, camp authorities in the secret police apparatus made surprising accommodations to allow for freedom of religion among those imprisoned for their religious beliefs.[28]

Religious Life among the Christian Laity

Solovki was home to inmates with a wide range of religious views. We know the most about Orthodox clerics' experiences (discussed shortly), because many wrote memoirs and nonreligious memoirists also often described them. We know far less about ordinary Christians—lay believers—who were imprisoned usually for nonreligious reasons but who found a direct challenge to their faith at SLON. Maintaining religious belief, let alone religious practice, at Solovki was difficult. Camp authorities were, to some extent, invested in turning ordinary prisoners into atheists. Camp society, dominated by criminals and unreligious political prisoners, also made maintaining faith difficult. But in the improvised and uncertain climate of Solovki, where the attitudes of guards and inmates toward religion varied widely, some inmates maintained or even strengthened their convictions.

For a few, spirituality at Solovki came in the form of religious conversion, with the camp experience provoking tough questions about the existence and nature of God. Yury Bessonov, the son of a tsarist general and a nominal Orthodox Christian, converted as he prepared to escape from Solovki.

54 FINDING GOD IN THE GULAG

He wondered if he had "the right to change my fate" and act according to his wishes rather than endure a trial sent by God. But he also questioned the very existence of God, asking the universal question, "Does he exist?" Bessonov consulted a priest to address his concerns, but as he later recalled, "I didn't understand anything." He eventually decided that an escape attempt would not thwart God's divine plan, and he and a few others successfully fled to Finland. While on this perilous journey, he credited his success as a manifestation of God's love. It is unclear whether Bessonov, had he been caught, would have seen this as a sign of God's disapproval of his actions or evidence that God must not exist. But his spiritual journey leading up to the escape attempt illustrates how inmates grappled with spiritual questions amid the deprivations of camp life.[29]

Other accounts of ordinary Christians imprisoned at Solovki include stories of both despair and faith. Zaitsev, an Orthodox believer, spoke of the torment but also the spirituality that Christians at Solovki experienced. As he recounted, "Only in places of suffering and anguish can one observe and feel for oneself the sincerity with which prayers are raised to the Lord God out of the depths of the soul, and the confidence with which the sufferers address the Heavenly Father. . . . Many praying inmates weep; sometimes you hear sobbing or hysterical cries." Yet in Zaitsev's observation, anguish was accompanied by spiritual comfort. He wrote, "After such moments of deep emotional outpouring, after a spiritual communion with the Lord Creator, unhappy inmates experience moments of tender affection, humble submission, and physical relief." The religious philosopher Likhachev experienced a similar juxtaposition after hearing the sound of prisoners being shot. As he later recalled, "That night was the turning point. I realized then that every day was a gift from God. I had to live day by day, be satisfied that I was alive for one day more and be grateful for every morning."[30]

This duality is also present in the memoirs of Andreyevsky, another lay Orthodox Christian. He expressed spirituality through frequent prayers to God, the Virgin Mary, his guardian angel, and various saints for deliverance from difficult situations. He also recalled discovering that one of the medical orderlies who worked with him, Jewish by birth, was a devout Christian convert. While enduring multiple days of work with hardly any sleep, together with an impromptu beating from a drunk officer, this coworker declared, "Don't worry about me. . . . I've had to endure much worse torture without any guilt, and for it I only praise God. . . . Remember, Saint John Chrysostom

THE SPIRITUAL LIFE OF SOLOVKI   55

said, 'Praise God for everything!'" Later, while walking through the forest, the two discovered an old deteriorating chapel. They entered, fell on their knees upon finding an icon of the Virgin Mary, and began praying. Joint suffering and devotion thus provided spiritual solace for Andreyevsky and his new friend.[31]

Some Christians maintained and expressed faith among suffering through poetry. In one poem, Mikhail Frolovsky, a former tsarist army officer who fought in the Red Army before being imprisoned by the secret police, depicts Solovki as a place of intense spiritual struggle:

> Stubbornly the generations went north
> Weary from the silent struggle,
> Exhausted but not defeated,
> Foretasting the delights of victory.
>
> *****
>
> The prison sleeps and breathes heavily.
> Every breath exudes longing and groaning,
> The incorruptible stone hears,
> It will tell God everything.

For Frolovsky, faith in ultimate spiritual victory helped him overcome imprisonment's torments, and poetry helped give voice to this eternal interpretation of his everyday struggles.[32]

In terms of religious worship, private holiday celebrations were common among lay believers, and even nonbelievers, who yearned to keep spiritual traditions alive. This was particularly true for Easter, the high point of the traditional Christian calendar. Political prisoner Andreev recalled in 1929 how he managed to purchase ingredients for traditional Easter cakes and had a friend secretly bake them. He also boiled eggs for the occasion, and a few friends came in their best clothes bearing sausage, cheese, and other treats. After a prayer, during which Andreev observed the joy this brought to his Orthodox companions, they exchanged the customary Easter greetings: "Christ is risen!" and "He is truly risen!" They eagerly consumed the Easter cake and eggs, and "peace and friendship reigned at our table." In the end, even the atheist Andreev took pleasure in the fact that "we celebrated the holiday as our feelings told us to, and not how the administration ordered!" For his Christian counterparts, though, the holiday celebration no doubt meant more than defiance; it meant maintaining a yearly ritual

56 FINDING GOD IN THE GULAG

of remembering and honoring the crucifixion and resurrection of their Savior.[33]

Among the varied lay believers at Solovki, Baptists were remarkably open about practicing and preaching their religious beliefs. One of the most detailed personal narratives of lay Christianity at SLON comes from Petrov, a Baptist who characterized himself and fellow inmates as "slaves, sacrifices of idiotic political experiments." Starting in 1927, he served a three-year term primarily on Myagostrov, an island distinct from the Solovetsky Islands but administered by SLON. He strove to live a good Christian life and noted how this helped to change the behavior of others:

> Later the overseers learned that we were believers, and whenever someone came to review our work or to accept our work, they constrained themselves and didn't swear in our presence and sometimes even stopped their rude conversations. The Spirit of Christ just by our presence, without words, compelled their unholy mouths to be quiet.

Petrov's fellow inmates, however, were numb to his more overt missionary labors. Of this, he wrote, "They didn't want to hear about God, saying, 'If he exists, then why does he allow such injustice? Why doesn't he destroy our enemies who torture us? Why does he look and not do anything to free us?' People were very disillusioned." Petrov's memoir thus helps capture not only his own attempts to follow the precepts of his religion but the despair and distance from God that many inmates felt.[34]

Yet Petrov recalled receiving help from others who sympathized with the plight of suffering Christians on several occasions. One kindly guard, during a search, advised him to hide his Bible to keep it from being confiscated. After arriving at a small village during a long transfer, he and a few other Baptist prisoners asked a different guard to let them room together. "Oh, I know some Baptists," the guard replied, "and will try to do this for you." He then placed them in the hut of a kind Orthodox widow, who fed them and joined them in prayers, spiritual discussion, and singing. This scene was repeated at another village, where the Baptists sang and prayed together at night and "talked about the Word of God with the local villagers." Through the assistance of guards and local villagers, they were physically and spiritually strengthened on their difficult journey.[35]

Petrov's writings express devotion to and trust in God. He found evidence of God in his stark yet beautiful natural surroundings: "If you walk in the early morning along the edge of the sea then from all sides you can hear the majestic bird choir, singing a hymn to the Creator." And when the suffering of hard labor became too much to bear, he was strengthened by the feeling of God's presence:

> While working we fixed our gaze on Heaven, on our Father of life, who gives us strength to fulfill the task given to us without complaining. Oh, these sacred minutes! It is impossible to forget them. It seemed to me that He was suffering with us: it seemed that I could hear his heavy sigh.... I wanted not only to take on myself this work that was beyond my strength.... With the help of God even this difficult night passed.

Indeed, Petrov and his fellow Baptists seemed to draw strength from suffering, acknowledging that "Satan often led even me into despondency and sorrow." But as he remarked after relating the depraved condition of the other prisoners, "We understood that we were located precisely where Satan's throne was. We saw how people threw off their false masks of piety and turned into wild beasts." Still, seeing such depravity lent strength to his own sense of spirituality. He said, "I have never been so penetrated by that renewing and saving power of my Lord as there, among the inexpressible chaos of suffering, tears, and offense. More than at any other time I understood what it means to be a new creation, born of God. Christ kept my heart at peace." Believing that they were on the front lines of the war between good and evil, Petrov and his "brothers" endured their trials at the labor camp.[36]

Religious Life among the Orthodox Clergy

Religious life among the imprisoned Orthodox clergy was on prominent display at Solovki. As discussed earlier in this chapter, they were permitted to wear their robes while working and to worship at the cemetery church. However, much of their spiritual life was private, often manifested in one-on-one interactions with other believers. Sometimes these conversations centered on how to interpret Bolshevik repression and their incarceration at Solovki. Archpriest Mikhail Mitrotsky, who served in the Duma in prerevolutionary Russia, counseled his fellow priests to remain firm in their trials, telling them that "the weak and the faint-hearted will fall away. Then

58   FINDING GOD IN THE GULAG

those who remain will be [the church's] support, as were the martyrs of the first centuries." The clergy's ministrations commonly expressed this idea of shared suffering and viewed Bolshevik repression as a refining fire that would damn the weak and exalt the strong. As one blind, elderly monk told a friend after receiving news of his release from Solovki, "I don't know what I did to make God so mad that he punished me so little. I am unworthy, apparently, of the martyr's crown, oh, unworthy." Ultimately, Orthodox theology and the monastic tradition of suffering in imitation of Christ helped them accept the burdens of incarceration.[37]

Clergymen also strengthened each other by sharing spiritual visions and prophecies. One bishop described a vision he had on a starry Christmas Eve in which the stars gathered into the shape of a crown that descended to the earth while growing in brightness until they hovered over the common graves that held martyrs' bodies. This sense that the spiritual world, which he characterized as "larger and more real than the visible world," surrounded the imprisoned clergy at Solovki spurred this bishop to increased devotion. Archimandrite Feodosy likewise recounted a "prophetic vision" he had one night while on guard duty in 1927. He saw a mother on her deathbed, surrounded by brothers and sisters. The woman was given an icon and, with it, blessed Feodosy twice and then died while pronouncing a third blessing. His interpretation of this dream was that he would live for two years on the Solovetsky Islands and then die on the third. This dream, even though seemingly tragic for him (he survived, in fact), caused him to cry out, "Glory to God!" Such direct manifestations from God gave the clergy spiritual resolve to serve Christ amid trial and sorrow.[38]

Church holidays provided a vital opportunity for priests to commune together, particularly for those unable to attend the officially sanctioned services in the cemetery church. Feodosy recalled privately celebrating the Intercession of the Theotokos with Archbishop Ilarion and Archbishop Petr in 1927 and 1928. As he described it, "Speeches, food, tea—it was cozy, edifying, and nourishing."[39] Archpriest Polsky attended a secret Easter gathering held in a supply depot overseen by Hegumen Pitirim (Krylov) from Kazan and other clerics. At one moment, camp commander Eikhmans arrived for an unannounced inspection and demanded, "What kind of a meeting is this?" Father Pitirim explained that it was an Easter gathering, and this explanation was apparently sufficient, as the commander left them in peace. Polsky credibly suggests that the camp commander was satisfied with the work that Pitirim and his associates were doing and did not want to

THE SPIRITUAL LIFE OF SOLOVKI   59

disturb the delicate balance between the secular authorities and the religious inmates.[40]

Many other memoirists relate similar secret gatherings for Easter. In 1926, Pavel Chekhranov celebrated Easter while incarcerated at SLON's transit camp on Popov Island. The camp was crowded, and religious observance was strictly forbidden, but the clergymen plotted holiday observance anyway. Archbishop Ilarion and one other cleric held Easter services in an unfinished bakery that had no roof, windows, or doors. The others resolved to worship on the top bunks of a barrack. Chekhranov threw in his lot with the first group, "so that at least during these minutes [of worship] I won't have to hear swearing." While other inmates turned a blind eye, they slipped outside, reached the bakery undetected, and began the Easter liturgy. For Chekhranov, the words of the ritual had special meaning in their state of confinement, particularly the recounting of Israelite suffering in bondage in Egypt. And when they reached the chorus of "Christ is risen," Chekhranov related, "I didn't know whether to cry or laugh from joy." After finishing the services undetected, they celebrated the next day with coffee and pieces of Easter bread that had been smuggled in. Remembering this Easter service later, Chekhranov decided that even though it was "by starlight, without miter or vestments, it was most precious to the Lord." Holiday services in companion with fellow clerics had a clear positive impact on the spiritual community at SLON.[41]

Along with ministering to one another's spiritual needs, the imprisoned clergy often ministered to lay believers who looked to them for guidance. Sometimes this was prohibited by SLON authorities or at least made difficult; one eyewitness reported that inmates were only allowed to visit a priest if they were seriously ill. But many clergymen, due to their positions as doctors, accountants, and guards, had passes that allowed them to walk freely around the camp and minister to the imprisoned laity. Religious inmates who had passes also sought out spiritual leaders. As one political prisoner recalled, his Orthodox cellmate was like "a barely-noticed shadow" because he spent so much time in the cells where the priests lived.[42]

Memoirs from Solovki provide myriad accounts of intimate spiritual ministering. Feodosy recalled that many inmates sought communion with Archbishop Petr in 1927 and 1928, although he was too busy to see them all. Inmate Vladimir Zotov recalled guards sending Father Vladimir to the penalty isolator as punishment for performing a baptism for a fellow inmate.

60   FINDING GOD IN THE GULAG

When told not to conduct any more baptisms, he replied to the commander, "As a priest I cannot refuse to conduct ordinances for a believer." Andreyevsky related that Bishop Viktor was endlessly warm to those who sought his spiritual guidance, comforting those in need. He regularly received packages from his home parish and distributed the contents to other inmates. Similarly, Boris Shiraev devoted several pages of his documentary novel to the long-suffering ministering of Father Nikodim, who served as teacher and confessor to common criminals. And Likhachev recalled receiving comfort from Father Nikolay Piskanovsky. As he wrote: "One can't call him 'a man of good cheer,' but always, in the most oppressive circumstances, he radiated an inner peace. I can't remember his laughing or smiling, but a meeting with him was always consoling."[43]

The most sought-after Orthodox cleric for personal communion, even among nonbelievers, was Archbishop Ilarion. Political prisoner Volkov fondly recalled meeting Ilarion, who greeted him with a blessing before they conversed about a range of topics, including the Orthodox Church. "One must believe that the Church will stand firm," Ilarion made clear to Volkov, for "without such faith one cannot live.... Without Christ people will devour each other." Ilarion coupled this firm belief with indifference regarding his own fate: "He didn't think about himself and was ready to drink from any cup." Mikhail Nikonov-Smorodin remembered Ilarion similarly. Ilarion received him generously on their initial meeting, gave him a spiritual book to read, and then took the time to converse with him frequently on subsequent encounters. Ilarion inspired Nikonov-Smorodin with his deep intellect and devotion to serving God at Solovki. He was "a firm warrior for the faith; no deprivations could cause him to waver." Ultimately, Ilarion's optimistic outlook on life and exuberance in standing up for the faith uplifted many. As Chekhranov recalled, "discussions with Ilarion greatly tempered our unhappy life."[44]

Clergymen employed in SLON's medical institutions found themselves in a special position to minister to the sick and dying. Serving as a doctor during a typhus epidemic in 1929, Bishop Maksim ensured that he witnessed each death. As one eyewitness reported, "he closed the eyes of everyone who died, folded their arms over their chests and stood silently, not moving for a few moments. Apparently, he was praying."[45] Maksim also used his position to protect several other priests, whom he requested to work with him at the SLON hospital, thus creating a spiritual community of coreligionists in an institution devoted to helping others. The secret police report on Maksim made clear that through his position, "he surrounded himself with priests, and, not lacking in strength, healed souls, conducting religious ordinances." For this and other misdeeds against the regime, the Soviets executed him in 1931.[46]

A few memoirists recalled ministering efforts among SLON authorities. Arnold Shaufelberger related that an Orthodox priest who worked in the camp office often heard confessions from local Communists and gave them blessings. One priest even reportedly baptized the infant of one of the senior camp commandants because his wife was a believer who often attended church services. Polsky likewise recounted how one of his guards, who often listened to the clerics talking and occasionally argued with them about religion, eventually changed his heart. He secretly confessed to Polsky and accepted communion. As Polsky reflected, "examples like this are very joyful. The soul is real, and it turns out that the image of God in it is indestructible even for these half-beasts, half-people who are called *chekists* [a colloquial term for Soviet secret policemen]." Such miracles, as the believing called them, demonstrated God's continued concern for his followers and helped build a community of faith.[47]

Conflict among Christians

The uncertain attitude of SLON administrators toward religious expression, together with the policy of incarcerating many religious authorities in the same place, were crucial to allowing such a vibrant Christian community at Solovki. Yet not all was harmonious among imprisoned Christians. Certainly, they had to contend with antireligious propaganda and sporadic abuse from belligerent guards and other inmates. But there was also conflict among Christians themselves.

Some conflict occurred between different Christian sects. Incarcerated Baptists or Catholics eager to preach their vision of Christianity could grate on their Orthodox companions who held Russian Orthodoxy to be the one true religion. Likhachev recounted that staunch Catholic Yulia Danzas, a former lady-in-waiting to Empress Alexandra, "was prepared even on Solovki to take a somewhat lofty attitude to the sufferings of the numerous Orthodox clergy and even to write in the camp press about the existence of an Inquisition in the Orthodox Church, thereby lending strength to the antireligious propaganda." But other accounts suggest that Catholics and

62   FINDING GOD IN THE GULAG

Orthodox Christians more often cooperated rather than competed with one another. The Russian Catholic priest Fedorov was placed in a cell with Ilarion and other Orthodox clerics, and they found common ground in intellectual discussions of Christianity rather than arguing about doctrinal differences. Another Catholic priest recalled that the shared suffering at Solovki meant Catholic and Orthodox believers had become "brothers in Christ, bearers of the light of Christ in the surrounding spiritual darkness."[48]

In fact, most tension among Christians at Solovki occurred within Russian Orthodoxy itself. Officially, the Orthodox clergy imprisoned at Solovki kept their ecclesiastical ranks but were removed from their pastoral positions when they were arrested; they thus did not belong to the formal hierarchical structure of the church and had only infrequent contact with church headquarters in Moscow. In such conditions, they elected their own leadership and organized an informal church council that operated independently. Starting with his arrival in February 1924, the elected leader of the Orthodox clergy at SLON was Archbishop Evgeny, who was succeeded after his release in 1926 by Archbishop Prokopy. After Prokopy's release in November 1928, the imprisoned clergy chose Archbishop Petr as their leader, but he died months later from typhus. Tensions within the Orthodox community and increased repression from camp authorities then prevented a new leader from being chosen.[49] (See figure 2.3.)

This elected leadership of the 1920s, however, often did not always represent the highest spiritual authority at SLON. In the conditions of hierarchical uncertainty that the prison camp environment created, the highest-ranking clergyman, Archbishop Ilarion, refused a formal leadership role. Imprisoned at SLON from 1924 to 1925 and again from 1926 to 1929 (with imprisonment elsewhere in 1922–1923 and 1925–1926), Ilarion was well known as secretary and adviser to the head of the Orthodox Church, Patriarch Tikhon. He had also gained widespread recognition for his attacks on the Living Church, the Bolshevik-formed alternative to Russian Orthodoxy. After Ilarion arrived in 1924, as one inmate described it, "he quickly acquired great popularity due to his goodness, his eloquence, and his entire behavior." Thus, although Ilarion did not hold a formal leadership position, most imprisoned clerics at SLON recognized him as their de facto spiritual leader and often sought his advice and blessing. Below Ilarion and the elected heads of the Solovki assembly, archbishops, bishops, priests, hegumen, monks, and deacons found themselves in an unstructured environment, much different from the strict hierarchy to which they were accustomed.[50]

Figure 2.3 Imprisoned Orthodox clergymen at Solovki. Seated in the middle are Archbishop Ilarion and Archbishop Evgeny. Wikimedia Commons.

Not surprisingly, given the pressures of the prison camp environment, the uncertain leadership structure, and the challenges facing the Orthodox Church in the Soviet Union at large, there were quarrels among the Orthodox clergy at Solovki. Feodosy recalled that some priests resented the bishops because the latter devoted more energy to serving the laity than to serving the lower-ranking clerics. Other clergymen argued over the meaning of the new Bolshevik regime. As explained by Andreyevsky, who witnessed several heated discussions between Bishop Maksim and Bishop Viktor, Maksim "was a pessimist and was preparing for the difficult trials of the last days, not believing in the possibility of a rebirth of Russia. But the Right Reverend Viktor was an optimist and believed in the possibility of a short but bright period, as a final gift from heaven for the tortured Russian people." Discussions of joint suffering thus did not always lead to a sense of spiritual unity; they could also drive coreligionists apart. Sometimes quarrels were simply a function of camp-level rivalries and patronage networks. Archimandrite Feodosy recalled a feud between the commander and the chief accountant at one labor detail, and he and Archpriest Grinevich ended up on opposite sides. The two ranks—archimandrite and archpriest—were roughly equal, leaving no easy way for the situation to be resolved. Upon seeing this, Feodosy quit

64   FINDING GOD IN THE GULAG

his position and asked for reassignment rather than be put into conflict with Grinevich.[51]

Other conflicts were more consequential. In 1929, not all approved of the election of Archbishop Petr as head of the Orthodox clergy. Petr's friend, Feodosy, tried to help in his accounting duties to give him more time to minister, but other clergymen—Bishop Grigory and Archpriest Pospelov—prevented this. Moreover, Feodosy recalled, Deacon Lelyukhin "informed about our meetings and conversations." Petr's opponents also got him transferred to share a cell with "his enemy," Grigory, and Lelyukhin unceremoniously threw Petr's belongings out onto the street. This was "an unheard-of scandal at Solovki" that ultimately prompted most high-ranking clergymen to side with Petr. Pospelov even bowed down to the earth in front of Petr, begging for forgiveness, but "forgiveness was not given." As Feodosy wrote recalling this episode, "this is a difficult memory. The human weaknesses of the leadership came out in full force. It was bitter." Other memoirists chose to omit this conflict from their remembrances, suggesting that similar clerical conflicts have been lost in the historical record. In any event, the fact that lower-ranking clergymen could act in such open opposition to an archbishop demonstrates the potential for hierarchical breakdown in the labor camp's repressive and alienating environment.[52]

The largest source of tension among the clergy at SLON in the 1920s, which almost certainly played a role in the actions directed against Archbishop Petr, was the question of whether conciliation with the Bolshevik regime was possible. In part, this issue manifested itself in the presence of a few clergymen of the Living Church at SLON. Klinger recalled one former Living Church bishop who had attempted to return to Orthodoxy. As part of his repentance process, he revealed the close relationship between the alternative church and the secret police, for which he was convicted of "revealing state secrets." At SLON, however, the Orthodox clergy rejected his penance, and he was shunned by other prisoners and tormented by guards. Feodosy also recalled two members of the Living Church clergy who ended up at Solovki. One tried to inform on the Orthodox clergy with little effect, but the other "was a scoundrel of the highest order" who ultimately had to be bought off to keep him from making trouble.[53]

Patriarch Tikhon's death in April 1925 and the subsequent election of the more conciliatory Sergius as acting head of the Orthodox Church brought the already contentious debate of church-state relations to a head. In May 1926, some of the imprisoned clergy, including archbishops Evgeny and Prokopy,

THE SPIRITUAL LIFE OF SOLOVKI   65

along with Ivan Popov, a well-known professor of the Moscow Spiritual Academy, composed a letter supporting Tikhon's hard-line approach toward the Bolshevik regime. But there was considerable disagreement about how strident a tone to take in the letter. Polsky, a staunch advocate of "preserving the dignity" of the church and suffering repression and death rather than colluding with the state, was disappointed that most other high-ranking clerics did not accept his uncompromising position. After his long and strident draft of the "Epistle of the Solovetsky Bishops" was widely criticized, with one bishop accusing him of wanting to die "as if to the accompaniment of music," he lamented that "the majority want to conduct negotiations with the authorities in the hope of a positive result. They think that it is not necessary to die, that no one requires this, that they can get by without it." In the end, Polsky remembered, "my draft was not accepted, it was seen as impractical, but is hope on agreement [with the authorities] really practical?"[54]

Ultimately, many Orthodox clerics agreed upon a revised "Epistle of the Solovetsky Bishops." While it was more conciliatory than Polsky would have liked, it still staked out a firm stance against the Bolshevik regime. It criticized the Living Church for abandoning Christian principles and lying to the world about the state of religious affairs in Russia and declared that "the Orthodox Church will never enter this unworthy path." It clarified that the issue was not legislation on the separation of church and state, which the Orthodox Church did not directly oppose. The problem, rather, was more fundamental. While the Orthodox Church had productive relations with many different governments worldwide, including those with separation of church and state and those with state religions other than Orthodoxy, this was impossible with the Soviets because of "materialism, the official philosophy of the communist party." This deeply held ideology affected all aspects of political, social, and family life and made conflict unavoidable. In fact, the epistle charged, the Bolsheviks broke their own law by violently pushing a program of atheism on the Russian people. Ultimately, the message was clear: "The Orthodox Church does not believe in loyalty to the Soviet state."[55]

This epistle, widely circulated in Russia and abroad, warned Sergius to continue to follow the oppositional stance of Tikhon. Sergius, however, issued a declaration of conciliation on July 29, 1927, allowing for a tenuous truce between the Soviet state and the Orthodox hierarchy. When this was read at SLON, many imprisoned clergymen remained loyal to the hierarchy and were known (as elsewhere in Russia) as "Sergiusites." According to Andreyevsky, a lay member who opposed them, the Sergiusite bishops

66 FINDING GOD IN THE GULAG

also became more conciliatory with SLON authorities and, in return, were treated better by the guards.[56]

However, many high-ranking clergymen imprisoned at SLON opposed Sergius and took on the name "Josephites," after Metropolitan Joseph, who opposed conciliation with the Soviet regime. Their ranks swelled in the late 1920s, as most clerics incarcerated after Sergius's declaration were "Josephites." The Josephites professed allegiance to the newly established Russian True Orthodox Church, also called the Catacomb Church, and from SLON they distributed additional epistles declaring their opposition to Sergius. Ilarion tried to maintain a middle ground, condemning Sergius's declaration and often joining the Josephites for worship services but also maintaining communication with Sergius as the head of the church. (Perhaps not surprisingly, given his spiritual stature, sources on Ilarion are mixed. Some memoirs place him firmly in the Josephite camp, while others claim he remained loyal to Sergius.)[57]

This compromise by Ilarion and the already tenuous nature of the hierarchy opened space for new leaders to emerge among the Josephite clergy: Archpriest Nikolay, who served as confessor for the breakaway movement, Bishop Maksim, and especially Bishop Viktor. Viktor had been sent to Solovki in 1928 for his strident opposition to Sergius and Soviet power. As described by Likhachev, who was sympathetic to the Josephite position, Viktor appealed especially to the younger clergy. He was "very cultured and owned printed works on theology, but in appearance reminded one of a rural parish priest. . . . He tried to help everyone and, what really mattered, was able to, so that everyone was well disposed toward him and believed what he said." And although he worked as a bookkeeper at SLON's farm (and occasionally pilfered food to give to his subordinates), Viktor refused to sacrifice his religious principles. When the camp commander ordered all Orthodox clerics to shave their beards off like the other inmates in 1929, he was among the resisters and was forcibly shaved. In this manner, though lower in ecclesiastical rank than Ilarion and others, Viktor managed through force of personality to become the imprisoned Josephite clerics' de facto leader at SLON.[58]

One immediate point of contention when the schism occurred on Solovki concerned church services. Viktor and most other imprisoned clerics stopped attending services at the cemetery church operated by the local nonincarcerated monks, who remained loyal to Sergius. According to

Feodosy, who sided with the Josephites, the Solovetsky monks "conducted themselves very proudly in the presence of the inmate clergy," resulting in sharp divisions between them. As for lay prisoners who continued to attend services whenever possible at the cemetery church, the Josephite-inclined Likhachev observed, "The only prisoners who went there were those who didn't really understand Church affairs and simply couldn't do without church services."[59]

In place of the cemetery church, Viktor invited Josephite clerics, Ilarion, and a few lay believers to a forest clearing or remote building at night to conduct secret worship services of the "Solovetsky Catacomb Church." Viktor and other Josephite clerics even conducted secret ordinations of "catacomb" bishops, cementing their break from the Sergiusite hierarchy. They were aided in this effort by Maksim, who became one of the first secret bishops of the Catacomb Church in 1927 while working as the head doctor of the Taganskaya Prison in Moscow. (When the secret police discovered this, they sent him to Solovki on a three-year sentence for counterrevolutionary propaganda.) In this manner, Solovki played a key role in cementing the schism of the Orthodox Church in the late 1920s.[60]

The bitter tension between Josephites and Sergiusites at SLON is conveyed by an incident related by the lay Josephite Andreyevsky. Archbishop Antony, a Sergiusite, asked to talk with Andreyevsky about the latter's visit to Sergius as part of a delegation that protested the 1927 declaration. Viktor and Maksim agreed that Andreyevsky could talk with Antony but counseled him to receive a blessing from Antony only if the latter expressed solidarity with the Catacomb Church. After a two-hour discussion, at the end of which Antony professed his continued loyalty to Sergius, Andreyevsky, as instructed, interrupted Antony's parting blessing and abruptly left. Upon hearing what had happened, Maksim approvingly declared, "The Soviet and the Catacomb Church are incompatible. The secret, monastic, Catacomb Church has anathematized the 'Sergiusites' and those who are with them." By the late 1920s, the religious hierarchy at Solovki had decisively split along the Josephite-Sergiusite line that was affecting Orthodoxy throughout Russia. But while the majority of clergymen outside the camps remained loyal to Sergius, SLON's imprisoned clerics mostly rejected his accommodationist stance.[61]

68   FINDING GOD IN THE GULAG

The Solovetsky Camp of Forced Labor of Special Significance served as a model penal facility for the Soviet regime, demonstrating to Soviet citizens and the global community alike the supposed superiority of Soviet corrections. Even famed writer Maxim Gorky was enlisted in this effort, reporting on the SLON's alleged virtues while ignoring the incarcerated clergy and portraying the local monks as uneducated simpletons and drunkards who had nothing to offer modern society. Yet, contrary to official propaganda, SLON was an institution rife with contradictions. Some guards were sadistically cruel, meting out torture and summary execution, but others were noted for their patience and humanity. Some inmates were subjected to back-breaking labor, while others worked as theater directors, newspaper writers, and museum specialists. Despite the official rhetoric of re-education and correction, few inmates converted to the gospel of socialism.[62]

Such contradictions were also on display concerning religion. Solonevich, in his memoir of Solovki, recounted a conversation with an imprisoned Orthodox priest, who wondered at the harsh repression meted out against the Orthodox Church. "You know, it's kind of funny," the elderly cleric expressed, "but they are so afraid of us, old men. . . . As someone once said, the most explosive material in the world is ideas and faith." The imprisoned community of believers at Solovki certainly validated this statement. SLON authorities and Christians from various denominations clashed on several issues as their incompatible worldviews came into conflict in this place of detention and deprivation. Camp commanders issued antireligious propaganda, at times forbade religious practice, and even deliberately offended the religious sensibilities of their prisoners. Some imprisoned believers, meanwhile, refused cooperation with the regime, and most viewed it as carrying out the work of Satan. Faith proved so explosive that it worked toward the internal splintering of the Orthodox hierarchy after the death of Patriarch Tikhon, causing discord among Orthodox clergymen at SLON.[63]

Yet, amid these clashes among inmates and guards, faith flourished. Contradictory policies concerning religion and the historical religious surroundings of the ancient monastery created an environment where, despite the acute deprivation and violence of imprisonment, beliefs could be maintained, even strengthened. Incarcerated Christians suffered physically and emotionally, and they struggled with depression and doubt. But communion with fellow believers, formal and informal worship services, holiday celebrations, and private religious practices ultimately worked toward creating spiritual communities that were constantly invigorated by a steady supply of new inmates. Rather than be "re-educated" toward socialism by labor, propaganda, and other correctional devices, most devout Christians maintained their faith.

This fact was not lost on the Soviet regime. If SLON was a penal experiment on which the Gulag would be modeled, one of the apparent lessons learned by Soviet authorities was that permitting church services and concentrating ardent religious believers in one place were detrimental to the goals of socialist re-education. As the following chapters will show, Stalin's Gulag would decisively rule against inmate worship and try hard to prevent the formation of spiritual communities. Such was the lesson of Solovki.

3

The War against Religion in the Gulag

Vladimir Lenin's death in 1924 set off a succession struggle among top Soviet leadership. Joseph Stalin ultimately defeated Leon Trotsky and other contenders and, with his opponents sidelined, embarked on a new economic program of rapid industrialization and the forced collectivization of agriculture. The goal was to develop a state-run, socialist economy capable of surpassing the capitalist economies of the West. Stalin proclaimed the first "five-year plan" toward this goal in late 1928 with great fanfare, promising new factories, railroads, mines, canals, and power plants. Over the following years, labor competitions, "shock work" brigades that moved from job site to job site to quickly complete production tasks, and later the Stakhanovite movement of setting new production records were instituted to spur Soviet workers to vastly increased productivity. The 1930s was a period of great optimism, particularly as the capitalist West became mired in the Great Depression. But it was also a period of intense repression. Waves of arrests of economic specialists, street criminals, peasants who resisted collectivization, and various other groups overwhelmed Soviet judicial organs. For top communist leaders, this presented no contradiction: Marxism taught that socialism was humanity's destiny, and those who stood in its way needed to be either reformed or eliminated.

This dramatic reorganization of Soviet life also featured a renewed assault on religion. The calculated retreat from overt religious repression during much of the 1920s resulted in sporadic religious revivalism. New policies in 1929, however, clamped down on missionary work, restricted property rights and the freedom of assembly for churches, and created a new workweek that forced people to labor on Sunday (though this last policy was largely reversed in 1931). The secret police destroyed or repurposed thousands of chapels, stripped cupolas of their gold to bankroll industrialization, and imprisoned or executed many clergymen and devout believers. Orthodox parishes in the countryside were particularly hard hit, as police arrested village priests for resisting collectivization and turned chapels into storehouses. Lay believers protested these new attacks, sometimes violently,

Finding God in the Gulag. Jeffrey S. Hardy, Oxford University Press. © Oxford University Press 2024.
DOI: 10.1093/9780197751701.003.0004

THE WAR AGAINST RELIGION   71

but some 80 percent of village parishes were forcibly closed in the late 1920s and early 1930s. Pressure on religious organizations in succeeding years hardly relented. In 1935, for instance, Soviet police agencies prosecuted several religious groups under statute 58-10 of the criminal code for "counterrevolutionary agitation on the grounds of religion and various sectarian teachings (sermons, citations from religious books, illegal meetings, and so forth)." If socialism meant a planned and collectivized economic system devoid of the remnants of capitalism, it also meant creating "new Soviet people" freed from the religious superstitions of the past.[1]

This chapter explores religion in Soviet prisons and camps during the 1930s, the decade of intense Stalinization. Somewhat paradoxically, even as antireligious repression increased in Soviet society, antireligious repression behind bars or barbed wire presented a mixed story. There were certainly episodes of heightened persecution against religious prisoners and, based on the experience of Solovki in the 1920s, more concrete rules prohibiting worship and special treatment. Yet the implementation of these regulations was sporadic, and antireligious propaganda was less prevalent than might be expected. With an overbearing focus on economic production, Gulag officials surprisingly often allowed imprisoned Christians to find ways to practice their faith. This was more difficult than in the 1920s, but it was still more possible than might be imagined in a totalitarian country intent on crafting an irreligious, if not atheistic, society.

The Creation of the Gulag

The radical changes beginning in the 1920s, together with the mass repression that accompanied them, necessitated, from Stalin's point of view, a vast new penal system. Using the experimental labor camp at Solovki as a model, Stalin in 1929 created the Main Administration of Camps (Gulag) within the secret police apparatus and ordered it to create an expansive network of new labor camps. The explicit purpose of the Gulag was twofold. First, it was designed to extract labor from convicts to assist in the country's rapid industrialization, particularly in remote, inhospitable locations where "free" workers were scarce. Gulag inmates built canals, factories, railroads, and hydroelectric dams; they operated large farms; they mined coal, gold, tin, and other metals; and they produced an array of industrial and consumer products. The Gulag's second purpose was to re-educate inmates

72 FINDING GOD IN THE GULAG

using a combination of collective labor, political indoctrination, vocational training, educational programs, and cultural events. Gulag camps featured newspapers, libraries, theater troupes, soccer teams, labor competitions, awards for good hygienic practices, literacy classes, and a host of other re-educational programs. In sum, Gulag inmates were supposed to help transform the country and, by so doing, be transformed themselves.

In reality, the first of these two aims almost always took precedence over the second. Though the Soviets never abandoned re-educational goals in the Gulag, a consistent re-educational program was rarely realized or prioritized. Gulag camp managers faced constant pressure to attain weekly, monthly, quarterly, and yearly production targets but were rarely chastised for missing re-educational targets (which could also be much more easily falsified). Fearful for their jobs and indeed their very lives—accusations of "sabotage" and "wrecking" could be wielded against anyone in the 1930s— these managers mandated long and hard labor for their inmates, often in harsh weather conditions. Many inmates died from exhaustion, malnutrition, exposure, and disease.

Meanwhile, despite its supposed focus on re-education, the Soviet regime talked more about its convicts as "class enemies," "counterrevolutionaries," "enemies of the people," and "labor power" than as redeemable citizens. This attitude prevailed among Gulag guards and officials and translated into sporadic violence against the prisoners. Ultimately, while all prisons are repressive and violent to some extent, the Gulag was exceptional for both its massive size and its deadliness. The Gulag quickly became the largest penal system in the world, with more than a million inmates by the end of the 1930s and more than two million by the end of the 1940s. It also claimed the lives of millions of people who died in the camps or shortly after release, a staggering death toll caused by a callous disregard for human life.

This massive and violent network of labor camps was where religious prisoners in the Soviet Union were sent in the 1930s. Determining how many Gulag inmates were religious during this volatile decade is impossible. The Gulag categorized its prisoners in numerous ways, and one can still find in the Gulag archives detailed records sorting inmates by crime, length of term, age, number of convictions, class status, educational level, gender, ethnicity, nationality, and, most important for camp bosses, work capability. But Gulag administrators in official reports did not categorize inmates according to religious belief. Reflecting broader attitudes of Soviet officialdom, they chose to ignore this facet of their inmates' lives, even though it could have been helpful for the purpose of re-education to understand each inmate's religious convictions (or lack thereof).

The only mention of religion among these statistics that one occasionally finds in the archive are tallies of how many inmates were sentenced according to laws regulating the separation of church and state or how many had previously served as "cult workers." According to one internal report from October 1939, for example, there were 5,273 former "cult workers" in the camps and colonies of the Gulag out of some 1.3 million inmates (a figure reported alongside 4,972 capitalists, 37,094 rich peasants, 1,993 tsarist army officers, 8,277 White Army officers and spies, and 850 tsarist policemen). But indicators like these are rare in the Gulag archive and likely undercount former clergymen, monks, and nuns (not to mention lay believers). Regardless of their exact numbers, religious believers in the Gulag of the 1930s were quickly subjected to the harsh realities of this new labor camp system.[2]

The Antireligious Turn at Solovki

As the secret police organized the Gulag camp network in 1929 and the early 1930s, it quickly became apparent that religious believers would not enjoy special privileges as they sometimes did in the 1920s. Whereas the first decade of Soviet power was a period of uncertainty concerning religious rights in places of confinement, the second decade of Soviet power moved decisively in the direction of antireligious repression. There would be no more debate about allowing Christians to attend worship services or whether large groups of clerics could live together. Although the level of antireligious repression and propaganda varied from camp to camp (true of many things in the Gulag), the direction from Moscow was clear: all manifestations of religiosity were to be eliminated.

This new antireligious attitude was first felt at Solovki, where conditions for religious prisoners began to worsen in 1928 and 1929. Guards conducted detailed searches and confiscated cassocks, prayer books, icons, and crosses. SLON authorities mandated that clergymen's beards be shaved to eliminate this visual reminder of their religious rank. Most willingly submitted to this humiliation, but several resisted and were beaten, tied up with belts, and forcefully shaved. Camp officials increasingly restricted the use of the cemetery chapel, before closing it for good in 1931. Several members of

74   FINDING GOD IN THE GULAG

the Dukhobor spiritualist movement were accused of "openly engaging in anti-Soviet agitation, organizing mass work refusals and disobedience against camp orders," and were executed. And most of the Orthodox and Catholic clergy were sent to the island of Anzer, where they were placed on hard labor and minimal rations. One account from a Catholic priest related, "Even though almost all of us priests are old and invalid, they often force us to do very difficult work like, for example, dig holes for the foundations of buildings, carry heavy stones, dig during winter in the frozen earth." In the new era of industrialization and repression, as socialism was actively being built by the Stalinist regime, the spiritual community that had thrived at Solovki in the 1920s would no longer be tolerated.[3]

In one fascinating anecdote from this period of repression on Anzer, Orthodox memoirist Olga Vtorova-Yafa recalled how the guards tried to use the socialist May Day holiday, which fell just after Easter, to punish certain clergymen. They gathered fourteen Orthodox and Catholic bishops and forced them to clear snow, haul sand, and otherwise prepare for the May Day political rally. Other inmates were not allowed to assist them, and nuns in the women's barracks looked on, crying and exclaiming, "Oh Lord, Lord! And now this, on Holy Thursday! They should be right now participating in the triumphal 'washing of the feet' service, but instead of that, see what they are doing!" But for Vtorova-Yafa, herself an Orthodox believer, this was a holy act of humility "of the true pastors of the Church, who to the end displayed self-denial and firmly held to their faith in Christ." Moreover, the bishops of the two competing denominations were "united in love and humility, regardless of any councils or dogmatic arguments." She felt privileged to witness the ordeals of these "passion-bearers," the triumph of "the human spirit, the victory of faith." She also felt some satisfaction when Easter had beautiful weather, but a storm on May Day turned the square the bishops had prepared into a muddy mess.[4]

Gulag authorities also noticed the ecumenism that Vtorova-Yafa recorded. As a November 1930 report made clear, "it has been observed that the borders between sectarians of various confessions are noticeably diminishing and they, having united for the most part in a home base, entrust leadership with the most experienced and deserving 'brother,' regardless of what sect he belongs to." Increased repression, it seems, helped forge stronger bonds of fellowship across denominational lines. SLON authorities did all they could to prevent religious bridge building. As the report continued, "every instance of agitation has been punished, and the priesthood groups . . . are being broken up, and their members are being distributed in various camp units." This method of isolating religious authorities would soon be facilitated by the creation of dozens of new camps across the Soviet Union.[5]

Investigatory files from the Solovetsky Camp in the early 1930s provide a few more examples of heightened repression against imprisoned clerics. The character file of the Polish Catholic priest Feliks, for instance, records how SLON officials intensified efforts to coerce priests to renounce their faith.

> 2/10/30—He does not recognize the camp order. Still holds to his religious convictions.
> 11/10/30—There are no indications of correction. At the current time his attitude toward labor is unsatisfactory. Completely knowingly and thoughtfully is committing crimes.
> 11/18/30—Ideologically mature and a staunch enemy of everything soviet. Deserves strict isolation.
> 7/30/31—Doubtful toward correction.

Such observations by guards and informants became increasingly common. SLON authorities' attempts to re-educate Feliks ultimately took a toll on his psychological well-being. One of his companions later recalled, "It was impossible not to notice that imprisonment very much burdened the priest Feliks, and he with rather undisguised impatience awaited the exchange of prisoners between Poland and the USSR." But as talks dragged on, he began to lose hope. In late 1931, he fell sick and died.[6]

Other religious authorities were likewise monitored and harassed. A character statement concerning Bishop Arkady from July 6, 1930, noted that "he has an anti-Soviet attitude, he gathers around himself servants of a cult. He conducts among them agitation against the living church. He requires strict isolation and incessant observation." Several months later, an informant complained of "the luxurious lifestyle of the priests, who are always receiving packages from outside the camp." Moreover, the informant continued, they held nightly meetings after work with the pretense of drinking tea, but these were actually "illegal meetings of an anti-Soviet organization . . . aimed at discrediting Soviet power under the guise of religious discussions." In response, the camp commander ordered continued undercover observation and thorough searches of the priests' barracks. A psalter, a copy of the liturgy, a New Testament, and one set of prayer beads were quickly confiscated, and an ensuing investigation led to the arrest of twenty-two inmates, including

76   FINDING GOD IN THE GULAG

one bishop, twelve priests, and nine lay believers. Charges against Arkady detailed his leadership in "secret worship services, where he preached about the strengthening of patience, with hope for the rapid end of Soviet power." The charges also spoke of his organizing a mutual aid network among the clergy. Arkady denied these charges, as did the other arrested clergymen, but they staunchly defended their faith when interrogated. As one responded, "I will not betray my convictions. As firm as they were before the camp and imprisonment, they remain so now." In the end, Arkady received an additional five years' imprisonment, six priests got two more years, and eight others received lesser punishments.[7]

Many Orthodox and Catholic priests tried to accommodate themselves to this newly repressive environment. When possible, they met secretly in the woods for prayer or held mass in secret. Catholic priest Donat later recalled, "we carefully covered the room's windows with raincoats so that it would not be noticed from the courtyard that at nights worship services were being held in the attic." There was very little wine, some of it painstakingly extracted from raisins, so they had to ration it carefully. This shortage resulted in heated theological arguments about whether to mix it with water and, if so, the maximum amount of water that could be permitted. They ultimately decided to allow just one drop of water for each six to eight drops of wine to preserve the sanctity of the ordinance. Even in this era of heightened repression, in other words, devout Christians continued to observe their religious practices as best they could.[8]

Antireligious Activity in the Gulag

As conditions for religious inmates worsened at Solovki, Soviet authorities sent newly arrested Christians to the growing number of Gulag camps in remote locations throughout the USSR. In contrast to the 1920s, few inmates were imprisoned in former monasteries. Several monasteries continued to be used through the 1930s, including the Solovetsky Monastery and the Kirillo-Novoozersk Monastery in Leningrad Province, which was given to the secret police to house prisoners on March 20, 1935. (The latter is still used as a prison in Russia as of the time of publication, housing dangerous inmates with life sentences.) But these were stark exceptions. The hastily constructed Gulag camps of the 1930s and beyond increasingly featured wooden barracks, barbed wire, and watchtowers rather than monastic cells, chapels, and centuries-old walls. No longer could Orthodox prisoners find spiritual comfort in being imprisoned in a formerly holy place.[9]

If the physical environment of incarceration changed under Gulag administration, so, too, did the general attitude toward religious practice. Whereas in the 1920s there was still some debate about allowing the free expression of faith in prison, the 1930s brought an end to all such pretenses. This is made clear in the first Soviet penology textbook of the decade, published in 1930 by leading criminologist Boris Utevsky. This tome explained to Soviet law students and penal officials that Quakers initially developed the penitentiary in the United States and the United Kingdom as a place of repentance. As it spread to other countries, including Russia before the revolution, "forcible religious manipulation continued in full." Obligatory prayers, worship services, and religious education were, according to Utevsky, a way of subjugating the common people of Russia. Then, engaging in a bit of revisionist history, he declared that "one of the first accomplishments of Soviet power in relation to prisons was to "make a permanent break with religious influence on prisoners." As explored in previous chapters, this was certainly not true. But now, in 1930, it was supposed to become true.[10]

A book on Soviet corrections that procurator general Andrey Vyshinsky published in 1934 also highlighted this central difference between Gulag camps and the prisons of the West and of the tsarist past. The latter featured religious preaching and literature in "a combination of juridical punishment and theological torture" that endeavored to destroy inmates' free spirits, but in Soviet penal institutions, "the prison churches have been turned into clubs" filled with music, theater, and instruction aimed at freeing inmates "from the dense web of religious preconceptions that still in many cases enmesh them." Here the continued religious faith of many inmates is frankly acknowledged, but so, too, is a policy of mandatory socialist culture that would eventually eradicate such beliefs. Ida Averbakh's criminological text *From Crime to Labor* (1936) likewise emphasized that "long and organized explanatory work" dedicated to exposing religious reactionaries as "representatives of the class enemy in the camp" was necessary to transform inmates into good Soviet citizens. As she concluded, "Overcoming religious prejudices is an important link in the chain of activities aimed at re-educating and remaking the consciousness of the camp-dweller and raising the cultural-political level of every prisoner."[11]

A similar conclusion is presented in the most famous piece of Gulag-related propaganda, *Belomor*, a widely distributed book by famed author

78 FINDING GOD IN THE GULAG

Maxim Gorky and others about prisoners laboring on the White Sea–Baltic Sea Canal. The authors depict incarcerated priests and mullahs as lazy, greedy, and arrogant, except for one who renounced his monastic vows and planned to enroll in a technical school after release. As for lay believers, one of the many intriguing (and perhaps embellished or even invented) stories from this volume concerns a group of six peasants who refused to work but rather prayed and sang psalms: "They sang of Jonah, standing amid the Karelian forests. They lauded the belly of the whale. They sang hoarsely of the wisdom of wild animals, the supreme love of the fishes, the good-hearted birds, and the blueness of the sky." But prison officials distributed rations based on labor performed, and the peasants received almost nothing to eat. They then began to quarrel until one finally exclaimed, "Ah, to the devil with the birds. What am I, anyway, a fool? Singing in the forest!" The next day, they abandoned their religious pretenses and went to work. The intended message was clear: freed from the pernicious influence of religion, wayward Soviet citizens can quickly become productive and rational members of society.[12]

In addition to works like *Belomor*, which reached a broad audience both domestically and abroad, prison officials disseminated antireligious propaganda in the camps. As the Gulag's statute on cultural-educational work instructed, "Antireligious work should be conducted by means of discussions, reports, lectures, reading antireligious literature, showing films, and so forth. For conducting discussions, reports, and lectures on antireligious themes propagandists from among the staff who have corresponding preparation should be chosen." As in the 1920s, speakers lectured on topics such as "the clerical crusade to overthrow Soviet power" and "the key role of religion as a weapon in oppressing the working masses." Officials stocked antireligious books in camp libraries, and visual propaganda declared things like "We need to destroy [religion] by destroying the priesthood as a class."[13]

Yet, perhaps paradoxically, even as Gulag regulations mandated antireligious propaganda, the amount of space devoted to atheism in Gulag newspapers fell. This was due to the overwhelming tide of production-related content in this decade, with "cultural-educational" officers in the Gulag committing most of their efforts to spurring inmates to meet plan targets. Some Gulag newspapers in the 1930s had no antireligious content for years. Surprisingly, this was true even of *New Solovki*, which in the 1920s had produced a steady stream of antireligious articles. A prominent front-page article on the cultural transformation of inmates from 1930, for

THE WAR AGAINST RELIGION 79

instance, completely omitted religion, as did another lengthy article on the history of SLON. Even those newspapers with editors inclined to wage a more active struggle against religion only featured three or four antireligious pieces per year. While antireligious messages still may have been shared in political and cultural discussion groups organized by the cultural-educational departments of each camp, they increasingly disappeared from the newspapers.[14]

So what remained, in those camp newspapers that did occasionally publish antireligious articles? As in the 1920s, there were a few poems with antireligious content, primarily highlighting the difference between the old and new ways of life. Writers attacked religious holidays, particularly Easter and Christmas but also Ramadan, as the Soviet state imprisoned more Muslims from Central Asia and the Caucasus. In one such article from the newspaper *Reforging on the Construction Site of the Moscow-Volga Canal*, the author frames Ramadan as just another tool in the oppression of the working class and calls Muslims to work hard rather than fast. After all, the article made clear, "workers should be free from all religious ways; they should not consider themselves slaves of a nonexistent god."[15]

The juxtaposition of religion and science also featured prominently in antireligious propaganda of the 1930s. A front-page article from 1933 makes this clear with a quote from Stalin himself: "The Party cannot be neutral in regard to religion. It conducts antireligious propaganda against any and all religious ideas because the Party is for science, but religious ideas go against science, for in every religion there is something that contradicts science." This idea was reaffirmed in the same newspaper a few months later in an article called "Did Christ Really Exist?" which begins: "Science has not left for us any traces of the existence of Christ." Another representative article on religion and science in Gulag newspapers comes from *Down with Illiteracy*, distributed to poorly educated inmates of the Dmitrovsky Camp. Published in 1935, it stated, "Religion teaches that man was created by God. Modern science . . . has demonstrated that mankind by natural means came about from animal predecessors and that only through labor has man become intelligent matter." The article further explains that "religion gets in the way of and harms the creation of socialist society. Faith in God and socialism are incompatible. Here in the Soviet Union even children do not believe in the Godly origins of mankind." So here the stark contrast is laid bare: science and religion are fundamentally incompatible.[16]

Gulag newspapers of the 1930s also continued to use real stories (or at least presented them as such) from within the camps to attack religion. On page

80 FINDING GOD IN THE GULAG

two of the October 23, 1934, edition of the newspaper *Lumberjack*, for instance, there is a letter addressed to the deputy commander of the Temnitsky
Camp that reads:

> Since the time I have been in the camp I have rethought my pre-
> vious convictions and have come to the conclusion that, as a sectarian,
> I had deeply erred. And by this I had brought great harm to socialist
> construction. . . . Now new prospects of a new, real life have been unfolded
> and I want to fight in the ranks of the working class for the realization of
> socialism and cut off all ties to sectarianism. I thank the commander of
> the camp for his sensitive attitude toward me, which has allowed me to re-
> structure my psychology. Signed V. Lebedev.

Readers found an editorial note accompanying the letter explaining
that the October Revolution of 1917 beneficially reformed the psychology
of millions of people. The editor explained that while "the remnants of
capitalism—religion and sectarianism—have still not been completely
stamped out, . . . with every day their ranks are diminishing; the blind now
see." Here a well-known Christian metaphor of the blind seeing is turned
on its head to talk about de-conversion from Christianity. The editor then
reached the crucial point: "In analyzing their own ideology, every sectarian
must behave exactly as Lebedev. A real person cannot fence himself off from
real life. He cannot stand outside this great construction, which will go
down in the annals of history as a shining example of new forms and relations among mankind." This intimate story and the accompanying editorial
form a call to action for other inmates. They, as builders of a massive canal
who were bringing socialism to the world, must not be deceived by religious
falsehoods. They must embrace the advance of modernity and progress and
let their lives be governed by socialist ideology.[17]

Gulag newspaper editors published several visual propaganda
pieces along with antireligious articles. One picture, without caption
or accompanying article, depicts churches in the background, clearly
symbolizing the old. In the foreground, construction activity shows that
the new socialist, economically oriented way of life is replacing the old, superstitious, unproductive way of life. In another illustration from the newspaper *Lumberjack*, the reader sees a "Cemetery of the Loafers." Three graves,
along with a vulture, signify that loafers would perish; in the Gulag in the
1930s, after all, rations were often tied to productivity. But it is also unmistakable that the crosses over the graves are Russian Orthodox crosses. The

clear implication is that those who retained their old ways and religiosity were prone to laziness, and their deaths would therefore not be mourned. The message of such propaganda was clear: a new socialist society could only rise in an atheistic environment free from the vices that religion supposedly inculcated in society.[18]

Like antireligious propaganda, antireligious repression in the Gulag was sporadic and uneven. To be sure, there was a marked increase in antireligious repression in the late 1920s and early 1930s. A Gulag circular issued in 1930 instructed camp leadership to remove priests and other counterrevolutionary prisoners from administrative and medical work and assign them to general labor. Religious inmates, along with other counterrevolutionary prisoners, were also explicitly excluded from a 1930 decree allowing early release for old, sick, and invalid prisoners. (Some religious inmates in this decade recalled being offered early release but only on the condition that they renounce their faith.) Those who attempted to practice their faith, whether through worship services or missionary efforts, were sent to solitary confinement in the penalty isolator. For instance, according to a Gulag report dated February 8, 1936, four women in the Baikal-Amursky Camp wrote in a letter to fellow Catholics, "We are strong in spirit, and no kind of camp or organ of the NKVD [People's Commissariat of Internal Affairs] can entice the faithful daughters and sons of the one Catholic Church from the true path. Even here we are trying to recruit similarly zealous supporters of the Catholic Church." Camp officials confiscated the letter, however, and sent the women to the penalty isolator, where one died.[19]

Other evidence, however, suggests that antireligious efforts in the Gulag were surprisingly uneven. On September 20, 1931, Gulag boss Lazar Kogan made this striking concession to religious believers:

Among the camp population there are individuals refusing to eat animal food (meat, fish, etc.). For the most part, these are sectarian fanatics. While not encouraging such views, but rather dissuading them through camp cultural and educational organizations, we still should not force them to eat animal food. The aforementioned individuals should receive natural food rations, with meat, fish, and animal fats replaced by other products totaling the caloric count of the ration.

By recognizing the legitimacy of religious dietary needs, Kogan made clear that antireligious repression had limits and that religious inmates retained some rights. Archbishop Yuvenaly, in the Sibirsky Camp in 1936, reported

82 FINDING GOD IN THE GULAG

that while he was not permitted to wear his religious clothing, he was allowed to keep his beard, a symbol of his religious calling. He was also, contrary to the 1930 circular concerning labor, given light work as a bookkeeper and a storeroom guard. Elena Chicherina likewise recorded that guards at the Sibirsky Camp did not confiscate her icon or religious books or interrupt her attempts to live a spiritual life. To some extent, this can be attributed to the chaotic nature of the camp, with few guards, large distances between camp zones, and a lax attitude toward monitoring the inmates. But it is notable that Chicherina also discovered a psalter, gospel, and prayer book in a house used by camp officials for visits by family members, which she was tasked with cleaning. Some Gulag employees, it appears, tolerated, or even held to, religious beliefs.[20]

Indeed, we know from other sources that some guards in the 1930s continued to identify as Christians. Lay believer Valentina Yasnopolskaya, arrested in 1930 for her activity in the True Orthodox Church, recalled that while she was being searched in the secret police prison in St. Petersburg, the female orderly twice yelled at her to remove her cross but then did nothing when Yasnopolskaya protested and left it on. Several nights later, Yasnopolskaya awoke to find this same orderly making the sign of the cross over her in her sleep, as if to impart to her a secret blessing of strength. When the woman noticed that Yasnopolskaya had awoken, she offered heartfelt words of comfort to her. Part of the issue here was that, as historian Lynne Viola explains, "local officials... were not necessarily ideologues or even true believers [in communism]." This certainly held true for the Gulag, where local bosses and guards often repeated the proscribed language of class warfare and socialist construction but were motivated by more pragmatic factors such as ensuring plan fulfillment and preventing escapes. In such an environment, religious beliefs held by Gulag guards could be concealed, and antireligious mandates could be ignored. And this, in turn, allowed some inmates to continue practicing their religion.[21]

Religious Life in Stalin's Gulag

The Gulag of the 1930s featured a wide variety of prisoners in terms of gender, ethnicity, age, family situation, social background, and criminal sentence. Prisoners also differed in how they coped with imprisonment. Some resigned themselves to eventual death, but others tried to escape.

THE WAR AGAINST RELIGION   83

Some joined gangs or other groups, while others kept to themselves. Some worked hard and strove to earn early release, and others tried to cheat the system (and often their fellow inmates) to make life easier on the inside. Some collaborated with the guards to spy on other prisoners, while others refused. Some who had previously been Party members retained their faith in communism, but others renounced it in whole or in part. In short, there were many choices to be made in the Gulag's high-pressure environment, and religious inmates experienced this same range of decisions. It should not be surprising, therefore, that some chose to hide their faith or use their position of trust as a clergyman to profit or simply survive. Indeed, one thing that I found striking as I pored over hundreds of Gulag memoirs and letters was how many inmates barely seemed to notice religious prisoners. These documents, typically written by nonreligious political prisoners, rarely include more than brief references to priests, nuns, or other religious figures in the camps. Many completely omit any mention of faith or religion. This absence can partly be attributed to the interests of the memoirists, who focused on their own personal experiences and circle of friends. But it may also reflect how many inmates chose not to display their religious beliefs in the Gulag. In the face of official opposition, where public devotion could bring punishment, many religious prisoners kept their faith private.

Many political prisoners who wrote letters home or later penned memoirs, however, did observe and write about the diversity of overt religious life in the camps. For example, ethnographer Vasily Smirnov remarked in a letter to his wife in 1930 that there were three basic types of religious believers. First, "some of them are self-confident, contemptuously bearing their own stupidity. . . . They sincerely consider themselves ideological martyrs." In this category fell a devout Old Believer who shared a bunk with Smirnov. With both curiosity and disgust, Smirnov detailed how this inmate never undressed for any reason, even to sleep, and "on principle refused to bathe." Smirnov complained about the smell and the noise made by the Old Believer as he scratched himself incessantly, until Smirnov finally found a different place to sleep. Strongly held religious beliefs did not always endear devout Christians to their bunkmates.[22]

Smirnov's second category of believers included clerics who "are quite worthless, long ago having taken off their ridiculous outfit and now willingly adapt to anything."[23] Here he had in mind a particular Orthodox deacon whom Smirnov despised for dressing in fine clothing, eating delicacies sent from admirers, remaining aloof to the needs of those around him, and

84   FINDING GOD IN THE GULAG

generally caring only for himself. "I decided that when I am free," Smirnov remarked with biting sarcasm, "I will become a deacon."[24] An Orthodox priest followed this same logic before ultimately receiving early release after signing an affidavit promising to renounce the priesthood upon release. In the pressure-filled environment of the Gulag, where survival was far from guaranteed, such men had lost sight of religion's redeeming qualities and lived at the expense of others or traded their faith for worldly gain.[25]

The third category of religious believers identified by Smirnov were "true martyrs, sincerely believing in their god and in the salvation of souls, and sincerely loving their unfortunate incarcerated family [those around them]."[26] Smirnov recalled in a letter, for instance, a "very touching" Easter celebration in his communal cell in the Ivanovo House of Correction. An Orthodox priest led the group in prayer, with everyone participating except for a few "educated people," including Smirnov. Even an atheist like Smirnov could feel the priest's genuine faith and love for his parishioners in such moments, and this won his genuine admiration.[27]

Other political prisoners identified these and other types of religious inmates. Petr Skachkov, for instance, recalled an old prisoner who, while they mined gold in Kolyma, suddenly declared, "The Scriptures correctly prophesied of us: 'Thou shalt walk among gold, and curse it.'" Yet rather than a sign of obdurate fanaticism, Skachkov viewed this paraphrase of Ezekiel 7:19 (where a prophet predicts that people will cast aside their gold because "it is the stumbling block of their iniquity" in the last days before Armageddon) as a sign of wisdom. As he ruefully recalled, "We all, having endured the difficult work in the mine truly did curse the gold that the brigade obtained through such hard labor." Religious inmates in this way could provide even atheist political prisoners with a fresh understanding of the world around them.[28]

The irreligious political prisoner Aleksey Yarotsky, also laboring in Kolyma in the 1930s, described another type of religious inmate. Having been sent to bring firewood back to camp, Yarotsky protested when his partner overloaded the horse-drawn sleigh. But the latter calmly said, "God will help us." When the sleigh refused to budge, however, the believer angrily threw off his hat and began to stamp on it while shouting toward the heavens, "How could you just watch me being tortured?" Other Christian prisoners undoubtedly experienced the palpable anger, bordering on despair, expressed by this prisoner at God's seeming indifference to his fate. Suffering from the effects of hunger and hard labor, these religious inmates underwent faith crises that at times led to a complete abandonment of their beliefs.[29]

Memoirs and letters by religious believers similarly portray a variety of personality types in the Gulag, along with a broad spectrum of religious experiences. Yasnopolskaya, for instance, confirmed that the kind of faith crises described by Yarotsky were common. She described experiencing deep spiritual loneliness while in prison in Leningrad, preventing her from attending to the most basic act of Christian devotion. "I tried to pray," she related, "but couldn't: a stone lay on my soul." What ultimately brought her out of this sense of despair was a renewed sense of struggle against the enemy. Summoned for interrogation, she defiantly proclaimed her Christianity to her tormentors, declaring that "the violent struggle against the Church stands as testimony to the [regime's] powerlessness before her spiritual power." For Yasnopolskaya, spiritual strength in the Gulag seemed correlated to the amount of direct opposition to it. Later, in the camps, Yasnopolskaya's faith again seemed tied to this idea of opposition. During Easter week, when guards watched closely for any manifestations of devotion, she managed to find a solitary place in the forest and recited what she could remember of the Easter liturgy. "In these moments I was happy," she recalled.[30]

This tension between faith and repression was explored in greater depth by the prominent religious philosopher Aleksey Losev, who was arrested in 1930 for his anti-Soviet writings shortly after he and his wife secretly took monastic vows. Losev told his wife by letter in late 1931 that he "prayed and cried a lot" while in solitary confinement in Lubyanka Prison for four months. His spiritual journey in the camps then became more difficult after receiving news that the secret police had confiscated his personal library. Despairing of his fate, he wrote:

> What is going on with me? I feel like I'm losing control and can no longer vouch for myself. Why does God allow such wild revenge and spiritual outrage? It makes me remember that atheist Walter, who said that if God can't overcome evil, then he is not all-powerful, and if he doesn't want to overcome evil, then he is not all good, and if he really is all-powerful and all good, then what is he looking at?

Continuing this line of questioning as he endured hard labor, insufficient rations, and failing health, Losev reported feeling that the traditional answer of how suffering indicated God's love "now sounds like mockery and

86 FINDING GOD IN THE GULAG

evil sarcasm." Unable to commune with God ("prayer is simply impossible here"), Losev despaired that "God has left us alone, and what is there to wait for other than death?"[31]

As the Lent season of 1932 approached, Losev seemed to make peace with God, writing to his wife that "we place everything in God's hands." But soon after, spiritual despair again encompassed his writing, brought on by the horrors and pressures of Gulag life and by years away from the conversations, rituals, and prayers that had formerly sustained him. "The most important thing," he wrote, "is that the objective treasures of life, religion, and love, have died and are dying. . . . My soul is becoming empty, it is becoming accustomed to darkness, being crucified with the tortures of despondency and despair." In another letter, he frankly acknowledged the wisdom of God and the need to submit everything to God's will. "But my God," he continued, "how unhappy this all is! How you, Lord, have taken from me every comfort in life, deprived me of the joy of accomplishment and of comfort in prayer."[32]

Losev's spiritual strength ultimately rebounded. Letters once full of despair became livelier as he discussed theology with his beloved wife. In one such letter, he drew on the experience of ancient Israel to make sense of his relationship with God, writing, "I sit in Babylonian captivity, unable to forget the lost sweetness of Jerusalem and its holy mountain of Zion." He then quoted Psalm 136 (137 in the Western biblical tradition) in its entirety, beginning with the line "By the rivers of Babylon, there we sat down, yea, we wept, when we remembered Zion" and ending with a plea for vengeance against the Babylonians. "Happy shall he be, that rewardeth thee as thou hast served us," the psalm concludes. And indeed, for Losev, this righteous indignation stirred his spirits. "Pray that my youth will be renewed like an eagle," he wrote, quoting other Old Testament scriptures, "and that Babylon will fall, the whore on the many waters."[33]

Yet it was not just the thought of God's vengeance being meted out against the Bolsheviks and his own potential role in such an act that helped Losev recover his spiritual strength. At the top of a letter from June 1932, written while being transferred to the Svirsky Camp, Losev wrote, "Love is stronger than death. We will see each other in eternity, free from parting or suffering." His wife's frequent letters of comfort and support—she was also at this time imprisoned—certainly helped him endure his physical and spiritual crises. And so did better living conditions at the Svirsky Camp, which prompted him in one letter to write, "God has sent me a good mood, which I haven't had in a while." And this good mood helped him to see "that some wise hand leads me to a great purpose. I bless my life, I bless all of my sufferings, I am thankful for everything." Through the depths of despair, Losev ultimately found reasons not just to survive but to rejoice in the inscrutable will of his God.[34]

Letters to and from home provided other inmates with a vital outlet for religious reflection. Vladimir Levitsky, sentenced to a ten-year term in 1931, began including brief references to God and faith in his letters home in the mid-1930s. These were tentative initially, as if to see if they would pass the camp censors who monitored mail for anti-Soviet sentiments. But even though they were brief, they created a spiritual connection between him and his wife, Natalya. The most that he wrote about his spiritual life (or at least the most that escaped the censors) came in a letter dated March 11, 1935: "I pray God only that he gives the strength and power necessary to last until that moment when they say that I am free and can go home." Unfortunately for Levitsky, he was executed in the camp two years later.[35]

Yuvenaly, imprisoned in the Sibirsky Camp in 1936 and then executed in 1937, wrote numerous letters filled with hope and faith to his congregation in Ryazan. These letters were much more detailed than those of Levitsky, and Yuvenaly almost certainly found a way to bypass camp censors. He did not disguise that camp life was hard but framed such difficulties as a struggle for spiritual survival. In one letter, he reported offering prayers only in his mind, which was "all that is possible right now." In another, he wrote of feeling spiritually lonely: "You are so kind to write, after all I am all alone here, there is no one to share my thoughts and worries with, as I live among other nationalities: Kyrgyz, Buryats, Kalmyks, and so forth." He then mused that whereas it was good to be alone with God, he sometimes wanted a fellow Orthodox believer with whom he could share his spiritual thoughts. He also wrote of the challenging labor assignments he had to complete. But still, the consistent message in his letters was that "everything that God does, he does for our benefit, and I thank Him for my current situation." After receiving a package of apples from his congregants, for example, he exclaimed, "In everything I see the hand of God, through your love that comforts me, a sinner. How precious it is here, when you feel that the Lord is not only nourishing you, but comforts and makes you joyful." Like many other religious prisoners, Yuvenaly found solace in the idea that an omniscient God still loved him: "In every step, in all troubles and trials, I see the protecting, saving, comforting, caressing, joy-inspiring hand of God."[36]

88 FINDING GOD IN THE GULAG

Chicherina's memoir illustrates the role religion played in the lives of female Christian inmates in the early 1930s. Having been born to a noble family, her religious activities in the early 1930s led to her arrest in 1933 and subsequent transfer to the Sibirsky Camp. On the march to the camp, the inmates faced a narrow, rickety bridge standing three meters above a river that frightened her. But, as she recorded, "I prayed to Saint Nicholas and decisively strode across the planks, not looking down, not noticing their shakiness, but looking straight ahead at the green meadow on the opposite bank." Throughout her imprisonment, she and her incarcerated sister found private places to pray and sing hymns. They kept an icon of the Mother of God of Kazan with them, along with the gospels and other religious books. For Christmas, the two sisters managed to reserve the bathhouse and had a quiet celebration there: "We sang everything we remembered; it was very comforting." When she feared a transfer to a different camp that would separate her from her sister, she prayed and was spared at the last minute. Singing songs of praise and thanks after this, she recorded, "My soul rejoiced. Such a clear mercy of our God."[37]

The presence of Chicherina's sister in the camp was no doubt an emotional and spiritual comfort, but there were also others with whom to share spiritual beliefs and practices. One year for Easter, while in a logging camp, Chicherina and other inmates celebrated and sang hymns. "It was as if Jesus Christ was with us and comforted us unseen," she remarked. She discovered three religious men in a different camp who visited and sang with her as often as possible. Other stories of friendly believers abound in Chicherina's memoir. On one occasion, a monk arrived in a convoy and visited her, but as he had been shaven and had his robes confiscated, Chicherina thought he was probably from the Living Church. The monk assured her that he was Orthodox, and they quickly became friends. Another time on a march, a fellow Orthodox woman, Tatiana, raised her hands in the air every time they started walking and shouted: "Lord, bless us all." At the Sibirsky Camp, at least, religious women and men could talk, sing, and pray together, strengthening each other's faith.[38]

One of the more remarkable stories from Chicherina, though, involved a solitary pilgrimage of sorts. She was laboring as a nurse and could occasionally travel without a guard escort to the hospital in the nearby town. Noticing on one visit that the town had a still-open Orthodox church, she found a priest and asked him to give her communion. "He opened the church immediately," heard her confession, administered the Eucharist, and concluded with prayers of thanksgiving. She barely returned to the camp in time, thanking God for his protection. Later she managed to visit the church again, this time joining the choir in singing praises to the Lord who had eased her burdens. Visits to a brick-and-mortar church while imprisoned in the Gulag were exceptional, but Chicherina's worship highlights the continued individuality of experience in the Soviet penal system that allowed for a wide variety of religious experiences. Believers could not count on it, but occasions still arose when they could practice their faith—sometimes even with others.[39]

This ability to worship despite the crackdown on religion in the 1930s is also on display in the memoir of the religious inmate K. Petrus, who was also incarcerated in the Sibirsky Camp. Like Chicherina, Petrus found many believers in the camp, some of whom were open about sharing their faith, while others were reserved and tried to avoid conflict with the guards and other inmates. Some of the most public with their belief were a group of nuns and the priest Berezkin of the Catacomb Church, all of whom refused to work and were often consequently thrown into the penalty isolator as troublemakers. On Christmas Day, one of these nuns appeared in Petrus's barrack, greeted the inmates in the name of Jesus Christ, and began to sing Christmas hymns. As he related, the room instantly grew quiet, and "immediately everyone felt as if the barrack walls had disappeared . . . and every one of us had on the rushing wings of trials been carried off far, far away from these 'oases' of death." They remembered their childhoods and families, how they celebrated holidays before imprisonment, and the prisoners began to cry one by one. They wished the nun a merry Christmas as she prepared to leave, but just then, a camp guard seized her. Soon after, guards threw all of the camp's nuns into the isolator, where they continued to sing and praise the Lord. Meanwhile, all was quiet in the barrack until one inmate yelled, "Death to the butchers," and another, "Cursed be the bloodthirsty Stalin and his gang."[40]

After release from the isolator for their Christmas demonstration, most of the nuns continued to refuse to work and received only starvation rations. But a few started laboring in the sewing workshop, except on the Sabbath and other holy days. One inmate named Masha, who worked hard to fulfill her daily quota and shared her rations with her sisters, left a lasting impression on Petrus. Masha constantly chatted while she worked, not fearing the possibility of informants being nearby. "For us the camp is a like a convent," she said, "except that in a convent we are obedient to the abbot and here we obey God himself. Whatever He wants we do, and what is abhorrent to Him we don't do, even if the NKVD is going to shoot us." She made clear that the nuns would celebrate Easter as best they could: "Could we really not give praise to the Resurrected One?" True to promise, the nuns started singing loudly in the camp early on the morning of the first day of Easter so that all would awaken to hymns. This was repeated after lunch, at which point the guards rounded them up and threw them in the isolator. They were then beaten and charged with a new crime: "organizing a counterrevolutionary group and conducting ... agitation among the prisoners."[41]

Looking back on these and other experiences, Petrus recalled that his time behind barbed wire was "the best time in my life. The cleansing power of suffering, which I underwent while imprisoned, and which I saw in my fellow inmates, opened up to me what before was out of reach." The Gulag, in other words, was a type of "purgatory," from which one emerged "either renewed and reformed or else burnt and dead." Only there could one understand "the mystical essence of the victory of the resurrected Christ over the powers of evil." Moreover, Petrus explained, the Gulag had a powerful ecumenical spirit where one could feel the love of all for God and God's love for all. On that Easter day, inspired by the bold actions of the nuns, "all of the 'religionists' of our little prison were united by joy in Christ: an old-belief bishop and Orthodox priests, nuns and lay believers, Catholics and Lutherans, Baptists and Pentecostals. In one impulse, in one spiritual triumph we praised God."[42]

After a tumultuous period of uncertainty and improvisation from 1917 to 1929, Stalin in the 1930s created a massive system of corrective-labor camps called the Gulag. Penal authorities in this new environment devoted overwhelming resources to economic production using the forced labor of inmates, but they also enacted a re-educational program that included a crackdown on inmate religiosity. This reflected a broader assault against religion in Soviet society generally and took the form of propaganda, prohibitions on worship, confiscation of religious clothes and literature, harassment from guards, and the dispersal of Christian clergy across various penal facilities. In the face of such repression, some Christians chose to hide or abandon their beliefs. Yet, as in broader Soviet society, where organized religion was persecuted but never fully stamped out, many religious inmates found ways to practice and openly share their faith. They sang hymns, wrote religiously infused letters, celebrated church holidays, secretly held worship services, and refused to engage in labor.

A few factors helped make such displays of faith possible. First, the communal nature of the Gulag meant that inmates lived and worked in close proximity and were often not monitored directly by guards. They always had to be on alert for informants and unannounced searches, but at times the busy life of communal barracks allowed for religious get-togethers. Second, Gulag officials at the ground level were so preoccupied with production demands that they sometimes turned a blind eye to minor disciplinary infractions such as religious observance. Third, some guards and other employees of the Gulag system retained their own hidden religious beliefs, prompting them to ignore or even facilitate religious observance among their inmates. Certainly, not all prisoners enjoyed such opportunities—some faced persistent and violent persecution for their displays of faith. But the amount of religious discussion, singing, and worship during the height of Stalinist fervor is surprising. Even in the Gulag, arguably the most repressive place within the Soviet totalitarian system, faith in God persisted.

4

Belief and Disbelief from the Great Terror to Stalin's Death

Like more than a million of her fellow Soviet subjects, the Muscovite actress Vera Shults was arrested during the Great Terror of 1937–1938. The secret police interrogated her at Taganskaya Prison in southeast Moscow and ultimately sentenced her to five years of exile in Central Asia for being a "socially dangerous element." During her time at Taganskaya, Shults was deeply impressed by one of her cellmates, an older religious woman named Tatyana Pavlovna, whom she described as "radiating kindness" while patiently accepting her unjust imprisonment. While pondering the meaning of religion during this time of great trial, Shults remarked in her memoir, "We all grew up as atheists, and so I have a hard time judging what role her faith played, but I think that Tatyana Pavlovna found solace in it."[1]

In the Gulag of the late 1930s to the early 1950s, solace was in short supply as the brutal system of incarceration and compulsory labor was rocked by the successive calamities of the Great Terror and World War II. The Great Terror, a horrific crime against humanity perpetrated by Joseph Stalin's regime, resulted in the execution, imprisonment, or exile of some 1.5 million people, many of them falsely convicted of conspiring against the Soviet Union. This was followed by the Second World War, a terrible war of attrition that ultimately caused more than 20 million Soviet deaths. More Stalinist repression followed the war, and long sentences for minor infractions such as petty theft swelled the ranks of the incarcerated. For those imprisoned in the Soviet Gulag, these successive waves of violence and repression brought chaos, overcrowding, suffering, and death to an already dangerous and desultory system.

Thousands of religious leaders were among the millions of people sent to the camps from the beginning of the Great Terror in 1937 to Stalin's death in 1953, along with untold numbers of lay believers. In the crucible of these darkest years of the Soviet Gulag, maintaining belief was difficult. The Gulag prohibited religious worship, guards and nonreligious inmates

Finding God in the Gulag. Jeffrey S. Hardy, Oxford University Press. © Oxford University Press 2024.
DOI: 10.1093/9780197751701.003.0005

mocked expressions of faith, and the matter of survival for many took precedence over all other concerns. Some believers ultimately lost their faith or were criticized by fellow inmates for selfish hypocrisy—preaching Christian charity while hoarding food, for example. Others hid their faith. Yet, like the Orthodox clergy imprisoned at Solovki in the 1920s, many managed to hold to their beliefs and share them with others, finding camaraderie, patience, peace, and joy. Such inmates were examples of Christian love and service in the Gulag's bleak and brutal camps.

The Great Terror

The Soviet Union employed violence against perceived enemies from the beginning, but Stalin exponentially expanded the use of terror starting in 1929. This reached its apogee from 1937 to 1938, a period known retroactively as the Great Terror. Sparked by investigations into the murder of top Soviet official Sergey Kirov, the Great Terror featured mass arrests, brutalizing interrogations, and quasi-legal prosecutions of millions of people accused of conspiring against the USSR. Around 750,000 were executed, and around 750,000 more were incarcerated or exiled. Additional millions were deeply affected as family members and witnesses, not to mention the psychological damage suffered by many of the perpetrators—policemen, judicial officials, jailers, interrogators, and political bosses. The Gulag left virtually no layer of society untouched. Among its victims were Party leaders, ambassadors, ballerinas, movie stars, musicians, professors, artists, collective farm bosses, factory managers, village troublemakers, peasants who had resisted collectivization, and representatives from every national and ethnic group. Secret police operatives faced intense pressure to fulfill conviction quotas, but eventually, they, too, became targets for repression in 1938 as Stalin ended the Terror by shifting blame for the arrests onto supposedly overzealous policemen.

Christians and other religious believers were among those punished for their perceived disloyalty to the regime during the Great Terror. On July 20, 1937, the secret police (NKVD) issued its infamous Operational Order No. 00447, which mandated mass repression against a long list of perceived enemies. "Church officials and sectarians" were expressly targeted, along with "sectarian activists, church-goers, and others who are now in prisons, camps, labor colonies, and colonies and who continue to conduct

94 FINDING GOD IN THE GULAG

disruptive anti-Soviet work." In response to this mandate, NKVD operatives across the Soviet Union arrested tens of thousands of devout Christians. Many were executed, while others were sentenced to long terms of incarceration. Meanwhile, hundreds of chapels were indefinitely closed. By the Great Terror's close, zero Seventh-day Adventist churches (there had been 600 Adventist congregations in 1928) and only two Catholic churches still operated in the Soviet Union, while the numbers of Orthodox congregations declined precipitously. [2]

The Great Terror affected religious life in the Gulag in several ways. Most immediately, camp officials carried out extrajudicial trials and summary executions of religious prisoners (alongside other "counterrevolutionary" inmates). At Solovki, for example, a series of informant reports on anti-Soviet statements by Catholic priests resulted in a broad investigation of all priests in the camp in 1937. One investigatory document on priest A. N. Kappes reported that "from the moment of arrival in the camp to the present time he has conducted active counterrevolutionary activity. He formed around him in the camp a group of other priests. He conducts illegal worship services, using them to bring together counterrevolutionary elements. He systematically conducts malicious counterrevolutionary agitation. He presents himself as an open enemy of Soviet power." Camp authorities accused another priest of establishing "connections with like-minded priests while conducting provocative counterrevolutionary agitation against the Soviet Government and praising fascism. After release, he intends to travel abroad to distribute various news of a provocative nature about the Soviet Union." Following these investigations, which readily accepted anti-Soviet statements reported by informants as evidence of treasonous conspiracies, Solovki officials executed thirty-two imprisoned Catholic priests.[3]

In some cases, the execution of religious inmates extended beyond 1937–1938. In Kazakhstan's Karagandinsky Camp, officials in 1939 noted the influence of incarcerated members of the True Orthodox Church. They talked openly about their faith, railed against the Soviet regime (one prophesied that Germany would destroy the USSR the following year), refused to work, and persuaded others to join their acts of disobedience. When interrogated about their activity, the defendants gave varied answers as to whether they were guilty of spreading anti-Soviet propaganda and sabotaging production. Some declared innocence, while others confessed to being active opponents of Soviet power. One professed, "I don't know if I'm guilty or not . . . but I can't work for Soviet institutions." Another clarified in his interrogation that "we are religious people who must fight against the antichrist and re-store private property on earth." The True Orthodox inmates also refused to sign transcripts of their interrogations, as was customary in Soviet legal practice, because even this act signified in their minds cooperation with the "godless" communists. In the end, officials prosecuted two supposed ringleaders and sentenced them to death in early 1940. Two others received five-year sentences that were tacked onto the end of their existing sentences. Being already in the Gulag, in other words, did not save religious inmates from the arrests, interrogations, and executions of the Great Terror.[4]

But if many Christians were killed in Stalin's camps during the Terror, many more were newly arrested and imprisoned. Given the harsh repression against religious officials during the Terror, one might think that Gulag leaders would devote more attention to promoting an atheistic worldview among the inmates. There is some evidence to suggest that this happened. Gulag officials reiterated that public displays of religiosity were forbidden and instructed guards to confiscate Bibles and other religious literature. A Gulag statute issued in April 1940 repeated that "sectarians and officials of religious cults," along with political prisoners, should not lead cultural-educational work in the camps. Yet other evidence suggests there was no sustained campaign to stamp out religious observance. Camp newspapers barely mentioned religion during the Great Terror, except for a few reprinted antireligious articles from national newspapers that had no direct connection with camp life. And an internal account of re-educational work in the Gulag showed that only 600,000 inmates in the first half of 1941 (out of well over a million prisoners) had heard an antireligious lecture or participated in an antireligious discussion.[5]

A report from the head of the Gulag's political department, dated April 16, 1941, confirms this inconsistency in antireligious re-education. The official praised some commanders for ensuring that inmates were taught atheism and prohibited from religious worship. Authorities at the Kuloisky Camp, for instance, provided a wealth of literature from the local cell of the Union of Militant Atheists and conducted 355 antireligious lectures and discussions in the fourth quarter of 1940 alone. Similarly, the Ukrainian network of corrective-labor colonies held 321 lectures and discussions that 24,000 inmates attended. Most Leningrad colonies had "atheists' corners," display cases with antireligious content, and periodic atheistic bulletins. And yet, the report lamented, many camps and colonies lacked appropriate atheistic literature and "qualified propagandists" and did not devote "the requisite

96 FINDING GOD IN THE GULAG

attention" to eliminating religion. This resulted in group prayers being held at the Onezhsky, Dzhezkazgansky, and other camps and inmates at many penal institutions refusing to work "out of religious convictions." Inconsistency regarding religious practice and belief continued to be the norm in the camps despite the purposeful repression of religious authorities during the Terror.[6]

Caught up in the tragedy of the Great Terror, many Christian prisoners clung to their beliefs to alleviate and make sense of their suffering, and this was often noticed and remembered by the political prisoners who were later most active in writing their memoirs. Menachem Begin, who eventually became prime minister of Israel, met a Christian doctor in the Pechorsky Camp whose wife had falsely informed on him so she could leave him for another man. Through this betrayal and subsequent incarceration, he retained his belief in God, telling Begin that he prayed for his children and that God would forgive his wife. "The truth is that I believe in God," he continued, "and no one can take my faith away from me." Christian beliefs thus helped this man accept and endure the intense suffering he experienced during the Great Terror. Similarly, Elena Lipper, a young Dutch idealist who traveled to work in the USSR in 1937 and was arrested just two months later, encountered during her transfer to the camps of Kolyma an elderly nun who had already been imprisoned for a long time. But, as Lipper discovered, "neither camps nor prisons had persuaded her that it would be better for her to renounce her religion. In her weary, resigned old voice, she would say, 'Now I've suffered almost as much as Jesus Christ. Now I will certainly be redeemed soon.'" The promise of eternal redemption through Christlike suffering brought comfort to those repressed for their faith.[7]

This conviction that belief in God eased the pains of imprisonment made a lasting impression on others. In 1937, the political prisoner Mikhail Rotfort met a Sorbonne-educated Christian philosopher in Kharkiv Prison who cited Isaac Newton, Leo Tolstoy, Blaise Pascal, and other scientists and writers to win arguments about faith. "True knowledge doesn't separate one from God, but brings one closer to him," the man would affirm. He also insisted that because of the belief in eternal happiness following this mortal existence, "it is easier for the believing Christian to endure tribulation and death." Although Rotfort did not share this belief, he still "with great pleasure listened to him." Petr Yakir, arrested in 1937 at age fourteen, experienced similar pleasure in the Astrakhan Prison, where he was placed in a communal cell full of Orthodox priests. They were arrested because of their support for Archimandrite Iliodor, who had fled the Soviet Union but still corresponded with those who supported his uncompromising opposition to Soviet power. As Yakir related, the priests were kind and attentive to his needs, not to mention indignant that "the sons of anti-Christ" were locking up teenagers for no apparent reason. They sang hymns in the evening with beautiful voices accentuated by the prison cell's acoustics. Even the wardens confessed to enjoying their singing. And one of them gave Yakir advice that stuck with him throughout his imprisonment: "Keep your spirit up, or else you will not survive—you will die. If your spirit is strong, your flesh will be strong also!"[8]

The experiences of Yakir and others demonstrate that, despite the supposed lesson learned at Solovki that religious believers should be isolated from each other, this was simply not possible during the Great Terror because of the mass arrests of Christians. Faith communities existed and helped alleviate suffering in the camps. In late 1937, for instance, the secret police placed the nonreligious political prisoner Zoya Marchenko in a prison cell along with four lay Orthodox women, four Orthodox nuns, and two Catholic nuns. And while the nuns did not impress her—"tiresome and worldly," she described them—she quickly grew to love the simple Orthodox women for their Christian kindness and service to others. For a Baptist imprisoned during the Great Terror, his first experience in a labor camp was a trip to the bathhouse, where he found an old inmate attendant quietly singing a hymn. The new arrival asked if he was a "brother" and in this way found the first of what became a small group of evangelical Christians. They often met in the camp's boiler room to teach each other and pray, but they were sorrowful that they "didn't have a Bible and how could we get one with such strict control in the camp?" Then one day, the inmate related:

> I received a parcel containing a bag of sugar and other things from my sister in Pskov. The contents were carefully examined, but not the bag of sugar. The censor threw the bag of sugar at me. To our great joy this bag contained a Gospel. We could now read the genuine living Gospel in the warm boiler room and did not need to depend on isolated verses that we had learned by heart.

Warmed by the boiler, scripture, and prayer-based fellowship, these Christians jointly discovered how to keep their beliefs strong in the brutal labor camps of Siberia.[9]

Olga Adamova-Sliozberg, an atheist and former Communist Party member arrested during the Great Terror, observed a similar sense of

98   FINDING GOD IN THE GULAG

spiritual community among a group of devout peasants at the Dalstroy Camps who had been prosecuted for refusing to work on Sundays. "They called one another sisters, slept, ate, worked, [and] prayed together," Adamova-Sliozberg recalled. Although they typically worked hard, they refused to work on Sundays or church holidays and were therefore often sent to the penalty isolator. Once, when one of the women received a package containing dried fish, promising needed nourishment for the near-starving inmates, the camp orderly said she could only have it if they all went to work on Sunday. "Whatever you wish," the inmate responded, "we are not going to work." Adamova-Sliozberg also remembered how one of their husbands traveled several hundred miles to visit his wife. He brought eggs and traditional Easter bread to celebrate the impending holiday, and he prayed and sang hymns with his wife and the others. This community of believers in the far northeastern corner of Russia survived in no small part because of their collective religious spirit. They lived for each other and for their God.[10]

One of the most famous memoirists of the Gulag, Evgenia Ginzburg, relied on literature and poetry to help survive after she was arrested at the height of the Great Terror in 1937. But Ginzburg also occasionally strayed into expressions of faith. She recalled praying in moments of deepest distress, such as while hearing the screams of other prisoners being tortured or during the voyage to Magadan when she fell gravely ill. "O Lord, spare me till we reach Magadan, I beg You," she remembered praying on the ship. "I want to be buried in the ground, not at sea. I am a human being, and You Yourself said: Dust thou art, and unto dust shalt thou return." A lifelong intellectual and atheist, Ginzburg in her darkest trials turned to God for help and comfort. It is likely that such prayers of desperation stemmed not only from her literary understanding of the Bible but from the Christians she encountered in the prisons and camps of the Gulag. She befriended a German Catholic inmate, who saved her from a camp orderly's sexual advances, and an Orthodox gravedigger who promised Ginzburg "a real Christian burial" if she died. She enjoyed long conversations with a Christian doctor who was put on "general work" because she attended a prayer meeting held by imprisoned Adventists. And she encountered a kind and simple Russian peasant who told her to "pray God you'll see your children again one day."[11]

Ginzburg was also inspired by a group of Orthodox women from Voronezh, perhaps the same ones observed by Adamova-Sliozberg, who worked hard cutting timber but refused to labor on Easter. As Ginzburg later related:

When the women refused to leave their hut, saying repeatedly, "It's Easter, it's Easter, it's a sin to work on Easter Day," they were driven out by rifle butts. When they got to the forest clearing they made a neat pile of their axes and saws, sat down quietly on the frozen tree stumps and began to sing hymns. Thereupon the guards, evidently on instructions, ordered them to take off their shoes and stand barefoot in the ice water of one of the forest pools, which was still covered with a thin sheet of ice.... I do not remember how long this ordeal went on. For the peasant women it was physical torture while we suffered only morally. They went on chanting as they stood in the icy water and we, dropping our tools, ran from one guard to another crying and sobbing, begging and beseeching. That night the punishment cell was jammed so tight that there was hardly any standing room.

To Ginzburg's amazement, these women dutifully reported to work the next day, exceeding the daily production quota by 20 percent. The spiritual inmate who made the most profound impression on Ginzburg, however, was the kind and intelligent German Catholic Anton Walter, whom she labeled the "jolly saint" for the way his religious foundation helped create moments of humor and joy in the camps. They quickly formed a friendship that blossomed into marriage after their release following the grim trials of the war years. Though not deeply religious herself, Ginzburg found in the Christianity of her fellow prisoners not just a strategy of survival but a sincere path to peace and joy during the Great Terror and beyond.[12]

The Great Patriotic War

The Second World War, known as the Great Patriotic War in the USSR and post-Soviet Russia, was a cataclysmic war of attrition that for the Soviets raged from June 1941 until May 1945. The Soviet people suffered terribly during the war; more than 20 million died, and millions more were wounded, deported to Germany as forced laborers, or starved in the multiyear siege of Leningrad. Soviet policies also imposed suffering as the regime imposed harsh military discipline and long working hours on the civilian population. Entire ethnic groups were also exiled to Central Asia for their perceived disloyalty during this time of national crisis.

As for religion, Stalin relaxed his harsh stance toward the Orthodox Church, making peace with the church hierarchy in exchange for its help in

100   FINDING GOD IN THE GULAG

mobilizing the Russian people against invading German armies. Orthodox leader Sergius fully supported this new church-state relationship; indeed, this was precisely what he had hoped to accomplish in 1927 when he pursued a policy of conciliation against the wishes of the Solovetsky bishops. In exchange, Stalin permitted Sergius to be ordained patriarch, allowed many churches and a seminary to reopen, released Orthodox clerics from the Gulag, and temporarily shuttered antireligious magazines. The Soviet regime also formally recognized a newly unified Baptist hierarchy, the All-Union Council of Evangelical Christians and Baptists. Meanwhile, the Soviet annexation of large swaths of territory in 1939–1940 brought millions of new, and often Christian, subjects into the country (to be discussed in chapter 5). As a result, a marked increase in religious observance took place during the Second World War.[13]

For the Gulag, war meant the hurried evacuation of prisoners in 1941 and, more fatally, starvation conditions for inmates in 1942–1943 as German armies occupied the USSR's most fertile farmland. Sickness multiplied, death rates spiked, and although some inmates were released into the army to help fight the enemy, Stalin preferred to keep most prisoners behind barbed wire. There they were compelled to toil for the war effort, with increased political discussions on the value of their work hardly compensating for reduced calories and longer labor hours. Without question, Gulag inmates made important contributions to the home-front production of food, ammunition, uniforms, coal, and other necessary goods. Yet this came at the cost of hundreds of thousands of inmates who perished.[14]

For the war years, as always, the number of religious inmates in the Gulag is impossible to quantify. The Gulag's correctional-labor colonies (the smaller counterparts to the corrective-labor camps) keep track of those classified as "clerics and sectarians," showing a range of between 568 and 1,144 such inmates between 1942 and 1945. As these figures capture only the colonies, typically reserved for prisoners with the lightest sentences, they are incomplete. It is also uncertain who precisely was included in this count. Gulag officials relied on sentencing statutes rather than self-identification and so doubtlessly undercounted the true number of "clerics and sectarians." It seems certain that many thousands of religious leaders were imprisoned in the wartime Gulag, in addition to unknown numbers of Christian laypeople.[15]

Gulag leaders during the war made some efforts to try to counter the influence of religion. Antireligious propaganda circulated among inmates, though propaganda generally tended to focus on explaining the war and the inmates' role in contributing to the war effort through their labor. For instance, a report on re-educational activity in the labor colonies of Krasnoyarsk Territory during the second half of 1941 lists twenty-two lecture topics discussed with the inmates. Most topics concerned the war with Germany, but the last one centered on "Religion [as] the opiate of the people." Similarly, the Berezny Camp in the first half of 1942 reported thirty-four delivered lectures, with only one on religion: "The Myth of Christ." The Georgian colonies were more active, sharing three lectures on religion's origins, Christmas, and "Religion—a tool in the hands of capitalists against the working class." Dozens of similar reports sent to Gulag headquarters during the war years, however, did not specify a single antireligious lecture.[16]

In terms of direct religious repression during the war, the secret police in 1942 ordered that guards and informant networks monitor "sectarians" and other counterrevolutionary prisoners more closely. While in Butyrka Prison in 1944, Genrikh Elshtein-Gorchakov related a case in which an informant pretended to convert to Christianity under his Christian cellmate's guidance in order to gain his confidence. Prison officials also continued punishing religious prisoners for refusing to work on Sundays or religious holidays. As Petr Skachkov, incarcerated in Kolyma, related of one such inmate, "Every evening he prayed for a long time. He wouldn't go to work on Sundays and for this [he] soon ended up in the BUR [the camp prison]." Sparse examples of such occurrences suggest that many Gulag officials ignored religious prisoners during the war as long as they stayed out of trouble and fulfilled their production quotas.[17]

Sometimes it was fellow prisoners who made it difficult to maintain faith. The secular Polish Jew Janusz Bardach frequently encountered anti-Semitism in the camps but also observed anti-Christian discrimination. For instance, he reported seeing two religious prisoners, a father and son, praying and crossing themselves on the prison train bound for the Far East. Bardach asked if they were Catholic, but they responded that they were Pentecostal. Bardach was curious, having never heard of this denomination, but "two other prisoners sitting on the opposite bench mocked them, calling them 'Jesus freaks' and 'little Christs.'" They then proceeded to imitate their bows and prayers, "crossing themselves in obscene places" and accusing them of being cowards who refused to enlist in the army when the war broke out. In another case later in his narrative, Bardach recalled how a deeply religious Orthodox Russian was similarly labeled "a religious freak"

102 FINDING GOD IN THE GULAG

by a fellow inmate. Bardach does not provide insight into how such bullying affected these inmates, but enduring with public expressions of faith in such circumstances must have been difficult.[18]

Other faith-related pressures were more introspective in nature. Dmitri Panin, an Orthodox Christian, found it hard to perform acts of Christian charity during the stark depravations of the wartime Gulag. All prisoners were preoccupied with their own struggles for survival, which made some inmates steal from or otherwise oppress their fellow prisoners. "I thought of how difficult it is in these circumstances for anyone to do an act of kindness," he mused as he debated whether to exchange bunks with a sick inmate to give him the preferable spot in the guarded train carriage carrying them to the camps, "even for a man professing to be a Christian." In the end, he changed places with the poor inmate and discovered that other incarcerated Christians, on occasion, did likewise. These prisoners, he mused, "held to a Christian viewpoint; they gained strength from prayer and set their hopes in the Divine Creator. They were always making an effort on behalf of others, either with a kind, meaningful word or by the example of their indomitable courage." Yet Panin struggled to maintain his Christian worldview. He described several fights and instances where he did not grant forgiveness to those around him who acted dishonorably. Indeed, his first two rules for survival in the Gulag were "1. Wipe out the stool pigeons. 2. Repay a blow with a blow." Only after this does one find the somewhat more Christian "3. Help the deserving." Panin's survival instincts were clearly on heightened alert as fellow inmates died from violence and exhaustion, and this made Christian morality difficult to uphold.[19]

Panin's rules for survival—a mix of faith, revenge, and charity for those deemed worthy—continued to guide his thoughts while incapacitated in the Viatsky Camp hospital. He remembered offering a "fervent prayer, during which I promised God to help carry out His sacred will, and thereby to bring aid to all men who had been deceived, to protect them against liars and murderers." Renewed faith sparked by his own near-death experience and a desire to fight against the hated Bolshevik regime gave him courage in his darkest hour. As he recalled, the result of this prayer was that he felt "with certainty and conviction that God would save my life, that I would have the ability and resolve to move mountains." Yet Panin's Christian faith was not just about fighting his enemies, or at least while he was in the hospital it underwent a transformation. Along with his initial prayer of vengeful courage, Panin began to engage in daily meditation that revolved around repeating and contemplating the Lord's Prayer. "I began reflecting on each word of it," he remembered, "discovering how nearly all the principal ideas of Christianity are contained within this prayer." As sickness ravaged his weakened body, he also "prayed to God with the intensity of a candle burning before His altar," but for more than a month, his condition only worsened. Finally, the sickness broke, and his strength returned. "Tears of rapture and gratitude streamed from my eyes," he related. "I praised Almighty God. He had taken notice of me!" This "miracle," Panin reasoned, could only be explained by divine intervention, a product of his heartfelt prayers and meditation.[20]

Tamara Petkevich related a similar experience of evolving and challenged faith during her time in the wartime Gulag. She found that "God and the devil, morals and immorality ceased to be stark absolutes. Each of these concepts built up its own 'anti-space' around them, which overlapped and penetrated each other. Ideas and principles were growing less and less clearcut until they became an impassable thicket." She found that retaining her morality and sense of humanity was extremely difficult in the atomizing and brutalizing labor camp. But through this moral haze, the sparks of faith at times burned bright, and not just for the repressed nuns who inhabited her camp. When she and her lover from the men's zone were about to be sent to different camp zones, on parting he asked, "Will you pray tonight?" As Petkevich noted, they had never discussed God or faith before, though Petkevich had been trying to pray daily. Both, it turned out, had been hiding their faith from each other right up to the moment of separation. In the end, they never saw each other again, and they no doubt wondered how many others were suppressing religious inclinations because of the circumstances of imprisonment.[21]

For some prisoners, the conditions of the wartime Gulag were simply too oppressive to build a relationship with God. Not a believer before her imprisonment, Hava Volovich experienced a yearning for God during the most brutal years of the war when she became pregnant and gave birth to a girl in the camp. This experience was not unusual—many camps had nurseries and children's homes for those born to imprisoned women (rape and prostitution were common in the Gulag, as were voluntary sexual liaisons). As Volovich recalled years after her imprisonment, "I believed neither in God nor in the devil. But while I had my child, I most passionately, most violently wanted there to be a God. I wanted there to be someone who might hear my fervent prayer, born of slavery and degradation, and grant me salvation and happiness for my child, at the cost of all possible punishment and torment

104 FINDING GOD IN THE GULAG

for myself, if need be." Despite Volovich's attempts to care for the child and her fervent appeals to God, little Eleonora died after sixteen months of starvation and illness. "God did not answer my prayer," Volovich sorrowfully concluded. For her, the intense physical and emotional suffering of the camps, together with only silence from the heavens, signified that no higher power was concerned with her plight.[22]

Many others no doubt experienced similar spiritual emptiness as they suffered and sometimes died in the wartime Gulag. As Aleksandr Solzhenitsyn related regarding his and others' experiences in the Gulag, hunger, violence, disease, exhaustion, lack of privacy, and lack of trust in others made it extremely difficult to carry on normal spiritual relations with others and with God: "Can you think about your own grief, about the past and the future, about humanity and God? Your mind is absorbed in vain calculations which for the present moment cut you off from the heavens—and tomorrow are worth nothing." To actively cultivate one's beliefs amid such stark physical and psychological torture was simply more than many could do, Solzhenitsyn himself included.[23]

Postwar Repression of Religion

The Soviet Union achieved a resounding victory over Nazi Germany in May 1945. Within just a few years, Stalin had installed pro-Soviet governments across Eastern Europe and the Cold War erupted, with the Soviet Union and the United States vying for power and influence in the international arena. Domestically, victory convinced Stalin that the Soviet system he had built during the 1930s required no significant policy shifts. Accordingly, the postwar era featured ideological retrenchment and an attempt to rapidly rebuild the country's infrastructure without substantial reforms. Growing the country's heavy industrial complex took priority, to the detriment of most Soviet subjects, whose poor living conditions were compounded by a devastating famine in 1946–1947.

These postwar developments meant that the Gulag remained a massive, secret institution bent on maximizing production and punishing the USSR's enemies. Gulag officials were tasked with major industrial projects aimed at helping the country compete with the West. They opened many new camps, and Gulag administrative structures were changed to emphasize economic tasks. At the same time, repression against the peoples from the western

BELIEF AND DISBELIEF 105

borderlands, combined with harsh antitheft laws passed in 1948, meant that the Gulag population reached its apex of roughly 2.5 million people in the early 1950s (plus another 2.5 million exiled to "special settlements"). Famine and ruthless economic exploitation meant that inmates' living conditions continued to be harsh in the late 1940s, although death rates declined following the war.

As for religion, the tentative wartime truce between Stalin and denominations officially recognized by the state continued into the postwar era. Surprisingly, the USSR in 1946 had 10,547 active Russian Orthodox churches served by 9,254 clergy. There were also seventy-five monasteries in the Soviet Union: forty-two for women with 3,424 nuns and thirty-three for men with 902 monks. The wartime concessions to Orthodoxy, in other words, allowed for significantly more religious worship than was possible at the end of the 1930s. These figures paled in comparison with the pre-Soviet Russian Empire, which in 1916 had 77,727 churches served by 117,915 clergymen, along with 478 monasteries for men with 21,330 monks and 547 for women with 73,299 nuns. Still, these changes represented a significant moderation in religious policy by the Soviet state.[24]

This moderation is reflected in the Gulag, where administrators only sparsely disseminated antireligious propaganda in the postwar era. Quarterly tallies of re-educational lectures rarely mentioned antireligious or scientific lectures. As a report on "cultural-educational work" in the Gulag for the first half of 1952 makes clear, "as before in many colonies and camps of the Gulag scientific-educational and atheistic propaganda is not organized." A 1952 inspection report from Ryazan Province concluded that the absence of antireligious propaganda opened the door for "nuns and sectarians to conduct corrupting work among the backward portion of the inmates." Meanwhile, a thirty-two-page analysis of propaganda at the enormous camp complex of Dalstroy omitted the topic altogether. Lectures and other forms of propaganda were organized on various issues, including production, foreign affairs, and sanitation in the camp, but inmates heard nothing concerning religion.[25]

Gulag leaders' primary concern regarding religious inmates was their tendency to refuse to work. One inspection report from 1946 at the Ustvymsky Camp, for instance, complained that "the absence of natural-scientific propaganda" to combat superstition contributed to the fact that "a fairly large group of sectarians" refused to work "out of so-called religious motives." Administrators in one camp unit hung a satirical drawing of praying

106   FINDING GOD IN THE GULAG

sectarians asking, "God, when will you bless us to go to work?" And beneath the illustration were the words "the lord was silent," implying that religious prisoners only simulated belief in a nonexistent God to escape labor duties. But "this vulgar form of antireligious agitation," the inspector decided, would be unlikely to do any good.[26]

Several years later, a 1952 report on inmates who refused to work found that religious believers were among "the so-called uncorrectable" inmates who persistently refused to perform compulsory labor. In an Amur Province colony, fourteen nuns refused to work for two years "out of religious motives." At the Dalstroy Camps, seventeen sectarians had not worked in a year. Similar examples abounded. The fact that officials considered such inmates "uncorrectable" and yet these prisoners were still alive after a year or two in direct opposition to camp regulations demonstrates that local Gulag officials were uncertain about what to do. The report, signed by Gulag boss Ivan Dolgikh, recommended various measures to end work refusals, but these did not include anything about antireligious propaganda or repression. To some extent, the Gulag recognized that some believing inmates were not susceptible to such influence and that it was better to focus efforts on nonreligious prisoners who could be persuaded to return to work.[27]

This lack of interest in promoting atheism even at the highest levels of Gulag leadership is surprising. With the inundation of inmates from the western borderland regions (discussed in chapter 5), religiosity in the Gulag was rising. Yet this neglect by Gulag authorities was a matter of priorities. With almost all efforts during and after the war geared toward production, antireligious work was little more than an afterthought. Believers in the camps were an occasional nuisance, but they were not considered a major problem. A statistical report on the Gulag population from late 1948, after all, listed just 1,993 "clerics and sectarians" out of more than 2 million inmates, or less than 0.1 percent of prisoners. This count did not include large numbers of lay believers, but it contextualizes why Gulag officials did not prioritize antireligious propaganda.[28]

At the camp level, camp officials likewise focused their efforts, including re-educational work, on production concerns, knowing that job security and potential bonuses were dependent on fulfilling their production plan. This neglect of religion can also be attributed to general apathy among the re-educational staff, who were generally underpaid and endured difficult living and working conditions in the remote camps. Most were not members of the Communist Party, or if they were, it was out of practical considerations rather than ideological conviction. As a representative report from the Karagandinsky Camp in the early 1950s made clear, many "cultural-educational" positions at the camp were vacant due to low wages; cultural-educational workers who were there, meanwhile, were corrupt drunkards who cared little about fulfilling their assigned tasks. In other words, inmates in many camps were subjected to minimal re-educational efforts because camp staff members were more interested in drinking, sleeping, and illicitly enriching themselves at the camp's expense.[29]

The result was that inmates in the postwar Gulag experienced a wide range of attitudes among their jailers concerning faith. Many guards simply ignored religion, but others exhibited more positive or negative tendencies. The archimandrite Pavel Gruzdev, a monk before his imprisonment in 1941, recalled secret worship services in the woods but also a church in a neighboring town where a few guards allowed inmates to attend on occasion in the postwar era. Far from Moscow, such leniency could be permitted if the inmates otherwise behaved well. On the other hand, Lidia Sooster recalled a guard named Pervak at the Peschanny Camp who persecuted imprisoned Christians in the early 1950s. As she recollected, they "refused to work and spent all their time praying. Pervak hated the believers with a fierce hatred, and persecuted and punished them." As with other facets of Gulag life, much depended on the whims of local officials.[30]

Worship and Spirituality in the Late Stalin Era

Memoir accounts of religious belief and worship in the postwar Gulag abound. This reflects not just the large body of memoirs covering this period but also reveals, contrary to the Gulag's official statistics, that there were large numbers of believers in the camps. The Jewish doctor Walter Kaufman, who was captured by the Red Army in Harbin in 1945 and then sentenced to twenty-five years' imprisonment, recalled the wide range of Christians in the camps of Kazakhstan. "There is no counting the number of Christian sects," he noted:

> "Sabbatarians," Adventists, "followers of Jehovah," some kind of "Christ-lovers," and on, and on. These were all persecuted in the camps. Their beards were sometimes forcibly shaven. Their crosses were seized, but they made new ones out of wood and some simply tattooed crosses on their

108   FINDING GOD IN THE GULAG

chest. They would refuse to work on holidays and were thrown in the penalty isolator on a bread-and-water penalty ration.

Lipper likewise wrote of many lay believers who "had not lost their faith, although they scarcely ever practiced the rituals of religion." Lipper was particularly impressed by former nuns who refused to work on Sundays and so spent them in the penalty isolator. Some refused even to give their name to agents of the Antichrist, as they called the guards, and were likewise punished.[31]

Religious believers in the postwar era feature in some of the best-known camp literature, including Solzhenitsyn's account of Alyoshka the Baptist (discussed in this book's preface). Equally famous is Varlam Shalamov's *Kolyma Tales*, a semifictional autobiographical account of the Dalstroy Camps of Kolyma, where Shalamov was incarcerated from 1937 to 1951. Like Solzhenitsyn's *One Day in the Life of Ivan Denisovich*, these tales must be treated carefully, since Shalamov liberally mixes fact with fiction. But taken as a whole, they are designed to impress on readers the types of people who inhabited the Gulag, including an interesting mix of religious characters. One inmate in these tales prayed regularly and loved to engage Shalamov in discussions about Christianity. Shalamov was not religious but had a basic knowledge of the New Testament, and when he corrected his interlocutor at one point, the latter became distraught that he needed "a stranger to point out my unforgivable mistake." Though the believer was still religious, the isolation of the camps had caused him to begin to forget the details of his faith. Shalamov also related encountering in the forest an imprisoned priest who was repeating liturgical prayers and crossing himself. The priest explained that these rituals provided him an escape from hunger, but Shalamov understood it was something more: "I know that everyone has something that is most precious to him, *the last thing that he has left*, and it is that something which helps him to live, to hang on to the life of which we were being so insistently and stubbornly deprived."[32]

But not all of Shalamov's interactions with Christian prisoners were so positive, such as the case of the sectarian Dmitriev, who refused to answer any questions from the guards, replying only, "God knows." Shalamov described how the sectarian got on everyone's nerves in the barracks. The prisoners all "hated the administration and the camp guards, hated each other, and most of all we hated the sectarian—for his songs, hymns, psalms. The sectarian sang in a hoarse voice as if he had a cold. He sang softly, but his hymns and psalms were endless." The sectarian explained that the hymns kept him alive, but this did not elicit sympathy. In the end, the prayers were not enough to counteract the brutal conditions of the camp and the bullying from other inmates. One day, the sectarian walked away from a work detail and refused to stop when ordered to halt. He was shot and killed.[33]

The variegated relationships between Christian and non-Christian inmates are also found in *To Be Preserved Forever*, the well-known memoir of the disillusioned former Communist Lev Kopelev. Imprisoned at the Unzhensky Camp in the late Stalin era after writing a scathing letter denouncing Red Army soldiers' unpunished crimes in occupied Germany, Kopelev made a detailed record of camp life, including his observations of imprisoned Baptists. Contrary to Solzhenitsyn's glowing portrait of Alyoshka, however, the portrayal here is more mixed. Kopelev writes of two Baptists constantly using religious phrases such as "As the Lord wills" and "God bless you." They prayed and sang hymns together and told of miracles they had experienced and conversions they witnessed in the camps. Kopelev writes that there was mutual respect between these believers and their non-believer counterparts until one incident changed everything. The older of the two, Nepichor, received a food parcel from home and was sharing it with other prisoners, but he did not give anything to his fellow Baptist, Iosip, claiming there was not enough to share with everyone. When the others protested that Iosip needed nourishment much more than they did, Nepichor responded, "That is the cross he has been given to bear. Whom the Lord loves he burdens with tests. Brother Iosip bears his cross humbly and gains virtue in the sight of God." At this, one of the prisoners unleashed a torrent of abuse on Nepichor and called him a "lousy bloodsucker." Following this incident, the Baptists, now viewed suspiciously as fanatics, kept their distance from Kopelev and the others.[34]

Kopelev's memory of an Easter celebration reflects more positively on imprisoned Christians. "Aunt Dusya," the female inmate tasked with cleaning the camp hospital where Kopelev labored, helped arrange a secret Easter service in one of the women's barracks along with an imprisoned Orthodox priest and two nuns. They used a table as an altar, found something to burn for incense, cobbled together a few homemade candles, and made vestments out of sheets. The priest performed the ceremony using an iron cross, chanting in the darkness before an assemblage of believers and nonbelievers alike, accompanied by a hastily assembled choir. The following day, several of them gathered for a small feast and exchanged the traditional greetings of

110   FINDING GOD IN THE GULAG

"Christ is risen" and "Truly he is risen." What touched Kopelev most was that Dusya insisted on inviting a known informant to the gathering, arguing:

> [W]ith his poor, lost, dark, sinful soul, where will he find a ray of light if we don't show it to him? Let him see that even here, in prison, the light of Christ still shines and there is pity even for such as he.... [And] if we invite him and treat him and exchange toasts with him, in Christ's holy name— for Jesus taught us to love and pity our enemies—he will see things differently, and he will not be able to repay good with evil.

The group celebrated with heartfelt toasts, Easter cake, and other delicacies and reaffirmed their love for all men and their desire to see Christians, Communists, and everyone else living peacefully together. As for the informant, he seemed to enjoy the celebration and indicated that he would keep the secret, but the next day, he squealed, and Dusya was transferred to a more difficult labor assignment.[35]

Less-well-known memoir accounts from religious and nonreligious inmates further attest to the multitude and diversity of imprisoned Christians and the variability of their experiences. Thomas Sgovio recalled a Russian inmate, who had married a German woman, quietly humming "Stille Nacht" ("Silent Night") on the worksite once in late December. Alla Andreeva wrote that in the early 1950s, in the Mordovian camps, a staunch member of the True Orthodox Church became friendly with her since she was also a Christian, but when she found out that Andreeva was not formally married to her common-law husband, she started calling her an "unwed mare" and cut off all ties with her. Yury Yurkevich, incarcerated in the Kungursky Camp near the city of Perm, was impressed by Vasily Ivanovich, a poorly educated and "deeply religious" farmer from Voronezh Province who had been captured by the Germans during the war before then being sent to the Gulag by the Soviets. Vasily lived "an intensely spiritual life" and was perpetually cheerful despite his fate (in addition to imprisonment, he was also missing most of his right arm, presumably from a wartime injury). He read the Bible often and always sought ways to serve and share with others around him.[36]

Walter Ciszek's memoir recalls how important Christian beliefs and practices were to him in the Gulag. Ciszek, a Polish-American Catholic priest arrested and imprisoned for conducting secret religious activity in the Soviet Union, spent many lonely days in Moscow's Lubyanka Prison in prayer. (See figure 4.1.) As he described his religious life there:

After breakfast I would say Mass by heart.... I said the Angelus morning, noon, and night as the Kremlin clock chimed the hours. Before dinner, I would make my noon *examen* [examination of conscience]; before going to bed at night I'd make the evening *examen* and points for the morning meditation, following St. Ignatius' *Spiritual Exercises*. Every afternoon, I said three rosaries—one in Polish, on in Latin, and one in Russian—as a substitute for my breviary. After supper, I spent the evening reciting prayers and hymns from memory or even chanting them out loud.... During these times of prayer, I would also make up my own prayers, talking to God directly, asking for His help, but above all accepting His will for me.

Later, in Butyrka Prison, he reunited with a Russian friend, a fellow Jesuit priest, and they followed this prayer ritual together, along with granting confession to each other and discussing theology. However, after being transferred to a larger cell with more inmates back in Lubyanka, he found praying and meditating more difficult, and his spirituality waned. But he held lengthy discussions with a convinced atheist, with whom he sparred over supposed contradictions in the Bible. When he was again transferred, to a solitary cell, he resumed his lonely routine of prayer and meditation. He recalled, "I learned there the lesson which would keep me going in the years to come: religion, prayer, and love of God do not change reality, but they give it a new meaning. In Lubyanka I grew firmer in my conviction that *whatever* happened in my life was nothing else than a reflection of God's will for me. And He would protect me."[37]

Anatoly Levitin-Krasnov's memories of faith in the Gulag are similar to Ciszek's in some ways, but they fit into a very different spiritual trajectory. Levitin-Krasnov was primarily raised by his believing grandmother in the 1920s and was very active in Orthodoxy and then the Bolshevik-sponsored alternative, the Living Church. During the 1930s, however, he immersed himself in education, specializing in Russian language and literature, and lost touch with his religious roots. His faith revived during the Second World War, and he was ordained a deacon in the soon-to-be-disbanded Living Church. But after the war, he again became immersed in secular teaching until his arrest in 1949 for anti-Soviet agitation. His spiritual life, as he related, had diminished significantly by this point: "Only drops of it remained." However, he experienced a spiritual rebirth in the Kargopolsky Camp, donning a cross, praying, and communing with fellow believers. And he refused to be an informant, since, as he explained to the recruiting officer,

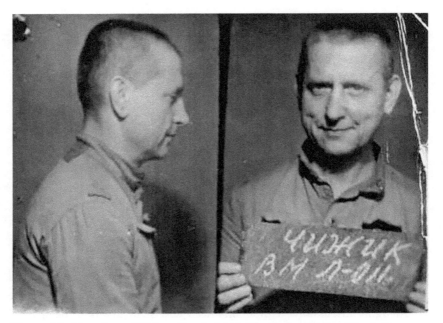

Figure 4.1 Mug shot of Walter Ciszek, 1941. The Father Walter Ciszek Prayer League.

"Because of my faith I cannot do evil to others." As he related, he "felt God—here, near, close by." His faith sustained him through the difficult years of the labor camp, and when informed of his release in the spring of 1953, he wrote, "Although it was not yet Easter, I still wanted to say: 'Christ is risen!'" Yet after his release from the Gulag, Levitin-Krasnov's faith again waned as "earthly human interests, ambition, egotism, and everything that is vulgar and worthless in my nature" reappeared and triumphed over spirituality. In other words, it was precisely the oppressive, black-and-white nature of the Gulag that provided fertile ground for faith to flourish, with periods of spiritual apathy standing on either side of that experience.[38]

As opposed to Levitin-Krasnov and Ciszek, who both entered the camps as believers, Vasily Kozlov entered as an unbeliever. He recounted in his memoir how he was imprisoned in the late 1940s because of a neglected childhood that led him to a life of crime. In the camps, he despaired, but among his fellow inmates, he wrote, "I happened to see other people who did have good morals and high ideals in life. These were Christians, believers. They had been sentenced and put among criminals for their living faith in God!" Although these Baptists had been imprisoned unjustly, they "did not despair. Life in the camp in these harsh conditions did not dismay them. They were shining with a spiritual beauty. . . . One could see Christ reflected in their faces! I, too, wanted to live just such a pure life with high ideals." Ultimately, Kozlov was persuaded to become a Christian. As he testified: "The Russian prisons and camps have become for many a place of spiritual regeneration and they have met Christ there. In 1953 I completely broke with my sinful past and with the world of sin. I became a Christian." Kozlov was released from the camps in 1954 but would later be imprisoned again, not for theft but for his efforts to share Christianity among the Soviet people. Such tales of conversion in the postwar Gulag are rare, but they do exist. By presenting an alternative system of values to that professed by the Soviet regime, Christian prisoners attracted those seeking stability and meaning in their lives.[39]

But not all such conversions were deeply rooted. Kaufman encountered a fellow inmate who was a devout member of the Communist Party before his arrest but then suddenly became religious in the camp. An Orthodox priest helped him make this transition, and soon "he would pray, cross himself, believed in the son of God Jesus Christ, and in the New Testament and Gospels." After a year and a half, however, he converted from Orthodoxy to Catholicism. To Kaufman, this all seemed artificially contrived, and he wondered whether this former Party member would return to the Party and a life of atheism after his release. "There were many such mutilated souls in the camp," Kaufman concluded, searching for hope or relief wherever it could be found. Memoirists Joseph Berger and Elena Lipper likewise noted the conversion, however temporary, of former Communists to Christianity in the camps. Christianity provided a path, not the only path but for some a viable one, toward psychological survival in the brutal world of the Soviet Gulag.[40]

Aleksandr Ugrimov's self-reflective account confirms this observation. His family fled the Soviet Union in the early 1920s, and he was educated in Germany and France. He joined the French Resistance during the Second World War, but immediately after the war, he and his wife were forcibly handed over to Soviet authorities because they were officially Soviet citizens. Upon the Ugrimovs' arrival in Moscow in 1948, the secret police arrested the couple; Ugrimov received ten years in the Gulag for supposed anti-Soviet activity, and his wife received an eight-year sentence. In a camp near Vorkuta, he suffered physically and psychologically. He was frequently lonely,

114 FINDING GOD IN THE GULAG

surrounded by few fellow inmates with whom he could relate, which left him a lot of time to think. During these periods of reflection, he discovered that although he had not been much of a believer before his arrest, he now often thought about God. Within a short time, he applied Christian teachings to help him cope with this new repressive environment. "I did not get angry," he later recalled. "I was ready to accept suffering as being sent by God for my sins." This sense of patience, and even justice, amid suffering served to calm his soul, and Christian teachings about love prompted him to re-evaluate his relations with his fellow inmates. Specifically, he felt prompted to "love my neighbor, regardless of his beliefs, convictions, or nationality."[41]

Several months later, Ugrimov experienced his first Easter behind barbed wire, which "few in my circle remembered or wanted to observe somehow." But he found one fellow Christian, and the two resolved to celebrate together. At midnight, when all was dark and quiet, they retreated to a corner of the barrack, sang Easter hymns, crossed themselves, and tried to feel the spirit of the traditional Easter liturgy. This brought some comfort and a sense of spiritual fulfillment. Ugrimov also discovered, as he became more enmeshed in camp society, that there were several other Christian inmates willing to openly discuss their faith, a stark contrast to imprisoned Communists who never dared to profess their beliefs. But while most other inmates generally respected their Christian beliefs, none of the nonbelieving inmates converted. Even one of his friends, whose father was a priest and who celebrated Easter with Ugrimov a few times out of respect for the tradition, remained an unbeliever.[42]

Living a Christian life in the postwar Gulag was challenging despite the potential benefits of providing hope and peace in a world of violence and corruption. One might think that ordained clergymen would be more immune to such pressures, but even some of them abandoned the faith or at least stopped practicing. For instance, a French Catholic priest noted in his memoir that the imprisoned clerics in his camp had no energy to serve as pastors, subjected as they were to the same insufficient rations and hard labor as the rest of the inmates. "As a result," he observed, "people had no other interests but the desire to somehow earn more money to buy a little more [food]." Berger similarly related how a Lutheran pastor from Moscow quickly abandoned his beliefs and started assimilating with the common criminals of the camp. According to Berger, "he blamed his degeneration on the NKVD and Soviet power and said he was merely adapting to adverse circumstances."[43]

Many clergymen, however, remained loyal to their callings and found ways to perform their religious duties. Michael Solomon, a devout Jew, described being impressed by an Orthodox priest at the Dalstroy Camps whom many prisoners loved for his benevolent pastoral care.[44] Vladimir Kabo, a secular Jew, was likewise attracted to an Orthodox priest with "the eyes of a prophet" who gave him a Bible to read. As he later related, this man alone awakened in him "religious feeling," for he exhibited "the essence of Christianity, expressed in the simple words 'God is love.' Love for God and for man—this is what determined his behavior, this is what glistened in his eyes, that is what he was always talking about."[45]

Meanwhile, Anatoly Zhigulin was drawn to an Orthodox priest named Mitrofan while awaiting sentencing in prison in Voronezh in 1949–1950. Whenever a warden came to the door, Mitrofan made the sign of the cross and said, "Get thee hence, accursed Satan." He was frequently beaten but bore it bravely, praying to and praising God while suffering. Mitrofan often recited the gospels to Zhigulin by memory and told Old Testament stories in his own words. The priest told him he was imprisoned for truth and would therefore, as the New Testament says, inherit the kingdom of God (even though Zhigulin himself was not religious). Coincidentally, they met once more in a transit prison, and Mitrofan again reminded Zhigulin, "Do not sorrow, for 'Blessed are they who are persecuted for the truth.'"[46]

For many believers in the postwar Gulag, faith was quiet and internal. Muscovite artist Andreeva, imprisoned at Lubyanka in 1947 before being sent to the camps, later recalled that there were few believers in prison and that she could not live any religious life. She did not read scripture or pray for anything concrete, such as release, but silently, in her heart, she prayed that God would "not abandon her." She believed these quiet acts of faith helped her survive her torments.[47] Gruzdev, who later joined the Orthodox clergy, similarly observed that "the camp with all its merciless reality proposes a choice: 'If you go right—you lose your life, if you go left—you lose your conscience.' And this choice must be made every day, every hour." And here, Gruzdev found, "on the very precipice of life and death is where faith is experienced." This was where ritual, ceremony, church hierarchy, and other trappings of religion no longer mattered. This was where, amid starvation, humiliation, and violence, "the example of unprecedented fortitude and the humble height of spirit is revealed." Suffering silently but faithfully, Gruzdev found strength in relying on God for spiritual salvation, even when physical salvation was not guaranteed.[48]

116   FINDING GOD IN THE GULAG

Others demonstrated their faith outwardly. John Noble recounted how three nuns in postwar Vorkuta refused to work in the brick factory to which they were assigned. The guards subjected them to penalty rations, straitjackets, isolation, and other forms of punishment. When even a regimen of eight hours standing in the Arctic winter for multiple days without hats or gloves yielded neither dead bodies nor working bodies, the camp commander finally gave up and accepted their refusal to labor. But by this point, tales of this miracle of survival "without the slightest trace of frostbite" had spread through the camp, and both prisoners and guards acknowledged "the hand of a Power that was not of this earth." Noble's memoir is full of such miracles, and the account here, related to him secondhand, is likely exaggerated through multiple retellings. But it still expresses a simple truth: imprisoned Christians sometimes acted in publicly defiant ways that laid bare their opposition to the Soviet regime. Believers then used such stories, in actual or exaggerated form, to buoy their faith and see the miraculous in their lives.[49]

In addition to memoirs, artifacts of religious observance from the postwar Gulag also testify to the spiritual life of imprisoned Christians. Dora Rogalskaya, incarcerated at the Karagandinsky Camp in the early 1940s, secretly crafted an embroidered icon of the Virgin with Child to help focus her prayers. (See figure 4.2.) Inmates at the Temnikovsky Camp and Dubravny Camp created prayer books and a homemade icon depicting the Virgin with Child. Other inmates in the late 1940s and early 1950s made Easter, Christmas, and "Angel's Day" greeting cards, sometimes using birch bark, straw, and other materials to adorn them. (See figure 4.3.) One of the most amazing religious artifacts still surviving is a vest from the Mineralny Special Camp, worn by a friend of Irina Ugrimova. It appears at first to be an ordinary padded vest, black on the outside and white on the inside. Upon closer inspection, though, one sees that the unknown owner had meticulously inscribed Orthodox prayers, liturgical texts, and scriptures from memory in blue ink on the inside liner, so they were only noticeable if the vest was turned inside out from the unsewn bottom hem. This ingenious arrangement allowed the inmate to keep the religious inscriptions physically close to her body during the day, providing a sense of spiritual protection, while allowing easy access to them in the barracks in the evening. Of course, they would be easily concealed during searches.[50] (See figure 4.4.)

These tangible expressions of faith were vital to the spiritual lives of many inmates. Old Believer Arseny Formakov, imprisoned in the Krasnoyarsky

BELIEF AND DISBELIEF 117

Figure 4.2 Virgin Mary with Child, sewn icon by Dora Moiseyevna Rogalskaya, 1942–1946. Memorial Museum, Moscow.

Camp during and immediately after World War II, requested of his wife by letter a calendar that noted religious holidays. After receiving it, he replied, "It turns out I celebrated Shrovetide a week early." In one letter to his wife, he remembered how for his first Easter in prison, he "made three Easter eggs of various sizes out of the inside of a piece of bread, dipped them in powdered sugar, and decorated each with a red ribbon and your monogram." He repeated this ritual on a later Easter holiday, making the best feast he could and sending a letter home through the camp censor (which let it through) adorned with dried flowers and the traditional Easter greeting, "Christ is

Figure 4.3 Easter card, unknown author, 1950. Memorial Museum, Moscow.

Figure 4.4 Vest with religious handwriting, unknown creator, 1949–1954. Memorial Museum, Moscow.

Risen." For historian Emily Johnson, these letters recording his private religious celebrations in the camp helped "[restore] family unity by reiterating, to the extent possible, beloved performative traditions." In other words, while the rituals themselves reinforced Formakov's family in the atheistic environment of the camps, the letters recreated a sense of spiritual connection with his family across their five time zones of separation.[51]

———————

As the Soviet state launched successive waves of repression against perceived enemies before, during, and after World War II, the number of Soviet subjects who experienced the Gulag rose dramatically. Many of these were religious, and while some experienced heightened antireligious repression in the camps, all endured terrible living conditions and violence during these deadliest years of the Gulag. While individual experiences varied widely, many believers in this pressure-cooker environment faced the dilemma of whether to publicly exhibit their faith, retain it introspectively, or else abandon it altogether. For some, the horrors of the Gulag made faith seem impossible. Others endured the trials of their spirit and their body quietly. For many, the increased presence of like-minded Christians provided a mutual support system that aided physical, psychological, and spiritual survival. Far from all survived, but many who did credited their faith and the faith of those around them.

5

Western Worshippers and Gulag Gangsters

One of the most significant ways that World War II affected the Soviet Union and the Gulag was the Soviet annexation of Estonia, Latvia, Lithuania, part of Finland, much of interwar Poland, and the Romanian territory of Bessarabia. The USSR brought these lands and their varied peoples into the Soviet "brotherhood of nations" by force after the short-lived Nazi-Soviet Pact of 1939 divided up much of Eastern Europe between the two countries. The Soviet Red Army, secret police, and other Soviet officials worked quickly to Sovietize these territories by holding Soviet-style elections, collectivizing agriculture, organizing Communist Party cells, establishing the Communist Youth League, and conducting mass purges of suspected enemies. Many government officials, military and police officers, wealthy landowners, "capitalists," professors, cultural figures, church leaders, and others were sentenced to the Gulag or sent into exile. Before this process of Sovietization was completed, however, invading German forces overran these territories in 1941, only for them to be reoccupied by the Red Army a few years later and reincorporated into the USSR.[1]

The annexation of these western borderlands, as they became collectively known, brought millions of Christians and other believers into the USSR. Polish Catholics, Estonian Lutherans, and other members of the predominant religions of these territories deeply resented the loss of national independence and the prospect of living in an avowedly secular state, seeing the national and religious struggle against Soviet occupation as the same. Others did not connect religious and national identity but opposed Soviet power as a manifestation of the Antichrist foretold in the Book of Revelation. Notably, despite various repressive measures, including the abolition of the Ukrainian Greek Catholic Church, religion remained a powerful societal force in the newly annexed territories. As the secret police in 1949 wrote of the situation in Moldova:

> Despite measures that have been taken, the influence of church authorities among the population is still significant. The majority of the local

Finding God in the Gulag. Jeffrey S. Hardy, Oxford University Press. © Oxford University Press 2024.
DOI: 10.1093/9780197751701.003.0006

population, especially the rural population, attend church and perform religious ordinances. This is also taking placing among a portion of the intelligentsia and the members of the Communist Youth League.

A similar assessment of strong church attendance was made in 1951; even some Communist Party members were found to be baptizing their infants, singing in church, and allowing priests to visit schools and teach the children about God.[2]

This chapter explores the persistence of this religiosity in the Soviet Gulag. Ukrainians, Moldovans, Poles, Latvians, and others practiced their faith and employed it not only to help them endure their suffering but to maintain their staunch opposition to the Soviet occupation of their homelands. Curiously, another group of inmates also displayed increased religious devotion in the postwar Gulag: gangsters. Adopting Russian Orthodox symbols, mainly through tattooing, they employed a ready language of opposition to Soviet rule even though the depth of their religious beliefs was usually shallow. These tattoos also highlighted a growing Russian nationalism, spurred in no small part by the sudden increased presence of Poles, Ukrainians, Jews, and other groups. Religion thus not only divided the new wave of western inmates from their jailers, but it operated as a source of division within inmate society.

A Mosaic of Believers from the West

The Gulag in the 1940s and early 1950s witnessed hundreds of thousands of new inmates arriving from successive waves of Soviet repression in the newly acquired western borderlands, and the devout religious beliefs of many of them made an immediate impact. As memoirist Mikhail Puzyrev wrote, most prisoners "from the west were believers in God. They put their utmost trust in him." He recalled how these Christians endured the ridicule of other inmates and "conducted collective prayers throughout entire nights. The youth among them were especially diligent in prayer." Despite being surrounded skeptics, including Puzyrev himself, these Christians believed that God was listening to their pleas in the brutal camps of the Soviet Gulag. Elena Lipper encountered a similarly religious woman "from some sect in the Ukraine" in her camp in Kolyma, who "radiated cheerfulness and kindness" and endured well the difficulties of camp life. Released from her first

122 FINDING GOD IN THE GULAG

prison stint, she was soon reimprisoned for refusing to work on religious holidays, accepting this new sentence as an acceptable price to pay for remaining loyal to God.[3]

The faith of the new arrivals likewise struck other Soviet inmates. Dmitri Panin wrote glowingly of a blue-eyed inmate from the west who gained a position of some authority after Ukrainian and Baltic inmates seized de facto control of the camp from a criminal gang. To Panin, this strong, fair-haired man "abided by the simple, clear-cut principles of Christian ethics." The most important result of these westerners taking power in the camp was enforced honesty in the kitchen and dining hall, where theft and corruption had previously run rampant. Christian morality was thus appreciated even by those who did not believe in God. Tamara Petkevich, meanwhile, described a group of Poles in her wartime camp whom she deeply admired for their joyful spirits and willingness to help others. As she explained, "The Poles refused to lose hope, nor would they taste humiliation . . . I could never forget their gallantry or their ability to hide the ugliness of camp reality behind the words 'God protect you!'" She also wrote favorably of Baltic prisoners who asked her "to hide their prayer books or Bibles, which they'd managed to hold on to." Although not religious herself, she remarked that "a respectful relationship gradually took root between us."[4]

Joseph Berger recalled meeting several believers and clerics in the camps. Among these, he singled out religious leaders from the western borderlands for their honesty and courage, describing them as "very defiant and militant in their attitudes, defending their faith with great devotion and even fanaticism." One of these, a Lithuanian Catholic priest, seized an opportunity when a large group of inmates had just arrived in the camp and were waiting for directions as to where they should go. Jumping up on a rock, he started preaching to them, peppering his admonitions with biblical verses and encouraging the inmates to disobey camp authorities. For this, he was arrested and given a new sentence, although he already had a twenty-five-year term.[5]

Similarly, the intellectual Zoya Marchenko encountered several Christians from western Ukraine in a Kharkiv prison in 1949. They courageously stood up to the guards and to the common criminals who stole from the other prisoners. They also renewed their "inner strength" with collective spiritual practices: "Crossing themselves, they would whisper prayers, and sometimes they gathered together and sang." This deep spiritual conviction of Ukrainian prisoners was also noted by another inmate who observed them regularly hold mass on Sunday, the typical day off from work:

In the morning, they would never breakfast until noon: they would patiently place their ration of bread and *balanda* on the bunks, and, dressed up as well as they could, their braids freshly combed, they would sit down at the long table and silently, intently pray. They would sing church songs in beautiful voices. Prayer and the celebration of the Holy Mass became a spiritual recharging, giving us strength and vitality.

Such "spiritual recharging" at the end of the workweek was certainly important in the Gulag, and here the spirituality imparted by such Sunday services affected not just the direct participants but those around them.[6]

An imprisoned American, John Noble, a nonpracticing Christian during his stint in the postwar Gulag, was for this reason happy to find himself in a camp made up largely of Christians from the western borderlands. As he recalled, there were "Roman Catholic priests from Lithuania, Greek Orthodox priests from the Ukraine, Lutheran pastors from Latvia and Estonia, a Jewish rabbi, a Mennonite bishop from the Volga Basin, Seventh-Day Adventist missionaries, [and] Jehovah's Witnesses." Soon after their arrival at the camp, the Lutherans began holding secret worship services in the room dedicated to drying wet clothes, and Noble joined them on occasion to revive his own religious beliefs. They prayed, conducted Bible study by memory, sang hymns, and discussed various topics, such as why God allows human suffering, especially among his followers. Other denominations soon began to hold their own worship services. Baptists typically gathered after dinner in a curtained-off corner of the dining room used for cultural productions. Jehovah's Witnesses, Adventists, Mennonites, and Ukrainian Greek Orthodox believers held their own smaller meetings. And the Lithuanian Catholics met during the work shift in the mines, where their priest would hastily administer the Eucharist using black bread and water with just a drop of wine added from a small vial. The guards typically ignored these gatherings, considering them unimportant as long as the work was being done. But on one occasion, a "militant atheist" prisoner discovered them and attacked the priest with a shovel, breaking his arm. In addition to his injury, the priest was forced to serve two months in solitary confinement, from which he emerged emaciated but firm in spirit. For Noble, these Christian meetings provided sorely needed spiritual support, making him feel as if "a great burden was lifted from my shoulders." As for relations among the different branches of Christianity, he discovered that "differences in denominations or creed were much less important in Vorkuta than in the

124 FINDING GOD IN THE GULAG

outside world. We were all standing together against the common foe." Out of many different national and religious groups came a unified desire to oppose Soviet power.[7]

Belief combined with anger at the political annexation of their homeland meant that many people from the western borderlands retained a strong sense of national and religious identity in the Gulag. This is exemplified in Polish inmates' religious ballads that expressed the pain of incarceration coupled with the hope that faith provided. One, for example, characterized Poland as a "holy land" and exclaimed, "Oh Jesus! You alone are with us." Another Polish ballad, "Prayer from the Taiga," written by a prisoner at Norilsk in 1944, expressed in greater detail both the agony of confinement and the hope of overcoming it through God-given strength:

> All-loving God, All-powerful God!
> Here, in Siberia, in the snowy hell,
> In hunger, in cold, in grief,
> From the depths of our hearts, humbly,
> We raise our prayers to the heavens:
> To your children in exile,
> Give strength to withstand,
> And draw spiritually near to you!
>
> God, make it so that to your glory,
> The gates of this hell were broadened!
> So that your people—half dead,
> Sick and humiliated,
> Scared and exhausted,
> Again obtained great strength!
> Our voice rises above the thorns,
> Be merciful to us, oh Lord!

The imagery of "children in exile" evoked the biblical story of "captive Israel," enslaved first in Egypt and then in Babylon. It also, no doubt, recalled the Polish revolts against the Russian Empire in the nineteenth century (1830–1831 and 1863–1864), which resulted in tens of thousands of Poles being exiled to Siberia. The prisoners of the 1940s thus asked their God for "great strength," along with spiritual and political salvation, just like their Polish and Hebrew predecessors.[8]

The recorded prayer of Ukrainian prisoner Anna Kotsur also reveals the union of religious belief and nationalism. Incarcerated at Taishet in the early 1950s, she poured out her soul to God for both individual and collective deliverance from Soviet repression:

> Redeem us, Oh God, and our families,
> Do not allow us to die in this difficult moment.
> Do not let us perish, we ask of you, Oh God,
> and You, Mother of God,
> and You, all the Saints at the Throne of God.
> We beg You, do not refuse us a better fate.
> All of You, please intercede for our beloved land,
> And have mercy on our people.

Such prayers on behalf of themselves, their fellow inmates, and their oppressed nations were typical among prisoners from the western borderlands. One memoirist recalled, "We prayed a lot and asked God to help us get through this and endure." Another related, "In the evening, lying on the bunks, our blue lips rustled, saying prayers. We believed, and we prayed sincerely." Vanda Horchynska similarly recalled, "Regardless of the severe camp regimen and our unbearable living conditions, we continued to defy all the moral prohibitions and to live the life of freedom by preserving the tradition of daily prayer."[9]

The Polish prisoner Stanislav Svyanevich recorded the effect of such practices. Mobilized into the Polish army to fight the Germans in 1939, Svyanevich was captured by the invading Soviets and sent to a prisoner-of-war camp. This camp was located in a former monastery, and the Polish inmates maintained a vibrant spiritual life with assistance from several army chaplains who were imprisoned with them. Open manifestations of worship were forbidden, so they gathered secretly to pray and partake of the Eucharist. Even many Poles not interested in religion before their incarceration, Svyanevich related, became so in the camps to assert national solidarity against the Soviets. Soviet incarceration thus turned at least some previously nonreligious people from the western borderlands to God in the name of national solidarity. After Svyanevich was convicted of anti-Soviet activity and sentenced to eight years in the Gulag, he was separated from his Polish comrades with whom he had practiced Catholicism in the prisoner-of-war camp. Still, he found many fellow believers, both Russian and non-Russian,

126 FINDING GOD IN THE GULAG

who provided meaningful interactions that helped him maintain his faith in God. These imprisoned Christians convinced him of the certainty of God's eventual triumph over evil, as long as "in each of these people there is the smallest part of the spark of God."[10]

The Polish-American Jesuit Walter Ciszek provided more detail on how Catholics from the western borderlands practiced their religion. After arrival at his first labor camp in Dudinka in 1946, Ciszek became friends with a Polish Catholic priest, Father Casper, renowned in the camp for holding mass with wine made out of raisins, bread from stolen flour, a whiskey glass for a chalice, and a watch part as the paten. He had the mass prayers written down and shared a copy with Ciszek, who remarked that "my joy at being able to celebrate Mass again cannot be described." Ciszek then joined with Casper to hear confession, give spiritual counsel, and otherwise function as a Catholic priest, primarily among Polish inmates. For this, he related, "I thanked God daily for the opportunity to work among this hidden flock, consoling and comforting men who had thought themselves beyond His grace."[11]

Transferring to a different camp in Norilsk gave Ciszek the chance to perform mass and hear the confessions of Polish and Lithuanian Catholic inmates almost daily. Camp authorities knew to some extent what was happening and occasionally questioned Ciszek, but they did not interfere with his religious observance. As long as production targets were met, they were content to turn a blind eye to religious practice. As Ciszek recalled, "We delivered sermons and exhortations walking up and down in a group in the yard, just like any group of prisoners engaged in a discussion or a bull session. . . . All in all, we had a thriving parish." This pattern of finding ways to perform mass, administer communion and confession, and otherwise engage in group religious practices continued in every camp zone Ciszek inhabited, with Ciszek often joined by other Polish, Lithuanian, and Ukrainian Greek Catholic priests.[12]

Wladyslaw Bukowinski, a Catholic priest who had presided over Saint Peter and Paul Cathedral in Lutsk (closed by Soviet authorities in 1946 and eventually turned into a museum of atheism), provides another story of Catholicism in the camps. Bukowinski was arrested in 1940 during the initial Soviet occupation, released in 1941, and then rearrested in 1945 with the Soviet reoccupation. Typical of many religious inmates, he saw his imprisonment as God's will; as he reasoned, "the will of God sometimes acts through atheists, who sent me where a priest was needed." In his first camp near Chelyabinsk, Bukowinski often heard confessions from Polish Catholics, typically at night after lights out to avoid detection by the guards. But one night, after hearing a confession and enjoying a pleasant conversation with a fellow Pole, he encountered a guard patrol while returning to his barrack. They recognized him as a priest, and one guard smacked him on the cheek and ordered him back to the barrack. As he recalled, this enraged him, and he had no thought of "turning the other cheek," as instructed in the New Testament. But then, after a few minutes, he realized that according to regulations he should have been immediately thrown into the penalty isolator for being out so late. So really, he concluded, the blow on the cheek could be defined as an act of mercy. It stung but only briefly, whereas inmates in the isolator often had to be taken straight to the hospital after the period of isolation. Bukowinski's faith and position as a priest thus allowed him to bring spiritual comfort to other inmates and to suffer the abuses meted out against him patiently.[13]

Religious Objects and Holidays

One aspect of religious life that was often noted by other inmates was the variety of religious objects made or obtained in the camps by newly arrived western worshippers. Orthodox inmate Aleksandr Solzhenitsyn observed Lithuanian Catholics in a transit prison crafting homemade rosary beads out of bits of bread, which were soaked, molded, and dyed ("black ones with burnt rubber, white ones with tooth powder, red ones with red germicide"). They were then strung and dried. Solzhenitsyn recalled helping them and also making his own rosary (even though rosaries are not typical in the Orthodox tradition) with their assistance, proffered out of "true brotherly love." Solzhenitsyn treasured the rosary from that point forward:

> I fingered and counted the beads inside my wide mittens—at work line-up, on the march to and from work, at all waiting times; I could do it standing up, and freezing cold was no hindrance. I carried it safely through the search points, in the padding of my mittens, where it could not be felt. The warders found it on various occasions, but supposed that it was for praying and let me keep it.

An account from an inmate from the western borderlands provides additional detail on the making of rosaries: "We prayed a lot on rosaries made out of bread. We would knead breadcrumbs in our hands to a consistent mass that we then formed into beads. Using the needle that, despite prohibitions, was well hidden in every cell, we would pierce each bead and slip it onto the thread." Having such tangible reminders of their faith helped these dislocated Catholic inmates preserve their attachment not only to God but to the spiritual home of their native lands. And to some prisoners, the spiritual protection of such objects was absolute. Ukrainian Greek Catholic inmate Ivan Lelekach kept a rosary dedicated to the Virgin Mary with him at all times and credited it for saving his life when the rest of his work brigade perished in a mine explosion. In his telling, the Virgin Mary, through the rosary, instructed him, "I will not let you perish, for I still have a plan for you." Crafted and kept in secrecy, rosaries provided prisoners with a physical anchor to their inner spiritual beliefs and a sense of divine security.[14] (See figure 5.1.)

Other religious objects provided similar feelings of comfort and belonging. Ukrainian Greek Catholic priest Volodymyr Senkyvskyi kept a handkerchief with the images of Mary and Jesus sewn onto it, along with

Figure 5.1 Rosary in a heart-shaped box belonging to a political prisoner, Magadan, 1950s. Museum of Occupations and Freedom Fights, Vilnius.

a toothbrush whittled into a cross, throughout his time in the camps. Both were given to him by fellow incarcerated believers. Family members and friends also sent religious items—crosses, icons, literature, and even wine for communion—to prisoners in care packages. In a stunning admission of confusion concerning policy regarding religious practice in the camps, one high-ranking Gulag administrator reported to the deputy minister of Internal Affairs: "Some camps confiscate all objects of religious ritual from packages and parcels, while others hand them over to prisoners. In regard to this matter there are no instructions." Christian inmates especially valued items that could not easily be created in the camps such as religious texts. As one prisoner remembered:

> A prayer book was a real rarity, so they were very much valued, because with them it was possible to recite one of the litanies. This meant an awful lot to those of us who prayed together! It seemed, then, as though you had been in church at least for a short time. The regular common prayer of the Ukrainians was usually led by one of the educated women. In our barracks this was an older woman of about fifty.

Olha Hodiak likewise recalled, "I was sent a missal [an instruction book for conducting mass], and Grandma sent me a rosary. . . . I kept that prayer book and rosary for ten years. Every Sunday we would say the Mass with it. Two of us would keep watch while we stood somewhere in the barracks." Religious objects sent from home provided for increased religiosity in the camps and a deeper, spiritual connection with loved ones back home.[15]

The risk of carrying such items, of course, meant possible confrontations with the guards, but like the disorganized policies surrounding incoming mail, guard attitudes about religious contraband in the barracks varied widely. Evhen Pelekh described how Lithuanian priests bribed the guards by distributing packages with food and other items to ensure that they received communion wine from home. The Ukrainian Greek Catholic Petro Herlyuk-Kupchynsky had his prayer book seized during a routine search, then returned to him by a different orderly who explained that he "didn't find anything anti-Soviet." But it was later confiscated again, and Herlyuk-Kupchynsky was punished with a difficult labor assignment for possessing it. Another Ukrainian Greek Catholic likewise had a prayer book seized but got it back after giving the guard tobacco sent from home. A third protested after his prayer book was confiscated, explaining to the camp commander, "I

130 FINDING GOD IN THE GULAG

am a priest, and I need to pray ... for my family, my parish, for all people, and for you citizen commander." Whether touched by this or simply wanting to avoid further trouble, the commander returned the book and instructed the priest, "Hide it [better], so they don't confiscate it a second time." The varied nature of guard attitudes and corruptibility in the Gulag meant that religious objects could often be kept or even reclaimed.[16]

Religious holidays also helped prisoners newly arrived from the western borderlands maintain their religious devotion. As long as prisoners were reasonably discreet, they were often able to celebrate these holidays in peace. Inmate Genrikh Elshtein-Gorchakov recalled Easter celebrations at the Sibirsky Camp, where many inmates from "the western territories" celebrated openly without interference from the camp authorities. This was especially true in the women's zone, which Elshtein-Gorchakov had free access to with his position as a senior accountant. As he related, "The girls dressed up in white, candles were lit, and dyed eggs even appeared from somewhere. They sang hymns and exchanged Easter greetings with everyone, even us." The actress Tatyana Leshchenko-Sukhomlina, imprisoned at the Vorkutinsky Camp, related a similar story. On Christmas Eve of 1950, she discovered a group of new inmates from western Ukraine who had everyone in the barracks kneeling while they sang hymns. She wrote, "I shall never forget the beauty of their singing, in four-part harmony, without music." After the carols, the inmates all shared saved-up treats and celebrated the birth of Christ under the direction of these fearless Ukrainian Christians.[17]

Other inmates likewise described how they observed Easter, Christmas, and other important dates on the Christian calendar as best they could, given the restrictions of the camp. As Horchynska related, "We knew the feast days, starting them with the hymn, 'God the Great and Only One,' to which we added our own stanza":

> May we return home,
> to where our brothers and sister are,
> in our native land with song,
> O Lord, we praise Thee."

The Polish Catholic Kazimierz Zarod recorded how two Christmas celebrations helped keep his faith alive while imprisoned in the Soviet Union. The first happened in 1939 in a church-turned-prison in western Ukraine when the guard on duty, perhaps a Christian himself, explicitly allowed the

WESTERN WORSHIPPERS AND GULAG GANGSTERS   131

celebration. An incarcerated priest performed the mass, bringing Zarod and his compatriots "a sense of peace." After the service, they sang carols and chatted merrily about memories of happier Christmases, until a changing of the guard brought a spiteful order to wash the cell floor. The following Christmas Eve, this time in a Siberian labor camp, a kind Jesuit priest led the traditional mass at night with lookouts posted to prevent detection. He concluded the service with this admonition: "My brothers, do not think that we are forgotten by Almighty God. He sees our suffering, and he has not forgotten us. . . . Don't give up hope. I give you God's blessing and may a little of the joy of Christmas lighten your hearts." After that, the inmates dressed a small Christmas tree but did not sing carols for fear of detection. They then worked as usual on Christmas Day, chopping down trees.[18]

For many, Christian holidays stood as a tangible representation of their faith that, when observed with conviction and passion, generated a powerful, transformative religious experience. As recorded by one western inmate about Christmas in the Gulag:

> The barrack was full of these grieving, heartsick prisoners. After their heavy work, they are lying down, it seems like no one and nothing will get them up. But Lina gets us all up long before wake-up and begins reading the Mass: 'The Lord is with us, know this, O people . . .' from the Matins, and then, like bells ringing, carol after carol. . . . It was as though something had transformed everybody. One after another they raised their heads, got up, and cried and rejoiced.

Russian inmate Alla Andreeva's transformative experience with western inmates observing religious holidays in a Mordovian camp in 1950–1951 was similar. A group of Ukrainian women invited her to celebrate Christmas, gathering at eight in the evening in a designated barrack after the workday was done. They convened on the upper bunks to softly sing and cry, remembering specifically how Herod (for them a symbol of Soviet power) had ordered a massacre of infants. An informant set off to alert the guards of this anti-Soviet gathering, but they had chosen the farthest barrack from the guard tower to give them as much time to celebrate as possible. Ultimately, it turned out the guard on duty was unconcerned, seeming to understand their need for spiritual release and loath to disrupt the tenuous prisoner-guard dynamic. The Christmas celebration went as planned, and Andreeva was deeply moved. Then, on Easter, in the absence of a priest, the Ukrainian

132 FINDING GOD IN THE GULAG

women and Andreeva wrote down what they remembered of the Easter prayers and then read them aloud. According to Church rules, Andreeva knew, "a woman is not allowed to read what a priest is designated to read. But I think," she concluded, "that we there, in the camp, did what was right." For Ukrainian women imprisoned in the Gulag, worshipping Christ was more important than worrying about dogmatic matters of priesthood authority.[19]

Conversion and De-conversion

Though for many it was sufficient to try to practice their own faith in the Gulag, some prisoners from the western borderlands attempted to proselytize, seeing the camp as an opportunity to fulfill Christ's admonition to "preach the gospel to all creation."[20] Camp society often made this difficult, with guards and other inmates at times mocking religious belief and repressing religious practice. But some found ways, often in quiet conversations with those willing to befriend imprisoned Christians. Yakov Etinger, a Jew who survived life in the Minsk Ghetto under German occupation and was arrested by the Soviet secret police in 1950, described a well-meaning Estonian Lutheran pastor who attempted to convert and baptize him in the camp. Meanwhile, his friend found himself incarcerated with Father Benedict, a Lithuanian Catholic priest, in the Kirov Transit Prison. After many engaging discussions on various topics, the priest invited him to convert to Catholicism and receive baptism in their cell, an offer he declined. Similarly, Mikhail Rabinovich related how he befriended a Ukrainian Greek Catholic priest while working in the camp library in the postwar years. This man, whom he described as "deeply religious, gentle, kind, and very firm in his convictions," always tried to steer conversations in a religious direction, "emphasizing the superiority of Catholicism as a religion over others." Such efforts failed, however, with Rabinovich remaining an unbeliever. Meanwhile, numerous inmates in their memoirs recorded the proselytizing activity of Jehovah's Witnesses, and Noble found that the Baptists in his camp were very active in preaching, "making converts among groups of all nationalities."[21]

Some inmates found success in these proselytizing and church-building efforts. The Ukrainian Greek Catholic priest Andriy Mykhailikha described to his daughter his several years in the Gulag: "We recruited many political prisoners and together managed to take a soulless, noticeably degraded youth, who lacked even a secular education and reeducate them with God's help into 'a people for God's praise.' " There may be a tendency to exaggerate here in terms of the number of converts made, but certainly some converted to Christianity under the influence of religious believers from the western borderlands. For instance, the Greek Orthodox bishop Yosofat Kotsylovsky converted and then ordained Herlyuk-Kupchynsky as a deacon and planned to ordain him as a priest before they were transferred to different camps. Bishop Viktor Novikov-Halikovsky similarly converted and ordained the young Pavlo Vasylyk as a deacon, who recalled that upon his ordination, "the world became different, the world became new." These and other accounts testify to the religious conversion of some trapped in a place of terrible religious oppression.[22]

Yet alongside such tales of conversion are accounts of de-conversion among believers from the western borderlands. Alexander Dolgun witnessed many prisoners lose hope and abandon their faith. In his anecdotal experience, "this seemed to happen more often with people from the Baltic states, I don't know why." Despair at the stark realities of the Gulag certainly affected Poles, Ukrainians, and others. The Ukrainian Greek Catholic priest Pavel Deresh, for instance, found only misery and seeming abandonment by God and died by suicide shortly after being sent to the Gulag in 1940. For some, as Zarod explained, "imprisonment and the cruelty they had endured meant the loss of their faith—they reasoned that God must have forgotten them." He witnessed how two Polish priests ended up in the same Siberian labor camp with him, but their paths quickly diverged. One was a kind, hardworking man who "always had a good word for everybody, even our guards and the few 'real' criminals amongst us. He brought hope, encouragement, and strength to those too ill to work simply by talking to them, smiling his gentle smile." The other priest, by contrast, was despised by the inmates, for "he gave no help, spiritual or physical to any of his fellow prisoners." He managed to keep a Bible with him all the way to Siberia, but once there, he sold the individual pages to prisoners for rolling cigarettes. Perhaps his faith was already weak before Soviet occupation brought arrest and imprisonment, and the Gulag quickly destroyed his spiritual self. Still, the believing Zarod had trouble condemning him, reasoning that "human beings have to feel the cold and suffer the pain of hunger before they know how they will conduct themselves under such circumstances."[23]

Janusz Bardach's spiritual journey in the Gulag began from a position of atheism. Although a communist sympathizer who initially collaborated with

134 FINDING GOD IN THE GULAG

the Soviets after their occupation of eastern Poland, he was soon arrested and exposed to the harsh conditions of Soviet imprisonment. There he experienced a sort of religious questioning, a desire to find out if the God he had always ignored really existed. This came suddenly at first, in a moment when he had been beaten senseless by a group of inmates and guards after attempting to escape. He recounted his short prayer of salvation in his memoir:

> Please, God, if You exist, take me now. I don't want to live. But please save my family. Keep them from being tortured and killed. There is no one else I can ask for help. I never believed in You. I thought You were only the goodness in my heart, the goodness inside a person. But now I know that wasn't right. There is no goodness in people's hearts. People are cruel, vicious, full of hate. I don't know if You exist, but if you do please save my family.

In the end, Bardach did not sense an answer to his prayers and maintained his atheism. As he later acknowledged regarding his time in the camps, "I saw too many terrible things to believe that God existed."[24]

Gustaw Herling and Nina Gagen-Torn

One of the best descriptions of religious life among new arrivals from the western borderland comes from Gustaw Herling, a Polish intellectual arrested in 1940 during the Soviet occupation of eastern Poland. Sentenced to five years in the Gulag, he was released after just two years due to the Sikorski-Mayski agreement that freed tens of thousands of Polish prisoners. But while in the camps, he made keen observations of prison life that were then published as a memoir in 1951. Herling was not a Christian, and in some of his observations his derision is palpable. He called the nightly prayers of one group of inmates "disjointed babblings" and their appeals to God's justice "irrational arguments." When a group of nuns refused to work and were thrown in the penalty isolator, he called their protests "mysterious madness." He also derisively recounted the story of one Russian peasant who went mad and declared, "I am Christ in the rags of a prisoner," before jumping into the fire and badly burning himself. For many nonbelievers like Herling, the more militant religious inmates of all nationalities and denominations seemed to irrationally multiply the hardships of the Gulag through their acts of faith.

And they did not hesitate to mock such believers both in the camps and in their subsequent memoirs.[25]

Still, some Christian inmates impressed Herling, including one who prayed quietly every night and a group of prisoners who celebrated Christmas surreptitiously and sincerely. One fellow Pole's patience in suffering and his devotion to "God, Poland, and his wife" made a particular impression. Herling found this man's prayers powerful and moving: "Sitting up on the bunk, his face hidden in his hand, he pronounced the words of prayer in a whisper so moving, so pregnant with tears and pain, that he might have been prostrated at the foot of the Cross in a trance of adoration for Him whose martyred body had never broken out with a word of complaint." When asked whom he prayed for, he responded, "For all mankind." And when Herling pressed on whether that included his jailers, the man thoughtfully responded, "No, those are not men." Christian admonitions to love one's neighbor clearly had their limits for those who experienced the brutality of Soviet repression firsthand. Later, when Herling was leaving the camp, this man (known only as "M") embraced him and whispered, "God won't abandon us."[26]

This sense of hope rooted in God, Herling noted, helped some Christians endure their suffering. Whereas intellectuals like him often had a hard time forgetting their previous life of liberty and were thus prone to bouts of hopelessness, "people of simple faith found life in the camp somewhat easier to accept, for they looked upon it as the natural culmination of their previously hard existence and with humbleness in their hearts awaited heavenly reward for their patience in suffering." But this statement seemingly applied only to some Christians. Others he found intensely disagreeable for giving in entirely to despair, constantly yearning for death. "Their Christianity," he concluded, "is not a belief in the mystical redemption of souls wearied with earthly wandering, but only gratitude to a religion which promises them eternal rest." By equating belief in God with simplicity of intellect, Herling perhaps sought to justify his rejection of deity or else make sense of his intense struggle with depression in the camps.[27]

Herling was unsparing in his criticism of religious leaders in the Gulag. One Polish priest, he wrote mockingly, "disguised his pastoral dignity under a prisoner's rags, whose fixed price for confession and absolution was 200 grammes of bread (100 grammes less than the old Uzbek who read fortunes from hands), and who lived among his parishioners in an aura of sanctity." Yet Herling also understood that the camps were unsparing in turning humans into animals. "I became convinced," he related, "that a man can be

136   FINDING GOD IN THE GULAG

human only under human conditions, and I believe that it is fantastic non-sense to judge him by actions which he commits under inhuman conditions." Herling focused mainly on the intense hunger experienced in those wartime years of famine and how it stripped away all morality, forcing people to do anything to alleviate its physical ravages. "If God exists," he wrote, "let him punish mercilessly those who break others with hunger."[28]

Herling's observations of Christianity in the Gulag during the terrible years of World War II are illuminating, even if colored by his disbelief. He found that faith buttressed by heartfelt prayer could help inmates make sense of their suffering and endow them with the patience necessary to outlive intense suffering. Yet not all chose this route; some actively sought a martyr's death through punishment rather than suicide. Faith provided moments of celebration and quiet reflection, yet it also opened opportunities for corruption. Herling ultimately remained an unbeliever, though he did consider becoming Christian a few times. This happened only when he came close to dying, the moment that "most disposes to religious conversion." Sensing the finality of death in the absence of religious belief, he "regretted the fact that the camp had hardened me so that I could no longer pray; I was like a barren, parched desert rock which will not stream with living water until it is touched by a miraculous wand." But once revived, he abandoned such thoughts and remained only an observer of religiosity in the Soviet Gulag.[29]

Nina Gagen-Torn's memoir provides a second illustrative account of believers from the western borderlands. A Russian ethnographer convicted of counterrevolutionary crimes during the Great Terror, Gagen-Torn was released in 1942 but then rearrested in 1947 and given a second five-year term. Sent to the Dubravny Camp, she entered a multiethnic milieu punctuated by Christians of various denominations. As she related, a host of faithful women gathered each morning after breakfast in a wooded area of the camp for prayers, with the Orthodox believers around one birch tree, Ukrainian Greek Catholics around another, then Baptists, Sabbatarians (an offshoot from Russian Orthodoxy that celebrated the Sabbath day on Saturday), and so forth. This system of separate yet communal prayer services worked well for the most part. As one of the Orthodox women, looking at the Ukrainian Greek Catholics praying, concluded, "They are like us. . . . Everyone prays a little different, but all are equal before God. And they sing well." In approval, Gagen-Torn concluded, "The uniting of churches is occurring."[30]

Gagen-Torn experienced this ecumenical spirit again early one morning when she walked to the wooded section of the camp and found the Baptist leader Annushka pouring out her soul to God. Staying hidden, she watched Annushka, with tears running down her face, cry out, "You see, You see how they suffer? Be merciful to them, Lord! There is no measure of the suffering of the world, but extend Your hand, Lord, and give comfort. With tears I pray to you and ask this of you, for all people I beg of you." Annushka's heartfelt prayer on behalf of her fellow inmates deeply touched Gagen-Torn, who remained hidden before tiptoeing out of the glade of trees. On the way back to her barrack, she met the Orthodox leader Katya Galovanova going to pray in the "birch temple." When Gagen-Torn told her of Annushka's prayer, Galovanova exclaimed, "May the Lord help her! I won't interrupt," and headed off to the washroom. Gagen-Torn clearly admired the aspect of Christianity that tended toward inclusiveness between Russians and the more recent arrivals from the western borderlands. In the face of sometimes brutal religious persecution, differences in creed and nationality faded against the more urgent backdrop of spiritual survival.[31]

Yet not all was harmonious, as Gagen-Torn soon discovered. The Baptists did not appreciate the repetitive nature of Orthodox prayers, and disputes also arose between the Baptists and the Sabbatarians, whose birch trees were close to each other. Tension further developed between certain religious inmates and their political counterparts. On one occasion, in Gagen-Torn's telling, when called to go outside the camp to collect firewood, a group of nuns who refused to work out of religious principle started singing. The camp commander became enraged and commanded the guard dogs to be set on them. But when the women stood still and crossed themselves quietly, the dogs, trained to attack fleeing or resisting prisoners, left them alone. Not everyone in the camp, however, admired how these religious inmates avoided the work that everyone else performed. Echoing Soviet rhetoric, some accused them of living parasitically at the expense of others. Eventually, Gagen-Torn persuaded one who lived in her barrack to at least help keep the barrack clean for the sake of the other inmates. This allayed some immediate concerns, but the broader dissatisfaction at the nuns separating themselves from the other inmates and implicitly accusing political prisoners and religious inmates of working for the Antichrist remained. Religious expression, it seemed, had the power to both unite and divide Gulag inmates.[32]

Yet sometimes the political prisoners aided their religious counterparts from both Russia and the western borderlands. In one example, a guard hoping to catch Christian inmates in a religious meeting was ultimately tricked by political prisoners who devised a way to protect their fellow

138   FINDING GOD IN THE GULAG

inmates. When he was seen approaching, a political prisoner started performing stretches in front of the barracks, while others sat around her and
sang songs. When the guard rushed up and accused them of holding a religious meeting, the stretching inmate indignantly yelled back that she was
an old Communist Party member and a convinced atheist. The rest claimed
they were simply singing, not worshipping. All the gathered inmates then
had a good laugh at the guard's expense, who conceded defeat and withdrew.
While musing on this and other experiences, Gagen-Torn recalled that
those with something to believe in found it easier to endure the camp. And
while some continued to believe in Marxism or some other secular ideology,
others, particularly those from the Baltics or western Ukraine, survived
thanks to their Christian beliefs and strong national identity.[33]

Religious Imagery among Gulag Gangsters

One last aspect of Gulag religiosity that flowered in the late Stalin era concerned the "thieves-in-law" and other gangsters. Criminal gangs had always existed in the Soviet penal system, but the late 1940s and early 1950s
were their heyday. Gangsters in many penal institutions rivaled guards and
administrators in terms of actual power, which allowed them to live comfort-
ably while refusing to work. They attracted young inmates to their criminal
lifestyle and performed theft and murder to gain "authority." In some camps,
fierce gang wars broke out, particularly the so-called bitches' war of the early
1950s, with camp administrators often favoring one side or the other in an
attempt to manage the violence. Other inmates, meanwhile, lived in constant
fear of the "thieves," who terrorized the camps with rampant thefts, beatings,
sexual violence, and murder. As one memoirist recalled of this reign of violence in the postwar era, "innocent people were savagely beheaded with axes
in broad daylight or stabbed to death with picks and shovels, and ... no other
prisoner or guard dared intervene to save the victim."[34]

It seems curious that criminal gangs would be at all interested in
Christianity. Most Russian gangsters before 1917 were ambivalent or outright hostile to religion and the Orthodox Church, seeing it as a branch of
the repressive tsarist state. But as the Bolshevik regime began imprisoning
Orthodox clergymen, opposition to Soviet power often took on a religiously
inflected Russian nationalism. Gradually, professional criminals began to
identify with imprisoned Christians and Russian nationalists as their fellow

sufferers, and this came to be reflected in their symbolic world, especially in the realm of tattooing. By the 1930s, some Soviet gangsters proclaimed themselves as "keepers of the true Orthodox faith," referred to their initiation rituals as baptisms, wore crosses around their necks, and tattooed religious images on their bodies. This adoption of religion fully flowered after the Second World War and persisted into post-Soviet Russia.[35]

But the story is a nuanced one, with Soviet gangsters in the Stalin era and beyond displaying a range of attitudes concerning religion. Some were completely irreligious and mocked those who believed in God. Others professed some beliefs, but this did not alter their behavior. Hava Volovich, for instance, witnessed a group of female gangsters stealing a pregnant inmate's extra ration on Easter and happily consuming it until one of them, with a cross around her neck, suddenly exclaimed, "Eh, girls, what have we done! We just robbed a pregnant woman on Easter Sunday!" After a brief pause, however, she thought better of her brief protest and muttered, "Never mind. God won't hold it against us." Varlam Shalamov likewise noted that some gangsters wore crosses around their necks as talismans but still murdered other prisoners.[36]

Other inmates observed how a mix of religious and superstitious beliefs led the thieves to treat overtly Christian prisoners better than the general mass of inmates. Aleksey Pryadilov, a young poet arrested in 1943 and sent to the camps on a seven-year term, recorded a lively conversation between a thief-in-law boss and a young religious inmate, where the gangster rejected the idea of Christ's atonement and most of the Ten Commandments. But when another thief accused the religious man of being a "counterrevolutionary" worthy of abuse, if not death, the boss defended him: "Don't touch this guy. You and I have our own faith, he has a different one. He's not stupider than we are." Later, when the Christian man died in the camp, the same gangster lamented his fate but accepted it as inevitable. "I told him that in the camp one must forget about loving one's neighbor.... Here the laws are camp laws, not Christian ones. You die today, and I tomorrow."[37]

Ciszek likewise encountered varied religious beliefs among gangsters, such as one who had been baptized Catholic as a child. As Ciszek related, this Yevgeny "had a very primitive idea of religion, mixed with any number of superstitions. He asked me, for instance, to bless a little cross for him, which he wore from then on. Yet he wore it more as a talisman or good luck charm. He did bless himself as he put it on, but he also pulled out a knife and warned the crowd around him, 'If anyone laughs at this cross, he'll get a knife right

140 FINDING GOD IN THE GULAG

in the belly.'" Ciszek eventually persuaded Yevgeny to accept communion on occasion, but that, combined with wearing a cross, was the extent of his religious devotion. Gulag memoirist Rabinovich described another gangster as superstitious in various ways but also religious. "In any case," Rabinovich wrote, "he believes in the divine origins of mankind and rejects Darwin's theory of evolution." But it was more than that, as the cellmate plainly told him: "God hears the prayers of the thief, especially in prison."[38]

Memoirists rarely comment on hearing any "prayers of the thief," but they did observe religious imagery in various forms in the underground world of Gulag gangs. Ballads, for instance, were a central form of expression in the evening hours, including among the criminal class, and sometimes drew on religious motifs. Modeled on prerevolutionary songs that vindicated those who committed crimes in good faith or had been sentenced unjustly, one song from the 1920s expressed the belief that "all thieves will end up in paradise," a direct reference to Jesus promising the two thieves crucified alongside him that "today you will be with me in paradise." Another song of this type, originally from the 1930s and modified in later years, went like this:

> Forgive me, a sinner!
> Save from the present order,
> From the long transfer,
> From the central isolator,
> From the Serbsky Institute,
> And the beastly hashish,
> From the Okhotsky Sea,
> From the Vologda convoy,
> From the landlord Demon,
> From the light rations,
> Oh Lord!
> Save me forever,
> From procurators,
> And people's courts,
> Amen.

Modeled on an Orthodox prayer, this song expresses the dual nature of salvation as spiritual and physical, with the petitioner pleading for temporal relief from suffering in the Gulag. Positioning himself in opposition to the state, the singer finds solace in this appeal to a higher, heavenly authority.

A similar, popular song from the 1940s continues this plaintive style, though with greater pessimism. "I know where we are being driven/Somewhere in the tundra, into the harsh frosts," it declares before solemnly concluding, "They will bury me without a prayer/Among the crooked Karelian birch trees." Brief references to God and prayer continued to be found in songs sung by criminals after Stalin's death. These occasional mentions of God and faith signify some understanding of and hope for Christian salvation.[39]

A more common emblem of criminal culture that reflected a religious understanding of the world was tattooing. Russian criminal tattoos predated the Soviet Union but became widespread in the 1930s as the Gulag ballooned in size. Political prisoner Thomas Sgovio, who was recruited as a tattoo artist in the Kolyma camps, described how needles were crafted out of pieces of wire, and ink was made by collecting the black carbon residue produced by burning rubber and then combining it with water and sugar. The resulting Soviet criminal tattoos, particularly after World War II, were rich in imagery. Gangsters placed various pictures, symbols, and phrases that reflected lives devoted to gambling, drugs, sex, and crime on their bodies (and sometimes forcibly onto others' bodies). Playing cards, animals, skulls, daggers, and pornographic images were widespread. Stars, epaulets, and other insignia denoted stature within the criminal world. Some inscribed explicitly anti-Soviet messages, such as "Slave of the USSR" or an image of Lenin as a devil.[40]

Religious images also featured prominently in gang tattoos starting in the 1920s but fully flowering after the Second World War. There are a few examples of sacrilegious tattoos, such as sexualized portrayals of Adam and Eve or "In God we trust" written on one inmate's penis. But far more express a positive view of religion and Russian Orthodoxy in particular. These talismans inked onto the bodies of Soviet-era gangsters, as well as some genuine lay believers, took many forms; angels, churches, crosses, candles, and images of Jesus Christ and the Virgin Mary were all common, as were brief texts such as "Holy Father, save and preserve this servant of God" and "Mother of God, forgive my sins." These tattoos, commonly found on the chest, back, shoulders, and fingers, had real spiritual significance for some gangsters. As historian Alexei Plutser-Sarno explains, "If the human body was created by God, then what is written on it is just as sacred as the inscription on an icon or the letters on a Christian cross. A tattooed autograph becomes a living word addressed to God." Even if other aspects of a gangster's life appeared devoid of religious content, their body bore testimony to at

142   FINDING GOD IN THE GULAG

least an idea of belief in God and hope in his protective power. Certainly, few people in the Soviet Union needed divine protection more than Gulag inmates.[41]

Like other tattoos, religious ones often had multiple meanings beyond affirmations of faith and prayers for protection. For instance, the tattooed letters B–O–G spelled out the word *Bog* (God), signifying a convict's reliance on God for salvation. But these letters could also stand for "I will rob again," denoting intent to continue a life of crime, or "I was sentenced by the government," suggesting opposition to the Soviet state. An image of the Madonna could represent the divine protective power of Christ's mother or signify that "prison is my home." And during the "bitches' war" of the early 1950s, when the thieves-in-law battled former gang members who formed rival gangs, that same Madonna could mean "'my conscience is clean before my friends,' [or] 'I will not betray.'" Churches and crosses were famous for having numerous meanings beyond symbols of faith and protection. For example, the number of cupolas on a tattooed church often signified the number of terms the convict had served, with an added cross on a dome meaning the sentence had not been shortened by parole or amnesty. As for crosses, as Plutser-Sarno explains, "Some crosses are badges of a thief's [rank], some record his 'trips to the zone,' some are oaths of vengeance, some are symbols of devotion to the idea of 'thiefhood,' some are emblems of his specialty as a thief, and some symbolize the need to preserve one's honour as a thief, even unto death." Such double meanings were varied and up to the wearer of the tattoo to define, but they typically merged expressions of faith with adherence to the thieves' code, which prized loyalty to fellow gangsters, refusing to cooperate with state officials, and devotion to living a life of crime.[42] (See figure 5.2.)

One of the central purposes of religious tattoos was to identify one's own clan along with one's enemies. Tattoo artists depicted Karl Marx, Joseph Stalin, and other Soviet authorities as devilish figures, consistent with how anti-Soviet Christians spoke of the Bolsheviks as servants of the Antichrist. Images of Saint George battling the dragon, one of Orthodoxy's most prominent patron saints, affirmed Russian nationalism and opposition to Soviet rule (with the slain dragon symbolizing the Soviet regime). One particularly elaborate tattoo depicted a devilish Vladimir Lenin crucified on an Orthodox cross while being burned to death atop Marx's book *Das Kapital*. Two archangels on either side preside over this execution, and accompanying texts read, "God's trial of the leader of the worldwide proletariat" and "The

Figure 5.2 A Russian man celebrating Epiphany in 2016. Note the religious tattooing that became widespread among Gulag gangsters in the 1940s and 1950s. Getty Images.

punishment of the boss of ghouls." The inmate clearly associated himself with God's angels, expressing his desire for revenge against the Soviet system in religious terms.[43]

In addition to the Soviets, Jews figured prominently among those targeted as enemies, with many Gulag tattoos expressing anti-Semitic messages through religious and nationalist phrases and symbols. Some appeared on Estonian or Latvian criminals and featured Nazi symbols or depictions of Jewish devils sexually assaulting Baltic women. Among Russian gangsters, tattooed messages such as "It was the Jews who sold Christ! Beat the Jews!" expressed long-standing anti-Semitic prejudices through an explicitly religious lens. A tattoo from the 1950s linked Jews with the Communist Party, depicting a devil's head with stereotypically Jewish features and a Star of David, along with the phrase "Curse you, Kolyma-Yid construction camp!" Another arranged skulls and crossbones in the shape of a cross surrounded by the words "The Jews in Russia created the GULAG and NKVD." The presence of Orthodox crosses and other religious images in many of these tattoos makes clear the association among Gulag gangsters between Christianity and a chauvinistic version of Russian nationalism.[44]

144 FINDING GOD IN THE GULAG

Prisoners also displayed this chauvinism in tattoos that expressed hatred toward the minority nationalities of the Soviet Union. Ethnic strife inflected by religion was common in the Gulag, and religious tattoos identified one's status. One tattoo from 1950, for instance, depicted a Russian peasant man sitting next to a devil with a Koran hanging around his neck being hung from the gallows. Above the image is the phrase "We Russians don't need non-Russian devils, only their land." Another tattoo discovered in Vladivostok in 1949 illustrated a devil's head with stereotypical Asian features being stabbed with a dagger. Above this image is an Orthodox cross, and below is the inscription "Beat, crush, and kill the yellow-faced monkey." A third displayed an Orthodox cross superimposed on the double-headed eagle, the symbol of tsarist Russia, surrounded by the phrase "We will purge Russia of all non-Russians." Jews, Muslims, and even Buddhists were thus targeted by gang tattoos borne by Russian gangsters who increasingly identified with an Orthodox-inflected Russian nationalism.[45]

Non-Russians also used religious imagery in anti-Russian tattoos. Jewish and Muslim tattoos depicted religious symbols such as the crescent moon or Star of David while calling for violence against, in one example, the "Russian swine." Those from the western borderlands similarly linked religious images to national identity in a chauvinistic way. In one found on a Latvian inmate, a simple Lutheran cross impales the head of a bear, a common symbol for Russia. In another, a cross stylized in Nazi fashion is surrounded by the words "For Lithuania without Communists, Russians, and Jews!" A third, discovered on a young Polish woman, depicts a grotesque piglike woman with an Orthodox cross around her chest and a hammer and sickle on her forehead. Surrounding this is a long text expressing hatred against Russians. Rising nationalism in the wake of World War II and Soviet annexations of new territories was thus emblazoned through spiritual symbols on the bodies of Gulag inmates.[46]

The Gulag of the late Stalin era was a massive and violent institution. Millions of inmates were forced into hard labor in terrible living and working conditions, and many never returned, killed by exhaustion, disease, or violent guards. Inmate society could likewise be violent and debasing, particularly as the criminal gangs increasingly gained power. Using religious imagery as a tool both to show defiance to Soviet authorities and to delineate national boundaries among inmates themselves, Gulag gangsters sharpened lines of division in the camps. Russian nationalist imagery in tattooed cathedrals, crosses, and images of the Virgin Mary helped them forge a national consciousness antithetical to the Soviet project. But beyond Soviet taskmasters, various others religious groups (Jews, Muslims, Buddhist, Catholics, and Lutherans) were targeted in this Russian Orthodox symbolism.

The arrival of hundreds of thousands of people from the western borderlands contributed to this social strife along ethnic and religious lines, with the visual explosion of Russian nationalist tattooing no doubt linked to this influx. But the surge in inmates from Poland, Ukraine, Moldova, and the Baltics also elicited, at times, a spirit of faith-based camaraderie against the Soviet regime. Religion among these new subjects of Soviet imperial expansion also reinforced their own sense of national identity. At a more personal level, though the resources and methods for conducting religious worship varied, western worshippers in the Gulag found ways to safeguard their hope in God and thereby to increase their chances of survival. Such was the case for a Ukrainian Greek Catholic believer who, after his release in 1956, told his wife that his time in the Gulag was ultimately worth the price: "I don't regret it, because I still love God now, but in the camp I learned how to love Him better, stronger."[47]

6

Khrushchev's Reforms and
the Camp for Sectarians

After almost thirty years as head of the Soviet Union, Joseph Stalin died on March 5, 1953. His successors waged a power struggle ultimately won by Nikita Khrushchev, who then ruled until 1964. The Khrushchev era was a period of relative liberalization compared with its Stalinist predecessor. Khrushchev's famous "secret speech" denounced Stalin's reign of terror and pledged an end to state-sponsored repression. Censorship was relaxed, more apartments and consumer goods were produced to raise the country's standard of living, and Khrushchev promoted "peaceful coexistence" in the realm of foreign affairs. This was a period of hope and optimism for the future, buoyed by Soviet successes in the Olympics and the space race.

As part of his promise to reduce repression, Khrushchev made significant efforts to reform the Soviet Gulag. Although often imagined as a defining Stalin-era institution, the Soviet Gulag as a hybrid prison–concentration camp system continued to exist after Stalin's death in 1953. But Khrushchev dramatically reduced the prisoner population from 2.5 million to under 1 million by the late 1950s and changed laws and police practices to ensure that the labor camps were not quickly repopulated. Many large camp complexes were shuttered in favor of smaller corrective-labor colonies. The post-Stalin Gulag also renewed focus on inmate re-education through educational, vocational, and cultural programs as Khrushchev attempted to reduce the brutality and overwhelming economic orientation of the Stalin-era camps. Reality ultimately fell far short of this ideal, but the Soviet Gulag was still substantively transformed.[1]

Khrushchev's reforms directly affected large numbers of religious inmates who were summarily released in the mid-1950s. However, some Orthodox priests reported being offered freedom only if they signed an oath of loyalty to the state, and a few high-profile inmates were only released thanks to outside political pressure, including Ukrainian Greek Catholic bishop Yosyf Slipy, released in 1963 thanks to the interventions of Pope John XXIII

Finding God in the Gulag. Jeffrey S. Hardy, Oxford University Press. © Oxford University Press 2024.
DOI: 10.1093/9780197751701.003.0007

and US president John F. Kennedy. Such difficulties in obtaining release stemmed in part from Khrushchev's renewed policy of antireligious repression, which primarily targeted Orthodox clerics outside the legalized church structure and various "sectarians," with Baptists, Pentecostals, Adventists, and Jehovah's Witnesses most prominent among them. Antireligious propaganda multiplied under Khrushchev, and Soviet authorities shuttered monasteries, seminaries, and around 10,000 churches, most of which had been reopened only at the end of World War II. Meanwhile, the officially recognized Orthodox patriarchate, infiltrated by the KGB and cowed into obedience by threats of removing its privileged standing, remained silent. Khrushchev's stance toward Christianity was "uncompromising."[2]

As always, the precise number of religious inmates in the Khrushchev era is impossible to determine. The Gulag in December 1953 identified 5,183 explicitly religious criminals, but it is unknown how many more devout Christians were not counted. Indeed, while the number of religious prisoners dropped alongside every other category of inmates in the 1950s, Khrushchev's antireligious campaign likely increased the number of religious prisoners in the early 1960s. And, as this chapter will demonstrate, while sweeping reforms to the Soviet Gulag made living and working conditions more bearable for inmates, the Gulag continued to be a place of repression against believers. Penal authorities ordered camp commanders and other personnel to preach the virtues of atheism and restricted the ability of Christians to practice their faith. As under Stalin, believers in the Khrushchev era often found ways to circumvent such restrictions, though individual experiences varied widely. Perhaps the most fascinating part of the Khrushchev era was the creation of camp zones at the Dubravny Camp explicitly designated for Christian "sectarians." Not since the penal experiment of Solovki in the 1920s had so many ardent Christians been deliberately concentrated in the Gulag. Dubravlag thus provides a fascinating window into religious group dynamics in the post-Stalin Gulag.[3]

Antireligious Propaganda under Khrushchev

In 1955, representatives from around the world met at the first United Nations Congress on the Prevention of Crime and the Treatment of Offenders, debating and ultimately approving a set of Standard Minimum Rules for the Treatment of Prisoners. Significant to this book's topic, the Minimum Rules

148 FINDING GOD IN THE GULAG

prohibited religious discrimination and dictated that prisoners should be allowed to attend religious services, read religious literature, and meet with representatives of their preferred religious denomination. Although these regulations were designed to be binding on all members of the United Nations, including the Soviet Union (which did not attend the 1955 congress but participated in every subsequent quinquennial congress), in reality, they were unenforceable. The Minimum Rules were filed, with no accompanying discussion, in the Gulag archive.[4]

Even under Khrushchev's policy of reviving international exchanges and dialogue, the Soviet Union was not going to buckle under international pressure to provide for religious liberty in places of confinement. When West German journalists in May 1955 visited the Kryukovsky Corrective-Labor Colony (a model colony kept suitable for foreign visitors), they expressed interest in religion and asked if prisoners could meet with a priest. They were told that inmates were allowed to participate in religious rituals but that there was no priest "because the church here is separated from the state and these are state institutions." While the second part of this statement was more or less accurate, the first part about religious rituals was an abject lie. Soviet officials clearly understood that they had constitutional guarantees for religious freedom and therefore needed to at least put on the appearance of ensuring this right even in penal facilities. In reality, however, the Khrushchev era did not change the established practice of the Stalin era; in fact, it spawned renewed enthusiasm for actively repressing religious belief.[5]

This revived antireligious attitude was evident just months after Stalin's death, when Gulag commander Ivan Dolgikh issued a decree concerning religion in labor camps. In this immediate post-Stalin era, the rash of releases and other changes to Soviet criminal justice prompted questions about whether regulations concerning religious practice would be altered. This document both hints at the extent of religiosity in the Gulag and signals a renewed determination to combat it. It strongly criticized Gulag facilities "where political work and scientific propaganda among prisoners is poorly organized," providing "fertile soil for the revival of alien ideologies, including religious sentiments." As before, one of the biggest problems posed by religion concerned labor, and Dolgikh wrote that in many camps, "sectarian prisoners refuse to work out of religious conviction and persuade other prisoners to do the same, which undermines labor discipline and introduces disorganization into the internal order of the camps and colonies." To combat this danger, the Gulag boss ordered his subordinates, "In every way possible strengthen natural-science propaganda among prisoners, orienting it around the formation of materialistic worldviews and the displacement of religious remnants. To this end, use lectures of the society for the spreading of political and scientific knowledge, the journal *Science and Life*, popular scientific films, and so forth." Thus, rather than using Stalin's death to modify their approach to religion, Gulag officials doubled down on their antireligious stances.[6]

Just a few months later, in September 1953, Dolgikh issued a follow-up directive ordering the immediate confiscation of religious literature and objects, although it allowed that such things should be "returned to their owners upon their release." He also directed that any "gospels, bibles, icons, crosses, and so forth found in packages and correspondence should not be given to the prisoners but returned to the sender." Curiously, care was to be taken to preserve religious objects or return them to relatives rather than demanding their immediate destruction. The Soviet Union did not prohibit religious literature or objects, but the condition of being a prisoner meant that this right had been forfeited. As Dolgikh unambiguously ordered, "Undertake measures that will exclude the possibility of religious literature and objects of religious rites from infiltrating the corrective-labor institutions." With these decrees, Dolgikh signaled that while many aspects of the Gulag would become more lenient under Khrushchev, its antireligious mission (even if inconsistently applied) would not.[7]

This staunch antireligious stance was reinforced in the late 1950s and 1960s in numerous pieces of internal propaganda. For example, an extensive 1959 article by L. Vyushina in a professional journal for Gulag workers declared that the Communist Party must hold a position of "militant atheism, and of an uncompromising ideological struggle" against religion. The author argued this was especially important in corrective-labor institutions because they served people with a "low cultural level" who were most susceptible to "religious superstitions and preconceptions." She encouraged penal institutions to use inmate self-governing bodies, including "comrades' courts," to shame religious inmates who distributed religious literature or refused to work. Perhaps most important, Vyushina directed camp workers to befriend religious prisoners and gradually influence them away from faith. On this note, Vyushina offered the example of one comrade Tsokur, who reported numerous conversations with two religious prisoners who refused to work, before finally, after several months of effort, "they presented him with their ripped-up religious texts, announced their rejection of religion, and

150   FINDING GOD IN THE GULAG

gave their word that they would labor honestly." Such was the desired outcome of antireligious efforts.[8]

Subsequent articles in the Gulag's professional journal continued this antireligious line. One from 1960 described how propaganda in camp newspapers could lead inmates away from religion. Citing an example from one camp, the author reported:

> the former leader of the Pentecostal sect . . . stopped religious propaganda, started to attend all cultural activities, and is working hard. Prisoner Sh., a Jehovahite, left the sect and is working without refusal. The former priest I., having broken with religion, is now an active member of the detachment council. Prisoner F. took off his cross in front of everyone. Such examples are becoming more common.

The accuracy of this story, of course, cannot be independently verified, but antireligious propaganda was clearly expected of camp authorities. This was reaffirmed in an official Gulag directive that called for propaganda efforts that "convincingly demonstrate the harm of religion and religious prejudices, expose religious groups who are sowing [the drug of religion] and interfering with our political-educational work, and educate readers in the spirit of a materialistic worldview."[9]

To aid local camp workers in this effort, central Gulag authorities outlined many discussions on atheism or "religious and its harm" and distributed them to the camps in the Khrushchev era. Of ninety lecture topics compiled for camp "cultural-political workers" in early 1954, for example, three centered on religion: "Marxism-Leninism on the Reactionary Essence of Religion," "The Irreconcilability of Science and Religion," and "Religious Superstitions and Their Harm," as well as two lectures on evolution and the origins of life on earth. The Gulag's political department shortly thereafter sent out preparatory materials for another antireligious lecture on "The Origins and Reactionary Essence of Religious Holidays," which included references to antireligious material from Marx, Engels, Lenin, Stalin, Gorky, and others. Even Leo Tolstoy's last novel, *Resurrection*, was recommended by an official who had apparently never read it (though anti-Orthodox, *Resurrection* advocates for Tolstoy's simple and compassionate form of Christianity). Then, when a further thirty-eight re-educational lectures were recommended to camp officials, sixteen of these concerned religion. This new list included such broad topics as "What is religion and how it

KHRUSHCHEV'S REFORMS AND THE CAMP FOR SECTARIANS   151

originated," "The communist development of workers and overcoming religious prejudices and superstitions," and "Scientific foresight and religious superstition." It also included lectures directed at specific religious denominations: "The reactionary essence of Islam," "Sectarianism and its reactionary essence," and "The Vatican in the service of warmongers." Officials also reissued instructions for how to set up "Book Exhibits on Scientific-Atheist Propaganda" in the Gulag's camps.[10]

Responding to these repeated orders and propaganda material, guards in some camps actively promoted atheism and repressed religion. Camp guard Lieutenant Radovenchik, for instance, used the Council of the Collective (a group of prisoners given some self-governing powers by the colony administration) to try to shame Jehovah's Witnesses into abandoning their beliefs. Josyp Terelya related that guards constantly disrupted their communal prayers and conversations. Other inmates recalled religious texts and objects being confiscated and being sent to the penalty isolator for celebrating Christian holidays.[11]

But far from all camp commanders or guards followed their antireligious orders. In August 1956, for instance, an inspection of the Unzhensky Camp found massive problems with inmate discipline and attributed them in part to unreformed "believing prisoners." In their defense, camp workers complained that they had no training in how to talk about religion and atheism with the inmates, and the library had no atheistic literature. As a result, the report continued, Christian prisoners retained their beliefs and converted other prisoners. Several inmates confessed to joining the Jehovah's Witnesses or Baptists, finding ways to worship together, read the Bible, and even be baptized in the camp. The most detailed of these accounts concerned inmate Chesnokov:

> Before imprisonment in the camp he "never thought about god," but as a result of discussion with one of the prisoners he entered into the sect of the "Pentecostals," and stopped smoking, drinking, and playing cards. He conducts himself well in the camp, but having accepted the teachings of the "Pentecostals," he has had on these grounds several work refusals on days of religious holidays. In discussion, Chesnokov declared that he doesn't think he would be able to take up arms to defend the fatherland, he believes that the world will end soon, and other heresies. Further, Chesnokov declared to the commission that he "is happy and content that he ended up in the camp," seeing as how the "Pentecostals" had supposedly made him a man.

152 FINDING GOD IN THE GULAG

For the visiting inspectors, the conclusions were clear: religious activity disrupted the work of re-educating inmates and turning them into loyal Soviet citizens. There was an urgent need, therefore, to conduct more antireligious propaganda among these young and impressionable prisoners.[12]

In Ukraine, an inspection of the republic's correctional institutions came to similar conclusions. It found that "atheistic propaganda among prisoners . . . is being neglected. The fact that among the prisoners there are hostile religious sects and groups, which act against the ideological work of the administration in re-educating prisoners, is not being taken into account." The starkest example of this came from Colony 48 of Lviv Province, located in the newly acquired western borderlands, where various Christians met in the evening unimpeded by the camp administration. More troubling, the inspection report continued, Jehovah's Witnesses "recruited into their sect impressionable prisoners, forbade them from participating in the social life of the colony, attending school, reading newspapers and books, and watching films, and forced them to worship the leaders of the sect, prisoners Kutsyn and Kuzma, as 'saints.'" In the absence of staunch antireligious activities, the report concluded, Gulag authorities were losing the spiritual struggle for the souls of men.[13]

Some local officials, it seems, simply did not know what to do with religious activity. Many were newly hired after a purge of Stalin-era personnel, and the aftermath of Stalin's death was a confusing time for Soviet officials. This is what an inspecting procurator in the Magadan region concluded in the mid-1950s when he discovered that the camp administration of a women's section for two years allowed a group of young religious prisoners (likely from the True Orthodox confession) to dress in black, conduct religious rituals, and keep crosses, icons, candles, and religious literature. They also refused to work. There had been efforts to stop such behavior, but the inmates complained to higher authorities, who, in the uncertainty of the time, instructed the camp to allow them to worship unmolested. The prosecutor found this intolerable and ordered them to live and labor like the other inmates. The "nuns," in turn, announced a hunger strike and only ended it after being threatened with forced feedings. Michael Solomon, a Jewish Romanian imprisoned in the same camp, offers additional detail about what happened next:

> The camp officials, fearing the influence of the strike on other women prisoners, determined to shift them to an ordinary work camp. Regulations

required that they appear before the camp photographer to have their photos taken. . . . When I reached camp they were all lying on the ground outside the photographer's hut surrounded by a dozen armed security soldiers. . . . They simply refused to have their pictures taken! The nuns remained as rigid as corpses and had to be carried like logs by the soldiers; some were pulled by their hair and dragged along, others pulled by the feet. Once in the photographer's cabin they refused to sit on the chair in front of his camera and continued to fight and gesticulate, spitting in the faces of those in charge of them. After an hour of complete pandemonium, the officials finally had to abandon the fight.

It is unclear what happened to these Christian women next, but the two memoirs affirm that religiosity in the camp, particularly in group form, caused serious problems for an uncertain administration.[14]

A decidedly secondary, though fascinating, reason some local authorities refused to repress religion in the camps was that some Gulag guards even in the Khrushchev era were themselves religious. On June 1, 1960, *For Peaceful Labor* (*Za mirnyi trud*), the weekly newspaper for employees of a network of corrective-labor colonies, published excerpts from a speech given by "atheist lecturer comrade Berezin," who complained that "among the workers of our enterprises there are still believers, who wear crosses, celebrate religious holidays, and participate in church ordinances." Famed novelist and former Gulag guard Sergei Dovlatov likewise noted that some guards and administrators believed in God or at least wrestled with the idea of belief in God. Perhaps it was a believing guard who turned a blind eye to a stool at a camp for recidivists in 1961 that had the image of Mary Magdalene carved into it. It is remarkable that although the environment of the post-Stalin Gulag was decidedly antireligious, there were still a few Soviet jailers who secretly wore crosses and a much larger number who were not interested in repressing religion. Four decades after the Bolshevik revolution, Soviet prison and concentration camp officials still had not imposed a concerted, consistent, or effective antireligious program.[15]

Religious Observance under Khrushchev

Many inmates were emboldened by Stalin's death and the confusion evident among Gulag officials. Yevgeny Yeminov found himself on a train from

154 FINDING GOD IN THE GULAG

Moscow to the Vorkutinsky Camp just days after Stalin died. There was lots of excited talking despite futile shouts from the guards to be quiet, but then a group of monks started singing "a gentle, prayerful melody." A young officer instructed them to stop, but the other inmates yelled and cursed at him. "Let them sing," they called out. At this, the officer remained quiet, and the monks continued to praise God through song. Catholic priest Walter Ciszek quickly noticed that the guards were much more permissive than under Stalin, and so "it was much easier to work as a priest. . . . Besides hearing confession, saying Mass and distributing Communion, I also began giving retreats again and I did a lot of spiritual counseling." This relative freedom resulted in more prisoners expressing interest in religion. As Ciszek related, "It was astonishing to note the number of men who proved religious now that there was no outward persecution, and religion was 'tolerated,' or at least winked at." This manifested itself openly during Christmas and Easter, which were celebrated in grand style without interference by camp authorities. (See figures 6.1 and 6.2.) Feasts, singing, mass, sermons, and prayers revived a religious spirit half hidden under the more repressive regime of the Stalin era.[16]

Revived religious belief combined with nationalism among inmates from the western borderlands played a prominent role in the Gulag uprisings of 1953–1954. Gorny, Rechnoy, and Stepnoy, all "special camps" for counter-revolutionary inmates, witnessed mass strikes in the aftermath of Stalin's death, with inmates protesting harsh living conditions, brutal guards, and, as they viewed it, the illegal nature of their incarceration. Inspecting officials later numbered 175 "members of church organizations" at the Gorny Camp, 594 at the Rechnoy Camp, and 377 "clerics and sectarians" at the Stepnoy Camp. This may not sound like a lot, as each camp had tens of thousands of inmates, but these camps held thousands of Ukrainians and Balts, many of whom were religious even if not categorized as priests or pastors. As one leaflet at the Gorny Camp leading up to the strike declared, in a spirit of religious nationalism, "In 1953 the Ukrainian nation celebrates the Birth of Christ in conditions of heavy oppression by the Bolshevik empire. . . . Let the Christmas of 1953 be a great holiday, celebrated . . . under the banner of solidarity of the Ukrainian people and all the oppressed nations of Europe and Asia. . . . Blood for blood! Death for death!" When guards killed two inmates, their fellow prisoners held a Christian funeral service, with prisoners crossing themselves and praying over the deceased. The strike then erupted.[17]

Figure 6.1 Christmas Eve supper at the Chuna Corrective-Labor Camp, Chukotka, 1950s. Museum of Occupations and Freedom Fights, Vilnius.

Clerics from the borderland regions played a significant role in encouraging and maintaining these uprisings. Priests were among those killed during the Rechnoy Camp strike, including Stepan Cheremukha of the True Orthodox Church and Ivan Cheipegi of the Ukrainian Greek Catholic Church. At the Stepnoy Camp, the strike committee included a group of four priests who served in the "Propaganda Department," teaching and preaching to their fellow prisoners. As the Gulag's investigatory report of the uprising noted, "These priests systematically conducted prayers and exhorted the prisoners to disobey the camp administration." Soviet police and military forces ultimately crushed the strikes, but they demonstrated the power of religious belief in the post-Stalin Gulag.[18]

Varied religious activity among inmates from the western borderlands continued throughout the Khrushchev era. Lithuanian inmate Regina Majoraitė in 1954 composed a prayer book containing Easter psalms while imprisoned at the Severo-Vostochny Camp. Also in 1954, an unknown female Ukrainian

Figure 6.2 Easter Mass in the ninth mine of the Inta Corrective-Labor Camp, Komi, 1955. Museum of Occupations and Freedom Fights, Vilnius.

inmate sewed an icon depicting the Virgin with Child, along with a prayer of protection in a Mordovia-area camp:

> O Mother of God
> Of unceasing aid,
> Take my children under your protection,
> And I beg of your son, Jesus Christ,
> To set all the prisoners free.

This intricate icon must have taken many hours to complete and stands as a testament to the enduring faith of its creator.[19] (See figure 6.3.)

Even in the early 1960s, during the height of Khrushchev's antireligious campaign, religious worship among inmates continued. In Estonia in 1962, for instance, Pentecostal prisoners in two corrective-labor colonies were identified as an ongoing challenge to colony operations. They were caught singing religious songs, and one was found to be writing psalms mixed in with mathematical formulas in a letter. Colony administrators monitored

Figure 6.3 Mother of God with Child, sewn icon, unknown creator, 1954. Memorial Museum, Moscow.

158 FINDING GOD IN THE GULAG

them with undercover agents, censored their correspondence, and reported that "all of them have been strictly warned about the impermissibility of all kinds of sectarian activity." But the prisoners persisted. As officials reported, inmates "continue to correspond with psalms, and are searching for various ways to establish illegal correspondence with sectarians-Pentecostals" outside the colony. Similar religious behavior abounded in Gulag colonies in Ukraine. Terelya, a Ukrainian Catholic memoirist, remarked that he participated in daily morning and evening prayers along with other Ukrainian and Baltic prisoners in the early 1960s. "It was those prayers," he suggested, "that let me see beyond the corruption and temptations [in the camp] to the Kingdom of our heavenly Father."[20]

One of the larger camp complexes of the Khrushchev era, the Ozerny Camp, housed many Christians who openly shared their beliefs. Political prisoner Irina Verblovskaya recalled that many of her fellow inmates in the early 1960s were Jehovah's Witnesses, Baptists, and True Orthodox believers. Anatoly Kuzin discovered the same phenomenon, adding that Jehovah's Witnesses in the camp came from various national groups but "were united by their faith." Kuzin related their numerous meetings, some of which featured a newer member of the faith being interrogated with various questions by the other members, "testing his readiness to participate in discussions." Others dissected the ways atheist propagandists would attempt to confuse them. Indeed, while the administration often tried to persuade them to renounce their beliefs, promising early release in exchange, Kuzin never heard of one accepting such an offer. For Kuzin, this was eye-opening. Raised a committed atheist, he had always considered believers old, weak, and ignorant, but in the Gulag, he found people of faith who were "strong, young, and firm in their faith." "Only an internally free person," he reasoned, "could truly become a Jehovah's Witness." And while Kuzin did not become a Witness himself, he "believed in the victory of their spirit," and this gave him internal strength.[21]

Tension between representatives of different denominations sometimes bubbled over at Ozerlag but only infrequently. In one stark example, Ukrainian Greek Catholic priest Stepan Tsybran approached an Orthodox counterpart to inquire about holding joint liturgical services, but the latter categorically refused, "because you're a Catholic-Uniate, and your world is tainted black." Tsybran then acrimoniously shot back, alluding to the Orthodox Church's legal status in the USSR, "And your world is what, red?" As Tsybran later recalled of this priest, "He didn't understand anything. He didn't know Church history, or the dogma. [He was] just so blind." This incident appears to have been exceptional, however, as other memoirists recalled much more cordial relationships between Orthodox and Ukrainian Greek Catholic clerics.[22]

Even though religious belief and practice were possible at the Ozerny Camp and other camps of the Khrushchev-era Gulag, not all Christians retained their beliefs. For example, a 1960 report on the work of camp trustees noted that they had persuaded inmate Zhiruk, a Jehovah's Witness, to abandon religion. "The activists on the recommendation of the camp administration systematically pointed out the error of his religious views and drew him into the cultural life of the subdivision," it explained, and "as a result of the diligent work with Zhiruk, he began to visit the cinema and other social activities, and then announced that he had stopped believing in god." There is no way to assess the veracity of this report, of course; it is possible this story was embellished or invented to make the camp's re-educational work appear successful to Gulag bosses in Moscow. But such instances are also occasionally noted in memoirs, suggesting that some religious inmates were persuaded to abandon their beliefs or at least pretend to in exchange for better treatment.[23]

The memoir of Vladimir Ablamsky, an Orthodox believer at the Ozerny Camp, explains why some inmates abandoned their beliefs. He experienced profound disappointment when the guards broke up a church holiday celebration held by inmates. Like others, he longed to connect spiritually with God and his fellow imprisoned Christians, but his life at the camp contributed to a gradual departure from belief. He described his gradual de-conversion that happened during and after release: "I believed in god, but now, after all I've been through, I no longer believe." He thought that God could have granted him happiness for enduring such suffering, but ultimately, "my wife left me, and I saw so much grief, so much death, so many innocent people. And he didn't help."[24]

Even as Ablamsky gradually lost his faith, others found theirs. Helene Celmina recounted the story of Clara, a longtime political prisoner, who converted to Christianity in Vladimir Prison after being taught by a "revivalist." As Celmina related, "Faith in God gave Clara's tortured soul balance." Yuri Mashkov, an idealistic young Marxist arrested and sentenced to seven years' imprisonment in 1958, recounted his own conversion in the camps. His first step was realizing that Marxism was fundamentally wrong, which caused him to "fall into a spiritual vacuum." This led to thoughts of suicide, spurred

160 FINDING GOD IN THE GULAG

on by other suicides of despair that took place in the camp. As Mashkov then recounted:

> And so I too was prepared for a tragic end (suicide or madness), were it not, to my great joy, on September 1, 1962, for the extraordinary miracle that occurred in my life. Nothing really happened that day, and there wasn't any influence from others—I was thinking by myself about my problem: "to be or not to be?" To this point I already knew of the saving faith in God, and I really wanted to believe in Him, but I could not deceive myself: I didn't have faith. And *suddenly* there came that second, when I as if for the first time perceived (as if a door from a dark room opened onto a sunlit street), and in the next second I already *knew* for sure that God exists and that God is the Orthodox Jesus Christ, and no kind of hindu, buddhist, or other god. . . . And it was through this miracle that my new spiritual life, which helped me survive another 13 years of camp and prison life, began.

For Mashkov, conversion was associated with a Russian national awakening, as he noted earlier in his account that Russians in the camp were surrounded by national minority groups who hated them. Associations of national identity and religion were common in the camps, though Mashkov's conversion from devout Marxist to Orthodox believer was decidedly less common.[25]

The Spiritual Life of Yuri Yakimenko

A fascinating case study of both conversion and at least partial de-conversion in the Gulag is that of Yuri Yakimenko, whose memoir and letters are notable because they were written by a common criminal rather than the political or overtly religious prisoners who make up the vast majority of Gulag memoirists. Born in 1929 in Vladikavkaz (near the Georgian border) and raised in a religious Molokane family, Yakimenko had a traumatic childhood that mirrored many others in the 1930s and 1940s. His father abandoned the family when he was an infant, they suffered greatly during the famine of the early 1930s, several family members were executed in the purges of the late 1930s, his grandfather was murdered, and then his mother and stepfather were both sent to the front when World War

KHRUSHCHEV'S REFORMS AND THE CAMP FOR SECTARIANS   161

II broke out. He never saw his stepfather again, but his mother returned a while later, only to be placed in a psychiatric ward due to her experiences in the army. During this tumultuous wartime period, without parents at home, Yakimenko's cousins introduced him to a life of crime. He spent a few years in and out of jail and juvenile detention facilities, until a theft conviction in 1947 sent him to the Gulag on a ten-year sentence. He became a thief-in-law gang member in the camps, and then, in March 1953, the same month Stalin died, he was falsely accused and convicted of murder in the labor camp and given a lengthy new sentence. It was at this point that Yakimenko's spiritual life began to be rekindled.[26]

A fellow gangster, perhaps one with religious imagery tattooed on his body, inspired Yakimenko's first steps in his return to faith. This man was sentenced to death for a camp murder and promptly announced, "I have repented before God, and want to die a believing Christian." This made a deep impression on Yakimenko, who began to remember his own religious upbringing. Then, in 1954, he met an old Ukrainian inmate who talked about how God would eventually free Ukraine from the Bolsheviks, and the church bells would ring again. At this, Yakimenko began to ponder, "Are we all God's creations?" An Italian inmate who had served as pastor, chaplain, and papal nuncio and who was arrested by the Soviet secret police after he entered the country illegally to conduct missionary work, also inspired Yakimenko. "After each of our discussions," Yakimenko recalled, "I became convinced that this man in his spiritual form stood higher than the rest of us suffering souls." These experiences and his growing frustration with gang life eventually persuaded him to leave the thieves-in-law. Yakimenko was then transferred to the Ozerny Camp in late 1958, and there, in the company of other Christians, he experienced a true spiritual awakening, believing what one of them told him: "If you give yourself to Christ you will triumph over all the adversity in your life."[27]

Yakimenko's conversion story comes alive in a series of letters he sent to his aunt. In his initial letter, dated October 28, 1958, he divided his life into two parts, the first punctuated by aimless wandering through the Gulag's camps, while the second, still in front of him, promised physical and spiritual freedom. As he expressed to his aunt, "My spiritual life is worth more than my physical life." This thought struck him later when imprisoned in a cell with a True Orthodox believer and a nonbeliever. One fasted, read from the Bible, and talked about Christianity, while the other mostly chatted about womanizing, liquor, and food. For Yakimenko, the difference between the

162   FINDING GOD IN THE GULAG

two was clear: "Spiritual life enriches one's thoughts, knowledge, and faith," while physical life only left one ignorant and unhealthy.[28]

Like many inmates straining to maintain a religious life and identity, Yakimenko sometimes despaired. In a letter from February 25, 1959, he expressed hopelessness at having another eighteen years to serve and sought to interpret this despair through a biblical framework of sons being punished for their father's sins. But he struggled to identify the grievous sins his father could have committed to have caused him so much suffering and concluded instead that "mankind is not as good as it should be, or was before." Then, when his aunt replied that she would willingly share his grief, he responded, "May God send you a blessed life in place of the suffering that you are ready to share with me." But he also confessed, returning to the theme of the physical versus the spiritual, "The hardest thing is to overcome the flesh, and I am struggling with this, even though it is impossible to completely overcome it. Man feels suffering more sharply than he does pleasure, and pleasure is less varied than suffering is." Using imagery of the flesh and the spirit from Paul's writing in the New Testament, Yakimenko saw his life only containing suffering and an inability to rise above physical temptation.[29]

This sense of hopelessness continued in the following letter to his aunt in August 1959:

Everything is the same: joyless prison days and nights drag on slowly and painfully. You treasure up hope of something good, that cannot be foreseen. But in the end, we have not power to change this mortal existence, which flows according to the will of God. Everything is in the Lord's hands, and we must turn to the Savior and pray so that he will bless us. The ways of our Heavenly Father are inscrutable. We must accept his will with humility, because we can't comprehend his wisdom. We should express good feelings, empathy, and condescension. My soul and my brain are tormented with suffering, from which only faith can free me. Faith forbids control over one's own life.

Yakimenko struggled with this Christian fatalism, not understanding why he was subject to such suffering yet yearning to place his will in harmony with God's. This was reinforced as he expressed love for the scriptures even though he did not have them in the camp because religious literature was forbidden. Because of this and his fading memories of reading the Bible as a

KHRUSHCHEV'S REFORMS AND THE CAMP FOR SECTARIANS   163

child, he felt ignorant about its teachings. In fact, because of this ignorance, he confessed he "had still not stood on that path [to God], and might never stand on it."[30]

A short time after this letter, Yakimenko got into a fight with another prisoner that ended with Yakimenko suffering a severe head wound. Yakimenko decided that he would kill this man, and the next time they met, he tried to stab the other's eye with a nail. Other inmates intervened to prevent this, but it is clear that despite his appeals of Christian conversion, Yakimenko found it challenging to adhere to one of Christianity's most fundamental tenets— thou shalt not kill—in the pressure-cooker environment of the Gulag. His next letter to his aunt omitted these details, but Yakimenko did ask her to visit the grave of his mother, who had recently passed away. "After all," he reasoned, "I am guilty of many things before her. But I know that her soul should forgive me, since none of this was my fault. Fate so decided, and it is stronger than us."[31]

Yakimenko's fatalism continued in his next letter, from early 1960. He envied those not yet born, confessed that "all my views are filled with pessimism," and reiterated that fate, rather than one's own choices, guides the lives of the living. Yet he also related that "God is love that is poured out on all of us. And it is worth it for each of us to give in to this Love." He despaired that he had not fully accepted the Holy Ghost into his life and had therefore not begun his true religious development. "I still live by command of my reasoning, and give little heed to the voice of my heart," he lamented. Suffering still encompassed his thoughts and feelings. "And when will the end come?" he wondered. "The end is not in sight!" Ultimately, Yakimenko viewed the conditions of his imprisonment as the central obstacle to his spiritual development: "If I was able to be freed right now, it seems to me I would be born again, a second time on this earth."[32]

After receiving a comforting letter from his aunt, Yakimenko's next letter was more upbeat about his spiritual development. He expressed a degree of comfort in the eternal nature of his soul and a desire to work on becoming perfect: "I will do as much as I can to develop my consciousness. And God will help me." As part of this, he reported reading some of Tolstoy's words on Christianity, which he admired for their simplicity. He also felt optimistic that Russia, learning from Tolstoy's teachings, could become a spiritual example to the rest of the world. This optimism was short-lived, however, as his next letter returned to the theme of no longer wanting to live in the

164   FINDING GOD IN THE GULAG

camp among "such spiritual depletion and such a fearful pursuit for material goods!" He found it difficult to ask others for forgiveness, as they tended to be "cruel" and "foolish." Still, he reported memorizing a lengthy Orthodox prayer that another inmate had taught him and feeling peace when praying for forgiveness.[33]

Yakimenko's final two letters to his aunt, from 1963, continued this ambiguous relationship with God and fate. "I thank God that he gives me patience," Yakimenko wrote, before then wishing for death rather than continuing to live among such darkness and suffering. He concluded, "Don't think that loneliness is misery; remember that God is near to the lonely." But in some ways, Yakimenko seemed to have changed. When he found himself placed in the same camp zone as one of the thieves-in-law whose false testimony had resulted in his murder conviction, Yakimenko forgave him. As he said, "I am no longer the same; if I was still holding on to my former life I would kill you." Then, in another instance when a fellow inmate tried to murder him in a case of mistaken identity, Yakimenko freely forgave him, saying, "God has spared me."[34]

Yakimenko presents a tortured struggle between the life of crime and sin—the physical life, as he called it—and the life of the spirit. For the most part, this struggle seems to have been internal. Yakimenko rarely mentioned other believers in the camp, leading the historian to wonder how many prisoners there were like Yakimenko, who experienced profound religious turmoil in the camps but shared such thoughts only in private correspondence, unrecorded conversations, or else not at all. Curiously, Yakimenko fails to mention God or fate when writing about his early release in 1964, a subsequent visit to his mother's grave, or the awaited reunion with his beloved aunt. Even though in one of his letters to his aunt he had written, "We should believe in our reunion and God will grant it," when the reunion actually came, it appeared to have occurred without any thanks to God. It seems that his spiritual journey, so pronounced and torturous during his last years in the Gulag, suddenly ceased to be important to him after release, just as it had been for most of his life before Ozerlag. The closest he could manage was to say that in the camps, "there appears a yearning for heavenly assistance, because how can you live when your reason is not enough?" Yakimenko's religiosity thus proved fleeting, a spiritual response prompted by despair that lasted only as long as his physical body remained tormented by the conditions of imprisonment.[35]

Dubravlag: The Camp for Sectarians

If Yakimenko's autobiography and letters tell a story of internal spiritual development and conflict, memoirs of the Dubravny Camp (Dubravlag) in the 1960s reveal a very different story of group religiosity. Since its inception, the Gulag, like all penal systems, experimented with different ways of categorizing and grouping inmates. Prisoners were separated by gender and could also be categorized by type of conviction, number of convictions, age, work capability, and gang affiliation. This was done primarily to facilitate labor organization but also served to isolate those deemed dangerous to the rest of the inmate population. Gulag officials separated political prisoners from other inmates in the late Stalin era, and this practice was first abolished and later revived under Khrushchev. Religious prisoners were often included among the politicals, but in the aftermath of camp uprisings in 1953–1954, Gulag boss Dolgikh ordered that "all priests, catholic priests, and active believers should be . . . concentrated in far-off camps or camp divisions." The point was to prevent religiously inspired resistance from spreading among the broader inmate population.[36]

Many religious prisoners were sent to the Ozerny Camp as a result of this decree, but from the late 1950s to the late 1960s, large groups of religious prisoners—primarily Christian "sectarians"—were concentrated at Dubravlag. As the Catholic priest Wladyslaw Bukowinski deduced, "Apparently, it was decided on high, that it was insufficient to isolate the believers from people who lived in freedom, it was also necessary to isolate them from other prisoners." This arrangement lasted for about a decade before religious prisoners were dispersed among various penal institutions in the 1970s, with Soviet officials concluding that placing Christians together only strengthened their convictions and made them more resistant to antireligious propaganda. But for the years when it was in operation, Dubravlag proved to be a fascinating case study in Gulag religiosity.[37]

Located in the Mordovian Autonomous Republic some 300 miles southeast of Moscow, Dubravlag was one of the few large camp complexes left after Khrushchev's reforms placed most inmates in smaller corrective-labor colonies. In early 1961, Dubravlag held more than 10,000 inmates, half of whom had been convicted of political crimes. Four years later, the camp had expanded to more than 12,000 inmates, including just under 4,000 political prisoners. Typically categorized as politicals, most male religious prisoners

166 FINDING GOD IN THE GULAG

were kept in a separate zone of Camp Division 7, with 527 held there as of March 1961. Later that year, they were transferred to Camp Division 1, which held 817 inmates, including 585 "sectarians convicted of especially dangerous state crimes." Meanwhile, Camp Division 10 (and later 17) for women had 231 inmates, including 140 religious prisoners. Other camp divisions held smaller numbers of religious prisoners.[38]

Nonreligious memoirists found the sheer number of Christian prisoners in these select zones astonishing. Upon arriving at Camp Division 17, Celmina discovered that "about seventy-five percent of the women were there because of religious practices, and only twenty-five percent were sentenced for political motives." Those incarcerated for religious reasons were quite varied. Valery Ronkin reported that "there were representatives of almost every confession in the world." Danylo Shumuk likewise recalled that Camp Division 1 was filled with religious prisoners, including "Jehovah's Witnesses, who were split into two rival groups—a sort of 'Bolsheviks' and 'Mensheviks' situation. There were also Pentecostalists, Seventh Day Adventists, Catholics, Russian Orthodox 'old believers,' and members of some other Russian Orthodox group." Curiously, there are almost no references to Muslims, Jews, or Buddhists at Dubravlag; this camp was designated for repressed Christians who did not belong to the official Orthodox Church. As for their age profile, as Anatoly Marchenko reported, they were "for the most part over sixty years old, although there were younger ones too."[39]

The presence of hundreds of committed religious believers posed unique challenges for Dubravlag officials, particularly in organizing antireligious propaganda in Christian-majority zones. In 1960, for instance, the camp official tasked with propaganda work among Ukrainian inmates sent letters to the Communist Party in their native country, asking to be sent "lectures, reports, and political publications containing materials about nationalist, religious-sectarian and other manifestations for use in political-educational work" in the camp. In response, Ukrainian officials sent various Ukrainian-language materials with titles such as "Religious Sectarianism and Its Ideology," "The Irreconcilability of Science and Religion," and "Scientific Views and Religious Prophecies." That camp officials asked for outside help in antireligious work suggests that their initial efforts did not bear much fruit.[40]

Indeed, inspection reports from Soviet procurators overseeing the Gulag give some sense of the camp's failures. One from March 1961 noted that Jehovah's Witnesses were the most active among the different denominations. In 1960 alone, camp authorities confiscated fourteen copies of the *Watchtower*, "various types of instructions, programs and directives," and 347 other "manuscripts with Jehovahite and religious content." Drawing strength from each other, the procurator continued, "Prisoners commit various types of regimen infractions; for example, prisoners from among the church-goers and sectarians are freely performing religious ordinances, conducting various types of meetings, at which they study forbidden Jehovahite literature, and write and distribute manuscripts." Part of the problem was that prisoners enjoyed unlimited correspondence because the camp had insufficient censors to monitor their mail. In 1960, the 1,500 inmates of Camp Division 7 sent 140,088 letters and received 139,432. This deluge of correspondence—including some in foreign languages—overwhelmed the camp's nineteen full-time censors and allowed inmates to maintain "criminal connections" with people outside the camp. As the procurator reported, "former leaders of the sectarian underground, in part from among the Jehovahite and Pentecostal sects, daily send to fellow believers a stream of letters with various kinds of directives." Camp administrators had the power to remove correspondence rights from individual prisoners, but they rarely used this authority.[41]

As for re-educational work, supposedly a major focus of Khrushchev-era Gulag operations, the inspecting procurator reported that it was going especially poorly among Dubravlag's religious prisoners. As he explained, ecclesiastical leaders among them exerted a strong influence over the others, and therefore "Jehovahites, Pentecostals and others openly ignore all educational activities conducted by the administration, refuse to attend lectures and reports, and do not desire to participate in and even thwart activities conducted toward the formation of self-governing organizations." In the procurator's view, Dubravlag administrators did too little to undermine faith and re-educate believers to make them good Soviet citizens.[42]

Despite these findings, little changed in the following months. A follow-up inspection from late 1961 found that "as before, not enough work is being done to cut off sectarian activity among the prisoners. In the 1st [men's] and 17th [women's] camp divisions there continue to be instances of illegal meetings of Jehovahites, the performance of religious ordinances, and the keeping and distributing of forbidden sectarian literature and manuscripts." During a search of Camp Division 1 in October 1961, "5 secret compartments were found, from which 56 notebooks and 61 sheets with writings of Jehovahite content were confiscated. At the same camp division

168   FINDING GOD IN THE GULAG

on the same day they confiscated from prisoner Kazartsev 15 notebooks with notes from the forbidden magazine 'The Watchtower.' " Religious inmates also disobeyed camp administrators in protest of their treatment, which contributed to significant tension between inmates and guards.[43]

Memoirists also noted sporadic and largely ineffective efforts at combating religious practice. Marchenko recalled reading newspaper articles about religious prisoners that were often patently false. Ronkin reported that antireligious lectures were held occasionally in the mid-1960s but that believers and most political prisoners refused to attend; the only ones who did were those anxious to try to impress the administration and obtain early release. In the one lecture Ronkin reported on, a local teacher employed a scientific experiment—putting an alkaline substance into a phenolphthalein solution to turn it red—to prove there was no God. Not religious himself, Ronkin surmised that no self-respecting believer would let such a simple chemistry demonstration undermine their faith.[44]

But at times, more forceful measures were used. Marchenko and others related how some believers were transferred to the feared Vladimir Prison as punishment for disobeying camp regulations; while there, those who wore beards out of religious convictions were forcibly shaved. Another example of antireligious activity comes from the memoir of Celmina, who explained how the secret police would try to coerce Jehovah's Witnesses into abandoning their beliefs. They would take them one by one, "half-starved for years in hard labor camps," to the nearby city of Saransk and promise them as much food and entertainment as they wanted, along with their immediate release, if they would renounce their religion. This tactic rarely worked, demonstrating the resiliency of the Witnesses' faith, but on at least one occasion, it did. A woman was taken away and not seen again until she returned some six months later, apparently healthy and happy, as an antireligious lecturer. No longer a prisoner, "she explained that when she accepted the faith she was not aware of what she was doing. . . . Convinced of her error, she now felt it her duty to lead her former sisters back to real life." According to Celmina, "the Jehovah's Witnesses were visibly upset" and "viewed her with scorn." But little came of this besides a depressed mood among the Witnesses that day; the former believer did not persuade any of her former coreligionists to join her.[45]

As in other camps, political, ethnic, and especially religious divides shaped inmate society at Dubravlag. Political prisoner Boris Sporov recalled that each Christian group was "like one big family" that did everything

KHRUSHCHEV'S REFORMS AND THE CAMP FOR SECTARIANS   169

together: they rested after work, drank tea, and shared the contents of their packages. Volodymyr Marhitych and his fellow Ukrainian Greek Catholics exemplified this. They often studied and held long theological conversations together, though at times the denominational boundaries broke down. As he related, "If we sat down there were a lot of various sect [members], especially Jehovah's [Witnesses], who would immediately sit down next to us and they loved to join in on our discussion." Meanwhile, Marhitych was preparing to be ordained as a priest, but no bishop or higher-ranking church authority could do this until the arrival of archbishop Yosyf Slipy, the head of the Ukrainian Greek Catholic Church who had spent many years in Soviet camps. On August 19, 1960, the ordination took place, with makeshift vestments crafted from a camp jacket, while other members of the faith kept watch for guards. As ordinations even outside the camps were forbidden— Soviet authorities did not legally recognize the Ukrainian Greek Catholic Church—camp ordinations such as this one helped preserve the church hierarchy and community.[46]

One of the activities that helped forge a sense of religious community was the large underground operation of producing religious texts. Boris Vail recalled that prayer books and sections of the Bible were copied and distributed "by the believing inmates, above all the Jehovah's Witnesses, Seventh-day Adventists, and Baptists." He was amazed by the tiny and precise writing in these texts, which was necessary to keep them small enough to hide during searches. As historian Emily Baran has documented, Jehovah's Witnesses called this "spiderweb writing," which allowed believers to reproduce large texts on very small pieces of paper. Sometimes the authorities would find and confiscate religious writings, but the devout could always reproduce new copies. Clearly, one of the benefits of such a large concentration of Christians was the availability of forbidden religious texts due to the inmates' ingenious ways of creating and hiding them. And the communal act of copying scriptures worked toward the formation of robust faith communities behind barbed wire.[47]

As for interpersonal relations between believers and political prisoners, the nonbelieving political prisoner Ronkin found that most believers would talk with him respectfully on primarily nonreligious themes. A few political prisoners forged closer bonds, such as Vladimir Osipov befriending a Baptist and a member of True Orthodoxy. While relations between political and religious prisoners were typically cordial but not close, politicals were mostly sympathetic to their religious counterparts, with several expressing their

170   FINDING GOD IN THE GULAG

outright admiration. Marchenko and others were amazed to find Christians interpreting imprisonment as a blessing: "It comforts them that they are imprisoned for God and for their faith, and they patiently endure suffering and torture." Marchenko was also impressed by their ability to fast, consuming only bread and water for days at a time when the camp diet was already so meager. Many political prisoners, including Lev Krasnopevtsev, saw the Christian prisoners' faith as a counterpart to their own political beliefs, providing an interpretive framework and a sense of identity to help them endure their Gulag sentences. "Believers in the camp were always respected for the strength of their actions and convictions," he observed. If the camps isolated people and often made them feel lonely or depressed, a community of believers counteracted such pressures, giving to Christian inmates a support network that strengthened their resolve.[48]

Looking at more specific examples of how the religious community at Dubravlag functioned and how relations between religious and political prisoners developed, Vail reported most admiring Lithuanian Catholic priests, who held an ecumenical Christmas celebration every year attended by religious inmates as well as atheists. As Vail reported, "Here, an atmosphere of friendship and brotherhood reigned supreme." Ecumenism was one way in which some religious prisoners earned the respect of their political counterparts. Others earned it through principled opposition to the Soviet regime. Yuri Belov was impressed by a True Orthodox clergyman, Father Mikhail, who, whenever a guard would appear, would "make the sign of the cross to all around him and shout out: 'Get out, Satan! Be gone foul Bolshevik!'" In another episode from Vail's memoirs, camp authorities tasked the inmates with constructing a camp prison. The Baptists and Jehovah's Witnesses refused to participate in the project but then started to argue about what constituted construction in the following days. Was it wrong to make bricks that would be used for the prison? What about carrying the bricks to the worksite? Ultimately, those who refused to work on the actual prison project were put in the penalty cell and denied various privileges. Still, Vail was impressed by their intellectually fascinating discussions and insistence that "to build the prison is forbidden, to string barbed wire is amoral."[49]

A similar spirit of admiration developed for some prisoners in the women's zone. Lyudmila Klimanova reported that older religious prisoners did everything they could to care for the young political prisoners. "They loved [us] and treated us like their own children or grandchildren," she recalled. "They were so old and yet they protected us as much as they could." In return, the political prisoners helped as lookouts when religious prisoners conducted secret study sessions and prayer meetings. Celmina's memoir, however, reveals that political prisoners did not look upon all believers with fondness. For example, a group of Old Believers who wore black robes and headdresses refused to work, receive medical assistance, or even bathe and were often sent to the penalty isolator or Vladimir Prison as punishment. They prayed for hours every day, made the sign of the cross before eating or sleeping, and fasted in preparation for Easter. And they were wholly devoted to their elderly abbess, making her bed, doing her laundry, and taking "care of her as well as possible in the camp." As Celmina wrote, "the faith of these nuns without education, and from peasant backgrounds, bordered on fanaticism." While some admired these inmates' convictions and willingness to endure suffering, others were frustrated by their refusal to work and general obstinacy toward guards and fellow inmates. As one political prisoner lamented after hearing how several died after refusing medical assistance, "This idiocy of theirs is to blame."[50]

Jehovah's Witnesses created the most mixed feelings among political prisoners at Dubravlag. Generally speaking, religious organizations at Dubravlag mirrored those on the other side of the barbed wire. Orthodox believers tended to be the least hierarchical and the least inclined to proselytize, while Jehovah's Witnesses tended to be structured, disciplined, and the most ardent missionaries. Catholics, Baptists, and others lay between these two extremes. Not only were the Jehovah's Witnesses the most organized and active, but they were perhaps the largest of the religious groups at Dubravlag. Shumuk reported their number in the men's zone to be more than 300, most from Moldova and western Ukraine.[51]

Many political prisoners expressed incredulity at the Witnesses' discipline. Belov wrote: "I remember being amazed by their zeal, when they would copy by hand long texts from the scriptures." Moreover, Belov continued, "You could trust any Jehovah's Witness with your life: they would hide any note, smuggle it out, or give a piece of bread to the hungry." Ronkin likewise admired their "iron discipline," reporting that at their meetings, each member was obligated in turn to discuss a particular text and then judged according to their performance. This practice undoubtedly deepened feelings of group solidarity and strengthened each Witness's theological understanding. Even those who found the Jehovah's Witnesses fanatical admired some things about them. Osipov, for instance, was not impressed by them in general but found them notable for consistently holding religious exercises

172 FINDING GOD IN THE GULAG

in the barracks and employing an effective system of lookouts that gave sufficient time to disperse if a guard approached the barracks. This ability to systematically deceive Gulag personnel was viewed positively by other Soviet prisoners.[52]

Celmina described one incident in particular that earned her admiration. The Jehovah's Witnesses in the camp zone were singing songs in the courtyard for a worship service (possibly in commemoration of Jesus Christ's death— the only "holiday" Witnesses observe) when the camp commander and a group of armed guards stormed in to stop them. The inmates disregarded all orders to cease and disperse, instead continuing to sing without responding to the agitated commander, even when she threatened to have them shot. The incident was finally resolved on the Witnesses' own terms: "When the women finished singing their three hymns, they left without even glancing at the director, as if nothing had happened." Celmina also admired the Witnesses because of the care several of them showed her when she suffered from spinal pain. She recalled, "No one ever nursed and pampered me like these young women." By the end of her time at Dubravlag, Celmina was convinced that the imprisoned Witnesses were, "with a few exceptions, good, charitable, virtuous, and extraordinarily strong in their faith."[53]

Many political prisoners expressed amazement at their ability to receive religious literature, especially *The Watchtower*. As Shumuk exclaimed, "I would often listen to them reading from *The Watchtower* or the Bible, both which they managed to get hold of while imprisoned." Belov and Osipov likewise recalled being impressed that they managed to figure out how to get smuggled copies of *The Watchtower* into the camp, in both Russian and Ukrainian, just a month after its publication in Brooklyn. Celmina found a similar phenomenon in the women's zone, noting the presence of *The Watchtower* in multiple languages and marveling that "no one has discovered how it gets into the camp." Recounting regular searches and limited contact with outsiders, she marveled that "despite this surveillance, the Brooklyn literature finds its readers." In Osipov's view, these facts made clear that "they had bought off the guard and administrative personnel." This may have been true, though they also received religious literature through personal visits, with visitors "bringing in minute versions of *The Watchtower* hidden 'in the heels of their shoes' or . . . 'braiding thin sheets of paper into their hair.' The imprisoned Witnesses then protected their texts during searches by hiding them, covered in plastic, under their tongues." Understandably, not even political prisoners in the camp zone knew about these methods; fearful of informants among the inmates, the Witnesses kept them secret until long after their release.[54]

Political prisoners' views of Jehovah's Witnesses' evangelizing activities ranged from indifference to contempt. Klimanova, otherwise favorable toward the Witnesses, singled them out as being the most active in trying "to take possession of [her] soul." The dissident Marxist Ronkin remarked that the Jehovah's Witnesses would appear unexpectedly, "as if out of the ground," to interrupt ordinary conversations with their proselytizing. One older Witness tried to use various scientific evidence to prove the truth of their faith, but this had little effect on Ronkin and his friends, who joked that the Witnesses should have been convicted by Soviet courts "for bearing false testimony." Attempts at persuasion continued, however, until the young political prisoners got fed up, and one of them blurted out, "God simply doesn't exist," at which the Witnesses finally left them alone. Valentyn Moroz likewise recalled how the Witnesses had converted a thief and tried, unsuccessfully, to convert Ukrainian nationalists like himself. Indeed, Moroz recalled that "having observed them closely, we found them to be our worst potential enemies, the most susceptible agents of Russification, because in becoming a Jehovah's Witness a Ukrainian becomes hopelessly deaf to the national problem. Yes, we found them to be extremely unsympathetic."[55]

Celmina likewise noted the Witnesses' missionary zeal. While recovering from an injury and being tended to by Jehovah's Witnesses, she wrote, "They sat at my bedside for hours trying to convert me. Although I said that I had been christened and had my own faith, they explained that it was their duty to share theirs." As one declared after Celmina mildly rebuked the Witnesses for being so active in their missionary efforts, "It is our duty to preach and gain new brothers and sisters. We should not be so egotistical to prepare only ourselves for the millennium on earth. All people should be informed so they can live in it. If someone refuses, that is their own business." Her Witness friends tried to convert her even after she recovered from illness: "They insisted that there were two gods, Jehovah and another, whom Jehovah would fight. No matter how hard they tried, using modern science, chemistry, and the newest findings in physics, they could not prove the existence of the other god to me." Celmina may have misrepresented Witness theology, but the imprisoned Witnesses' tenacity is clear. Feeling called to preach, they worked to convert other inmates using a variety of methods to persuade others to accept their unique conceptions about God and the destiny of mankind.[56]

174   FINDING GOD IN THE GULAG

One of the few Christian memoirs from Dubravlag likewise criticized the Witnesses for their stubbornness and missionary zeal. Bukowinski, a Catholic priest, recalled that relations were mostly harmonious among the various Christian confessions and nationalities at Dubravlag, with many committed to ecumenism. But Bukowinski was incensed by the Witnesses, "who threatened God's punishment against everyone except for themselves." To highlight the arrogance and ignorance of the Witnesses, he recalled an instance when a Witness stirred up trouble by condemning Catholics for the Crusades. When asked if he knew when these events occurred, the Witness responded, "During the time of Alexander the Great, of course." Bukowinski then contemptuously retorted, "Why don't you just admit that you're off by a whole 1,500 years?" As this account and many other memoirs were written long after these events, the details of such conversations may be distorted. Nevertheless, it is clear that Jehovah's Witnesses caused the most inter-confessional trouble at Dubravlag among both political prisoners and religious inmates.[57]

To be fair, however, it was more than just the Jehovah's Witnesses who tried to convert others to their faith. Bukowinski recalled priests of various denominations, including Catholics, performing secret baptisms of converts. "Young men, educated in atheism, converted," he related, "and they were primarily intelligent youth, students, Komsomol members." Klimanova remembered how one inmate converted to Sabbatarianism and then refused to work on Saturdays. As she admiringly recollected, "She considered herself one of the faithful and that was that. She would refuse to work, and they'd take her off to the punishment block without any fuss. She had everything ready—her pockets were full of tobacco and whatever else she needed. On Sundays she would come back." Fascinating here is Klimanova's judgment that the transition to religious believer was a positive step for this formerly isolated inmate, who now had strong convictions and a support network of fellow believers. Although Klimanova remained an atheist, she approved in principle of religious believers' active proselytizing of those who surrounded her.[58]

Shumuk, who started his incarceration in a zone full of political prisoners before being transferred to Camp Division 1 with its hundreds of avowed Christians, talked of conversion in a more personal way. Thrust into this multi-confessional religious milieu, Shumuk reported that "they made a very positive impression on me because they were all basically good people who tried to lead their own 'religious' way of life." At the time, Shumuk was a committed atheist, but in this camp, he later recalled, he converted at least to the idea of God, "not in the traditional sense of the word, but the philosophical." Communing with various Christians at Dubravlag helped him become tolerant of all religions and accepting of the possibility of God's existence. After his release, these experiences eventually help lead to his conversion to Orthodoxy.[59]

––––––––

Dubravlag proved to be a fascinating experiment in Soviet penal policy. The premise was simple enough: concentrate several hundred "sectarian" Christians into one corrective-labor camp to prevent them from sharing their faith with other prisoners or providing an example of how to disobey Gulag officials; this would also allow Gulag authorities to focus the bulk of their antireligious efforts in one location. While the first goal of isolation may have been effective, as publicly devout Christians were no longer present in many Gulag institutions, the second aim of re-education was not realized. Antireligious efforts at Dubravlag were consistently weak, and religiosity in various forms—worship services, study sessions, production of religious texts, and even proselytizing—abounded.

When asked about his experience as an inmate at Dubravlag in the mid-1960s, one Jehovah's Witness "described the camp as a 'school' for studying his faith." Indeed, evidence from both Gulag documents and memoirists makes clear that the concentration of believers at this camp made it much easier for religious groups to find spiritual strength in unity and for religious leaders to minister to their flocks. While the Soviet state's decision to imprison the most overtly Christian convicts at Dubravlag may have made it more difficult for believers to proselytize to other inmates throughout the Gulag system, it simultaneously made it easier for them to maintain their own beliefs. Then, upon release, having endured the "theological seminary" of the Gulag, they were in a better spiritual position to be faith leaders in their communities and to share their beliefs with other Soviet subjects. The USSR's ultimate decision in the late 1960s to again disperse convicted believers across many Gulag institutions confirms that Soviet authorities eventually came to the same conclusion. The lesson of Solovki was thus learned a second time.[60]

7

Religious Dissidents under Brezhnev

In 1975, a female Baptist inmate wrote a letter detailing her experiences in the Brezhnev-era Gulag. Whether she smuggled the letter out of the camp or was lucky that camp censors did not check it is not clear, but the Council of Relatives of Evangelical Christian-Baptist Prisoners soon published her message of hope and faith in its underground newsletter. "You are no doubt worried about me," she counseled, "but don't worry, because He in whose hands our lives are, He knows what each of us needs." The inmate, kept anonymous to protect her from retaliation should the authorities discover the newsletter, included just a few mundane details of camp life, paying more attention to inspirational messages designed to uplift her fellow believers. She then closed the letter with words of attachment: "I am always thinking about you. I so hope that God preserves you and that you remain faithful to Him until death. I long for you all so much and I so want to know if you are all alive and well." For this inmate, the spiritual state of her fellow believers outside the Gulag mattered more than her own trials behind barbed wire. Though imprisoned, she projected a message of steadfast faith, calling on her friends to remain true to the beliefs that resulted in her imprisonment. Mortal life in the camp was bearable and thus of secondary concern to the eternal life that awaited them.[1]

As detailed in chapter 6, the Khrushchev era's chaotic reforms substantively altered the Soviet penal system. By the time of Leonid Brezhnev's ascension to power in 1964, it was considerably smaller and economically less significant than under Stalin. Yet, while the Brezhnev-era Gulag was more humane than its Stalin-era iteration in many respects, it remained a penal system enmeshed within a repressive political structure. Few inmates died during this period, but most complained of poor rations, insufficient medical care, and abusive and corrupt guards. The inmate population of the Brezhnev era averaged around 900,000, most of whom had been convicted of crimes such as theft, robbery, "hooliganism," rape, and murder. But a few thousand were political prisoners, often called dissidents by foreign observers, who were persecuted because of their opposition to the Soviet regime.

Finding God in the Gulag. Jeffrey S. Hardy, Oxford University Press. © Oxford University Press 2024.
DOI: 10.1093/9780197751701.003.0008

RELIGIOUS DISSIDENTS UNDER BREZHNEV   177

Religious prisoners were much less visible in the Western press than po-litical dissidents, though they were hardly less insistent or principled in their opposition to Soviet power. No precise statistics detailing the number of inmates convicted because of their religious practices or beliefs in this era are available. The leading unregistered Baptist organization through the 1970s counted between 100 and 200 Baptist inmates in any particular year. Pentecostals counted just five incarcerated bishops and preachers from their denomination in 1977, with a typical sentence of five years' imprisonment followed by five years of exile. Starting in the late 1970s, the Oxford-based Keston Institute began tracking reports of known religious inmates, and its lists included between 200 and 400 prisoners in the late 1970s and early 1980s. Since some undoubtedly escaped the notice of these monitoring or-ganizations, it is reasonable to conclude that in any given year in this period, between 250 and 500 Christians were behind bars or barbed wire explicitly for their religious practices. In contrast to the Stalin era, sentences were typi-cally short, with a three-year term being the most common sentence for reli-gious prisoners. This led to a constant flow of religious inmates in and out of the Brezhnev-era Gulag.[2]

This chapter is devoted to these inmates and their jailers in what became known as the "era of stagnation." Indeed, relative stability was a feature of the Brezhnev era for religious life in the Gulag. After the harsh repression of the Stalin era and the experimentation of the Khrushchev era, the Brezhnev era featured the establishment of a tenuous modus vivendi between guards and religious inmates. Mostly, they all knew their roles and acted out their parts. Administrators and guards engaged in periodic antireligious propa-ganda and repression against various religious manifestations without ex-cessively tormenting the inmates. Religious prisoners found ways to practice and share their faith, including through active correspondence with friends and family. The Brezhnev era's religious dissidents thus maintained their spiritual lives, while the authorities could claim that they were trying to re-educate religious inmates while treating them justly and in accordance with Soviet laws.

More than other chapters in this book, this chapter relies heavily on letters to, from, and on behalf of imprisoned Christians, particularly Baptists. These letters are fascinating and valuable to historians because of their closeness to actual events—they were written while their authors were imprisoned. Of course, they were also written for particular audiences, and many are best un-derstood as representing a middle ground between reality and a constructed

178 FINDING GOD IN THE GULAG

archetype (which could be either positive or negative, depending on the audience and purpose of the letter). This does not detract from their usefulness, however, as they show the message that Soviet believers wanted to project. They illustrate the believers' hopes and dreams and the types of Christians they yearned to be.

Official Attitudes toward Religious Prisoners

Official Gulag propaganda during the Brezhnev era affirmed that religion would continue to be viewed with suspicion, if not outright hostility. The monthly journal for Gulag workers, *Toward a New Life*, for example, periodically related the supposed dangers of religion. Various articles depicted Christians disrupting socialist society, corrupting impressionable young minds, and refusing to perform their duties as citizens. One article from 1968 told of Agafya Shnyrka, a devout but hypocritical Pentecostal who recruited others to the sect and coerced them into frenzied prayer meetings and long periods of fasting. Sentenced to three years for enriching herself from parishioners' donations, she ended up in a corrective-labor colony, where she refused to perform any work. Clearly, the article's author mused in exasperation, "The deceiver just doesn't understand." Religious believers, in Soviet parlance, led a parasitic way of life, expecting the full benefits of the Soviet system without working. But according to Soviet logic, they deserved no special treatment; rather, they deserved to be treated as conniving (and perhaps brainwashed) peddlers of deceit.[3]

Occasional lectures and newspaper articles in penal facilities reflected these attitudes, focusing on the superstitious origins of religion and claiming that religious views "will undoubtedly disappear after the social roots of religion have been destroyed." Camp newspaper articles mustered the teachings of Marx, Lenin, Tolstoy, Gorky, and even Sun Tzu and Voltaire to convince Gulag inhabitants of the errors of religion. As one camp newspaper article made clear, "Christianity remains an anti-science, anti-Marxist teaching." An "atheist lecturer" taught that even though the Soviet Union allowed for religious liberty, it was clear that religious individuals actively opposed the creation of communism and thus deserved to be repressed.[4]

Official policies continued to discriminate against known believers in Brezhnev's Gulag. Georgi Vins recalled that a commission sent in 1967 refused to grant amnesty to a group of Baptist inmates because they had been praying and preaching in the camp. "Either prayer or freedom—choose!" one commission member demanded. When they chose prayer, they were denied amnesty and separated into different camps. Then, in 1972, an amnesty celebrating the fifty-fifth anniversary of the 1917 revolution explicitly excluded those convicted of Articles 142 and 227, the two sections of the criminal code dealing with the separation of church and state. Meanwhile, the subsequent 1977 amnesty commemorating the sixtieth anniversary was applied to those convicted of Article 227, but few religious inmates were convicted under that article alone. Thus, religious inmates had a much harder time than other inmates in securing early release; viewed by the state as parasites, they were denied opportunities to rejoin Soviet society.[5]

The camp experience also continued to be more difficult for those who openly attempted to practice their faith. When some Jews started to wear the yellow Star of David in the Perm-35 Colony (in pointed imitation of those worn by Nazi prisoners), the commander ordered their removal and somewhat ironically declared, "Only one religion is allowed in our country—the Orthodox one; only crosses may be worn." Yet numerous accounts from the mid-1970s confirm that wearing crosses was typically not allowed. They were forbidden in Vladimir Prison according to a Ministry of Internal Affairs order from 1972, under which several inmates had their crosses confiscated in subsequent years. Imprisoned Orthodox priest Vasily Romanyuk likewise reported in the late 1970s that jailers tore off crosses worn around prisoners' necks in the Mordovian camps. But guards were not always consistent in confiscating crosses. Irina Ratushinskaya reported that in some camp zones, they turned a blind eye to her cross.[6]

Religious literature was likewise forbidden. Gleb Yakunin had Bibles, psalters, a prayer book, and a church calendar confiscated. Boris Perchatkin had two Bibles confiscated and only managed to keep a third by hiding it in the camp library with the inmate librarian's assistance. Gabriel Superfin's Bible and prayer book were confiscated in 1976, and in protest he went on a hunger strike that lasted thirty-three days. He submitted many complaints to various authorities but was repeatedly told that the commander was within his rights to confiscate forbidden literature. Similarly, Orthodox inmate E. I. Pashnin-Speransky recounted that camp officials in Mordovia "repeatedly confiscated from me a prayer book, an Orthodox Calendar, the four Gospels . . ., and Metropolitan Makari's *Extracts from Orthodox Dogma*." When he protested, a camp administrator replied, "Prisoners are forbidden to possess literature of this type, even if it is handwritten."[7]

180 FINDING GOD IN THE GULAG

Guards justified confiscating religious literature by referring to a decree from the USSR Ministry of Internal Affairs that permitted inmates to possess only literature published by government agencies. Because the Orthodox Church was considered a private organization, its publications, including the Bible, were prohibited. But some Gulag officials came up with different reasons for confiscating religious literature. One commander of a corrective-labor colony in Rostov Province wrote to family members of a religious inmate, "Prisoners are forbidden from receiving from family members scientific and other literature. We have sufficient fictional, scientific, technical, and other literature, and for this reason the administration returns to you the 'Gospel,' since receiving books by prisoners is forbidden." Another camp official simply reported to an inmate's wife that he "cannot be allowed to read the 'Gospels' and thus continue his 'criminal activity.'" Such an explanation did not accord precisely with Gulag regulations, but the essence of his statement was certainly on point.[8]

Prohibitions on religious literature also extended to correspondence; any mention of religion could get the letter returned to the sender by camp censors. In late 1971, Baptist inmate Lidia Vins instructed her family to avoid words and phrases such as "God," "Jesus Christ," "May the Lord God keep you," "May the Lord bless you," and "Merry Christmas." In early 1976, inmate Yuri Vudka had a letter returned to him because it contained psalms and, as Captain Doynikov of Vladimir Prison confirmed, "Psalms are forbidden." Nijole Sadunaite reported the confiscation of hundreds of her letters. Attempts by inmates to protest such rules rarely succeeded. Two Baptist inmates in 1975 complained about being denied correspondence rights on religious grounds, for instance, and when they attempted to discuss the issue with a camp administrator, the latter "used uncensored swearing and threatened: 'If it were not for the West, we would have long ago done away with you.'"[9]

Even though the post-Stalin Gulag was supposed to be a place where inmates were treated with respect, verbal abuse from guards and administrators was common. A Baptist told of how, on his first day in the labor colony, the commander made no secret of his hatred of religious prisoners, shouting things like "You forced children to pray!" and "You led astray the youth!!!" He then ordered the Baptist to join a hard-labor brigade, remarking, "Here we will oppress you." Another warden reportedly told an imprisoned Christian, "Forget your Jesus Christ! There's only one true religion—communism—and only one God—Lenin! In Stalin's time, I used to shoot people like you!" Although guards infrequently inflicted physical harm in the Brezhnev era, they often designated religious prisoners for difficult labor assignments or sent them to the penalty isolator. As one camp commander reportedly told an elderly Catholic priest in the early 1980s, "We have the right to place all Catholics up to age 90 in a punishment cell. Priests don't get a discount for old age."[10]

Guards sometimes provoked disputes between nonreligious and religious inmates. In 1974, Baptist inmate Adam Dubitsky complained that all his papers with religious content, even letters from home, were confiscated during a search. But more than this, the guards planted material to make it appear that Dubitsky was "an American spy," which turned the other inmates against him. Pentecostal inmate Denis Karpenko related that one of his administrators cynically instructed the other prisoners that if religious inmates "went around covered in bruises, then the administration will forgive them and God will forgive them too." Another official told the inmates at roll call that believers "cram the administration's doorstep with denunciations against the other prisoners." Statements like this had predictable consequences. Baptist inmate B. M. Zdorovets lodged an official complaint that such subversion by the administration in a Kharkov Province penal institution resulted in other inmates beating him up. When he reported the incident, the official on duty coldly replied, "You deserved it. They did correctly."[11]

Gulag officials also often forbade prayer and associating with fellow religious inmates. As Karpenko related, "From a photograph of twenty-two believers they made two displays and stood them in camp headquarters and in the main gate of the camp in order to familiarize the sergeants and officers with the faces of the believers so as to not permit them to congregate in the camp territory." Even praying in private could earn direct reprisal. Dubitsky wrote in a complaint to his camp commander in July 1970:

> Returning from work I bathed, after which I went into the brigade's changing room to say a prayer. . . . While saying my prayer the warder Yakimov with senior lieutenant Popov stormed into the room with the shout of "What is this?" After which he hit me and began to use uncensored swearing. I continued to pray, but he hit me a second time. . . . After completing my prayer I went out, but he continued his swearing with threats that he would put me in the penalty isolator.

182 FINDING GOD IN THE GULAG

One can only imagine Dubitsky's despair at not being allowed to pray in a private, secluded space. As for holidays, E. I. Pashni-Speransky recalled an attempt to celebrate Easter together in 1975, but warders almost immediately broke up the gathering and sent the participants to the penalty isolator. "So, by the order of the servants of the MVD," he lamented, "our holy days are turned into humiliation and suffering."[12]

Official justifications for discrimination against religious inmates in Brezhnev's Gulag varied, but a commonly cited one was that religious inmates refused to participate in the camp's cultural life. Gulag officials designed cultural activities to "re-educate" inmates, and while this often included activities such as musical concerts or plays, it also included political indoctrination sessions and antireligious propaganda. Dubitsky reported that despite always overfulfilling the labor quota, he was constantly harassed by guards because he refused to participate in the camp's cultural life and was therefore deemed not "on the path to correction." Similarly, Pentecostal inmate Vasily Barats wrote in a letter that because he refused to renounce his faith, the guards pestered him and wrote in his file that he "had not stood on the path of correction." When inmates' families complained of poor treatment, Gulag commanders were not shy about using this justification. As one responded to a Baptist prisoner's wife, "he doesn't admit his guilt, he openly shares his religious views, and he doesn't participate in the avocational organizations of the institution, [therefore] he has been put on the rolls of the difficult-to-reeducate, about which he has been informed."[13]

Yet not all Gulag officials treated religious inmates poorly. Baptist prisoner David Klassen related in one letter, "Dear friends! You can imagine how happy I was when I arrived here in the north, and one of the soldiers greeted me not with the butt of his rifle, but instead gave me a brotherly handshake through the barbed wire." A kind prison photographer in Saransk likewise told Sadunaite that he was a believing Christian, although he could not divulge this publicly. Other Gulag officials were sympathetic to the plight of suffering believers out of more general humanitarian concerns. For example, in 1968, the Ukrainian Greek Catholic believer Josyp Terelya was sent to the penalty isolator for speaking in Ukrainian, not Russian, with the camp administration. As he was praying out loud in the isolator, including on behalf of his jailers, one of the guards stormed in and demanded, "Why are you praying for me?" But he then softened and said, "I will give you a warm blanket so that you can put it on the ground and at night I will give you some hot water to drink." The next morning, he told Terelya, "You know, we

RELIGIOUS DISSIDENTS UNDER BREZHNEV   183

must repress you, but please forgive us." Though exceptional, sympathetic guards such as these undoubtedly made camp life more bearable for Terelya, Klassen, and others.[14]

Religious Worship and Identity in the Brezhnev Era

Although the Brezhnev-era Gulag made it difficult for religious prisoners to maintain a spiritual life, numerous inmates reported finding spiritual fulfillment in the camps. For instance, Orthodox inmate Pashnin-Speransky remembered how difficult it was for him and fellow Orthodox believers because the daily religious schedule of prayers and observances conflicted too much with the camp's regimented schedule. Individual prayers said in private were sometimes possible, but, as he stated, "Orthodox prayers are in fact intended for corporate use, for reading together." It proved almost impossible for two or more of them to meet to pray, but a few opportunities arose. On one occasion, he and another Orthodox believer said evening prayers together at night next to the latrine. "To avoid this unpleasantness," he recalled, "we moved nearer to the bath-house, where Kalinin laid a sheet of plywood on the ground and used another as a shield from the wind and from the prying eyes of vigilant informers. And there we began to read our prayers." Another incident related by Pashnin-Speransky confirms the length to which believers had to go to say communal prayers: "How overjoyed I was when in January 1975 A. A. Petrov, A. I. Romanov, and I succeeded in entering unobserved an empty refrigerated truck, which stood by a warehouse ready to be loaded. We threw ourselves on our knees on the icy floor and gave praise to Jesus Christ. But such moments of joy were few and far between during our life in captivity."[15]

The presence of coreligionists in the camp was a source of great comfort and support to prisoners of faith. As the Baptist Georgi Vins recalled of discovering two other Baptists in the camp in 1967:

> Finding another Christian in the harsh surroundings of a desolate labor camp gave me joy beyond words. How difficult it is to be in bonds! But if there are two or three believers imprisoned together—*that* makes a church! A very small one, perhaps, but still God's precious church! There were now three believers in our camp. We could whisper encouragement to one another from the Word of God written in our hearts.

184 FINDING GOD IN THE GULAG

The three of them spent their free time copying Bible verses, praying to-gether, quietly singing hymns, and even receiving communion together after Vins's wife visited and smuggled in a vial of wine for that purpose. As Vins later shared of that occasion, "We felt a special significance in this ordinance. The Lord had instituted it just before his own arrest, when he faced the suf-fering and torture of death on the cross. Now he had given us, his followers, the privilege of experiencing bonds for his holy name." After blessing the bread and wine and eating it, "We knelt together and thanked the Lord for his great sacrifice of love on the cross of Golgotha, for salvation and eternal life given to us through his suffering, death, and glorious resurrection. Then quietly, brokenly, with overflowing hearts, we sang a hymn of thanksgiving and praise to our lovely Redeemer."[16]

The Lithuanian Catholic Sadunaite vividly described a group of old True Orthodox women, convicted of various crimes against what they called "the Satanic government." They prayed earnestly, abstained from food with an-imal fat in it while fasting, refused to perform labor, and, most poignantly for Sadunaite, sang hymns. As she recalled, "Once I learned them, I used to join in. I would feel as though I were in some shrine, such goodness and light would my soul experience. Not without reason it is said that prayer in common reaches heaven." Camp guards often punished the True Orthodox women for their refusal to work, so they spent much time in the penalty iso-lator, where cold and hunger sapped their strength but never broke their spirits. As Sadunaite marveled, "When I recall such spiritual giants as the pleasant little brunette, Nadia Usoyeva, I am reminded of the words from the gospel, 'If God is for us, who can be against us?' It is possible for one who is deeply rooted in God and lives by love to bear all things. Love is uncon-querable." This sense of solidarity across denominational lines was experi-enced in particular by female prisoners, whose gatherings may have been viewed by guards as less dangerous than those attempted by male Christian prisoners. As Ratushinskaya wrote, "What a mixed bunch we are: a Catholic, a Pentecostal, several Orthodox, an unbeliever . . . later we were to be joined by a Baptist. Yet we were always deeply respectful of one another's convictions. And God did not turn His face away from our small patch of Mordovian soil."[17]

This feeling of solidarity helped imprisoned women celebrate Christian holidays, despite the differences in religious denomination. As Ratushinskaya remembered:

We gather around the table, and the words of the Lord's Prayer ring out in Lithuanian, Latvian, Russian and Ukrainian, although Orthodox Christmas is still to come. Mrs. Jadvyga divides up a Communion wafer from Lithuania, so that there is a bit for everyone. This wafer, no thicker than a sheet of paper, was sent to her by relatives in an envelope. The censor let it through: either she had no idea what it was, or refrained from confiscating it without a direct order to do so. "Silent night, holy night," sing Galya and Mrs. Lida in two languages. And we, despite our various creeds, never doubted for a moment that God was looking down on us all at that moment.

Celebrating holidays across denominational lines also found expression during Epiphany. "After 'lights out,'" Ratushinskaya related, "when all the others had gone to bed, we dragged buckets of water and a tub into the snow outside, and set them down among the drifts. The frost fairly crackled, but the stars were unbelievably bright, and we felt so excited on this special night." Although it was twenty-five degrees below zero, the younger women of the group of believers stripped naked, ran through the snow, and doused themselves with buckets of water. "No, we were not out of our minds that Epiphany eve," Ratushinskaya concluded, "we were just—young.... And as tradition maintains, we came to no harm, not one of us developed so much as a sniffle."[18]

Ukrainian national activist Iryna Stasiv-Kalynets also celebrated religious holidays such as Easter and Christmas in the Brezhnev-era Gulag, although for her it was less a celebration of ecumenical spirit than one of national solidarity. In a letter written soon after her release, she recalled how a small group of Ukrainians set up a small Christmas tree, enjoyed a modest feast, and sang carols. "And Ukraine was near us," she recalled, "and all our distant and close countrymen." Food, song, and even a small group of like-minded inmates thus conjured a spirit of religious nationalism among those who lamented the seizure of their homeland by the USSR. Although there were fewer overt nationalists from the western borderlands in the Brezhnev-era Gulag compared with the 1940s and 1950s, many remained imprisoned for their opposition to the Soviet regime.[19]

On rare occasions, family members' visits provided spiritual communion. These were almost impossible due to the grueling travel involved and policies that restricted such meetings. According to Georgi Vins, "few of the convicts'

186　FINDING GOD IN THE GULAG

wives will risk the journey." In fact, many "Gulag wives" simply abandoned their husbands following their convictions. "Wives of Christian prisoners, however," Vins continued, "always try to visit their husbands, even at the most distant camps." When Mikhail Khorev's family made the long journey to visit him for Easter in 1984, for instance, they were told the visit had been rescheduled for three weeks later. Only after persistent complaining and threats to involve higher authorities were they able to meet as planned. As recounted by Khorev's daughter, "The first thing he said to each of us were these wonderful words, 'Christ is risen!' We all responded in unison each time, 'He is indeed risen!'" After this ceremonial Easter greeting, Khorev taught from the scriptures and prayed with them. His daughter recorded part of his poignant prayer: "Only help us, O Lord, to remain wholeheartedly true to you here on earth, because when we reach eternity there will be no more prison, deprivations or lawyers or any other way to demonstrate to you our loyalty, because there will be no more fines, or arrests and nothing will separate us from your love." Such a visit from his wife and children no doubt strengthened Khorev's resolve to survive his ordeal and remain true to his convictions.[20]

Despite various ways to socialize with fellow believers, most spiritual fulfillment in the camps took the form of individual communion with God. Ratushinskaya recalled that "in camps—especially political camps—the primary aim of the administration and the KGB is to break the prisoners spiritually, make them renounce their principles and convictions.... When I came to the camp I realized very quickly that the most important thing is not to allow hatred into your heart." Ratushinskaya relied on prayer and poetry to remain spiritually strong. One typical poem expressed how she felt the support of fellow Christians who prayed on her behalf as she suffered:

> Believe me, it was often thus
> In solitary cells, on winter nights
> A sudden sense of joy and warmth
> And a resounding note of love
>
> And then, unsleeping, I would know
> A huddle by an icy wall
> Someone is thinking of me now
> Petitioning the Lord for me

My dear ones, thank you all
Who did not falter, who believed in us!
In the most fearful prison hour
We probably would not have passed
Through everything—from start to end—
Our heads held high, unbowed,
Without you valiant hearts
To light our path.

As for prayer, she stated that her prayers were typically short because of the nature of the prison camp regimen. Yet, despite this, she felt spiritually nourished by these brief chances to direct her thoughts toward God. She experienced, in her words, "an active flow of strength, a sort of warmth, and bearing in mind the icy conditions of punishment cells, this warmth could only have been the force of prayer, sustaining and protecting us."[21]

For Orthodox inmate Aleksandr Ogorodnikov, communion with God while in the "truly satanical" Gulag system often took place through meditative practices in the cold and dismal conditions of the penalty isolator:

In the morning I would pray. Then I would begin a hesychastic type of prayer, the Jesus Prayer, and I would practice it so that the Jesus Prayer would continually grow. I would observe myself very carefully that I would perform it correctly. The isolation cell is actually very small; you can only make three small steps diagonally. So I began to take walks back and forth and see to it that the Jesus Prayer would be connected with my breathing.

Anatoly Levitin-Krasnov reported a similar ritual:

The basis of my whole spiritual life is the Orthodox liturgy, so while I was in prison I attended it every day in my imagination. At 8:00 in the morning I'd begin walking around my cell repeating its words to myself. I was then inseparably linked to the whole Christian world.... At the central point of the liturgy I felt myself standing before the face of the Lord, sensing almost physically his wounded, bleeding body.... After this, I felt all day an exaltation of spirit—I felt purified within.

Repeating contemplative prayers in the confined spaces of the penalty isolator attuned Ogorodnikov and Levitin-Krasnov to the ancient monastic

188 FINDING GOD IN THE GULAG

tradition within Russian Orthodoxy. Ignoring their physical suffering, they effectively, if only temporarily, tempered the effect of punishment by focusing instead on an intense spiritual communion with God.[22]

Communion with God could also mean admiring the camp's natural surroundings. As Georgi Vins thought after being transferred from prison to a Siberian labor camp, "The beauty and majesty of God's creation is truly amazing! What invigorating, fragrant air! The pure heavens—what a boundless, distant blue! It was wonderful to be moved overnight from the dark, dirty, stinking prison to the open, snow-clean forest." His fellow inmates were less thrilled at this observation, but Vins was not affected. As he recalled, "My heart was filled with such joy and light. I even seemed to feel a little warmer as I thought of God. I knew who had created this amazingly beautiful winter forest. I knew who had created me, who had created all of us. I knew that God loves us, is ever mindful of us, and offers salvation and eternal life to all men!" As he shared these feelings of rapture about the beauty of the Siberian ecosystem with his fellow inmates, one remarked, "You Baptists are strange. For you everything is God. They put you in prisons and camps and freeze you on these forest roads, and all you do is talk about God and try to make others believe."[23]

Indeed, one remarkable part of religious life in Brezhnev's Gulag was the active preaching of Christianity. Terelya of the Ukrainian Greek Catholic Church remarked, "We were always trying to convert people in prison. Even if you only convert one soul, the fruit is bountiful and sweet."[24] The energetic young Orthodox inmate Ogorodnikov engaged in preaching, and Hermann Hartfeld recounted how he participated in the conversion of a young man who had been wrongly convicted of murder. This man had heard that an Orthodox believer had miraculously healed Hartfeld's injured arm in the camp and sought them out to learn more about Christianity. After many long conversations about prayer and why God allows evil things to happen, the young man "was gloriously saved." Shortly after, he was freed when the actual murderer confessed to the crime. As Hartfeld said of the man's release, "Before he left the camp he came to the Christians and asked the brethren to pray for him. They laid their hands on him and blessed him and he dedicated his life to serving the Lord."[25]

Baptists were especially active in attempts to convert others. Georgi Vins related that he and other Baptists attracted other inmates to their discussions, leading one guard to reportedly exclaim, "If we don't take decisive measures, in another six months half the camp will be Baptists!" Even Vins acknowledged that this was a humorous exaggeration, but still, "it was obvious that the atheists were very disturbed. Every day, lively discussions would spring up regarding faith in God." The Baptist G. V. Kostyuchenko recounted having converted several prisoners, including one young man convicted of burglary who asked him why he refused to smoke. As Kostyuchenko later said, "I with joy told him about the Lord. The next day I gave him a passage from the Gospel of John to read; he couldn't put it down. . . . We started praying together; the seed of the Word of God grew in his soul." But then a spiritual crisis beset Kostyuchenko when he was informed that he would be placed under administrative supervision after release. Other prisoners teased him about how unjustly God treated him, and he began to question God, feeling "complete spiritual powerlessness." The young man whom he had converted turned against him, saying: "What have you done with me? . . . I thought that this was the true path. People know that I believed, but now I'm completely empty." In the end, though, Kostyuchenko's faith was reaffirmed, and he and his convert enjoyed a spiritual reconciliation marked by prayer and forgiveness. This story, published as a faith-promoting anecdote, is not just interesting because it involves a conversion story in the Gulag, but it also illustrates the potential for de-conversion, with both Kostyuchenko and his convert undergoing stark trials of faith marked by doubt and despair.[26]

Evident in many accounts was an unspoken rule to preach to atheists but not try to convert other Christians. Pentecostal prisoner Anatoly Vlasov, for instance, found himself housed in a tent with a Baptist, an Adventist, a Jehovah's Witness, and an Orthodox believer in a small, localized experiment reminiscent of Dubravlag under Khrushchev. The purpose was apparently to allow the inmates of different denominations to fight against each other. But, as Vlasov related, "There was no hostility—only love. Nobody tried to 're-educate' the other, and everyone prayed according to his beliefs." Upon discovering this, Vlasov reported, the camp administrators broke up this congregation of Christians, dispersing them to various work gangs. Ratushinskaya observed a similar phenomenon, writing that "we all understood each other, because we all knew that there is one God, and the individual paths by which we find Him are not all that important: the thing that matters is whether you go *to* Him, or *away from* Him. So there were never any denominational tensions among us, any arguments on religious themes."[27]

One of the most fascinating accounts of religious belief in the Brezhnev-era Gulag, which ties together these varied themes of conversion, prayer,

190 FINDING GOD IN THE GULAG

communion with fellow believers, and repression from the camp guards, comes from Yevgeny Vagin. Vagin was a writer and political prisoner with religious inclinations who converted to Orthodox Christianity while serving an eight-year sentence in Mordovia in the 1970s. "Only in the camp," he reported, "did I learn to pray for real, and discovered and felt for myself the power of prayer."[28] According to Vagin, incarcerated Christians' religious life was surprisingly rich and "full of intensity" in the face of repression. Despite prohibitions on Christian literature, he found a vibrant tradition of copying and distributing scriptures, prayers, and other religious writing. Sometimes this was aided by the official camp library. "With the help of Tolstoy's 'Criticism of dogmatic theology,' which is not banned," he explained, "the Orthodox catechism could be reconstructed." And believers always strove to find ways to worship together. The priest Boris Zalivako, for example, "read the liturgy every Sunday during walks with 3 or 4 inmates" and was eventually punished for this with two years in Vladimir Prison. Vagin also tells of numerous Lithuanian Catholics, True Orthodox Christians, Jehovah's Witnesses, Baptists, Adventists, and Pentecostals who "often meet in groups and you can see them praying together, especially in the evening." And he recalled celebrating Christmas and Easter with such varied Christians, reporting that "generally the guards pretend not to notice, almost as if they respected the believers' feelings." Between them all, "the question of proselytizing didn't arise: We respected each other and learned to respect strange convictions."[29]

Vagin also told of how nonreligious inmates converted to Christianity in the camps, including the human rights activist Varsonofy Khajbulin and the convicted murderer Victor Tartinsky (who got fifteen years added to his twenty-year sentence for resisting a camp official who tried to rip off a cross from around his neck). Christianity offered a system of beliefs and values that stood at odds with those of Marxism-Leninism, and this proved attractive to many behind barbed wire. As Vagin related:

> The younger prisoners, especially those who belong to neo-Marxist groups, start by being amazed at these activities. They look in astonishment at those who make the sign of the Cross before meals. But little by little they get used to it and they too begin to cross themselves. At first it is a purely mechanical, external gesture, but after a while they become more seriously attracted towards religion, and not infrequently they become sincere Christians.

For Vagin, such conversions resulted from the persistent devotion of the believers and the natural inclination of humans to yearn for God amid harsh trials. As he described it, "The very atmosphere of the camp, the closeness to people who have suffered a lot, brings the believers to a quite special emotional state. It is hard to put into words: it is a sort of passion which is hard to explain to anyone who hasn't lived behind barbed wire."[30]

Petitioning for Freedom of Religion

In order to increase the "passion" that Vagin and others brought to their spiritual lives in the Soviet Union's penal institutions, prisoners of faith and their families filed many complaints to both Soviet and international authorities. Such a practice was not new; Soviet prisoners, including religious inmates, had long availed themselves of Soviet guarantees of petition. But in the Brezhnev era, these petitions became more common and increasingly adopted the legalistic arguments made famous by imprisoned political dissidents. Indeed, Russian Orthodox dissidents of the Brezhnev era often made common cause with the human rights movement. Orthodox priests Sergei Zheludkov and Anatoly Levitin-Krasnov and human rights campaigners such as Anatoly Marchenko, Aleksandr Solzhenitsyn, and Andrey Sakharov, for instance, explicitly linked the Soviet government's violation of human rights and its refusal to allow religious liberty. The fact that religious and political prisoners under Brezhnev were often imprisoned together provided the opportunity to exchange experiences and tactics, such as appealing to the Soviet constitution, other Soviet legislation, and even international law to lobby for freedom of religious worship.[31]

Camp friendships and a sense of mutual suffering resulted in the plight of religious prisoners often being included in political prisoners' petitions. In December 1971, for instance, nine political prisoners petitioned the International Red Cross for assistance in redressing a litany of complaints, among them an appeal on behalf of Orthodox priest Zalivako. The petition also complained that the camp authorities had forbidden reading, sending, and receiving religious literature, which they characterized as a "violation of articles 18 and 19 of the Declaration of the Rights of Man" (referring to the United Nations' Universal Declaration of Human Rights). Similar petitions, rooted in appeals to national and international law, followed. G. I. Butman's appeal to the Perm Camp boss in 1976, for instance, specified numerous

192 FINDING GOD IN THE GULAG

complaints of wrongdoing, including an incident where the religious prisoner Orlovich had his head shaven while handcuffed. Likewise, a 1975 declaration signed by sixty-seven inmates from Vladimir Prison, the Mordovian Camps, and the Perm Camps dealt primarily with how the regime treated its incarcerated ideological enemies. But one of the document's provisions argued that prisoners should have "the right to individual and collective performance of religious ordinances, and also to the fulfillment of other needs tied to their religious convictions; to receiving and using religious literature and objects of their religious cult, and so forth." Moreover, they should enjoy "the right to form societies by confession, and also to invite priests for their participation in religious cult ordinances and religious holidays." Notably, the language used here is rooted not in religion but in Soviet law. But more important is the content: Brezhnev-era dissidents largely accepted those persecuted for their religious convictions as engaged in a common cause of opposing the Soviet regime.[32]

The widely publicized signing of the Helsinki Accords, which supposedly guaranteed a host of civil liberties including the right to religious worship, provided new grounds for launching complaints. Six Baptist inmates in a September 1975 petition to the Presidium of the Supreme Soviet, for example, expressed the hope that conditions would improve after the Helsinki Accords were signed, but instead, they got worse. They viewed the continued prohibition against religious literature in the camps as "an infringement of our freedom of confession, and also the freedom of thought and conscience," which violated the seventh principle of the Helsinki Accords (which covered freedom of thought, conscience, and religion). Similarly, five Baptist prisoners in 1976 signed a petition complaining of the confiscation of religious literature and the practice of not allowing religious inmates to talk together. They specifically pointed to the Helsinki Accords, asserting that their human rights were being violated at their corrective-labor colony in near Omsk.[33]

Baptist prisoners were aided in their petitions by the underground organization Council of Relatives of Evangelical Christian-Baptist Prisoners (hereafter Council of Relatives), which fired off numerous missives to Soviet agencies and powerbrokers. In November 1976, for instance, it sent an urgent telegram to Brezhnev with the complaint that the ailing N. G. Baturin was assigned hard labor because he refused to disavow his belief in God. Beyond immediate relief from labor, the complaint also struck at the heart of his imprisonment: "On the basis of the Helsinki Accords, Baturin should be released immediately since he has been serving a sentence based on religious motives since 1972." Several years later, in 1982, Baturin made a similar appeal to the procurator over the correctional facilities of Kemerovo Province. "This year, when in Madrid there is a Conference on reviewing compliance of the Helsinki final act," he began, before detailing various abuses he had suffered because of his religious convictions. The Soviet Union signed the Helsinki Accords, each complaint suggested, so it needed to comply with its statutes.[34]

More often than the Helsinki Accords, however, religious prisoners and their supporters relied directly on Soviet law to justify their appeals. Nadezhda Shostenko sent a Bible to her husband's camp commander, asking him to pass it along, since freedom of conscience was explicitly enshrined in Article 124 of the Soviet Constitution. In a 1975 petition addressed to various Soviet agencies, the Council of Relatives similarly declared, "In *Soviet Corrective-Labor Law* [a well-known criminology textbook] it is written: 'Those who are deprived of freedom are guaranteed their constitutional right of freedom to practice religious cults and antireligious propaganda (Article 124 of the Constitution).' Indispensable to this is reading the Bible, praying, and partaking of the Lord's Supper (Communion)." Having established the legal basis for their claim, the Council of Relatives reported that "our relatives in prisons and camps are deprived of this right and experience a continual hunger for the word of God, for which they are suffering and even giving their lives. They are not permitted to have a Bible or New Testament with them, these are counted as forbidden books." After this attempt to argue that Ministry of Internal Affairs orders prohibiting religious texts in the camps were unconstitutional, the petition continued with another reference to the constitution and to Soviet legal scholar Yury M. Tkachevsky to protest the censoring of correspondence. It then concluded by bolding declaring: "We insist that their rights be respected! . . . We would remind you that we Christians, as citizens with equal rights, have never given the authorities the right to strangle freedom of conscience and to harass believers. We consider this to be a crime deserving punishment both by man and by God."[35]

Other petitions for redress centered on lofty idealism or even on Christianity itself. One letter from 103 Baptists to the chairman of the Presidium of the Supreme Soviet concerning the plight of religious prisoners declared indignantly, "And who would think that in the age of civilization and progress there could exist such savage, coarse medieval methods of

194 FINDING GOD IN THE GULAG

fighting against believers?!" Meanwhile, Vasily Kozlov, a hardened criminal who had converted to evangelicalism, wrote directly to the Kremlin about the benefits of faith:

> Our criminals don't need the morality of atheism, they need Christ. If you didn't prevent believers in your prisons and camps from speaking about Christ to this sinful world, you wouldn't need to maintain your million lecturers upholding atheist morality. . . . Then there'd be fewer drunkards and thieves and less crime. The camps where you hold men in concrete cages like wild animals would empty and you wouldn't have to maintain them anymore.

Likewise, a 1975 petition by Baptist inmate Ivan Fedorchenko arguing for unhindered religious practice in the camps ended with the following blessing, rooting his appeal firmly in Christian belief: "May Your Lord turn your heart to do good, may He make you wise to act prudently, according to truth. Glory and praise to our Savior, the Lord Christ, that He loves all people, including us, and you, and died for everyone."[36]

Most such appeals, whether rooted in international obligations, Soviet law, or Christian morality, fell on deaf ears. For complaints of specific abuse, however, the Brezhnev era's evolving standards of legality meant that the state typically conducted an investigation and gave an official, if cursory, response. After Valentina Baturina petitioned to have her husband transferred from a camp in the far north to his home province of Rostov on account of his poor health, a Gulag authority responded that "because there is no basis rooted in law, your request for the transfer of [your husband] cannot be satisfied." In another example, Nadezhda Vins, wife of the imprisoned Baptist preacher Georgi Vins, complained to Alexei Kosygin, chairman of the Council of Ministers, that her husband had been deliberately poisoned in the camp with mercury. She alleged that he had been threatened by a KGB operative, who showed him a copy of a foreign newspaper with his picture in it and a handwritten inscription that read, "Use strong measures against Vins." In response, Nadezhda Vins received a short reply from a Gulag official stating that her husband was in good health, that no poisoning had occurred, and that he was not in any way being discriminated against because of his beliefs. Just a few years later, however, he would be awakened in the middle of the night, flown to Moscow, and turned over to the United States along with

Figure 7.1 Georgi Vins in 1979, shortly after his expulsion from the USSR. From left to right, the exchanged prisoners are Aleksandr Ginzburg, Valentyn Moroz, Edward Kuznetsov, Georgi Vins, and Mark Dymshits. Alamy.

four other dissidents in exchange for two imprisoned Soviet spies.[37] (See figure 7.1.)

Occasionally, responses to petitions from Christian prisoners or their supporters were more detailed. In response to a letter complaining of interrupted correspondence, for instance, one prisoner's mother received the following reply in the late 1960s:

> In reply to your letter I inform you that your son Yuri Ivanovich Mikhalkov is in a place of confinement and every method of re-education is being applied to him to turn him into a person useful for our socialist society and not for your circle of God-worshippers. For this reason, all your letters containing prayers and quotations from church books are being withheld.... Your son has a higher education and you as his mother have succeeded in dragging him into a swamp from which for the second time he has landed in a place of confinement, which fact should worry you and make you influence him to take the right path, but you are only dragging him further into the swamp.... For violation of the established regime,

196   FINDING GOD IN THE GULAG

your son is deprived of food parcels until he begins to reform.... Therefore, my request to you is to help me to release Yuri early so that in accordance with his education he can take his place in our socialist society and not in your narrow circle of God-worshippers, and live with his family and not separated from it. You as his mother must take all measures to educate Yuri so that he becomes not "Yuri the martyr," but Yuri Ivanovich, industrial engineer.

Here the officially mandated program of re-education, together with the perceived necessity of repressing religious belief, is made clear. Relying not on statutes or the Soviet constitution, the camp commander rooted his response in a moral understanding of socialism that would produce a modern, productive, and atheistic society.[38]

In contrast to this long and overtly antireligious message, a few responses from Brezhnev-era Gulag authorities awarded some redress for purported wrongs suffered. After T. M. Pshenitsynaya complained to various authorities, she finally received a letter from the camp commander stating that her husband's Bible had been returned to him and that he had been released from the penalty isolator. In this case, it seemed, persistence paid off. This case also highlights the at-times-conflicting interpretations of what was permissible in the camps, in this instance, possession of scripture. Although the Brezhnev-era Gulag was far more systematized than the Stalin-era camps, which were run largely at the whim of their commanders, there was still a fair amount of discretion and confusion concerning antireligious regulations.[39]

Letters to and from Home

In addition to petitions to Soviet and international authorities, religious inmates also engaged in (or at least attempted to engage in) correspondence with friends and family. This was a primary means of outwardly expressing one's convictions and feeling the support of loved ones beyond the barbed wire, and it was particularly important for those without fellow believers in their penal institutions. Inmates' letters are remarkable for their messages of hope, faith, and optimism. Indeed, they were intentionally crafted to convey such emotions, providing spiritual comfort to those suffering in solidarity with their imprisoned comrades. The following is just a sampling of the many letters that still exist, testifying to a much more active correspondence than was possible under Stalin, despite the continued presence of camp censors on the lookout for religious content.

Most letters from Christian inmates expressed confidence in God's guiding hand. As one Lithuanian Catholic woman expressed in a letter from prison, "The Good Lord truly knows best what I need.... And how good it is that the small craft of my life is being steered by the hand of the good Father. When He is at the tiller—nothing is to be feared.... And I can say that the year 1975 has flown by like a flash but that year is my joy. I thank the good Lord for it." The message here is clear: do not worry about me—I am in God's care. Barats, in the early 1980s, composed a similar message to two women from his Pentecostal congregation when detailing his transfer to a different colony. Noting that he had received little food for the journey, he wrote, "The Lord gave me strength to endure this trial, and now I have already made peace with the small prison ration.... Although it has been difficult for me, and perhaps will still be, I am glad that I came to know the value of bread, and God helped me overcome my flesh." He also detailed a few health complaints and asked for medicine to be sent but concluded: "I am already relying on the Lord, for only He can help me in my situation.... The Lord in His mercy will not abandon us."[40]

The staunch Ukrainian Greek Catholic Terelya also testified to his reliance on God. He wrote in a 1983 letter to his home congregation: "Dear Brothers and Sisters! Another year of captivity has passed. Thank God, I will again see the dear and familiar faces of friends and family, of my little children and my beloved wife." Terelya then quickly shifted from his own status as a prisoner to the duty of all Christians, whether in bondage or free. "We live on earth in order to praise GOD and to attain eternal happiness," he told his friends and fellow believers, "and therefore I wish to remind you: beware of evil, do good deeds.... St. Paul says: 'All who want to live a blessed life in Jesus Christ will be persecuted' [2 Timothy 3:12]. The entire life of a Christian is the cross and martyrdom if he wants to live according to the Gospel.... And I beg you to remember: the LORD GOD does not abandon him who trusts in HIM." This statement that the righteous Christian can always trust in God was intended as a message of hope and praise, coupled with encouragement of righteousness and obedience.[41]

Baptists were particularly prolific letter writers, filling their correspondence with messages of love and hope amid trial, constantly reminding those at home that their suffering was only temporary and worked toward God's

198   FINDING GOD IN THE GULAG

glory. For instance, an inmate identified only as Vania wrote to his fellow Baptists back home: "Don't let your spirits fall, don't give up. The Lord is with US. To us is given not just to believe, but to suffer. The disciples in Jerusalem, while suffering, rejoiced." Dubitsky, in a letter home, rejoiced in his suffering in the camps and stated: "The Christian must know that the truest path in life is the path of the cross, and this path was shown to us by the lord of life—Christ. . . . And so we live on earth not for this life but to strive toward eternity." Four female Baptist inmates in 1970 likewise wrote a letter full of hope to their fellow believers, declaring, "Glory to God for this temporary separation, glory to Him for the storms! . . . Our temporary suffering of today is nothing compared with that glory that awaits us! . . . Dear friends, don't let anyone fall in spirits, don't despair. Remember the sinful world is watching us. We should reveal Christ to it. Our faces, our eyes should gleam with joy." Similarly, Khorev in his letters home reminded his family to remain faithful, without despair. Despair was never an acceptable emotional state, he taught, because although "our pathway goes through suffering, separation, distress and deprivation, our goal is glorious—the kingdom of Heaven. And the wearier we become upon this pathway, the more precious, pleasant, and beloved will be that place of rest."[42]

Baptist letter writers constantly thanked their friends and families for their letters and their prayers on their behalf. As Oleg P. wrote to fellow believers back home, "Above all I thank you for your prayers. Christ leads me by the hand on this new path for me. . . . Do not worry about me. Everything is wonderful." Such sentiments of comfort and gratitude were repeated in a 1981 letter from Sergei V. to the Council of Relatives. Focusing on his bond with fellow believers that persisted despite their enforced separation, he wrote: "I very strongly felt today a good, warm feeling of kinship with you in the Lord. And I knew, of course, that many thousands of souls who love the Lord, both young and old, are praying for me, but to receive another letter from friends, whom I did not know while living in freedom—this brings about such a special feeling. My friends, I am very thankful that you have given me so many happy minutes and brightened up my loneliness!" He continued, "You wanted to know how someone who has been torn away from everything feels, and by what miracle he is able to hold on to faith and to find joy, wonderment, and thankfulness. This is accomplished through your prayers; these are his breath; these are his atmosphere, and in them is his home!" Similar letters abound between Baptist prisoners and their fellow believers, showing

RELIGIOUS DISSIDENTS UNDER BREZHNEV   199

that despite limitations on correspondence, genuine spiritual relationships between prisoners and "free" citizens were maintained. And those in prison camps took strength in the knowledge that others were thinking about them and praying for them.[43]

One of the best examples of a devotional prison letter was sent in 1981 by "the least brother-prisoner of Jesus Christ, G" (a single letter to protect the anonymity of the sender). It combines tales of suffering, humility, miracles, rejoicing, and warnings to those outside the barbed wire to remain faithful. Its tone and message mimic the New Testament epistles of the apostle Paul, the quintessential Christian prisoner. The anonymous Baptist thanked the Lord for the trial of being sent to the "house of rest" (the penalty isolator) for his efforts to proselytize among the inmates; for a while, it brought physical suffering, but in the big picture, it was a spiritual blessing. He reported a miracle of being fed by other inmates who pitied him. He cited scripture, such as James 5:16: "The fervent prayer of the righteous can accomplish much." And he ended with another scripture: "My wish: 1 Corinthians 15:58." This reference forced his readers to consult their own Bibles to discover his desire: "Therefore, my dear brothers and sisters, stand firm. Let nothing move you. Always give yourselves fully to the work of the Lord, because you know that your labor in the Lord is not in vain."[44]

In addition to containing messages of hope and spiritual guidance, letters sent by imprisoned Christians could also be quite tender. One letter from an anonymous inmate to his son, for instance, is full of encouragement to live a good Christian life, but it also contains the devoted love of a parent for his child. It reads, in part:

> I think about all of you, and especially about you. Yes, in the last ten years I have seen you so little. . . . But that warmth in my soul that I have not been able to give you during the years of my wandering and imprisonment has in abundance been given to you by my Father and your Father. And even when I am no longer on this earth, my prayers and my love for you, my children, and for you, my dear son, will accompany your path in life, for God's blessing for you I have asked and now ask the Father. And He has promised to answer.[45]

Letters in return often echoed such tenderness. As Georgi Vins said of a fellow Baptist, "The children's letters always refreshed Konshaubi, especially

200   FINDING GOD IN THE GULAG

those from the younger ones. They told him about the worship services and youth meetings. Their letters sparkled with the joy of the Lord and with a vibrant faith."[46]

The messages of faith and love contained in these letters between Christians demonstrate a shared commitment to endure, and even welcome, physical suffering in imitation of Christ. Drawing on scripture and mutual support to help bolster faith and spiritual resolve, religious prisoners voiced their willingness to, as they saw it, bear their trials with the type of hope-filled joy expected of the disciples of Christ. Such messages capture only part of the story of imprisoned Christians, who also suffered doubt and occasional despair. But the mutual desire to exude optimism and strengthen the faith of others through correspondence was an essential part of their story. In the face of repression, many imprisoned believers continued to boldly profess their faith, both to their captors and to their friends and family.

Far less common were letters that betrayed doubt or depression. Even as Ogorodnikov attempted to keep his faith alive through monastic prayers and communion with fellow believers, the harsh repression meted out against him took its toll. In one moment of despair, he wrote a heart-rending letter to his mother in the mid-1980s, bemoaning the fact that he rarely received letters from friends and family and lamenting that "occasionally it seems to me that I should school myself to accept the idea that my welfare does not interest anyone but God . . . I feel so alone, so forgotten." After recounting some of the suffering he had endured and the prospect of more to come, he confessed:

> You must see that death appears to be the only way to end my agony, the only release. I have already committed the mortal sin of attempting to commit suicide: on the 1st, 9th, and 17th of May, 1984. I secretly cut my veins, but every time I was discovered, unconscious, but still alive, so they gave me blood transfusions. So I beg of you again—please appeal to the Presidium of the Supreme Soviet to show me a measure of mercy by ordering my execution by firing squad to put an end to the prospect of life-long, painfully slow torture. . . . They even forbid me to pray, and my cross has been torn from around my neck on countless occasions. I have spent a total of 659 days on hunger strike to protest their refusal to let me have a Bible and a prayer-book, and 411 days in the internal camp prison. . . . It is sad to realize that you are of no use to anyone, that you are doomed to lose your life without compassion, in total oblivion; to lose life full of energy,

enduring hunger, cold; without books, in dark cells, where even the sacred gift of God—life itself—is turned into torture.

No doubt other imprisoned Christians experienced such feelings of abandonment by both fellow believers and God and yearned for an end to their suffering in whatever form that end might take. But as despair and especially suicide were considered signs of spiritual weakness, few in their letters home or subsequent memoirs confessed to such thoughts.[47]

Religious believers in Brezhnev's Gulag endured various forms of repression that inflicted physical and psychological pain, particularly extended stays in penalty isolators featuring poor nutrition, exposure to cold, and isolation from fellow prisoners. Still, camp officials were more restrained than their Stalinist predecessors. Very few religious prisoners died in captivity in this era, and, though imperfect, the Soviet system of petitions and investigations meant that guards and administrators were careful about not pushing repression too far. As for the believers, their own letters and memoirs, along with documents produced by the Soviet regime, demonstrate that religious life could be vibrant despite such repression. They found ways to read holy texts, pray, commune with fellow believers, celebrate religious holidays, and smuggle letters with religious content past the camp censors. They preached when the occasion arose, with a few reporting successful conversions of other inmates. And they reported satisfaction in imitating the apostle Paul and other Christian martyrs who rejoiced in the chance to suffer for Christ.

Religious inmates reflecting on their time in the Brezhnev-era camps often focused on the spiritual growth they experienced while imprisoned. Khorev wrote to a friend, "I have to admit to you that prison is a very useful school for our education and for the testing of the genuineness of our faith. I'm grateful to the Lord for this school and for his leading." Stepan Germanyuk wrote, "This three-year course in God's school, was extremely important for me. Throughout my life I have never thought so much about the Christian life and the ways in which the Lord leads as when I was in prison. I had never before had so many blessings as then and never before had I sensed such closeness to God."[48] Zoya Krakhmalnikova, the publisher of the underground Orthodox journal *Hope*, found her early-1980s prison experience similarly illuminating. "Prison is the back side of human existence," she mused, "a

202   FINDING GOD IN THE GULAG

good thing instituted by the world for its own protection; it is a road to hell, a road to heaven, a black tunnel illuminated by the light of Divine love. Into this hell, into this bottomless pit came the risen Christ. That's why on this threshold of hell one may get a chance to reach paradise." This assessment expresses joy but also implies the experiences of doubt and despair shared by Ogorodnikov and a few others. Imprisonment was a crucible that both caused inmates to lose hope and produced Christians educated and even encouraged by their trials.[49]

8

Christianity as a Re-educational Program

"One's Cross," a newspaper article in the November 24, 1991, edition of *The Moscow News*, could not have been published just a few years previously. Appearing a month before the collapse of the Soviet Union, it told about the infamous Matrosskaya Tishina prison and the labors of Father Vasily, an Orthodox priest and newly installed member of the Moscow City Council. Father Vasily, the article stated, "proposed distributing Bibles and other literature to all Moscow prisons a year ago, and insisted that prisoners, like all people, have the right to baptism, communion, church weddings, and confession." This call to religious action bore immediate results, and religiosity in the prison soon flourished. He then challenged the prison administration to turn the "Lenin room" of the prison into an Orthodox chapel, and they dutifully "refurbished it, changed out the portraits of Lenin and Gorbachev for icons with the face of Jesus Christ, [and] outfitted it with electric candle holders." From then on, the article explained, prisoners worshipped Christ rather than the leading figures of communism. And while the staff was nervous about organizing a baptismal ceremony, the first was held on November 15, 1991, with several infants born to female inmates receiving the ordinance. The transformation of Matrosskaya Tishina was dramatic, changing in just a few years from an institution where Christians were incarcerated on account of their beliefs to a place where criminals were being purposefully converted into Christians.[1]

When Mikhail Gorbachev came to power in 1985, he promised to inject new life into the stagnating Soviet system. At first, his program for reform was limited, and he did not envision the sweeping changes that would radically alter and then destroy Vladimir Lenin's socialist experiment. But the nuclear meltdown at Chernobyl dramatically affected Gorbachev, deepening his drive to substantially revitalize the Soviet system. Soon after this catastrophe, he relaxed censorship and initiated public conversations about what was wrong in the Soviet Union and how it could be fixed. He restructured the planned economy, resurrecting elements of capitalism that had been absent in the USSR since the 1920s. He also introduced more democracy, including

Finding God in the Gulag. Jeffrey S. Hardy, Oxford University Press. © Oxford University Press 2024.
DOI: 10.1093/9780197751701.003.0009

204 FINDING GOD IN THE GULAG

multi-candidate elections, into Soviet governance. Gorbachev remained a convinced believer in the superiority of the Soviet socialist system over the capitalism of the West, and these reforms were designed to breathe new life into all aspects of the Soviet Union. Ultimately, however, the Gorbachev era was an exciting but destabilizing time. Soviet citizens began participating in elections whose outcomes were uncertain, they engaged in entrepreneurial economic activity, and they consumed all manner of formerly censored media. But they also had endured a wrenching loss of community spirit, rising crime, economic collapse, and the gradual abandonment of a compelling ideology and state support structure that had governed their lives for generations.

Amid these destabilizing reforms, a dramatic religious awakening swept the Soviet Union. Religious believers quickly took advantage of Gorbachev's new policies of relaxed censorship and lessened state repression against perceived enemies of the regime, becoming increasingly vocal in asserting beliefs in public settings. In the midst of this, the Soviet state actively participated in the celebration of one thousand years of Christianity in Russia by promoting a series of public events to commemorate the baptism of Prince Vladimir of Kyiv in 988 CE. By 1989, Gorbachev had allowed foreign missionaries into the country, where they quickly began proselytizing faith-starved Soviet subjects and establishing outposts of dozens of Christian denominations. Perhaps most strikingly, the Communist Party itself began exploring how religious devotion could perhaps facilitate the perfection of socialism.

Gorbachev also reimagined the decaying Gulag and the broader criminal justice system, though initial steps were tenuous and funding for reform was in short supply. Like former Soviet leaders, Gorbachev was reluctant to admit that his country imprisoned people for their political and religious beliefs, telling the French newspaper *L'Humanité* in early 1986 that political prisoners "do not exist in our country, just as the persecution of citizens for their beliefs does not exist." Of course, this would have been news to the hundreds of people still locked up in Soviet penal establishments for their ideological opposition to Soviet rule or for their active worship of God. The Keston Center had files on 398 expressly religious inmates in 1985, including 333 Christians, and this count was almost certainly incomplete. By the end of 1986, however, things began to change. It started with the release of a few high-profile religious inmates and culminated with the wholesale abandonment of atheism as a re-educational principle in the Gulag. And penal

CHRISTIANITY AS A RE-EDUCATIONAL PROGRAM   205

officials did not just become neutral regarding religion; by the early 1990s, they began actively embracing religion, particularly Christianity, as the most effective way of turning prisoners into good, honest citizens. The transformation could not have been more dramatic. In just a few years, guards and administrators went from confiscating Bibles and breaking up surreptitious prayer meetings to inviting priests and pastors into their camps, organizing Bible study groups, and building chapels.[2]

The Early Gorbachev Era

The early part of Gorbachev's reign departed little from the status quo that had been developed under Leonid Brezhnev. There was talk of reform and a very real campaign against alcoholism, but the fundamentals of the Soviet system appeared safe. Gorbachev was still consolidating his power and, as even he would later admit, did not feel the deep urgency for reform that he would after the Chernobyl nuclear accident. For religious believers, particularly those who opposed the officially sanctioned hierarchies, repression by the secret police continued apace. As late as June 1986, for instance, Orthodox activists were being arrested and sentenced to imprisonment because they publicly criticized the Soviet-sanctioned Orthodox patriarch.[3]

For those in the prisons and camps of the Soviet Gulag, the repression chronicled in chapter 7 continued unabated. For instance, when guards sent Orthodox mathematician Valeri Senderov to the penalty isolator in early 1985 for refusing to work after his Bible had been confiscated, deputy camp commander V. I. Bukin explained that his Bible "is not permitted, since it is an object of a religious cult. And conducting religious ordinances in the [corrective-labor colony] is forbidden in the interests of re-educating the prisoners." Senderov ultimately spent more than a year in the isolator during the early period of Gorbachev's reign and endured several hunger strikes to get his Bible back. Looking back, he recalled that pursuing his Bible's return was a spiritual war against "heathens" and that "a feeling of righteousness sustained me." Ultimately, he concluded, "The Bible sustained me the whole five years [of imprisonment]. The Bible and my struggle for it."[4]

Other religious inmates chronicled similar consequences when seeking to practice their religion. In late 1985, Irina Ratushinskaya spent time in the penalty isolator for participating in a hunger strike, where guards handcuffed and beat her until she lost consciousness. She was then punished further

206   FINDING GOD IN THE GULAG

for "simulating a concussion." Her health deteriorated over the following months due to receiving only starvation rations while officials denied visits from her mother and husband. Similarly, Aleksandr Ogorodnikov in August 1986 petitioned the procuracy of Khabarovsk Territory for redress against "the lawlessness reigning in Corrective Labor Colony No. 13." He specifically complained that guards had confiscated his cross, beaten him, thrown him into the penalty isolator, and denied him medical treatment.[5]

Camp administrators and KGB operatives also pressured religious prisoners to renounce their faith. Josyp Terelya related that one KGB officer tried to prove that it was impossible, according to scientists, to love everyone, so Christianity was ultimately a futile exercise. "People like you are masochists who find pleasure in being tortured," his interrogator insisted, before adding, "We don't believe Christ existed or that God existed. That's for childish minds." Another was more direct regarding Terelya's immediate situation: "Why doesn't your Jesus help you? Here we throw you into solitary, we beat you, and Jesus doesn't help you." Amid such abuse, even Terelya confessed that his faith was challenged, and "there were moments of doubt— when I complained about myself and my destiny."[6]

Some inmates reported that Gulag officials enlisted other prisoners to encourage de-conversion through physical abuse. Such efforts occasionally proved effective. In January 1986, the imprisoned Orthodox Christian Sergei Markus, convicted in 1984 according to Article 190-1 (covering anti-Soviet slander) for distributing religious literature, formally recanted on Soviet television. He was not forced to renounce his beliefs but admitted that he knowingly broke the law (an important point of distinction for Soviet authorities, who took pains to argue that they did not persecute people for their convictions, only for their illegal actions). In fact, Markus used religious language throughout his public confession, in which he admitted, "At first, I was convinced that I had been convicted for my faith. But after long and agonizing doubts I reassessed the past and saw that this was not at all so. I understood the fact that my illegal activity had harmed not just the State but the Church too." He and his wife had four young children, and his confession earned his release.[7]

A similar case involved Boris Razveyev, sentenced in 1984 to three years' imprisonment, who was approached in the camp in 1986 by newspaper reporter and KGB operative Nikolai Dombkovsky. Dombkovsky ultimately persuaded Razveyev to renounce his faith and attack other religious prisoners, such as accusing Ogorodnikov of being a pedophile

CHRISTIANITY AS A RE-EDUCATIONAL PROGRAM   207

and rapist (trumped-up charges previously made by the KGB based in part on Ogorodnikov's pre-Christian life as a Soviet "hippie" interested in Eastern mysticism). His confession and accusations appeared in the *Labor* newspaper in April 1986 and were repeated in a subsequent television interview. Razveyev aimed another attack at Alexander Men, whom he outed as an Orthodox priest (Men had been operating as a popular Christian preacher up to that point). KGB agents then approached Men and pressured him into a "confession" that appeared in *Labor* just a week and a half later.[8]

Other imprisoned Christians, however, resisted such pressure. Orthodox deacon Vladimir Rusak refused to sign a document promising early release in exchange for renouncing his attacks on the official Orthodox hierarchy. Though it meant the continuation of his suffering and the possibility that time could be added to his sentence, Rusak remained committed to his spiritual ideals. Orthodox prisoner Zoya Krakhmalnikova also refused to cooperate in exchange for liberty. As she related after her ultimate release:

> The authorities offered me release. It was all very simple. I had only to renounced my service to God. . . . Then I thought: "What can you offer me in place of the Resurrection, in place of eternal blessedness, in place of the Kingdom which has been promised to me by my God? Why do I need this freedom?" It was right there in prison that I began to understand spiritual freedom, in that fire of constant repentance.

Although some religious inmates confessed in exchange for release, Rusak, Krakhmalnikova, and others drew strength from their ability to resist that temptation, focusing instead on their spiritual growth while incarcerated.[9]

As in previous eras, some inmates converted to Christianity while imprisoned in the first years of Gorbachev's reign. One fascinating anecdote from this era involves a convicted murderer, Vladimir, who began to pray in prison in the 1980s and then came upon an antireligious article in the Soviet illustrated weekly magazine *The Flame*. The article told of a Baptist woman, Tanya, whose husband had left her because of her Christian beliefs. Vladimir managed to locate Tanya using the information in the article and sent her a letter. Through subsequent correspondence, she taught him the Baptist gospel, and their acquaintance blossomed into love. The staunchly atheist prison warden discovered Vladimir's conversion and punished him with months in the penalty isolator, but there "he prayed and sang, evangelizing

208   FINDING GOD IN THE GULAG

to his cellmates about Jesus and giving thanks to God." Refusing promises of better treatment if he renounced his new religion, Vladimir was denied letters from Tanya. But eventually, one of his letters proposing marriage got through the censors, and she accepted. They were forbidden to meet, and the warden tried to prevent the wedding, but in the end he was compelled to permit it. They met and were officially married on the same day.[10]

Releases and Changing Conditions, 1986–1988

The marriage of two believers in a Soviet penal facility would never have been possible before the radical reforms that came to define the Gorbachev era. The first sign of change regarding imprisoned believers came at the opening of the famed Reykjavik Summit of October 1986, when Gorbachev released Ratushinskaya, who at that point was well known in the West, as a sign of good faith. (See figure 8.1.) Months later, in February 1987, the Gorbachev regime issued a mass pardon to more than 100 political prisoners convicted of "anti-Soviet agitation and propaganda" and "anti-Soviet slander," including seventeen religious prisoners. The Soviet state, however, continued to deny that political prisoners existed, instead claiming that "unlike legislations in Western states, Soviet laws do not allow prosecution for political dissent." More pardons followed. According to the records of the Keston Center, more than 100 religious prisoners were granted early release in late 1986 and early 1987. By late summer 1987, only 299 known religious prisoners remained in the Soviet Union.[11]

The growing pace of change sparked some misunderstandings. In September 1987, Konstantin Kharchev, chair of the Soviet Council for Religious Affairs, told US senator Richard Lugar that all "prisoners of faith" would be released by November 1987. There was, in fact, another amnesty in November 1987 for the seventieth anniversary of the Bolshevik Revolution, but not all religious inmates were freed. When pressed on this, Kharchev backtracked, claiming he had been misquoted. By early 1988, the Ministry of Internal Affairs claimed it only held eighteen people for "violating laws on religious practice," but the Keston Center had files on more than 200 individuals who were still imprisoned. Many were prosecuted under different statutes, such as "causing a public disturbance" or refusing military service out of religious conviction, and so were not included in the state's official tally.[12]

CHRISTIANITY AS A RE-EDUCATIONAL PROGRAM 209

Figure 8.1 Irina Ratushinskaya with her husband shortly after her release in 1986. Alamy.

The 1988 celebration of one thousand years of Russian Orthodoxy was a pivotal moment in Gorbachev's relationship with Christianity. During the elaborate state-sponsored celebrations, which witnessed a massive outpouring of religiosity among the Soviet population, Gorbachev met with the Orthodox patriarch in the Kremlin, talked about having "common cause" with the church, and promised new legislation that would guarantee true religious liberty. This legislation, which fully legalized all church activities, including the teaching of religion in schools, ultimately passed after lively public debate in September 1990. In the meantime, the state allowed 2,815 Orthodox parishes to officially open in 1989, and thousands more followed over the next two years.[13] Meanwhile, the USSR continued releasing religious prisoners and instructed the police and courts to stop prosecuting people for practicing their faith. Christian prisoners released during this era often joined new Christian ministries or returned to ecclesiastical hierarchies in the Orthodox, Catholic, and other churches. A few, after the fall of the Soviet Union, entered politics: Orthodox priest Gleb Yakunin was elected to the Russian Duma, and the Ukrainian Greek Catholic activist Stepan Khmara was voted into the Ukrainian Parliament.[14]

210   FINDING GOD IN THE GULAG

By March 1989, the Keston Center knew of only seventy-six inmates whom it considered repressed for their religious convictions, almost all of whom had been prosecuted as conscientious objectors to military service. In late 1990, the Jehovah's Witnesses reported that twenty-six inmates from their denomination were still incarcerated for refusing military service. With that important exception, the Soviet Union in the late 1980s had completely abolished imprisonment for religious belief and practice. By late 1990, the Soviet penal system still held between 700,000 and 800,000 inmates, down from more than 1 million under Brezhnev, but virtually none was serving time because of their faith.[15]

In this new climate of tolerance, repression eased for the remaining religious prisoners of the late 1980s. Correspondence and visitation rights increased, and letters with religious content began to be allowed through the prison censors, even those sent to international addresses. In 1988, the USSR allowed Gideons International to distribute Bibles in Soviet penal facilities and permitted lay believers to visit and meet with imprisoned spiritual authorities later that year. As one Pentecostal parishioner reported after meeting with his incarcerated pastor in early 1988, "I went into the meeting room. When Viktor was brought in a few minutes later, I felt a pang in my heart at the sight of him: he was thin and pale and most of his hair had turned grey. But he was full of hope for the future. He told me that he had never doubted that the church of God could overcome everything and stand fast." Father Sigitas Tamkevicius, who later became archbishop of the Catholic Church in Lithuania, wrote of his time in penal colonies in the relaxed state of the Gorbachev era: "In my free time, I read and pondered in my heart the Lord's words. When I lived in freedom, I had many chores and concerns and many things remained unexamined. God brought me to the Urals and provided the setting for a long retreat, that I might better hear the Lord's word."[16]

Christian Ministering in Soviet Places of Confinement

While believers sentenced for their religious practices were set free from the Gulag, other inmates in the late Gorbachev era increasingly converted to Christianity with the blessing of Gulag administrators. This is perhaps the most striking aspect of Gorbachev's penal reforms—that the ideology of corrections quickly swung from being staunchly antireligious to explicitly proreligious. The turning-point year for this ideological transformation

CHRISTIANITY AS A RE-EDUCATIONAL PROGRAM   211

was 1989. The camp newspaper *Rhythm of Work* on April 10, 1989, shared one of the first experiences of prisoners with the return of organized religion to Soviet penal institutions. It described the visit of the Latvian Christian Mission of Mercy, an evangelical organization founded in 1988, to a women's colony. As the author of the newspaper article—an inmate and self-described atheist—described it:

> The whole hall waits with bated breath. The recital (or should I call it a service?) lasts three hours. I want to applaud, but hold myself back—after all, this isn't a concert! They tell us about charitable work, about themselves, about God and people. They sing most beautifully. They have come to us with open hearts and preach about acts of mercy. This is the most important teaching in the Christian faith. They speak about children, mothers, families. A woman sings. I have a lump in my throat. I try to smile, but when I glance around I see that the whole hall is sobbing. For there is something bright, pure, and personal in every soul, which is inexpressible and painful. . . . Maybe this meeting will be the beginning of a new era, an era of mercy, and may our hardened souls become better and more pure.

Indeed, as the author described, this was the beginning of a new era in Soviet corrections. And whether the introduction of Christianity had a noticeable effect on recidivism is unknown, both inmates and guards agreed that it had the potential to make life in the Gulag more tolerable.[17]

Similar missionary activity soon followed. US congressmen Frank Wolf of Virginia and Chris Smith of New Jersey in mid-1989 toured the Perm-35 Colony for political prisoners. They were given full access to the facilities and inmates, and Wolf took pride that the Americans "gave Bibles to everyone that wanted one." At about the same time, a convicted murderer wrote to Orthodox Archbishop Yuvenaly (who worked covertly as a KGB agent in the 1980s), inviting him to visit the corrective-labor colony where he was being held. "I am an atheist probably out of ignorance," he confessed, while expressing a desire to find in religion a sense of morality that Soviet society had not given him. Yuvenaly successfully petitioned the camp commander to allow the visit, and a second letter from the inmate thanked the archbishop for coming and asked for continued visits from a local priest.[18]

A more public acknowledgment of religion's reintroduction into Soviet penal facilities came in July 1989, when the widely read *Literary Gazette* published an article on the visit of Metropolitan Filaret of Kyiv, the

212 FINDING GOD IN THE GULAG

second-highest-ranking Orthodox leader, to the Bucha Maximum-Security Prison. This visit was facilitated by a local government official, who declared, "For several decades our penal corrective system remained unchanged and contributed nothing to the re-education of the inmates. We are now trying to humanize the system. . . . We plan to experiment with letting the Church cooperate with us in the spiritual re-education of incarcerated criminals. We hope the experiment will be successful." Filaret was permitted to address an audience of some 700 inmates, with more listening by radio, and an attending journalist found the prisoners to be receptive to his message. As one remarked, "We have committed faults, but we have been completely rejected. If the Church can help us to regain confidence and to win the trust of the people, I am ready to accept the Ten Commandments of which I had heard in my childhood from our village priest. I am ready to try and make them part of my life."[19]

After the metropolitan's visit, Bibles were added to the prison library, and inmates were allowed to wear crosses. The journalist, meanwhile, wondered if this was the start of a broader trend or if the Ministry of Internal Affairs would clamp down on such local experiments. "Might not some professional atheist [in the upper ranks of the Ministry] even today," he wondered, "consider that the participation of the Church in prison life would adversely influence the scientific, materialist worldview of the prisoners?" But readers of this article were left with no doubt as to the viewpoint of this influential publication: "The Church cannot replace those who are appointed by the state to prevent crimes and to punish for them. But the Church can and must assist those who are incarcerated. It must appeal to their heart and their conscience. I am sure that representatives of all faiths would agree with me."[20]

The first steps of 1989 were soon followed by a rush of evangelizing activity in 1990 and 1991, along with official proclamations that the Gulag administration had embraced religion as a means of re-education. The 1990 law "On the Freedom of Confession" legalized religious practice in places of confinement, and the Corrective-Labor Code was subsequently modified to include a provision for "Securing the Freedom of Conscience of Prisoners." Gulag newspapers such as Tomsk's *On the Right Path* publicized these reforms to ensure that inmates were aware of their new rights. *On the Right Path* also ran a series of articles on "Traditions of the Russian People" which included discussions of important Christian holidays in the Russian Orthodox tradition. The one on Christmas, for instance, noted that "According to the Christian faith this day marks the beginning of the earthly life of God, who came to earth to save mankind." While such a statement is relatively neutral in tone, the article went into great detail about Christmas traditions and then concluded with the thought: "Christmas day is returning to us, and along with it the unbroken thread, which connects us to the spiritual treasures of Russia and the Christian world." Mention of "treasures" leaves no doubt that the author's appraisal of Christian holidays was positive. It is not coincidental that prisoners formally organized a Sunday school at Colony 1 in Tomsk around the same time as these articles appeared.[21]

This dramatic shift in correctional philosophy from being staunchly antireligious to becoming remarkably pro-religious is likewise chronicled on the pages of *Correction and Law and Order*, the monthly professional journal for Soviet penal administrators and guards. The first hint of this shift came only in early 1990, more than a year after priests, pastors, and Bible distributors began visiting correctional facilities. After propagating antireligious messages for decades, the chief Gulag propagandists in Moscow clearly had difficulty adjusting to the new reality. And the first article on religion in 1990 reflects some lingering uncertainty. While it reported on Metropolitan Filaret's visit to the Bucha colony and noted that Orthodox priests, Baptists, and other Christians were visiting penal institutions in Kyiv, Yakutia, and elsewhere, the author's tone is quite hesitant throughout, as if to report on these events but not officially condone them. Still, he did include (while not explicitly agreeing with) a striking quote by the chief political officer of the Kirov Province Department of Internal Affairs, who said, "Lectures and political education can expand one's horizon, but they can't open one's heart. In correctional-labor institutions we need psychologists, but priests are also appropriate."[22]

A few months later, the journal published a much more pro-religious article on the Orthodox convent where a correctional-labor colony was located. It lamented the convent's seizure and the confiscation of valuables by "the heavy hand of the builders of the new society," who failed to understand that "without faith there is no point in life." They destroyed much of the convent and its history, maiming "the people's soul, its memory and history." Criticizing the colony's lack of culture and spirituality, the author concluded, "I am convinced: only by resurrecting spirituality can one talk about re-educating individuals." This explicitly pro-religious message that at once condemned the early days of the Soviet regime and promoted a religious program of correcting inmates was a striking reversal made possible only by the new climate of the late Gorbachev era.[23]

214   FINDING GOD IN THE GULAG

Still, some within the penal apparatus were unconvinced. In June 1990, *Correction and Law and Order* wrote that "more and more often we are receiving letters from [penal] workers, who are speaking out from different, often diametrically opposed, points of view concerning the growing cooperation between our system and the Church, about the participation of religious figures in the re-education of convicts." An attached editorial by experienced Gulag propagandist V. Kalinin then opined that while there were many different opinions regarding religion in prisons, the experience of the West had shown that religion was not some panacea in re-educating inmates. The author mused that the state should not have to pay for spiritual work in the colonies but that inmates should be able to acquire religious literature, wear crosses around their necks, and have specially designated places for prayers in the colonies. However, Kalinin concluded, there should also still be atheistic lectures in the colonies, and the penal system should not allow the Orthodox Church to become involved in decisions concerning early release. Such a statement is unsurprising, as Kalinin represented the old guard in the Gulag apparatus, having served since at least the 1960s. Like others, he was skeptical that introducing religion was a good idea, and contextual clues point to him being a devout atheist.[24]

Yet this marked the last time the Gulag's official propaganda organ would be so conflicted about the place of religion in Soviet prisons and penal colonies. A front inside cover photograph of priests visiting a colony just a few months later, for example, contained the following caption: "Visits by cult workers to correctional-labor institutions, their meetings, conversations with those serving sentences have become fairly regular occurrences in our reality. As a rule, such contacts have a strong positive influence on the convicts. It is not coincidental that of late they have noticeably raised their labor productivity and improved discipline." While the use of the word "cult" was anachronistic, reflective of the atheistic training of whoever wrote the caption, the remainder was unambiguously supportive. Gulag officials were instructed to invite priests to achieve better institutional and re-educational outcomes.[25]

The clearest example of the Gulag's official turn to religion as a re-educational device came toward the end of 1990 in a six-page spread in *Correction and Law and Order* detailing the experience of a corrective-labor institution in Leningrad Province. There had been growing antagonism between the administration and inmates at this colony when the commander, Sergey Matyukhin, decided "we cannot live like this any longer." To defuse

CHRISTIANITY AS A RE-EDUCATIONAL PROGRAM   215

the situation, he invited in a local Orthodox seminary rector, who brought several seminarians with him to meet with the inmates and staff. According to the report, "no activity had ever gathered so many people as this memorial meeting." The meeting was challenging but ultimately productive. Several believing inmates asked for confession and communion, and one asked to be baptized. Over a series of subsequent meetings, religious literature was brought in, space for a new chapel was located, and the ordinances of baptism, confession, and communion were performed. All of this reportedly had a pronounced effect on the internal climate of the colony. Guards and inmates started reading the Bible and working toward building the chapel, and the typical gang-related divisions among prisoners broke down. Even some of the worst-behaved inmates began to change their attitudes. The message here was clear: penal institutions should form close relations with local religious authorities, build chapels, and reap the rewards of improved discipline and better success at transforming criminals into honest, God-fearing citizens.[26]

This point was driven home in another article from early 1991. It told of visits by Orthodox and evangelical Christians to various places of confinement and reported that the spiritual nourishment they brought was "as necessary as air." A recently converted inmate declared, "I want from this day forward, having rejected Satan and having given God an oath to do good deeds and acts, to begin a new life." To confirm this sentiment, a colony commander reportedly said, "Christianity has always given Russians strong spiritual fulfillment. The need for this is especially sharp in places of deprivation of freedom, where the relations between people are seriously deformed." The author then summarized this sentiment of adopting a new Christian worldview: "Militant atheism at one point divided us into two parts—believers and nonbelievers. But really, we are all people, we are all 'brothers and sisters.'"[27]

Similarly to Gulag officials in Moscow, some camp administrators had a difficult time adjusting to these rapid changes of 1989–1990. As late as mid-1990, one Christian prisoner claimed that guards had beaten him up because he owned a Bible, which they had confiscated. An account of two sisters in the Christian mission called "Agape" lamented that the commander of a strict-regimen colony in Komi was extremely reluctant to allow missionaries to visit one of his inmates. Another inmate expressed in a letter to Heather Keston just five days before Gorbachev's resignation, "Here many believe in God and Jesus Christ, but for us here there is very little

216 FINDING GOD IN THE GULAG

Divine literature. . . . And we would like to know more about my country, about God and about everything holy." Clearly, there was some variability across institutions and individuals regarding how this new emphasis on religion should be administered. But incidents of beatings and confiscated religious literature became rare as the Gorbachev era progressed. Increasingly, Gulag workers seemed to accept the new emphasis on spirituality behind bars. The *Lutheran World Herald* reported in August 1990 that, with the assistance of Gideon International and with no resistance from camp administrators, "two hundred inmates of the Moscow prison No. 2 have each been given a copy of the New Testament at the personal wish of the prisoners themselves."[28]

The year 1990 marked a dramatic expansion of Christian ministries to Soviet places, often with the intended effect of converting inmates. The Orthodox and True Orthodox churches were active, as were various "charismatic churches," particularly youth-oriented Pentecostal groups. One organized "a large-scale evangelization train that covered several thousand kilometers in Siberia on its journey from Abakan to Khabarovsk, stopping for prison visits on the way." In Minsk and Kyiv, local Baptist pastors told of letters from inmates all over the USSR requesting Bibles and ministering visits. As described by pastor Jacob Dukhonchenko, who visited a penal institution in Kyiv, the prison officials first mocked the guests, doubtful that the inmates would listen to their religious message. Indeed, Dukhonchenko remembered feeling "the tension" of religion and politics as they entered the room. But after a two-hour service in front of 700 inmates, "I finally asked those who wanted to join us in prayer to stand up, [and] everyone did!" One inmate after the meeting said to him: "We have lost faith in everything and have never met anybody who really cared for us. We can never become what you are, but after today neither will we ever be the same again."[29]

Not surprisingly, Baptists were among the most active in ministering to Soviet prisoners. A report on the operation of the women's section of the Evangelical Christian Baptist Church described the effect of these operations:

> As 1989 ended, the doors of labour camps and prisons opened to believers and they went in to witness to sinners about the Word of God "to take the light to those who sit in darkness." With love, wisdom, patience, and often tears, the sisters witness to convicts—men, women, and teenagers. From everywhere comes the call "Visit us in prison!"

CHRISTIANITY AS A RE-EDUCATIONAL PROGRAM   217

Already we have established a good relationship with the administration of several prisons. The women witness through services, church music concerts, one-to-one talks, and pen-pals who write to the prisoners. Many letters find their way to churches and missions. They speak of all kinds of human experiences—doubt, despair, hope.

And there are questions, questions, questions. . . . How can I find God? How can my faith grow, living like this? Where do I find the strength so I can fight against evil? Our sisters write back to these imprisoned brothers and sisters in Christ. Often they write at night, the only time they have free from their families. For they believe the Word of God is not barren, but that it bears fruit. Already they can see those fruits.

Several prison administrators report that their prisoners have changed beyond all recognition. Sheep have been made of wolves. In these confined spaces, prisoners are being baptized in the faith.

This report then described a hunger strike and potential riot in one prison averted only when a beloved Baptist couple called to mediate the dispute chastised the inmates and admonished them to replace their hunger strike with fasting and their disobedience with reliance on God. Religion could, in fact, be used as a disciplinary device.[30] But it was also a very intimate source of hope and joy. A letter sent by inmate Victor Volkov to the Baptist publication *Brotherly Messenger*, which by this point was being distributed in many penal institutions, illustrates the deeply personal effect of these ministries. The author wrote of his gratitude to his "brothers and sisters in Christ" who traveled from Ukraine to visit. "I am grateful that they brought light with them, the word of God, and goodness to us sinners, isolated as a punishment for our crimes before God, before mankind, and before the law." Especially poignant for him was one of the Baptist women singing at the event:

She stood on the stage among her brothers and sisters, and sang for us and wept. Her tears pierced the very depths of my soul. At the end of the concert, I went up to her and asked "Why are you crying?" She replied that not long ago her daughter had been murdered. The murderer is soon to be tried, but she has already forgiven him. The tears and words of this suffering woman touched me to my very soul. I tried to comfort her, said I was sorry, but the words stuck in my throat. For I myself murdered a man five years before. I am repenting for this act before God.

218 FINDING GOD IN THE GULAG

A similar letter from a female inmate, Natasha, likewise thanked a Baptist woman for bringing her to the knowledge of Christ. "Dear Vera," she wrote, "how much I have lost, how late I have come to know our Saviour! And yet I did come to know Him, thanks to you." She reported studying the Bible, drawing religious sketches to submit to the *Brotherly Messenger*, musing on the ability to forgive those who mistreat you, and desiring to share the gospel of Jesus Christ with those around her. Then, at the end of her letter, betraying the novelty of her newfound faith, she asked her spiritual mentor about convents, wondering if there was "a chance of striking up a correspondence with a nun." Although she did not yet understand the difference between the various Christian religions, conflating the historical practice of monasticism in Russian Orthodoxy with that of her new Baptist faith, Natasha demonstrated enthusiasm for her new religious worldview.[31]

Seventh-Day Adventists also quickly organized prison ministries in 1989–1990 in places as distant as the Baltics and Siberia. According to one account, the first sanctioned chapel in a Soviet place of detention was created after petitions from Adventist inmates for a dedicated prayer room were approved. Another account of Adventists ministering to inmates in a camp in the Ural Mountains concerned the prisoner Nikolai Koroblyov, who asked to be baptized after a period of Bible study. An Adventist pastor from Sverdlovsk was permitted into the camp to perform the baptism, but some confusion ensued when the pastor insisted that it take place in a nearby river, outside the camp's confines, so that it could be performed by total immersion according to Adventist beliefs. In granting approval, camp authorities no doubt thought that the baptism would be done through the sprinkling of water according to the Orthodox tradition. After four days, approval to hold the baptism in the river was finally granted, and the pastor recounted of the ceremony: "On the riverbank stood the guards with a dog beside them, while Nikolai and I walked into the freezing water of the river Sosva, which had recently thawed. . . . We felt the presence of God." Koroblyov was then permitted to hold a prayer meeting in the camp, and the camp administration reportedly even asked for a recording of the meeting so it could be broadcast on the camp radio.[32]

In the Caucasus and elsewhere, inmates and prison staff began building mosques in places of confinement, but evangelical groups also visited these traditionally Muslim areas of the Soviet Union. Inmate A. Sidikov in Tajikistan, for instance, reported in the local camp newspaper in late 1990 that a group came and showed a film titled *Jesus*. As he wrote, "Before the showing and after it the representative of the society talked a lot about God, who in their estimation, really does exist. The same people gave us the Gospels and personal Bibles, along with the book *Where is Truth?*" According to Sidikov, such efforts had a transformative effect. "I don't know about others," he wrote, "but they convinced me that God was, is, and will be. I understood that the most important thing in life is to keep one's spirits up, be brave and patient, just like the Lord was, and he will support us. Let's stop engaging in dirty affairs, and instead bring all our efforts to make things better for those who stand in need of help. Let's ourselves be clean, just as Jesus Christ was!"[33]

Christian groups from Europe and the United States were also active in ministering to Soviet inmates. In late 1991, the American pastor Joe Harmon visited a colony in Tomsk and distributed a pamphlet about how God loves all people, regardless of their sins, and how he stands ready to save all people. Harmon then talked about his life spent preaching a simple, nondenominational Christianity in prisons in the United States. "As a teacher," he reportedly told the Soviet prisoners, "I just consider it my duty to help prisoners understand who Jesus Christ is, I teach his teachings so that these people can follow his teachings and discover how they can lead better lives. In general, I think that this is more than teaching because it brings to prisoners a kind of happiness. They start to think much better about themselves." He then concluded his thoughts by saying, "I would like for people to accept faith in Jesus Christ, because this faith is the answer to all difficult questions. . . . It makes life much easier, it provides a goal in life, a meaning."[34]

William Cedfeldt, a member of the American Bible Society, reported in 1991 that he visited a penal facility outside Leningrad and found an Orthodox priest, Father Vladimir, bringing Bibles to the inmates and ministering to them. As Cedfeldt described it, "It was clear that the commandant had a deep affection for Father Vladimir, and he said that the prison had become much easier to run since his visits because many prisoners have become Christians, and the atmosphere is far better overall with less fighting and trouble." In fact, the prisoners had already begun building a chapel. Cedfeldt also visited a women's facility in Estonia and reported, "I was amazed by the number of women who were interested in 'religion,' particularly among the younger inmates. As I talked about the purpose of our visit, and assured them that we are all God's children, created by him, and that he loves us regardless of our past, or future, many nodded their heads in agreement, and some were

220   FINDING GOD IN THE GULAG

deeply moved." He left, having arranged to provide more Bibles for these incarcerated Soviet inmates.[35]

But while Baptists, Adventists, and others from both the USSR and abroad actively ministered to Soviet inmates in the late Gorbachev era, the Orthodox Church was the most involved in introducing spirituality into the Soviet Gulag. This sprang naturally from its thousand-year history of spiritual dominance in Russia and its official recognition by the Soviet state. In Zagorsk (soon returned to its pre-Soviet name of Sergiyev Posad), which housed the most famous monastery in Russia, Orthodox priests and young seminarians began visiting inmates at the local prison in 1989. During the brutal winter of 1989–1991, when societal breakdown resulted in food shortages, they brought provisions for inmates. And upon discovering that camp authorities had converted a former chapel in the prison building into two separate cells, they persuaded the commander to restore it. Although hesitant initially, he soon became enthusiastic and even "had a video made to record the positive impact of religion within the prison regime." The restored chapel was dedicated through a liturgical service on Pentecost in early 1991 that was marked by a sparrow entering a window of the chapel. Drawing on the biblical parallel to God's Spirit descending like a dove on Jesus Christ, Father Nikodim instructed the inmates, "Today God has seen fit to grace us with a sparrow, for even though we are prisoners we are loved by him." When asked about his prison's respectful and peaceful state sometime later, the commander credited the priests, remarking that "they have touched us and brought us peace."[36]

Similar occurrences happened all over the Soviet Union. Moscow's infamous Butyrka Prison illustrates the swiftness with which some penal officials embraced Orthodoxy, though many Orthodox activists initially came from outside the official hierarchy. The first priest—Father Stepan from the Bogorodichny Center (a popular though unsanctioned movement within Russian Orthodoxy at the time)—began visiting inmates already in 1989. According to one account from shortly after the fall of communism, "his visits to the prison have been so successful that Gennady Oreshin, the prison governor, asked for a priest to join his staff. 'We will give him everything! We will build a chapel!' he cried." Yakunin, another Orthodox priest who positioned himself outside the confines of the official Orthodox hierarchy, also visited Butyrka to conduct liturgical services. For Yakunin, a prisoner from 1980 to 1987 for his attempts to defend freedom of conscience and

CHRISTIANITY AS A RE-EDUCATIONAL PROGRAM 221

religious worship in the Soviet Union, this must have felt like a personal triumph of religion over atheism. And he was far from alone. Yakunin and other former inmates no doubt relished the chance to return to Soviet prisons and camps and preach the very things that they were forbidden to openly discuss while they were incarcerated.[37] (See figure 8.2.)

Figure 8.2 Gleb Yakunin (center, in priestly garb) at the dedication of the Solovetsky Stone, Lubyanka Square, Moscow, October 30, 1991. Wikimedia Commons.

222 FINDING GOD IN THE GULAG

Believers and outside observers marveled at how quickly the Soviet Union generally and the Gulag specifically abandoned the ideology of atheism in favor of Christianity. In just five years, the country went from locking people up for openly expressing their beliefs to allowing Christian groups into the prisons to convert felons to the gospel of Jesus Christ. Meanwhile, disillusionment with Soviet-style socialism snowballed rapidly, and so even as Gorbachev and others hoped to use religion to infuse new life into socialism and to bring peace and productivity into Soviet penal facilities, religious conversion more often helped persuade people to reject Soviet-style socialism altogether. Decades of persecution and ridicule from communist authorities could not be forgotten in just a few years. Even religious figures previously loyal to the USSR began calling for its downfall.

For many believers, the collapse of the Soviet Union on December 25, 1991—Christmas Day for Catholics and Protestants—bore the hallmarks of a sign from God that the government of the Antichrist had been defeated. No doubt some of them, particularly those who had endured repression and imprisonment, felt gratified that they had played a small role in its demise. They undoubtedly also remembered those who perished in the fight to maintain religious life in the Soviet Union generally and in the Gulag specifically. Flung into unmarked graves throughout the vast expanse of Soviet space, they made the ultimate sacrifice in imitation of Jesus Christ. Whether Orthodox, Catholic, Lutheran, Baptist, Adventist, or Jehovah's Witnesses, Christians throughout the Soviet era chose prison or death as martyrs rather than abandoning their beliefs. As they viewed it, whether they died prematurely or outlived the Soviet Union, they had overcome Satan.

Epilogue

But I, while still living,
To love and to toil,
Will not name their names,
Let them before God repent.
　　　—Vladimir Trubitsyn, *Ochnaia stavka* (The Confrontation)[1]

Continued religious revivalism across the various successor states, including the Russian Federation, accompanied the collapse of the Soviet Union. The government returned many churches and monasteries appropriated by the Soviet state to the Orthodox Church, which also constructed hundreds of new chapels across the country. Attendance at church services soared, as did the sale of religious literature. It became fashionable for politicians, businesspeople, and young people to be baptized and publicly wear crosses around their necks. Foreign missionaries from dozens of Christian denominations erected churches and competed for converts. Millions of Russians, after seven decades of communist rule, embraced faith as a vital component of everyday life.

In the Russian prison system, which in many respects changed little following the collapse of the Soviet Union, officials and propagandists deepened their embrace of religion as a means of effecting personal transformation and creating a more docile inmate population. The Tomsk newspaper for inmates, for instance, chronicled visits by foreign evangelical groups, discussions about religious holidays, and visits by local Orthodox priests and spoke of religion as an unambiguously positive force in transforming humankind for good. On January 5, 1993, the editorial board instructed its readers, "You well know that lately here in Russia all efforts have been made to renew Russian spirituality and culture. And if each of you brings your thoughts to order, then you will understand that this is a very important and necessary process. And each of us, turning to religious culture and

224 EPILOGUE

immersing themselves in it, will anew obtain kindness, faith, and hope." Marxist theories of economic determinism had been replaced by spiritual nationalism.[2]

A similar message was broadcast to post-Soviet guards and administrators in their monthly professional journal, *Correction and Law and Order*. One chronicled new regulations issued by the Ministry of Internal Affairs for working with religious organizations, mandating that a specific building or room be devoted solely to worship and that study groups, Sunday schools, and other religiously themed events should be organized. Others told of spiritually triumphal visits by American evangelicals or local Orthodox priests. But perhaps most poignant was the cover page of the third issue of this journal in 1993. It featured the image of a Renaissance-era Madonna with Child and, in a smaller inset picture, a close-up of an inmate mother (evident by the tattoo on her breast) nursing an infant. The symbolism of associating a female convict and her son with the Virgin Mary and Jesus is unmistakable: even the worst of sinners can become pure like Mary. Upon opening the front cover, readers found a large photo montage depicting an Orthodox chapel, an inmate inside the chapel, icons adorning its interior walls, and a prisoner kissing a relic with other inmates and a priest looking on. The associated caption declared: "Services are held triumphantly in the Orthodox church constructed by prisoners on the territory of one of the colonies in Saratov Province. Belief in God can help anyone find spiritual comfort."[3]

By the mid-1990s, worship services, Bible classes, confession, baptisms, weddings, and visits from local priests and foreign missionaries played a significant educational and social role in Russian places of incarceration. One women's colony in 1994 reported being affiliated with a local convent, with much interaction between the inmates and the nuns. An inmate in another penal facility in Nizhny Tagil in 2001 remarked to a visiting journalist that "the chapel here makes a real difference. It is the only thing of beauty and the only place where prisoners and guards are all the same." This was no exaggeration. Massive funding shortages meant that the penal system remained dilapidated, disease-ridden, violent, and corrupt during the 1990s and beyond. Amid such stark realities, religion for some inmates helped temper the acute pains of imprisonment, though it never fully delivered on the promises of order and personal transformation made in the optimistic era of the early 1990s.[4]

In the 2000s, the initial surge of interest in religion in post-Soviet Russia subsided to some extent, but Vladimir Putin hastened a process begun by his predecessor, Boris Yeltsin, to forge ever-closer ties between the state and Russian Orthodoxy. For Putin, this was a matter of promoting his ruling ideology of Russian nationalism, with Orthodoxy becoming the de facto state religion. At the same time, various efforts were made to curtail the activities of "foreign" churches—especially Scientology and the Jehovah's Witnesses. As part of this campaign to strengthen Orthodoxy, Putin made numerous well-publicized visits to holy sites, funded restoration efforts at temples and monasteries across Russia, and cultivated a close friendship with Patriarch Kirill, head of the Russian Orthodox Church starting in 2009.

This process of strengthening ties between church and state was not wholly unforeseen. As one observer in 1992 discerned, the religious flowering in Russian places of confinement would inevitably bring conflict as the Russian Orthodox Church reasserted its dominance in public life: "It is only a matter of time before an attempt is made to install Orthodox priests as the official representatives of Christianity in prisons. But the Protestants still hold some winning cards. They are a more active group; they suffered greater repression and are renowned among prisoners—and therefore they have greater opportunities for outreach." Yet, though energetic, Protestant groups were slowly removed from the life of Russian prisons as Orthodoxy cemented its position as the dominant religion endorsed by the state. The first post-Soviet head of the Russian Orthodox Church, Patriarch Alexy II, took pride in this work and remarked that ministering to prisoners in Russia "has long and deep traditions that were, unfortunately, largely severed in the years of totalitarianism but which are now, by God's mercy, being again revived." For Alexy, prison service was a noble, God-given labor of love that brought sinners to repentance and a new spiritual life marked by righteousness and honesty. It was also, he wrote, a necessary part of correctional institutions, calling on guards to "remember the souls of those entrusted to them" and on Christians everywhere "to extend a hand to the fallen." By the early 2000s, virtually every place of incarceration in Russia had an Orthodox chapel or prayer room, while visits from other groups quickly diminished.[5]

Observers of contemporary Russian prisons, however, note that Christianity under Putin, perhaps precisely because the state co-opted it, played an increasingly minor role in a system better known for violence, corruption, forced labor, and the withholding of proper medical and psychological services from prisoners. Alexei Navalny, then a well-known political prisoner for his opposition to Putin's dictatorial regime, bitterly remarked in 2023, "Russia's prison system is just like the Soviet Gulag, only with a chapel

226   EPILOGUE

in every zone." To some extent, Orthodox Christianity has become the functional equivalent of Marxist propaganda in the Soviet era, with neither the modern Russian regime nor the Soviet Union able to wield them effectively to re-educate their inmates. Under both regimes, inmates remain skeptical of heavy-handed efforts by prison officials to indoctrinate them.[6]

Sites of Memory

The legacies of Christian life in the Gulag not only persist in the post-Soviet Russian penal system; they are also evident in numerous monuments dedicated to Gulag victims. Not all Gulag monuments bear religious symbolism, but many do. One of the largest and earliest Gulag monuments is the Mask of Sorrow, erected in the far northeastern city of Magadan in 1996. It depicts a montage of distressed faces alongside a prominent cross carved into the granite on the front side; the back displays a bronze statue of a prisoner being crucified on a second cross while a young girl weeps beneath. Below the central monument, religious insignia of varied faiths—Orthodoxy, Catholicism, Islam, Judaism, and Buddhism—are carved onto several smaller stones (with the Jewish Star of David bearing anti-Semitic graffiti on the day I visited in the late 1990s). The central message is unmistakable: this is a place where the faithful were tortured and killed. (See figure E.1.)

Similar religious imagery abounds in other monuments erected in the 1990s and beyond. In Norilsk, the Golgotha memorial complex replicates this idea of Christian suffering in its name—a reference to the hill where Christ was crucified—and the numerous crosses (and a menorah) scattered on the large site. In Yekaterinburg, a massive cross dedicated to Gulag victims stands near the site of a mass grave. In Omsk, an Orthodox chapel stands on a former Gulag camp to commemorate those who died. Countries outside Russia also employ religious imagery in Gulag monuments. In Kengir, Kazakhstan, Christian crosses adorn a windswept hill where the camp cemetery once stood. And in Warsaw, the Monument to the Fallen and Murdered in the East depicts an old flatbed rail car laden with dozens of large crosses (as well as a few Jewish and Muslim symbols), symbolizing Poles who died in the Gulag and at the hands of the Soviet secret police.[7]

The most evocative site memorializing Christians killed or sent to the Gulag by the Soviet regime is at Butovo, on the outskirts of Moscow. Butovo was the site of mass executions during the Great Terror and a burial place

Figure E.1 Mask of Sorrows, Magadan. Wikimedia Commons.

for Gulag prisoners in the following years. Tens of thousands of people of various nationalities and faiths lie buried there, but beginning in 1995, the Orthodox Church has gradually turned this site into a shrine dedicated to the "new martyrs"—Orthodox clerics killed by the secret police. An enormous cross brought from Solovki marks the connection between different

228 EPILOGUE

eras of Soviet repression, and numerous other crosses and monuments commemorate victims of the Gulag and the Great Terror. Most stunning is the ornate Temple of the New Martyrs and Confessors of Russians, which features several colorful frescoes depicting Soviet agents gunning down innocent Christians. (See figure E.2.) To the outside observer, this appears as jarring imagery in a place of worship, but it is in line with Putin's spiritual-nationalist vision for Russia, which embraces violent imagery to cement ideas of both triumph and victimhood. Butovo is not just a place of mourning; it is a place for church and state to construct a particular narrative about both past and present.[8]

Not surprisingly, the Gulag's memory is hotly contested in Russia. At Butovo, those of other faiths or of no faith who were killed are hardly remembered amid the memorials to Orthodox victims. However, Christian victims of Stalinist terror are surprisingly absent at other memorial sites, including the state-funded Gulag Museum in Moscow. The public memory of the Gulag, told through memoirs, monuments, and museums, is fragmented, but perhaps this is the only possible outcome of such a complex phenomenon that touched every layer of Soviet society.

In June 2016, I spent several days on the Solovetsky Islands, visiting the sites of worship and suffering that so many Soviet inmates experienced nearly one hundred years previously. Scaffolding, wheelbarrows, freshly

Figure E.2 Fresco from the interior of the Temple of the New Martyrs and Confessors of Russians, Butovo. Author's photograph.

whitewashed walls, and a host of busy construction workers bore testament to Solovki's transformation. After decades of neglect, the monasteries were being restored to their former glory, with funding from the Orthodox Church and the Russian government. A cramped museum in a former prison barrack exhibited artifacts, photographs, and documents from the labor camp. Monuments in a small city park commemorated members of various ethnic and social groups who served time there in the 1920s. Bookstores sold memoirs of former inmates. Tour guides at the monastic-outposts-turned-penalty-isolators at Sekirnaya Gora and Bolshoy Zayatsky Island told of the brutal conditions and violence experienced by unfortunate prisoners. And cemeteries of marked and unmarked graves testified to those who never returned from the wastelands of the Far North. The religious infrastructure of the ancient monastery, erased by the Soviet regime, is being rebuilt. So, too, is the memory of the countless imprisoned Christians who, both at Solovki and throughout the Soviet space, suffered and died for their faith.

Notes

Preface

1. Solzhenitsyn, *One Day in the Life*, 28, 120, 181, 198; 1 Peter 4:16, King James Version.
2. Hardy, *Gulag after Stalin.*

Acknowledgments

1. Hardy, "Religious Identity, Practice, and Hierarchy."

Introduction

1. GARF, f. A-353, op. 3, d. 737.
2. Likhachev, *Reflections on the Russian Soul*, 98.
3. Dennen, "'And I Will Tell,'" 170.
4. Adams, *Politics of Punishment*; Gentes, *Exile to Siberia*; Beer, *House of the Dead*; Garland, *Punishment and Modern Society*; Morris and Rothman, *Oxford History of the Prison.*
5. Cooper, "English Quakers"; Skotnicki, *Religion.*
6. Jakobson, *Origins of the Gulag*, 18–90; Applebaum, *Gulag*, 3–17.
7. Kokurin and Petrov, *Gulag*, 15–17; Vinogradov, Litvin, and Khristoforov, *Arkhiv VChK*, 145–147.
8. GARF, f. R-4042, op. 4, d. 158, ll. 210–211; Jakobson, *Origins of the Gulag*; Shelley, "Soviet Criminology."
9. Hardy, *Soviet Gulag*; David-Fox, *Soviet Gulag.*
10. Gregory and Lazarev, *Economics of Forced Labor.*
11. Alexopoulos, *Illness and Inhumanity.*
12. Kokurin and Petrov, *Gulag*, 14; Vinogradov, Litvin, and Khristoforov, *Arkhiv VChK*, 83, 339–341.
13. Ellis, *Russian Orthodox Church*; Strickland, *Making of Holy Russia.*
14. Lenin, "Attitude of the Workers' Party," 402; Vinogradov, Litvin, and Khristoforov, *Arkhiv VChK*, 84, 104, 295; Rendle, "Mercy amid Terror"; Peris, *Storming the Heavens*; Froese, *Plot to Kill God.*
15. Husband, "Godless Communists," 3–68.
16. Roslof, *Red Priests.*
17. Lobanov, *Patriarkh Tikhon*; Husband, "Godless Communists," 130.
18. Orsi, *History and Presence*, 66.

Chapter 1

1. GARF, f. R-393, op. 89, d. 203, l. 36.
2. GARF, f. A-353, op. 4, d. 382, l. 88; GARF, f. A-353, op. 8, d. 8, l. 13.
3. Kelly, "Socialist Churches."
4. GARF, f. R-393, op. 89, d. 240, ll. 20–24; GARF, f. A-353, op. 6, d. 55, l. 49; Ivanova, *Istoriia GULAGa*, 133.
5. GARF, f. R-4042, op. 1a, d. 11, ll. 46, 53, 80–85.
6. GARF, f. R-4042, op. 1a, d. 11, ll. 3, 55–56; GARF, f. R-4042, op. 1a, d. 18, l. 78.

232 NOTES

7. GARF, f. R-393, op. 89, d. 203, l. 193; GARF, f. R-4042, op. 1a, d. 16, ll. 2a, 6, 18, 27, 32; GARF, f. R-4042, op. 1a, d. 32, l. 141; GARF, f. R-4042, op. 2, d. 284, l. 36; GARF, f. R-4042, op. 1a, d. 2a, l. 37a; GARF, f. R-4042, op. 1a, d. 18, l. 26; GARF, f. R-4042, op. 1a, d. 26, l. 183; Tolstaia, *Probleski vo t'me*, 51.
8. GARF, f. R-4042, op. 1a, d. 39, l. 69.
9. GARF, f. R-393, op. 89, d. 87, l. 6; Kurakina, "Vospominaniia kniagini T. G. Kurakinoi," 211.
10. GARF, f. R-393, op. 89, d. 246, l. 4.
11. GARF, f. A-353, op. 3, d. 638, l. 30.
12. GARF, f. A-353, op. 3, d. 640, l. 1.
13. GARF, f. A-353, op. 3, d. 640, ll. 2–41.
14. GARF, f. A-353, op. 3, d. 640, ll. 10, 12, 25–28, 32–33, 35.
15. GARF, f. A-353, op. 3, d. 640, ll. 5–7.
16. GARF, f. A-353, op. 3, d. 640, ll. 11, 14, 18.
17. GARF, f. A-353, op. 3, d. 640, ll. 18, 33.
18. GARF, f. A-353, op. 3, d. 640, ll. 25–26, 27–38.
19. GARF, f. A-353, op. 3, d. 638, l. 51; GARF, f. A-353, op. 3, d. 641, l. 5.
20. GARF, f. A-353, op. 3, d. 636, ll. 6–7.
21. GARF, f. A-353, op. 3, d. 636, ll. 5, 8.
22. Martsinkovsky, *Zapiski veruiushchego*, 169–171.
23. MEMO, f. 2, op. 2, d. 39, ll. 5–21.
24. Martsinkovsky, *Zapiski veruiushchego*, 130–134.
25. Martsinkovsky, *Zapiski veruiushchego*, 153–157, 181–184, 186–191.
26. Martsinkovsky, *Zapiski veruiushchego*, 175–177.
27. Fudel', *Sobranie sochinenii*, 86–89, 92–95.
28. Freeze, "Subversive Atheism," 27.
29. Kokurin and Petrov, *Gulag*, 30–31, 41; Zakliuchennyi, "Pervyi shag bezbozhnika," *Golos zakliuchennogo*, no. 99 (February 1926).
30. GARF, f. R-4042, op. 4, d. 3, ll. 17–18.
31. GARF, f. R-4042, op. 4, d. 64, l. 23; GARF, f. R-4042, op. 4, d. 139, ll. 2, 360, 366–368; GARF, f. R-4042, op. 4, d. 146, l. 43; GARF, f. R-4042, op. 1, d. 123, ll. 23–26; GARF, f. R-4042, op. 4, d. 76, ll. 2–3.
32. Martsinkovsky, *Zapiski veruiushchego*, 148.
33. GARF, f. A-353, op. 6, d. 68, l. 70; GARF, f. R-393, op. 89, d. 204, l. 57; GARF, f. R-4042, op. 4, d. 4, ll. 42–43; GARF, f. R-4042, op. 4, d. 25, l. 9; GARF, f. R-4042, op. 4, d. 79, ll. 1–96, 152; GARF, f. R-4042, op. 4, d. 139, ll. 360, 366; U. V. Ch., "Programma kruzhka bezbozhnikov," *Golos zakliuchennogo*, no. 101 (April 1926).
34. Gorcheva, *Pressa Gulaga*, 25–42; GARF, f. A-353, op. 6, d. 48, l. 5; GARF, f. R-4042, op. 4, d. 28, l. 98.
35. GARF, f. A-353, op. 6, d. 48, ll. 7, 10, 19, 28–29.
36. St. Plotnik, "Ia molilsia," *Za zheleznoi reshetkoi*, 1923, no. 4 (September), 31; St. Plotnik, "Spasibo," *Za zheleznoi reshetkoi*, 1923, no. 6 (December): 6; M. Tanygin, "Dva kuma," *Za zheleznoi reshetkoi*, 1924, nos. 2–3 (March): 66.
37. Shafiro, "Bezbozhie rastet," *Golos zakliuchennogo*, no. 57 (January 1925).
38. Stepanov, "Bezbozhnik," *Golos zakliuchennogo*, no. 57 (January 1925); Verak, "Antireligioznoe," *Golos zakliuchennogo*, no. 73 (May 1925).
39. Akimov, "Otzhivshii apostol," *Golos zakliuchennogo*, no. 57 (January 1925); Shparberga, "Bros', batia!," Priamoi, *Golos zakliuchennogo*, no. 63 (February 1925); "Obmanutaia popami," *Golos zakliuchennogo*, no. 100 (March 1926).
40. Skorodumov, "Dela grekhovnye," *Golos zakliuchennogo*, no. 43 (October 1924).
41. GARF, f. A-353, op. 3, d. 330, l. 14; GARF, f. R-4042, op. 4, d. 183, ll. 53–59.
42. GARF, f. R-4042, op. 1, d. 14, l. 130.

Chapter 2

1. Rakhmankulov, "Nasha federatsiia," *Golos zakliuchennogo*, no. 21 (March 1924); Nagan, "Stranitsa geografii," *Golos zakliuchennogo*, no. 22 (April 1924).
2. David-Fox, *Showcasing the Great Experiment*, 148–158; Solonevich, "Molodezh' v GPU," 374; Soshina, *Na Solovkakh protiv voli*, 163–164; Vtorova-Iafa, "Avgurovy ostrova," 397.
3. Robson, *Solovki*, 6–196; Florenskii, "Solovki," 63–85.

NOTES   233

4. Robson, *Solovki*, 197–206; Florenskii, "Solovki," 86–97; Kokurin and Petrov, *GULAG*, 29–30; Brodskii, *Solovki: Labirint preobrazhenii*, 49–50; Smirnov, *Sistema ispravitel'no-trudovykh lagerei*, 317.
5. Berkman, *Letters*, 211.
6. Klinger, "Solovetskaia katorga," 104; Mal'sagov, "Adskii ostrov," 379; Bessonov, "Dvadtsat' shest' tiurem," 462–463; Sapir, "Puteshestvie v severnye lageria," 138–139.
7. Klinger, "Solovetskaia katorga," 52, 105–106; Sapir, "Puteshestvie v severnye lageria," 138; Mal'sagov, "Adskii ostrov," 401; Zaitsev, "Solovki," 261; Osipova, 'V iazvakh svoikh', 50–51; Rozanov, *Solovetskii kontslager'*, 233; Leonardovich, "Na ostravakh pytok i smerti," 629; Soshina, *Na Solovkakh protiv voli*, 21, 147, 196–197; Rayner, *Criminal Code*, 30–31; Pol'skii, "Publikatsii o Solovkakh," 60–61; Feodosii, "Moi vospominaniia," 96; Brodskii, *Solovki: Dvadtsat' let*, 211.
8. Chirkov, *A bylo vse tak*, 12–13, cited in Gullotta, *Intellectual Life*, 78; Likhachev, *Reflections*, 90.
9. Brodskii, *Solovki: Dvadtsat' let*, 49; Kureishi, "Piat' let," 118; Berkman, *Letters*, 189.
10. Pol'skii, "Publikatsii o Solovkakh," 55–57; Vtorova-Iafa, "Avgurovy ostrova," 396.
11. Vtorova-Iafa, "Avgurovy ostrova," 406; Klinger, "Solovetskaia katorga," 58, 90–92; Rozanov, *Solovetskii kontslager'*, 233; Pol'skii, "Publikatsii o Solovkakh," 59–60; Likhachev, *Reflections*, 95; Volkov, "Pogruzhenie vo tmu," 236; Sederkhol'm, "V razboinnom stane," 702; Brodskii, *Solovki: Dvadtsat' let*, 215.
12. Zaitsev, "Solovki," 223, 262, 269–272; Mal'sagov, "Adskii ostrov," 413; Olekhnovich, "V kogtiakh GPU," 555; Andreevskii, "Katakombnye bogosluzheniia," 311; Petrov, "Vospominaniia izgnannika," 71, 99.
13. Sederkhol'm, "V razboinnom stane," 700–701.
14. Likhachev, *Reflections*, 122; Rozanov, *Solovetskii kontslager'*, 246–247; Nikonov-Smorodin, "Krasnaia katorga," 157–159; Olekhnovich, "V kogtiakh GPU," 560–561.
15. N. Mikhailov, "Monakhu," *SLON*, no. 5 (July 1925): 42; "Proshchai Bog!" *Novye Solovki*, April 12, 1925; Kai, "Paskha," *SLON*, no. 3 (May 1924): 12–13.
16. "Karrikatury—vera," *SLON*, no. 5 (July 1924): 66.
17. "Solovetskii Kreml' i dok" and "Trud pobedil," *Novye Solovki*, June 7, 1925.
18. Soshina, *Na Solovkakh protiv voli*, 33–34; Szabados, *Dvadtsat' piat' let v SSSR*, chap. 23; Brodskii, *Solovki: Dvadtsat' let*, 233; Zaitsev, "Solovki," 207–209; Vtorova-Iafa, "Avgurovy ostrova," 464–465; Kiselev-Gromov, *S.L.O.N.*, 47.
19. Zaitsev, "Solovki," 225; Pol'skii, "Publikatsii o Solovkakh," 61; Petrov, "Vospominaniia izgnannika," 102.
20. Robson, *Solovki*, 221; Zaitsev, "Solovki," 262; Klinger, "Solovetskaia katorga," 79; Likhachev, *Reflections*, 94, 103; Pol'skii, "Publikatsii o Solovkakh," 71; Andreev, "Solovetskie ostrova," 126; Volkov, "Pogruzhenie vo t'mu," 237; Feodosii, "Moi vospominaniia," 77–78, 81–85; Cherkasov, *Solovki*.
21. Klinger, "Solovetskaia katorga," 79; Rozanov, *Solovetskii kontslager'*, 259; Petrov, "Vospominaniia izgnannika," 102–103; Chernavin, "Zapiski 'vreditelia,'" 319.
22. Andreevskii, "Gruppa monakhin," 323–327.
23. Feodosii, "Moi vospominaniia," 77–78, 81–85, 88.
24. Leonardovich, "Na ostravakh pytok i smerti," 617–618.
25. Zaitsev, "Solovki," 264–268.
26. Feodosii, "Moi vospominaniia," 96–97.
27. Volkov, "Pogruzhenie vo tmu," 238–239; Cherkasov, *Solovki*; Zaitsev, "Solovki," 264–267; Andreev, "Solovetskie ostrova," 178; Shaufel'berger, "Solovki," 649–650; Nikonov-Smorodin, "Krasnaia katorga," 189–190, 204.
28. Brodskii, *Solovki: Dvadtsat' let*, 221–222; Olekhnovich, "V kogtiakh GPU," 554.
29. Bessonov, "Dvadtsat' shest' tiurem," 469, 480.
30. Zaitsev, "Solovki," 265–266; Likhachev, *Reflections*, 119.
31. Andreevskii, "Pravoslavnyi evrei-ispovednik," 316–320.
32. *Solovetskaia muza*, 9–10; Gullotta, *Intellectual Life*, 262–264. Translations of these poems, with only a few minor modifications, are by Andrea Gullotta.
33. Andreev, "Solovetskie ostrova," 111, 178–182.
34. Nikonov-Smorodin, "Krasnaia katorga," 192; Petrov, "Vospominaniia izgnannika," 76, 101, 103.
35. Petrov, "Vospominaniia izgnannika," 72, 86–88, 92.
36. Petrov, "Vospominaniia izgnannika," 68–69, 72, 81, 85, 93–94, 99, 100–101, 105.
37. Volkov, "Pogruzhenie vo t'mu," 238; Reznikova, *Pravoslavie na Solovkakh*, 14; Andreevskii, "Na Kommunisticheskoi katorge," 295.
38. Vtorova-Iafa, "Avgurovy ostrova," 482–483; Feodosii, "Moi vospominaniia," 83–84.

234 NOTES

39. Shaufel'berger, "Solovki," 649–650; Rozanov, *Solovetskii kontslager'*, 249; Solonevich, "Molodezh' v GPU," 404–405; Feodosii, "Moi vospominaniia," 91.
40. Pol'skii, "Publikatsii o Solovkakh," 71–72.
41. Chekhranov, "Dve tiuremnye Paskhi," 713–715.
42. V. N. I., "Solovetskii kontslager," 58; Andreevskii, "Vospominaniia o episkope Viktore," 330; Andreev, "Solovetskie ostrova," 124.
43. Feodosii, "Moi vospominaniia," 91; Brodskii, *Solovki: Dvadtsat' let*, 230; Andreevskii, "Vospominaniia o episkope Viktore," 331; Shiriaev, *Neugasimaia lampada*, 249–270, 357–359; Rozanov, *Solovetskii kontslager'*, 255; Likhachev, *Reflections*, 168.
44. Volkov, "Pogruzhenie vo tmu," 248; Nikonov-Smorodin, "Krasnaia katorga," 170–171; Kureishi, "Piat' let," 135; Chekhranov, "Dve tiuremnye Paskhi," 712–713.
45. Leonardovich, "Na ostravakh pytok i smerti," 614–615.
46. Andreevskii, "Episkop Maksim Serpukhovskoi," 334; Soshina, *Na Solovkakh protiv voli*, 25–26.
47. Shaufel'berger, "Solovki," 650; Pol'skii, "Publikatsii o Solovkakh," 80.
48. Likhachev, *Reflections*, 140–142; Brodskii, *Solovki: Dvadtsat' let*, 232; Osipova, *'V iazvakh svoikh'*, 55.
49. Reznikova, *Pravoslavie na Solovkakh*, 23; Pol'skii, "Publikatsii o Solovkakh," 72; Feodosii, "Moi vospominaniia," 91.
50. Kureishi, "Piat' let," 135; V. N. I., "Solovetskii kontslager," 59; Volkov, "Pogruzhenie vo t'mu," 248; Klinger, "Solovetskaia katorga," 106; Solonevich, "Molodezh' v GPU," 385–386; Nikona, "So slov ochevidtsa," 53; Pol'skii, "Publikatsii o Solovkakh," 64–71; Umniagin, "Sviashchennomuchenik Ilarion," 332–341.
51. Feodosii, "Moi vospominaniia," 86, 99; Andreevskii, "Vospominaniia o episkope Viktore," 331.
52. Feodosii, "Moi vospominaniia," 91–93.
53. Klinger, "Solovetskaia katorga," 107; Feodosii, "Moi vospominaniia," 99.
54. Pol'skii, "Publikatsii o Solovkakh," 76–78.
55. "Obrashchenie Solovetskikh episkopov," 102–107.
56. Andreevskii, "Episkop Maksim Serpukhovskoi," 337–339.
57. Brodskii, *Solovki: Dvadtsat' let*, 217; Reznikova, *Pravoslavie na Solovkakh*, 26–27; Likhachev, *Reflections*, 167; Osipova, *'Skvoz' ogi' muchenii'*, 14–15; Ioann, *Tserkovnye raskoly*, 128–129.
58. Likhachev, *Reflections*, 167–168, 173.
59. Brodskii, *Solovki: Dvadtsat' let*, 240; Feodosii, "Moi vospominaniia," 97; Likhachev, *Reflections*, 170, 177; Andreevskii, "Vospominaniia o episkope Viktore," 330.
60. Andreevskii, "Vospominaniia o episkope Viktore," 330–331; Andreevskii, "Katakombnye bogosluzheniia," 312–313; Andreevskii, "Episkop Maksim Serpukhovskoi," 336–339.
61. Andreevskii, "Episkop Maksim Serpukhovskoi," 339; Ioann, *Tserkovnye raskoly*, 195–236.
62. Gor'kii, *Sobranie sochinenii*, 203–207.
63. Solonevich, "Molodezh' v GPU," 385.

Chapter 3

1. Husband, *"Godless Communists,"* 135–158; Freeze, "Subversive Atheism," 40–49; Kozlov, *Istoriia stalinskogo GULAGa*, vol. 1: 239.
2. GARF, f. R-9414, op. 1, d. 1140, ll. 228–233.
3. Solonevich, "Molodezh' v GPU," 405; Feodosii, "Moi vospominaniia," 95–97; Brodskii, *Solovki: Dvadtsat' let*, 211; Reznikova, *Pravoslavie na Solovkakh*, 10; Nikonov-Smorodin, "Krasnaia katorga," 190, 221–223; Olekhnovich, "V kogtiakh GPU," 554; Nikona, "So slov ochevidtsa," 53; Andreevskii, "Na Kommunisticheskoi katorga," 295; Osipova, *'V iazvakh svoikh,'* 65; Kozlov, *Istoriia stalinskogo GULAGa*, vol. 6: 111.
4. Vtorova-Iafa, "Avgurovy ostrova," 416–418.
5. Kozlov, *Istoriia stalinskogo GULAGa*, vol. 6: 105–113.
6. Osipova, *'V iazvakh svoikh,'* 60–64.
7. Osipova, *'Skvoz' ogi' muchenii'*, 236–239; Osipova, *'V iazvakh svoikh,'* 66.
8. Osipova, *'V iazvakh svoikh,'* 62; Brodskii, *Solovki: Dvadtsat' let*, 242.
9. GARF, f. R-5263, op. 1, d. 1040, ll. 1–14.
10. Utevskii, *Sovetskaia ispravitel'no-trudovaia politika*, 20–23, 48, 78, 167–169.
11. Vyshinskii, *Ot tiurem*, 173–175, 206, 365, 438; Averbakh, *Ot prestupleniia k trudu*, 4, 36, 77, 186–188.

NOTES 235

12. Gorky, Auerbach, and Firin, *Belomor*, 51–55, 61–63, 79–80, 84–85, 177–179, 316.
13. Kokurin and Petrov, *GULAG*, 122; Vyshinskii, *Ot tiurem*, 265; "Shire antireligioznuiu propaganda," *Perekovka na stroitel'stve kanala Moskva-Volga*, April 16, 1933.
14. "Potoropimsia," *Novye Solovki*, April 17, 1930; "USLON, ego istoriia, tseli i zadachi," *Novye Solovki*, March 16, 1930.
15. M. Sagiduplik, "Uraza—prazdnik vragov sovetskoi vlasti!" *Perekovka na stroitel'stve kanala Moskva-Volga*, December 25, 1933.
16. "Shire antireligioznuiu propaganda," *Perekovka na stroitel'stve kanala Moskva-Volga*, April 16, 1933; S. Osokin, "Sushchestvoval li na svete khristos?" *Perekovka na stroitel'stve kanala Moskva-Volga*, December 25, 1933; "Plan uroka po estestvoznaiiu," *Doloi negramotnost'!*, June 22, 1935.
17. V. Lebedev, "Zam. Nachal'nika Upravleniia T. Matveevu," *Lesorub'*, October 23, 1934; V. Idlin, "Lebedev ushel ot sektanstva," *Lesorub'*, October 23, 1934. For a similar story, see Pulia, "Religioznik Mishin, pokonchiv s predrassudkami, stal khoroshim udarnikom," *Perekovka* [BBK], August 7, 1935.
18. Untitled illustration, *Za stakhanovskii Volgostroi*, no. 1 (January 1937): 35; "Cemetery of the Loafers," *Lesorub'*, May 25, 1934.
19. GARF, f. R-9414, op. 1, d. 1132, ll. 1–2; GARF, f. R-9414, op. 1, d. 1133, ll. 12–13; Petrus, *Uzniki kommunizma*, 133; Osipova, *'V iazvakh svoikh,'* 43–44.
20. Khlevniuk, *History of the Gulag*, 47; Iuvenalii, *Pis'ma iz lageria*, 22, 24; Chicherina, "'Po vere vashei,'" 94, 97, 104, 107.
21. Iasnopol'skaia, "Schastlivyi sluchai," 525, 531, 539; Viola, *Unknown Gulag*, 91.
22. MEMO, f. 2, op. 2, d. 84, ll. 38, 42.
23. MEMO, f. 2, op. 2, d. 84, l. 42.
24. MEMO, f. 2, op. 2, d. 84, ll. 22, 28–29, 33.
25. MEMO, f. 2, op. 2, d. 84, l. 28.
26. MEMO, f. 2, op. 2, d. 84, l. 42.
27. MEMO, f. 2, op. 2, d. 84, l. 28.
28. MEMO, f. 2, op. 2, d. 82, l. 20.
29. Iarotskii, *Zolotaia Kolyma*, 62.
30. Iasnopol'skaia, "Schastlivyi sluchai," 532–533, 554.
31. Losev, *Zhizn'*, 368, 376, 379–380.
32. Losev, *Zhizn'*, 382, 392, 394, 399.
33. Losev, *Zhizn'*, 404–405; Psalms 137:1, 8, King James Version.
34. Losev, *Zhizn'*, 407–409; Postovalova, "Christian Motifs and Themes," 84–85.
35. Kozlova et al., *Papiny pis'ma*, 159–160.
36. Iuvenalii, *Pis'ma iz lageria*, 20, 24, 27, 29, 42.
37. Chicherina, "'Po vere vashei,'" 92, 94–97, 101, 104, 107.
38. Chicherina, "'Po vere vashei,'" 92, 98–100, 107, 114.
39. Chicherina, "'Po vere vashei,'" 115–116.
40. Petrus, *Uzniki kommunizma*, 71–74.
41. Petrus, *Uzniki kommunizma*, 74–76.
42. Petrus, *Uzniki kommunizma*, 77–78.

Chapter 4

1. Shul'ts, "Taganka," 201–202.
2. Getty and Naumov, *The Road to Terror*, 473–475; Osipova, *'V iazvakh svoikh,'* 67; Sapiets, *True Witness*, 48, 59.
3. Osipova, *'V iazvakh svoikh,'* 67.
4. These archival notes from the Procuracy Archive of Karaganda Region (f. Karlag, d. 3663, ll. 1–246) were graciously provided to me by Steven Barnes. His own summary of this case can be found in Barnes, *Death and Redemption*, 112–113.
5. Kokurin and Petrov, *GULAG*, 120; "Pravda 'o rozhdestve khrustovom,'" *Za avtomagistral'*, January 7, 1940; Mikhail Zoshchenko, "Poslednee rozhdestvo," *Za avtomagistral'*, January 7, 1940; "Pochemu my boremsia protiv religii," *Za avtomagistral'*, January 7, 1940; "Iz besedy tovarishcha STALINA s pervoi amerikanskoi rabochei delegatsiei," *Za avtomagistral'*, January 7, 1940; GARF, f. R-9414, op. 1, d. 1434, l. 52.

236 NOTES

6. GARF, f. R-9414, op. 1, d. 1432, ll. 12–13.
7. Begin, *White Nights*, 157; Lipper, *Eleven Years*, 80.
8. Rotfort, *Kolyma*, 15; Yakir, *Childhood in Prison*, 36–37.
9. Z. Marchenko, "The Way It Was," 207; KCA, general subject files, box 54.3, folder SU 12/4.8 Prisons and Religion (2 of 2), "God Is in the Prison Camp."
10. Adamova-Sliozberg, *My Journey*, 111–114.
11. Ginzburg, *Journey into the Whirlwind*, 222, 303, 358, 387–394.
12. Ginzburg, *Journey into the Whirlwind*, 412–414; Ginzburg, *Within the Whirlwind*, 40, 45.
13. Fletcher, *Soviet Charismatics*, 49–50; Fletcher, "Soviet Bible Belt," 91–106.
14. Bell, *Stalin's Gulag at War*; Barnes, *Death and Redemption*, 107–154.
15. GARF, f. R-9414, op. 1, d. 1155, ll. 45–49; Kokurin and Petrov, *Gulag*, 426–427.
16. GARF, f. R-9414, op. 1, d. 1437, l. 33; GARF, f. R-9414, op. 1, d. 1441, l. 28; GARF, f. R-9414, op. 1, d. 1444, l. 86; GARF, f. R-9414, op. 1, d. 1466, l. 30.
17. MEMO, f. 2, op. 2, d. 82, l. 39; Kozlov, *Istoriia stalinskogo GULAGa*, vol. 6: 144–146, 157–158; Gorchakov, *L-I-105*, 83–84.
18. Bardach and Gleeson, *Man Is Wolf to Man*, 155, 210–211.
19. Panin, *Notebooks of Sologdin*, 42, 85, 240.
20. Panin, *Notebooks of Sologdin*, 167–169.
21. Petkevich, *Memoir of a Gulag Actress*, 171, 278, 350.
22. Volovich, "My Past," 261–264.
23. Solzhenitsyn, *Gulag Archipelago*, vol. 2: 619–620.
24. GARF, f. R-6991, op. 1, d. 80, ll. 68–77. For approvals for churches to reopen during the war according to new regulations, see GARF, f. R-6991, op. 1, d. 80, ll. 194–200.
25. GARF, f. R-9414, op. 1, d. 1535, l. 232; GARF, f. R-9414, op. 1, d. 1666, l. 48; GARF, f. R-9414, op. 1, d. 1717, l. 135; GARF, f. R-9414, op. 1, d. 1668, l. 106; GARF, f. R-9414, op. 1, d. 1631, ll. 1–32; Lavinskaia and Orlova, *Zakliuchennye na stroikakh*, 349, 363–364, 373.
26. GARF, f. R-9414, op. 1, d. 1468, l. 66.
27. GARF, f. R-9414, op. 1, d, 1668, l. 180.
28. Kozlov, *Istoriia stalinskogo GULAGa*, vol. 4: 116.
29. GARF, f. R-9414, op. 1, d. 1668, ll. 64–65.
30. Chernykh, *Poslednyi starets*, 243–247; Sooster, *Moi Sooster*, 27.
31. Kaufman, *Lagernyi vrach*, 247–248; Lipper, *Eleven Years*, 142–144.
32. Shalamov, *Kolyma Tales*, 52–54, 103–104.
33. Shalamov, *Kolyma Tales*, 436–442.
34. Kopelev, *To Be Preserved Forever*, 149–150.
35. Kopelev, *To Be Preserved Forever*, 155–156.
36. Sgovio, *Dear America*, 211; Andreeva, *Plavanie k Nebesnomu Kremliu*, 157; Iurkevich, *Minuvshee prokhodit*, 214–215.
37. Ciszek and Flaherty, *With God in Russia*, 52–53, 97, 103–104.
38. Levitin-Krasnov, "*Ruk tvoikh zhar*," 260, 264–266 283, 287–288, 293.
39. KCA, general subject files, box 54.3, folder SU 12/4.8 Prisons and Religion, "A Criminal Becomes a Christian in a Russian Prison."
40. Kaufman, *Lagernyi vrach*, 260; Berger, *Nothing but the Truth*, 145–146; Lipper, *Eleven Years*, 142–144.
41. Ugrimov, *Iz Moskvy v Moskvu*, 181, 185.
42. Ugrimov, *Iz Moskvy v Moskvu*, 186, 201, 271–272.
43. Osipova, '*V iazvakh svoikh*,' 130–131; Berger, *Nothing but the Truth*, 145–146.
44. Solomon, *Magadan*, 62.
45. Kabo, *Doroga v Avstraliiu*, 190, 192, 194.
46. Zhigulin, *Chernye kamni*, 108.
47. Andreeva, *Plavanie k Nebesnomu Kremliu*, 153–154.
48. Chernykh, *Poslednyi starets*, 242.
49. Noble and Everett, *I Found God*, 113–117.
50. Tikhanova, *Tvorchestvo i byt GULAGa*, 68, 167; Memorial Society Museum, f. Grafika, "Paskhal'naia otkrytka," "Otkrytka 'Khristos voskres!'" and "Pozdravitel'naia otkrytka 'S novym godom!' na latyshkom"; Memorial Society Museum, f. Tiuremno-lagernyi byt, "Bezrukavka so vyshitymi rukopisnymi tekstami."
51. Johnson, "Performing Family Unity," 255, 258–259; Formakov, *Gulag Letters*, 127–128, 193.

NOTES   237

Chapter 5

1. Gross, *Revolution from Abroad*.
2. Pasat, *Pravoslavie v Moldavii*, 419–422, 550–556.
3. Puzyrev, *I pokatilsia kolobok*, 55; Lipper, *Eleven Years*, 144–146.
4. Panin, *Notebooks of Sologdin*, 231; Petkevich, *Memoir of a Gulag Actress*, 189, 301.
5. Berger, *Nothing but the Truth*, 144–145, 193.
6. Z. Marchenko, "The Way It Was," 209; Kis, *Survival as Victory*, 240.
7. Noble and Everett, *I Found God*, 108, 118–124, 126–128, 134–147.
8. Bakhtin and Putilov, *Fol'klor i kul'turnaia sreda GULAGa*, 108, 111.
9. Kis, *Survival as Victory*, 229–230, 246.
10. Svianevich, *V teni Katyni*, 94–114, 185–187, 204–213.
11. Ciszek and Flaherty, *With God in Russia*, 139.
12. Ciszek and Flaherty, *With God in Russia*, 161–162.
13. Bukovinskii, *Vospominaniia shviashchennika*, 10–12, 19.
14. Solzhenitsyn, *Gulag Archipelago*, vol. 3: 100–101; Kis, *Survival as Victory*, 235; Mattila, "Sedition and the Sacred," 327, 352.
15. GARF, f. R-9414, op. 1, d. 1501, l. 10; Kis, *Survival as Victory*, 211, 235; Mattila, "Sedition and the Sacred," 327.
16. Mattila, "Sedition and the Sacred," 355–358.
17. Kis, *Survival as Victory*, 246; Gorchakov, *L-I-105*, 232; Leshchenko-Sukhomlina, "Selections from 'My Guitar,'" 239.
18. Zarod, *Inside Stalin's Gulag*, 43–45, 118–119.
19. Kis, *Survival as Victory*, 243; Andreeva, *Plavanie k Nebesnomu Kremliu*, 185.
20. Mark 16:15, New International Version.
21. Etinger, *Eto nevozmozhno zabyt'*, 193; Rabinovich, *Vospominaniia dolgoi zhizni*, 336; Noble and Everett, *I Found God*, 135.
22. Mattila, "Sedition and the Sacred," 313–314, 359–360.
23. Dolgun, *Alexander Dolgun's Story*, 223, 239, 251; Mattila, "Sedition and the Sacred," 315; Zarod, *Inside Stalin's Gulag*, 42, 116–117.
24. Bardach and Gleeson, *Man Is Wolf to Man*, 118, 319.
25. Herling, *A World Apart*, 151, 191, 202–203, 226.
26. Herling, *A World Apart*, 141, 218–220, 227.
27. Herling, *A World Apart*, 98, 146.
28. Herling, *A World Apart*, 131–133, 136, 141.
29. Herling, *A World Apart*, 204–205.
30. Gagen-Torn, *Memoria*, 208–209.
31. Gagen-Torn, *Memoria*, 211–212.
32. Gagen-Torn, *Memoria*, 152–154.
33. Gagen-Torn, *Memoria*, 205–207, 209–211.
34. Solomon, *Magadan*, 138–139.
35. Sidorov, "Russian Criminal Tattoo," 23–25, 35–36.
36. Volovich, "My Past," 267; Shalamov, *Kolyma Tales*, 7.
37. Lipper, *Eleven Years*, 189; Priadilov, *Zapiski kontrrevoliutsionera*, 52–54, 63.
38. Ciszek and Flaherty, *With God in Russia*, 167–168; Rabinovich, *Vospominaniia dolgoi zhizni*, 257.
39. Luke 23:43, New International Version; Jacobson and Jacobson, *Pesennyi fol'klor*, 52, 80, 113, 165, 204, 352, 261–262, 407, 458.
40. Sgovio, *Dear America*, 168.
41. Sidorov, "Russian Criminal Tattoo," 23–25, 35–36; Plutser-Sarno, "Language of the Body," 35, 37; Murray and Sorrell, *Russian Criminal Tattoo Encyclopedia*, vol. 1: 132–135, 147–148, 184, 186, 210–213, 304–311; vol. 2: 163, 202, 210, 292–293; vol. 3: 133, 150–151, 164–169, 244–245.
42. Plutser-Sarno, "Language of the Body," 29, 35; Murray and Sorrell, *Russian Criminal Tattoo Encyclopedia*, vol. 3: 313; Sidorov, "Russian Criminal Tattoo," 36.
43. Plutser-Sarno, "Language of the Body," 41; Murray and Sorrell, *Russian Criminal Tattoo Encyclopedia*, vol. 3: 270.
44. Plutser-Sarno, "All Power to the Godfathers," 44; Murray and Sorrell, *Russian Criminal Tattoo Encyclopedia*, vol. 1: 177, 229, 312 vol. 2: 186, 200; vol. 3: 267, 271.
45. Murray and Sorrell, *Russian Criminal Tattoo Encyclopedia*, vol. 1: 141, 250–251.

238 NOTES

46. Murray and Sorrell, *Russian Criminal Tattoo Encyclopedia*, vol. 1: 263, 267, 269, 315; vol. 3: 211, 246.
47. Mattila, "Sedition and the Sacred," 385.

Chapter 6

1. Hardy, *Gulag after Stalin*.
2. GARF, f. A-461, op. 11, d. 574, ll. 166, 190a; Bourdeaux, "Persecution, Collusion, and Liberation," 55–56, 59.
3. GARF, f. R-8131, op. 32, d. 4303, l. 12; Bourdeaux, "Persecution, Collusion, and Liberation," 54; KCA, denominational subject files, Uniates, box 1, folder 2, "Cardinal Ex-Prisoner to Visit UK"; KCA, denominational subject files, Uniates, box 1, folder 2, "Eastern Catholics in the Ukraine"; GARF, f. R-9492, op. 2, d. 196, l. 190.
4. GARF, f. R-9414, op. 1, dd. 1795–1796.
5. GARF, f. R-9401, op. 1a, d. 465, l. 93; Hardy, "Gulag Tourism."
6. GARF, f. R-9414, op. 1, d. 1716, ll. 112–113.
7. GARF, f. R-9414, op. 1, d. 1716, l. 226.
8. V'iushina, "Antireligioznaia propaganda," 23–30.
9. Monakhov, "V bor'be s religioznim durmanom," 76–77; GARF, f. R-9414, op. 3, d. 140, ll. 67–70.
10. GARF, f. R-9414, op. 1, d. 1764, ll. 177, 201, 312; TsDAGO, f. 1, op. 82, d. 174, l. 58; GDA MVS, f. 6, op. 2, d. 393, l. 117; GARF, f. R-9414, op. 2, d. 48, ll. 97–102, 248–271; GARF, f. R-9414, op. 2, d. 49, ll. 49–51, 56–62.
11. GDA MVS, f. 6, op. 2, d. 382, l. 198; Terelya, *Witness to Apparitions*, 85, 87.
12. GARF, f. R-9401, op. 2, d. 481, ll. 428–430, 434.
13. GARF, f. R-8131, op. 32, d. 7036, l. 53.
14. Pantiukhin, *Stolitsa Kolymskogo Kraia*, 68–69; Solomon, *Magadan*, 173.
15. "Usilit' ateisticheskuiu propaganda," *Za mirnyi trud*, June 1, 1960; Dovlatov, *The Zone*, 28–30; GARF, f. R-8131, op. 32, d. 6733, l. 7.
16. Eminov, *Smert'—samoe strashnoe*, 322; Ciszek and Flaherty, *With God in Russia*, 205, 211–212.
17. Kokurin and Petrov, *GULAG*, 628–629; Kozlov, *Istoriia stalinskogo GULAGa*, vol. 6: 365, 513; Osipova, *'V iazvakh svoikh*,' 141–143.
18. Kozlov, *Istoriia stalinskogo GULAGa*, vol. 6: 304, 519–523, 529, 567, 630, 634; Osipova, *'V iazvakh svoikh*,' 143.
19. Memorial Society Museum, f. Rukodelie i remeslo, "Ikon ana tkani. Bogomater' s mladentsem."
20. ERAF, f. 17sm, op. 4, d. 267, ll. 70–71, 255; KCA, denominational subject files, Uniates, box 2, folder 7, "Press Conference with Josyp Terelja"; Terelya, *Witness to Apparitions*, 85, 87.
21. Verblovskaia, "Pis'mo byvshei uznitsy," 153; Kuzin, *Malyi srok*, 76.
22. Mattila, "Sedition and the Sacred," 366.
23. GARF, f. A-461, op. 11, d. 588, l. 20.
24. Ablamskii, "Kharbin—Vikhorevka," 253, 258.
25. Celmina, *Women in Soviet Prisons*, 184; Mashkov, "Golos s rodiny," 12–21.
26. MEMO, f. 2, op. 3, d. 66, ll. 1–130.
27. MEMO, f. 2, op. 3, d. 66, ll. 156–157, 268.
28. MEMO, f. 2, op. 3, d. 66, ll. 269–270.
29. MEMO, f. 2, op. 3, d. 66, ll. 277, 281.
30. MEMO, f. 2, op. 3, d. 66, l. 287.
31. MEMO, f. 2, op. 3, d. 66, l. 298.
32. MEMO, f. 2, op. 3, d. 66, ll. 300–302.
33. MEMO, f. 2, op. 3, d. 66, ll. 311–312, 318–319.
34. MEMO, f. 2, op. 3, d. 66, ll. 330, 337–338, 343.
35. MEMO, f. 2, op. 3, d. 66, ll. 5, 319.
36. Osipova, *'V iazvakh svoikh*,' 143.
37. Bukovinskii, *Vospominaniia sviashchennika*, 98.
38. GARF, f. A-461, op. 11, d. 574, ll. 47, 51; GARF, f. A-461, op. 11, d. 577, l. 9; GARF, f. A-461, op. 11, d. 765, ll. 32a, 40a; GARF, f. A-461, op. 11, d. 1607, l. 2; Barnes, *Death and Redemption*, 79–106.
39. Celmina, *Women in Soviet Prisons*, 115; Ronkin, *Na smenu dekabriam*, 244; KCA, general subject files, box 54.3, folder SU 12/4.8 Prisons and Religion, "25 August 1987 Interview with D. Shumuk"; A. Marchenko, *Zhivi kak vse*, 117; Baran, *Dissent on the Margins*, 91–98.

NOTES   239

40. Kashirin, "Protestant Minorities," 299–300.
41. GARF, f. A-461, op. 11, d. 574, ll. 47–51, 53.
42. GARF, f. A-461, op. 11, d. 574, l. 53.
43. GARF, f. A-461, op. 11, d. 765, ll. 5, 17, 33.
44. A. Marchenko, *Zhivi kak vse*, 117; Ronkin, *Na smenu dekabriam*, 244.
45. A. Marchenko, *Zhivi kak vse*, 117; Celmina, *Women in Soviet Prisons*, 133, 227–236.
46. Mattila, "Sedition and the Sacred," 361, 363; Sporov, "Pis'mena tiuremnykh sten," 85.
47. Vail', *Osobo opasnyi*, 267–268. Baran, *Dissent on the Margins*, 83.
48. Ronkin, *Na smenu dekabriam*, 244; Osipov, *Dubravlag*, 64–65; A. Marchenko, *Zhivi kak vse*,
    117–118; Krasnopevtsev, "... U nas bylo svoia tochka zreniia," 69.
49. Vail', *Osobo opasnyi*, 267–268, 288; Belov, "Sviashchenniki v lageriakh," 27.
50. Klimanova, "My Meetings," 167–168; Celmina, *Women in Soviet Prisons*, 135–142.
51. Sporov, "Pis'mena tiuremnykh sten," 85; Ronkin, *Na smenu dekabriam*, 244; Klimanova, "My
    Meetings," 168; KCA, general subject files, box 54.3, folder SU 12/4.8 Prisons and Religion, "25
    August 1987 Interview with D. Shumuk."
52. Belov, "Sviashchenniki v lageriakh," 28; Ronkin, *Na smenu dekabriam*, 244; Osipov,
    Dubravlag, 64–65.
53. Celmina, *Women in Soviet Prisons*, 127, 129, 132.
54. KCA, general subject files, box 54.3, folder SU 12/4.8 Prisons and Religion, "25 August 1987
    Interview with D. Shumuk"; Belov, "Sviashchenniki v lageriakh," 28; Osipov, *Dubravlag*, 65;
    Celmina, *Women in Soviet Prisons*, 126–127; Baran, *Dissent on the Margins*, 83–84.
55. Klimanova, "My Meetings," 168; Ronkin, *Na smenu dekabriam*, 244–245; Moroz, *Boomerang*,
    49, 71–72, 82.
56. Celmina, *Women in Soviet Prisons*, 129–131.
57. Bukovinskii, *Vospominaniia shviashchennika*, 98–99.
58. Bukovinskii, *Vospominaniia shviashchennika*, 98; Klimanova, "My Meetings," 168.
59. KCA, general subject files, box 54.3, folder SU 12/4.8 Prisons and Religion, "25 August 1987
    Interview with D. Shumuk."
60. Baran, *Dissent on the Margins*, 83; Fletcher, *Soviet Charismatics*, 52.

Chapter 7

1. Letter from a female prisoner, undated," *Biulleten'*, no. 25 (1975): 24.
2. KCA, Samizdat Collection, folder SU/Pen 6, "Fakty i tol'ko fakty," December 1977; Keston
   Center, *Christian Prisoners*.
3. Usov, "Nedoumenie 'sviatoi' Agaf'i," 48; Usachev, "Mrakobes," 80.
4. Ronkin, *Na smenu dekabriam*, 298–299; "Proiskhozhdenie religii," *Za novuiu zhizn'*, November
   18, 1965; A. Kedrov, "Chto znaet istoriia ob Iisuse Khriste?," *Za novuiu zhizn'*, January 31, 1970;
   V. Konstantinov, "O tak nazyvaemom rozhdestve khristovom," *Za novuiu zhizn'*, January 6, 1968;
   N. Radchenko, "O religioznykh prazdnikakh," *Za novuiu zhizn'*, January 13, 1969; P. Sumarev, "A.
   M. Gor'kii o religii," *Za novuiu zhizn'*, September 16, 1967; "O religii i sueveriiakh," *Za novuiu
   zhizn'*, July 1, 1968; V. Krivenkov, "Svoboda sovesti v SSSR," *Za novuiu zhizn'*, January 21, 1969;
   V. Krivenkov, "Kto takie baptisty," *Za novuiu zhizn'*, June 17, 1969.
5. Vins, *Konshaubi*, 73; KCA, general subject files, box 48.2, folder SU 4/8 1977–1978 Prisons and
   Labor Camps, untitled note on amnesties.
6. "V tiurmakh i lageriakh," 86; "Dnevnik lageria No. 35"; "Segodnia sovetskikh kontslagerei";
   "Vladimirskaia tiur'ma"; "Iz pisem sviashchennika Vasiliia Romaniuka."
7. KCA, individual clergy files, Orthodox, box 24, folder 10, "Gleb Yakunin Goes on Hunger Strike";
   Perchatkin, *Ognennye tropy*, 212–213; "Vladimirskaia tiur'ma," 22; "V tiurmakh i lageriakh," 87;
   "Russian Orthodox Prisoners."
8. "Russian Orthodox Prisoners"; letter from Iu. Churbanov, deputy commander of the Political
   Department of the ITU MVD SSSR in Moscow, to P. S. Rogozhina of Rostov-na-donu, April 9,
   1917, *Biulleten'*, no. 1 (1971): 20; letter from Zhelobkovich, head of penal facility UCh-398/7 of
   Rostov Province, to N. V. Shostenko of Rostov na-Donu Province, *Biulleten'*, no. 1 (1971): 22;
   letter from the deputy commander of the department of the MVD (Odessa) to Z. F. Palamarchuk,
   April 5, 1971, *Biulleten'*, no. 2 (1971): 32.
9. Excerpt from a letter by Lidiia Mikhalovna Vins to her family, December 29, 1971, *Biulleten'*, no. 7
   (1972); "Vladimirskaia tiur'ma," 22; Sadunaite, *A Radiance in the Gulag*, 91–97; Ratushinskaya,

240 NOTES

"Someone Is Thinking of Me Now," 12; letter from E. K. Artiuk and Z. N. Artiuk to Procurator General of the USSR Rudenko and others, undated, *Biulleten'*, no. 27 (1975): 18.

10. Letter from a brother prisoner returned from prison, undated, *Biulleten'*, no. 25 (1975): 27; Vins, *Konshaubi*, 29; Perchatkin, *Ognennye tropy*, 187; KCA, general subject files, box 54.3, folder SU 12/6.8 Imprisonment and Exile (2 of 3), "True Orthodox Believers, USSR"; KCA, denominational subject files, Uniates, box 6, folder 10, "Chronicle of the Catholic Church in the Ukraine, No. 1" and "Chronicle of the Catholic Church in the Ukraine, No. 2."

11. Open letter by Adam Iosifovich Dubitskii, March 14, 1974, *Biulleten'*, no. 14 (1974): 61; KCA, Samizdat Collection, folder SU/Pen 6/8, "Poselok trudovoi"; statement by the EKhB believers of Kharkov Province to the General Procuracy of the USSR, January 1976, *Biulleten'*, no. 31 (1976): 5.

12. KCA, Samizdat Collection, folder SU/Pen 6/8, "Poselok trudovoi"; open letter to all believers of the Evangelical-Baptist confession," *Biulleten'*, no. 1 (1971): 6.

13. Open letter from Adam Dubitskii, undated, *Biulleten'*, no. 23 (1975): 19; KCA, Samizdat Collection, folder SU/Pen 6/8, "Pis'mo s etapa v lager"; letter from Head of the Political Department of Institution I-299 A. A. Ponomarev to Liubov' Vasil'evna Rumachik, 7.12.1976, *Biulleten'*, no. 39 (1977): 27.

14. David Davidovich Klassen to the Council of Prisoners' Relatives, September 5, 1971, *Biulleten'*, no. 7 (1972): 7–8; Sadunaite, *Radiance in the Gulag*, 91–97; KCA, denominational subject files, Uniates, box 2, folder 7, "Press Conference with Josyp Terelja."

15. "Russian Orthodox Prisoners," 264–266.

16. Vins, *Konshaubi*, 19–20, 59–60.

17. Sadunaite, *Radiance in the Gulag*, 73–81; Ratushinskaya, *Grey Is the Colour of Hope*, 102.

18. Ratushinskaya, *Grey Is the Colour of Hope*, 102, 248–250.

19. KCA, general subject files, box 54.3, SU 12/4.8 Prisons and Religion, "Letter from Iryna Stasiv-Kalynets."

20. Vins, *Konshaubi*, 57–58; Khorev, *Letters*, 204–208.

21. Ratushinskaya, "'Someone Is Thinking of Me Now,'" 13–14.

22. KCA, denominational subject files, Orthodox, box 5, "Exclusive Again Interview with Russian Prisoner of Conscience Alexander Ogorodnikov"; KCA, Michael Bourdeaux papers—uncatalogued, Michael Bourdeaux radio broadcast, March 2, 1980.

23. Vins, *Konshaubi*, 12, 14.

24. Terelya, *Witness*, 101.

25. KCA, denominational subject files, Orthodox, box 5, "Exclusive Again Interview with Russian Prisoner of Conscience Alexander Ogorodnikov"; KCA, general subject files, box 54.3, folder SU 12/4.8 Prisons and Religion, "Prison Camp Miracle."

26. Vins, *Konshaubi*, 68–69; Khorev, *Letters*, 137; Kostyuchenko, "Poedinok."

27. Lebedev, "Chained Freedom," 14; Ratushinskaya, "Someone Is Thinking of Me Now," 14.

28. Hornsby, *Protest, Reform and Repression*, 147–148; Vagin, "Interv'iu 'vestniku RKhD.'"

29. KCA, general subject files, box 54.3, folder SU 12/4.8 Prisons and Religion, "Religious Life behind Barbed Wire"; KCA, general subject files, box 54.3, folder SU 12/4.8 Prisons and Religion, "How Soviet Citizens Turn to God."

30. KCA, general subject files, box 54.3, folder SU 12/4.8 Prisons and Religion, "Religious Life behind Barbed Wire"; KCA, general subject files, box 54.3, folder SU 12/4.8 Prisons and Religion, "How Soviet Citizens Turn to God."

31. Tapley, "I Hasten to Establish," 142–146; KCA, Samizdat Orthodox subject files, box 43, folder 10.

32. KCA, general subject files, box 54.3, folder SU 12/6.8 Imprisonment and Exile (2 of 3), "Letter of political prisoners of institution ZhKh-385/3-1 to the International Red Cross"; KCA, general subject files, box 48.2, folder SU 4/8 1974 Prisons and Labor Camps, "Interview with political prisoners of the Perm Camp VS 389/35" and "Soviet Political Prisoners demand judicial and practical recognition of them as such, they demand the status of political prisoners"; KCA, general subject files, box 48.2, folder SU 4/8 1975 Prisons and Labor Camps, "Declaration by prisoner G. I. Butman to the head of the Perm Division of corrective-labor institutions (ITK-35)"; KCA, general subject files, box 48.2, folder SU 4/8 1975 Prisons and Labor Camps, "Day of the Political Prisoner" pamphlet.

NOTES   241

33. Letter from prisoners of Corrective-Labor Institution No. 8 in Omsk to the chairman of the Presidium of the Supreme Soviet of the USSR Podgornyi and others, September 12, 1975, *Biulleten'*, no. 27 (1975): 41–43; "Open Letter of the EKhB Prisoners," *Biulleten'*, no. 33 (1976): 62–63.
34. Telegram to General Secretary of the TsK KPSS Brezhnev, 17.11.76, *Biulleten'*, no. 3 (1976): 12; "Polozhenie uznikov," *Biulleten'*, no. 101 (January 1982): 32–33.
35. Declaration from Nadezhda Vasil'evna Shostenko to the head of the corrective-labor colony p/ia 398/7-2 of Rostov Province, April 5, 1971, *Biulleten'*, no. 1 (1971): 21; KCA, general subject files, box 38.2, folder SU 4/8 1975 Prisons and Labor Camps, "Declaration of the Council of Relatives of ECB Prisoners sentenced for the Word of God in the USSR."
36. Statement by 103 people to the chairman of the Presidium of the Supreme Soviet of the USSR comrade N. V. Podgornyi, *Biulleten'*, no. 16 (1974): 5; KCA, Michael Bourdeaux papers— uncatalogued, Michael Bourdeaux radio broadcast, March 2, 1980; letter from Ivan Ivanovich Fedorchenko to the chairman of the Presidium of the Supreme Soviet and others, undated, *Biulleten'*, no. 28 (1975): 23–24.
37. Head of the UITU MVD Komi ASSR Shurganov to V. M. Baturina, *Biulleten'*, no. 27 (1975): 23; letter from Nadezhda Ivanovna Vins to the chairman of the Council of Ministers of the USSR A. N. Kosygin and others, 6.6.77, *Biulleten'*, no. 44 (1977): 31–36.
38. Harris and Howard-Johnston, *Christian Prisoners*, 58–59.
39. Correspondence, *Biulleten'*, no. 27 (1975): 15–17.
40. KCA, general subject files, box 49.1, folder SU 6/8 Imprisonment 1977, "Prison Thoughts of Nijole Sadunaite"; KCA, Samizdat Collection, folder SU/Pen 6/8, "Pis'mo s etapa v lager."
41. KCA, denominational subject files, Uniates, box 2, folder 5, "Letter from a Prisoner."
42. Letter from prisoner Vania to the Church, undated, *Biulleten'*, no. 33 (1976): 61; open letter from Adam Dubitskii, undated, *Biulleten'*, no. 23 (1975): 17; KCA, Samizdat Collection, folder Su/Ini 11/4 CPR Second Congress, "Sbornik dokumentov Vtorogo Vsesoiuznogo s'ezda rodstvennikov uznikov Evangel'skikh khristian-baptistov v SSSR, chast' 1," 38; Khorev, *Letters*, 162.
43. Letter from Oleg P. to the Council of EKhB prisoners' relatives, 20.12.81, *Biulleten'*, no. 101 (1982): 38; "Polozhenie uznikov," *Biulleten'*, no. 101 (January 1982): 35–36.
44. Letter from "the least brother-prisoner of Jesus Christ, G," undated, *Biulleten'*, no. 101 (January 1982): 38–41.
45. "Inmates Write," *Biulleten'*, no. 37 (1976): 19–20.
46. Vins, *Konshaubi*, 46.
47. Walters, "From Community to Isolation"; KCA, denominational subject files, Orthodox, box 5, "Letter from Alexander Ogorodnikov to His Mother."
48. Khorev, *Letters*, 9; KCA, Michael Bourdeaux Papers—uncatalogued, untitled pamphlet clipping.
49. Lebedev, "Chained Freedom," 14; Krakhmalnikova, *Listen, Prison!*, 25.

Chapter 8

1. KCA, general subject files, box 54.3, folder SU 12/4.8 Prisons and Religion (2 of 2), "Svoi krest."
2. KCA, Michael Bourdeaux papers—uncatalogued, translation of February 1986 interview of Gorbachev published in *L'Humanité*; Keston Center, *Christian Prisoners* 1985.
3. KCA, denominational subject files, Orthodox, box 12, folder 22, "Orthodox Christian Arrested in Kiev"; KCA, denominational subject files, Orthodox, box 12, folder 27, "Dissentient Deacon Sent to Prison."
4. Senderov, "Bog i tiur'ma," 173–176, 180; KCA, denominational subject files, Orthodox, box 12, folder 29, "O subd'be R. Evdokimova i V. Senderova" and "Valeri Senderov in Poor Health."
5. KCA, Samizdat Orthodox subject files, box 43, folder 11; KCA, individual clergy files, Orthodox, folder 11/2, "Declaration by A. I. Ogorodnikov to the Procurator of Khabarovsk Territory, 21 August 1986."
6. Terelya, *Witness*, 199–201.
7. "News Round-Up"; KCA, denominational subject files, Orthodox, box 5, folder 14, "Hard Labour and Prisons for Soviet Believers" and "Sergei Markus Released."

242 NOTES

8. Daniel, *Russia's Uncommon Prophet*, 232–240; KCA, denominational subject files, Orthodox, box 12, folder 24, "Recantation by Former Orthodox Activist."
9. KCA, denominational subject files, Orthodox, box 12, folder 27, "Deacon Rusak Still in Lefortovo"; Krakhmalnikova, "Trial by Fire."
10. "Love behind Bars."
11. Bourdeaux, "Persecution, Collusion, and Liberation," 69; "More Releases!"; "Prisoners of Faith," 23; Antonov, *"Prisoners of Conscience,"* 7.
12. "Prisoners of Faith."
13. Bourdeaux, "Persecution, Collusion, and Liberation," 70–73.
14. "From Prisons to Palaces."
15. "A Happier Burden"; "News of Prisoners"; *Za novuiu zhizn'*, October 4, 1990.
16. "An Easter Greeting from Russia"; "We Went to See Our Pastor—in Prison" Loviniukov, "Svoboda sovesti v ITU," 42; "A Happier Burden," 22.
17. "Breaking Barriers."
18. KCA, general subject files, box 49.2, folder SU 6/8 1984 (1 of 3), transcript of News Network International interview; Daniel, *Russia's Uncommon Prophet*, 240; KCA, general subject files, box 54.3, folder SU 12/4.8 Prisons and Religion (2 of 2), "Syn."
19. Kiselev, "Russian Bishop Visits Soviet Prison."
20. Kiselev, "Russian Bishop Visits Soviet Prison."
21. Buzhak, "Dusha obiazana trudit'sia"; "Postanovlenie Verkhovnogo Soveta SSSR: 'O vvedenii v deistvie zakona SSSR o svobode sovesti i religioznykh organizatsiiakh,'" *Na vernom puti*, October 30, 1990; "Traditsii Russkogo naroda: novyi god," *Na vernom puti*, January 25, 1990; "Traditsii Russkogo naroda: rozhdestvo Khristovo," *Na vernom puti*, January 8, 1991; A. Zakharov, "Veriu v dobrotu i liubov'!" *Na vernom puti*, September 29, 1992.
22. Nazarov, "Mitropolit Filaret."
23. Vergel', "Po kom ne zvonit kolokol."
24. Kalinin, "O religii—bez predrassudkov."
25. *Vospitanie i pravoporiadok*, no. 8.
26. Kolomeets, "Bog v pomoshch.'"
27. Lepikhin, "Stanet li greshnik pravednikom?"
28. "Prison Ordeals Made Public"; KCA, general subject files, box 54.3, folder SU 12/4.8 Prisons and Religion (2 of 2), "Nitochkoi liubvi priviazannaia k nebu"; KCA, general subject files, box 54.3, folder SU 12/4.8 Prisons and Religion (2 of 2), Aleksandr Ivanovich Smirnov to Heather Rodd Keston, 20 December 1991; Lebedev, "Chained Freedom," 15.
29. Lunkin, "The Charismatic Movement in Russia"; KCA, general subject files, box 54.3, folder SU 12/4.8 Prisons and Religion (2 of 2), "Moscow Prisoners Given New Testaments"; KCA, general subject files, box 54.3, folder SU 12/4.8 Prisons and Religion (2 of 2), "The Gospel behind Locked Doors."
30. Kadayeva, "Harvest Time in Russia."
31. "Within These Walls."
32. "Seventh Day Adventists"; Lebedev, "Chained Freedom," 14.
33. KCA, general subject files, box 54.3, folder SU 12/4.8 Prisons and Religion (2 of 2), "Na puti k dukhovnomu prozreniiu"; A. Sidikov, "Ia poveril v Boga," *Za novuiu zhizn'*, November 22, 1990.
34. "U nas v gostiakh Dzho Garman," *Na vernom puti*, December 2, 1991.
35. KCA, general subject files, box 54.3, folder SU 12/4.8 Prisons and Religion (2 of 2), "Prisoners Build Their Own Chapel."
36. "Pentecost in Prison."
37. Lebedev, "Chained Freedom," 15.

Epilogue

1. Vilenskii, *Poeziia uznikov GULAGa*, 744.
2. B. Karpov, "K dukhovnym traditsiiam," *Na vernom puti*, June 2, 1992; A. Zakharov, "Veriu v dobrotu i liubov'!" *Na vernom puti*, September 29, 1992; editorial, *Na vernom puti*, January 5, 1993; I. Smirnova, "Rozhdestvo Khistovo," *Na vernom puti*, January 5, 1993; V. Strokov, "V poiskakh dukhovnogo schast'ia," *Na vernom puti*, January 5, 1993; A. Bilibin, "Veriu v cheloveka," *Na vernom puti*, January 5, 1993; "Ianvar' v narodnom i pravoslavnom kalendariakh," *Na vernom puti*, January 12, 1993.

NOTES 243

3. Loviniukov, "Svoboda sovesti v ITU"; Lepikhin, "Pust' Iisus istselit"; Baidakov and Burdyko, "Doroga v khram"; *Vospitanie i pravoporiadok*, no. 3.

4. Buzhak, "Dusha obiazana trudit'sia"; Baidakov, "Voznesenie k vere"; Kyrke-Smith, "Nightmare in Siberia."

5. Vasilenko, *Tiuremnye khramy*, 6–7; Lebedev, "Chained Freedom," 15; Vasilenko, *Tiuremnye khramy*, 4, 7, 13.

6. Navalny, "11/11 Tak chto tiuremnaia Sistema Rossii ..."

7. Bogumił, *Gulag Memories.*

8. Fedor and Sniegon, "The Butovskii Shooting Range."

Bibliography

Archival Sources

Note: Post-Soviet archives are typically organized by collection (*fond*,abbreviated as f.), inventory (*opis'*, abbreviated as op.), folder (*delo*, abbreviated as d.), and page (*list*, abbreviated as l. or ll. for multiple pages). Thus, a reference to a report that is found on page 6 of folder 12 of inventory 2 of collection A-353 of the State Archive of the Russian Federation would read: GARF, f. A-353, op. 2, d. 12, l. 6.

ERAF: Branch of the Estonian State Archive. - *Eesti Riigiarhiivi Filiaali.*
Collection 17sm: Secretariat of the Ministry of Internal Affairs, Estonian SSR.

GARF: State Archive of the Russian Federation. *Gosudarstvennyi arkhiv Rossiskoi Federatsii.*
Collection A-353: Ministry of Justice, RSFSR.
Collection A-461: Procuracy, RSFSR.
Collection R-393: People's Commissariat of Internal Affairs, RSFSR.
Collection R-4042: Main Directorate of Places of Confinement of the People's Commissariat of Internal Affairs, RSFSR.
Collection R-5263: Standing Central Commission on Matters of Cults of the Presidium of the Central Executive Committee, USSR.
Collection R-6991: Council for Religious Affairs of the Council of Ministers, USSR.
Collection R-8131: Procuracy, USSR.
Collection R-9401: Ministry of Internal Affairs, USSR.
Collection R-9414: Main Administration of the Places of Confinement of the Ministry of Internal Affairs, USSR.
Collection R-9492: Ministry of Justice, USSR.

GDA MVS: State Archive Branch of the Ministry of Internal Affairs of Ukraine. *Galuzevii derzhavnii arkhiv Sluzhby bezpeki Ukrainy.*
Collection 6: Administration of Corrective-Labor Camps and Colonies of the Ministry of Internal Affairs, Ukrainian SSR.

KCA: Keston Center Archive.
Denominational subject files.
General subject files.
Individual clergy files.
Michael Bourdeaux papers.
Michael Bourdeaux papers—uncatalogued.
Samizdat Collection.
Samizdat Orthodox subject files.

MEMO: Archive of the History of Political Repressions in the USSR (1918–1956), Memorial Society. *Arkhiv istorii politicheskikh represii v SSSR (1918–1956), Obshchestvo "Memoriala."*
Collection 2: Memoirs and literary works.

246   BIBLIOGRAPHY

Memorial Society Museum, Moscow.
Personal collections.

TsDAGO: Central State Archive of Public Organizations of Ukraine. *Tsentral'nii derzhavnii arkhiv gromads'kikh ob'ednan' Ukraini.*
Collection 1:   Central Committee of the Communist Party of Ukraine.

Newspapers and Newsletters

Note: The majority of newspapers used can be found in the State Library of the Russian Federation and in the microfiche collection *Gulag Press, 1920–1937*, which reproduces material from the collections of the State Archive of the Russian Federation. Other Gulag newspapers are cited in this book using the archival reference to where they are found.

Biulleten': Biulleten' soveta rodstvennikov uznikov evangel'skikh khristian-baptistov SSSR.
Doloi negramotnost'! (Dmitrov, Moscow Province).
Golos zakliuchennogo (Penza).
Lesorub' (Iavas, Mordovian Republic).
Na vernom puti (Tomsk).
Novye Solovki (Solovki).
Perekovka (Belemorsko-Baltiiskii Kombinat NKVD).
Perekovka na stroitel'stve kanala Moscka-Volga (Dmitrov, Moscow Province).
SLON (Solovki).
Za avtomagistral' (Vyazma).
Za mirnyi trud (unknown labor colony network).
Za novuiu zhizn' (unknown labor camp).
Za stakhanovskii Volgostroi (Perebory, Iaroslavl Province).
Za zheleznoi reshetkoi (Vyatka).

Articles and Books

"A Happier Burden." *Frontier*, May–June 1989, 20–22.
Ablamskii, V. P. "Kharbin—Vikhorevka." In *Ozerlag: kak eto bylo*, edited by L. S. Mukhin, 252–258. Irkutsk: Vostochno-Sibirskoe knizhnoe izdatel'stvo, 1992.
Adamova-Sliozberg, Olga. *My Journey: How One Woman Survived Stalin's Gulag.* Translated by Katharine Gratwick Baker. Evanston, IL: Northwestern University Press, 2011.
Adams, Bruce. *The Politics of Punishment: Prison Reform in Russia, 1863–1917.* DeKalb: Northern Illinois University Press, 1996.
Alexopoulos, Golfo. *Illness and Inhumanity in Stalin's Gulag.* New Haven, CT: Yale University Press, 2017.
"An Easter Greeting from Russia." *Frontier*, March–April 1988, 5.
Andreev, Gennadii Andreevich. "Solovetskie ostrova (1927–1929)." In Umniagin, *Vospominaniia*, Vol. 3: 117–188.
Andreeva, A. A. *Plavanie k Nebesnomu Kremliu.* Moscow: Uraniia, 1998.
Andreevskii, Ivan Mikhailovich. "Episkop Maksim Serpukhovskoi (Zhizhilenko)." In Umniagin, *Vospominaniia*, Vol. 3: 332–342.
Andreevskii, Ivan Mikhailovich. "Gruppa monakhin' v Solovsetskov kontslagere." In Umniagin, *Vospominaniia*, Vol. 3: 322–329.

BIBLIOGRAPHY   247

Andreevskii, Ivan Mikhailovich. "Katakombnye bogosluzheniia v Solovetskom kontslagere." In Umniagin, *Vospominaniia*, Vol. 3: 309–313.

Andreevskii, Ivan Mikhailovich. "Na Kommunisticheskoi katorge." In Umniagin, *Vospominaniia*, Vol. 3: 293–295.

Andreevskii, Ivan Mikhailovich. "Pravoslavnyi evrei-ispovednik." In Umniagin, *Vospominaniia*, Vol. 3: 314–321.

Andreevskii, Ivan Mikhailovich. "Vospominaniia o episkope Viktore (Ostrovidove)." In Umniagin, *Vospominaniia*, Vol. 3: 330–331.

Antonov, Boris. *"Prisoners of Conscience" in the USSR and Their Patrons*. Moscow: Novosti Press Agency Publishing House, 1988.

Applebaum, Anne. *Gulag: A History*. New York: Doubleday, 2003.

Averbakh, I. L. *Ot prestupleniia k trudu*. Moscow: Sovetskoe zakonodatel'stvo, 1936.

Baidakov, G. "Voznesenie k vere." *Prestuplenie i nakazanie*, no. 6 (1994): 48–51.

Baidakov, G., and V. Burdyko. "Doroga v khram." *Vospitanie i pravoporiadok*, no. 7 (1993): 36–38.

Bakhtin, V. S., and B. N. Putilov. *Fol'klor i kul'turnaia sreda GULAGA*. St. Petersburg: Fond 'Za razvitie i vyzhivanie chelovechestva,' 1994.

Baran, Emily. *Dissent on the Margins: How Soviet Jehovah's Witnesses Defied Communism and Lived to Preach about It*. Oxford: Oxford University Press, 2014.

Bardach, Janusz, and Kathleen Gleeson. *Man Is Wolf to Man: Surviving the Gulag*. Berkeley: University of California Press, 1998.

Barnes, Steven. *Death and Redemption: The Gulag and the Shaping of Soviet Society*. Princeton, NJ: Princeton University Press, 2011.

Beer, Daniel. *The House of the Dead: Siberian Exile under the Tsars*. New York: Knopf, 2017.

Begin, Menachem. *White Nights: The Story of a Prisoner in Russia*. Translated by Katie Kaplan. New York: Harper & Row, 1957.

Bell, Wilson T. *Stalin's Gulag at War: Force Labour, Mass Death, and Soviet Victory in the Second World War*. Toronto: University of Toronto Press, 2019.

Belov, Iu. "Sviashchenniki v lageriakh." *Posev*, no. 5 (1980): 26–28.

Berger, Joseph. *Nothing but the Truth*. New York: John Day, 1971.

Berkman, Alexander, ed. *Letters from Russian Prisons*. New York: Albert and Charles Boni, 1925.

Bessonov, Iurii Dmitrievich. "Dvadtsat' shest' tiurem i pobeg s Solovkov." In Umniagin, *Vospominaniia*, Vol. 1: 451–514.

Bogumił, Zuzanna. *Gulag Memories: The Rediscovery and Commemoration of Russia's Repressive Past*. Translated by Philip Palmer. New York: Berghahn, 2018.

Bourdeaux, Michael. "Persecution, Collusion, and Liberation: The Russian Orthodox Church from Stalin to Gorbachev." In *The Dangerous God: Christianity and the Soviet Experiment*, edited by Dominic Erdozain, 51–73. DeKalb: Northern Illinois University Press, 2017.

"Breaking Barriers." *Frontier*, January–February 1990, 11.

Brodskii, Iurii. *Solovki: Dvadtsat' let osobogo naznacheniia*. Moscow: ROSSPEN, 2002.

Brodskii, Iurii. *Solovki: Labirint preobrazhenii*. Moscow: Novaia Gazeta, 2017.

Bukovinskii, V. *Vospominaniia sviashchennika Vladislava Buovinskogo*. Translated by M. Shmidtlain. Moscow: Tsentr po izucheniiu religii, 2000.

Buzhak, V. "Dusha obiazana trudit'sia." *Prestuplenie i nakazanie*, no. 6 (1994): 46–47.

Celmina, Helene. *Women in Soviet Prisons*. New York: Paragon House, 1985.

Chekhranov, Pavel. "Dve tiuremnye Paskhi." In Umniagin, *Vospominaniia*, Vol. 1: 711–715.

Cherkasov, A. A., ed. *Solovki*. Moscow: Sovkino, 1928.

Chernavin, V. V. "Zapiski 'vreditelia.'" In Umniagin, *Vospominaniia*, Vol. 5: 304–495.

Chernykh, N. A. *Poslednyi starets: zhizneopisanie arkhimandrita Pavla (Gruzdeva)*. Iaroslavl': Kitezh, 2004.

Chicherina, E. V. "'Po vere vashei da budet vam . . .'" In *U Boga vse zhivy: vospominaniia o danilovskom startse arkhimandrite Georgii (Lavrove)*, edited by E. V. Chicherina, 9–133. Moscow: Danilovskii blagovestnik, 1996.

248 BIBLIOGRAPHY

Chirkov, Iu. I. *A bylo vse tak…* Moscow: Politizdat, 1991.

Ciszek, Walter J., and Daniel L. Flaherty. *With God in Russia.* New York: McGraw-Hill, 1964.

Cooper, Robert Alan. "The English Quakers and Prison Reform, 1809–23." *Quaker History* 68, no. 1 (Spring 1979): 3–19.

David-Fox, Michael. *Showcasing the Great Experiment: Cultural Diplomacy and Western Visitors to the Soviet Union, 1921–1941.* Oxford: Oxford University Press, 2012.

David-Fox, Michael, ed. *The Soviet Gulag: Evidence, Interpretation, and Comparison.* Pittsburgh: University of Pittsburgh Press, 2016.

Daniel, Wallace L. *Russia's Uncommon Prophet: Father Aleksandr Men and His Times.* DeKalb: Northern Illinois University Press, 2016.

Dennen, Xenia. "'And I Will Tell of the Best People in All the Earth': Faith and Resilience in the Gulag." In *The Dangerous God: Christianity and the Soviet Experiment,* edited by Dominic Erdozain, 170–186. DeKalb: Northern Illinois University Press, 2017.

"Dnevnik lageria No. 35." *Chronicle of Current Events,* no. 38 (December 31, 1975): 45–49.

Dolgun, Alexander. *Alexander Dolgun's Story: An American in the Gulag.* New York: Alfred A. Knopf, 1975.

Dovlatov, Sergei. *The Zone: A Prison Camp Guard's Story.* New York: Alfred A. Knopf, 1985.

Ellis, Jane. *The Russian Orthodox Church: A Contemporary History.* Bloomington: University of Indiana Press, 1986.

Eminov, E. A. *Smert'—samoe strashnoe.* Moscow: Penates-Penaty, 1999.

Etinger, Ia. *Eto nevozmozhno zabyt': vospominaniia.* Moscow: Ves' mir, 2001.

Fedor, Julie, and Tomas Sniegon, "The Butovskii Shooting Range: History of an Unfinished Museum." In *Museums of Communism: New Memory Sites in Central and Eastern Europe,* edited by Stephen M. Norris, 305–343. Bloomington: Indiana University Press, 2020.

Feodosii (K. Z. Almazov). "Moi vospominaniia." In Umniagin, *Vospominaniia,* Vol. 3: 73–103.

Fletcher, William C. "The Soviet Bible Belt: World War II's Effects on Religion." In *The Impact of World War II on the Soviet Union,* edited by Susan J. Linz, 91–106. Totowa, NJ: Rowman & Allanheld, 1985.

Fletcher, William C. *Soviet Charismatics: The Pentecostals in the USSR.* Bern: Peter Lang, 1985.

Florenskii, P. V. "Solovki: Monastyr'-Lager'-Muzei-Monastyr.'" In *Prebyvaet vechno: Pis'ma P. A. Florenskogo, R. N. Litvinova, N. Ia. Briantseva i A. F. Vangengeima iz Solovetskogo lageria osobogo nazacheniia,* Vol. 1, edited by P. V. Florenskii, 61–178. Moscow: Mezhdunarognyi Tsentry Rerikhov, 2011.

Formakov, Arsenii. *Gulag Letters.* Edited and translated by Emily D. Johnson. New Haven, CT: Yale University Press, 2017.

Freeze, Gregory L. "Subversive Atheism: Soviet Antireligious Campaigns and the Religious Revival in Ukraine in the 1920s." In *State Secularism and Lived Religion in Soviet Russia and Ukraine,* edited by Catherine Wanner, 27–62. New York: Oxford University Press, 2012.

Froese, Paul. *The Plot to Kill God: Findings from the Soviet Experiment in Secularization.* Berkeley: University of California Press, 2008.

"From Prisons to Palaces." *Frontier,* July–August 1992, 20–21.

Fudel', Sergei Iosifovich. *Sobranie sochinenii.* Vol. 1. Moscow: Russkii put', 2001.

Gagen-Torn, N. I. *Memoria.* Moscow: Vozvrashchenie, 1994.

Garland, David. *Punishment and Modern Society.* Chicago: University of Chicago Press, 1993.

Gentes, Andrew A. *Exile to Siberia, 1590–1822.* Houndmills, UK: Palgrave Macmillan, 2008.

Getty, J. Arch, and Oleg V. Naumov, eds. *The Road to Terror: Stalin and the Self-Destruction of the Bolsheviks, 1933–1938.* Translated by Benjamin Sher. New Haven, CT: Yale University Press, 1999.

Ginzburg, Eugenia. *Journey into the Whirlwind.* Translated by Paul Stevenson and Max Hayward. San Diego, CA: Harcourt, 1967.

Ginzburg, Eugenia. *Within the Whirlwind.* Translated by Paul Stevenson and Max Hayward. San Diego, CA: Harcourt Brace Jovanovich, 1981.

Gorchakov, G. N. *L-I-105: vospominaniia.* Jerusalem: Ierusalimskii izdatel'skii tsentr, 1995.

BIBLIOGRAPHY 249

Gorcheva, A. Iu. *Pressa Gulaga: spiski E. P. Peshkovoi*. Moscow: Izdatel'stvo Moskovskogo universiteta, 2009.

Gor'kii, M. *Sobranie sochinenii*. Vol. 17. Moscow: Gosudarstvennoe izdatel'stvo khudozhestvennoi literatury, 1952.

Gorky, Maxim, L. Auerbach, and S. G. Firin, eds. *Belomor: An Account of the Construction of the New Canal between the White Sea and the Baltic Sea*. New York: Harrison Smith and Robert Haas, 1935.

Gregory, Paul R., and Valery Lazarev. *The Economics of Forced Labor*. Stanford, CA: Hoover Institution Press, 2003.

Gross, Jan T. *Revolution from Abroad: The Soviet Conquest of Poland's Western Ukraine and Western Belorussia*. Expanded ed. Princeton, NJ: Princeton University Press, 2002.

Gullotta, Andrea. *Intellectual Life and Literature at Solovki, 1923–1930: The Paris of the Northern Concentration Camps*. Cambridge: Legenda, 2018.

Hardy, Jeffrey. *The Gulag after Stalin: Redefining Punishment in Khrushchev's Soviet Union, 1953–1964*. Ithaca, NY: Cornell University Press, 2016.

Hardy, Jeffrey. "Gulag Tourism: Khrushchev's 'Show' Prisons in the Cold War Context, 1954–1959." *Russian Review* 71, no. 1 (January 2012): 49–78.

Hardy, Jeffrey. "Of Pelicans and Prisoners: Avian-Human Interactions in the Soviet Gulag." *Canadian Slavonic Papers* 60, nos. 3–4 (September–December 2018): 375–406.

Hardy, Jeffrey. "Religious Identity, Practice, and Hierarchy at the Solovetskii Camp of Forced Labor of Special Significance." In *Rethinking the Gulag: Identities, Sources, Legacies*, edited by Alan Barenberg and Emily D. Johnson, 19–42. Bloomington: Indiana University Press, 2022.

Hardy, Jeffrey. *The Soviet Gulag: History and Memory*. London: Bloomsbury Academic, 2023.

Harris, Rosemary, and Xenia Howard-Johnson. *Christian Prisoners in Russia*. Wheaton, IL: Tyndale House, 1969.

Herling, Gustaw. *A World Apart*. Translated by Andrzej Ciolkosz. New York: Penguin, 1986.

Hornsby, Robert. *Protest, Reform and Repression in Khrushchev's Soviet Union*. Cambridge: Cambridge University Press, 2013.

Husband, William B. *"Godless Communists": Atheism and Society in Soviet Russia, 1917–1932*. DeKalb: Northern Illinois University Press, 2000.

"'I Was in Prison and You Visited Me,'" *Frontier*, January–February 1988, 5–6.

Iarotskii, A. S. *Zolotaia Kolyma*. Zheleznodorozhnyi: RUPAP, 2003.

Iasnopol'skaia, V. N. "Schastlivyi sluchai: vospominaniia." In *Mironositsy v epokhu GULAGa: 1918–1932: svidetel'stva, memuary*, edited by P. G. Protsenko, 465–607. Nizhny Novgorod: Izdatel'stvo Bratstva vo imia sviatogo Aleksandra Nevskogo, 2004.

Ioann. *Tserkovnye raskoly v russkoi tserkvi 20-x i 30-x godov XX stoletiia*. Sortavala: Sortoval'skoi knizhnoi tipografiia, 1993.

Iurkevich, Iu. L. *Minuvshee prokhodit predo mnoiu...* Moscow: Vozvrashchenie, 2000.

Iuvenalii Riazanskii. *Pis'ma iz lageria*. Moscow: Izdatel'stvo imeni Sviatitelia Ignatiia Stavropol'skogo, 1995.

Ivanova, G. M. *Istoriia GULAGa, 1918–1956*. Moscow: Nauka, 2006.

"Iz pisem sviashchennika Vasiliia Romaniuka." *Vestnik Russkogo Khristianskogo Dvizheniia* 129, no. 3 (1979): 281–283.

Jacobson, Mikhail, and Lydia Jacobson, eds. *Pesennyi fol'klor GULAGa kak istochnik (1917–1939)*. Moscow: Sovremennyi gumanitarnyi universitet, 1998.

Jakobson, Michael. *Origins of the Gulag: The Soviet Prison Camp System, 1917–1934*. Lexington: University Press of Kentucky, 1993.

Johnson, Emily D. "Performing Family Unity: Holiday Celebrations in the Labor Camp Correspondence of Arsenii Formakov." In *Russian Performances: Word, Object, Action*, edited by Julie A. Buckler, Julie A. Cassiday, and Boris Wolfson, 252–261. Madison: University of Wisconsin Press, 2018.

Kabo, V. P. *Doroga v Avstraliiu*. New York: Effect Publishing, 1995.

250 BIBLIOGRAPHY

Kadayeva, Vera. "Harvest Time in Russia." *Frontier*, March–April 1991, 13–14.

Kalinin, V. "O religii—bez predrassudkov." *Vospitanie i pravoporiadok*, no. 6 (1990): 18–19.

Kashirin, Alexander. "Protestant Minorities in the Soviet Ukraine, 1945–1991." PhD diss., University of Oregon, 2010.

Kaufman, A. I. *Lagernyi vrach: 16 let v Sovetskom Soiuze: vospominaniia sionista*. Tel Aviv: Am Obed, 1973.

Kelly, Catriona. "Socialist Churches: Heritage Preservation and 'Cultic Buildings' in Leningrad, 1924–1940." *Slavic Review* 71, no. 4 (Winter 2012): 792–823.

Keston Center. *Christian Prisoners in the USSR*. Oxford, UK: Keston Center, 1979–1987.

Khlevniuk, Oleg. *The History of the Gulag: From Collectivization to the Great Terror*. Translated by Vadim A. Staklo. New Haven, CT: Yale University Press, 2004.

Khorev, Mikhail. *Letters from a Soviet Prison Camp*. Eastbourne, UK: Monarch, 1988.

Kis, Oksana. *Survival as Victory: Ukrainian Women in the Gulag*. Translated by Lidia Wolanskyj. Cambridge, MA: Harvard University Press, 2021.

Kiselev, S. "Russian Bishop Visits Soviet Prison." *Literaturnaya gazeta*, July 19, 1989.

Kiselev-Gromov, N. *S.L.O.N.: Solovetskii les osobogo naznacheniia*. Arkhangel'sk: Tur, 2009.

Klimanova, Liudmila Vasilevna. "My Meetings with Anna Petrovna Skripnikova." In *Remembering the Darkness: Women in Soviet Prisons*, edited and translated by Veronica Shapovalov, 165–174. Lanham, MD: Rowman & Littlefield, 2001.

Klinger, Anton. "Solovetskaia katorga: zapiski bezhavshego." In Umniagin, *Vospominaniia*, Vol. 1: 48–120.

Kokurin, A. N., and N. V. Petrov, eds. *GULAG: Glavnoe upravlenie lagerei, 1918–1960*. Moscow: Mezhdunarodnyi fond "Demokratiia," 2000.

Kolomeets, S. "Bog v pomoshch'. . ." *Vospitanie i pravoporiadok*, no 10 (1990): 44–49.

Kopelev, Lev. *To Be Preserved Forever*. Translated by Anthony Austin. Philadelphia: Lippincott, 1977.

Kostyuchenko, G. V. "Poedinok." *Vestnik istiny*, no. 3 (1980): 22–26.

Kozlov, V. P., ed. *Istoriia stalinskogo GULAGa: konets 20-kh—pervaia polovina 50-kh godov*. 7 vols. Moscow: Rosspen, 2004.

Kozlova, Alena, Nikolai Mikhailov, Irina Ostrovskaia, and Svetlana Fadeeva, eds. *Papiny pis'ma: pis'ma ottsov iz GULAGa k detiam*. Moscow: Agei Tomesh/WAM, 2015.

Krakhmalnikova, Zoya. *Listen, Prison! Lefortovo Notes, Letters from Exile*. Translated by Olga Koshansky. Redding, CA: Nikodemos Orthodox Publication Society, 1993.

Krakhmalnikova, Zoya. "Trial by Fire." *Frontier*, July–August 1989, 23.

Krasnopevtsev, L. N. ". . . U nas byla svoia tochka zreniia . . ." *Karta*, nos. 17–18 (1997): 65–70.

Kurakina, T. G. "Vospominaniia kniagini T. G. Kurakinoi, urozhdennoi baroness Vrangel', 1918–1921 gg." In *Russkaia letopis': kniga piataia*, 178–292. Paris: Russkyi ochag, 1923.

Kureishi, Said. "Piat' let v sovetskikh tiur'makh." In Umniagin, *Vospominaniia*, Vol. 2: 90–148.

Kuzin, A. N. *Malyi srok: vospominaniia v forme esse so svobodnym siuzhetom*. Moscow: Rudomino, 1994.

Kyrke-Smith, Neville. "Nightmare in Siberia." *Catholic Herald*, September 21, 2001.

Lavinskaia, O. V., and Iu. G. Orlova. *Zakliuchennye na stroikakh kommunizma: Gulag i ob'ekty energetiki v SSSR*. Moscow: ROSSPEN, 2008.

Lebedev, Valeri. "Chained Freedom." *Frontier*, July–August 1992, 14–15.

Lenin, V. I. "The Attitude of the Workers' Party to Religion." In V. I. Lenin, *Collected Works*, translated by Andrew Rothstein and Bernard Isaacs, Vol. 15, 402–413. Moscow: Progress, 1973.

Leonardovich, Mechislav. "Na ostravakh pytok i smerti: vospominaniia s Solovkov." In Umniagin, *Vospominaniia*, Vol. 1: 596–632.

Lepikhin, S. "'Pust' Iisus istselit vam razbitye serdtsa.'" *Vospitanie i pravoporiadok*, nos. 11–12 (1992): 44–46.

Lepikhin, S. "Stanet li greshnik pravednikom?" *Vospitanie i pravoporiadok*, no. 4 (1991): 48–49.

Leshchenko-Sukhomlina, Tatyana. "Selections from 'My Guitar.'" In Vilensky, *Till My Tale Is Told*, 228–239.

BIBLIOGRAPHY   251

Levitin-Krasnov, A. E. *'Ruk Tvoikh zhar' (1941–1956)*. Tel Aviv: Krug, 1979.

Likhachev, Dmitry S. *Reflections on the Russian Soul: A Memoir*. Budapest: CEU Press, 2000.

Lipper, Elinor. *Eleven Years in Soviet Prison Camps*. Translated by Richard Winston and Clara Winston. Chicago: Henry Regnery, 1951.

Lobanov, V. V. *Patriarkh Tikhon i sovetskaia vlast': 1917–1925 gg*. Moscow: Russkaia panorama, 2008.

Losev, A. F. *Zhizn': Povesti, rasskazy, pis'ma*. St. Petersburg: Komplekt, 1993.

"Love behind Bars." *Frontier*, July–August 1992, 26–27.

Loviniukov, A. "Svoboda sovesti v ITU." *Vospitanie i pravoporiadok*, nos. 11–12 (1992): 42–46.

Lunkin, Roman. "The Charismatic Movement in Russia." *East-West Church & Ministry Report* 13 (Winter 2005): 1–3.

Maddox, Steven. "Gulag Football: Competitive and Recreational Sport in Stalin's System of Forced Labor." *Kritika: Explorations in Russian and Eurasian History* 19, no. 3 (Summer 2018): 509–536.

Mal'sagov, Sozerko Artaganovich. "Adskii ostrov." In Umniagin, *Vospominaniia*, Vol. 1: 370–444.

Marchenko, A. T. *Zhivi kak vse: moi pokazaniia*. Moscow: Vest', 1993.

Marchenko, Zoya. "The Way It Was." In Vilensky, *Till My Tale Is Told*, 200–210.

Martsinkovsky, V. F. *Zapiski veruiushchego: iz istorii religioznogo dvizheniia v Sovetskoi Rossii (1917–1923)*. Prague: Izdatel'stvo avtora, 1929.

Mashkov, Iu. T. "Golos s rodiny." *Russkoe vozrozhdenie*, no. 4 (1978): 12–21.

Mattila, Kathleen Hiatt. "Sedition and the Sacred: The Political Repression of Religious Figures in Stalinist Ukraine, 1930–1955." PhD diss., Indiana University, 2016.

Monakhov, V. "V bor'be s religioznim durmanom." *K novoi zhizni*, no. 2 (1960): 76–77.

"More Releases!" *Frontier*, July–August 1987, 24.

Moroz, Valentyn. *Boomerang: The Works of Valentyn Moroz*. Baltimore: Smoloskyp Publishers, 1974.

Morris, Norval, and David J. Rothman, eds. *The Oxford History of the Prison: The Practice of Punishment in Western Society*. New York: Oxford University Press, 1998.

Murray, Damon, and Stephen Sorrell, eds. *Russian Criminal Tattoo Encyclopedia*. 3 vols. London: Fuel, 2004–2008.

Navalny, Alexei (@navalny). "11/11 Tak chto tiuremnaia Sistema Rossii." Twitter, January 31, 2023. https://twitter.com/navalny/status/1620435946406813697.

Nazarov, M. "Mitropolit Filaret: 'Ia prishel otkryt' vashi dushi.'" *Vospitanie i pravoporiadok*, no. 1 (1990): 55–57.

"News of Prisoners." *Frontier*, September–October 1990, 25.

"News Round-Up." *Frontier*, January–February 1987, 22.

Nikona (Osipenko). "So slov ochevidtsa . . ." In Umniagin, *Vospominaniia*, Vol. 3: 52–54.

Nikonov-Smorodin, Mikhail Zakharovich. "Krasnaia katorga." In Umniagin, *Vospominaniia*, Vol. 5: 228–255.

Noble, John, and Glenn D. Everett. *I Found God in Soviet Russia*. New York: St. Martin's, 1959.

"Obrashchenie Solovetskikh episkopov." *Sever*, no. 9 (1990): 101–107.

Olekhnovich, Frants Karlovich. "V kogtiakh GPU." In Umniagin, *Vospominaniia*, Vol. 5: 506–577.

Orsi, Robert A. *History and Presence*. Cambridge, MA: Belknap Press, 2016.

Osipov, V. N. *Dubravlag: predo monoiu ikona i zapretnaia zona* . . . Moscow: Nash sovremennik, 2003.

Osipova, I. I. *'Skvoz' ogi' muchenii i vodu slez . . .': goneniia na Istinno-Pravoslavnuiu Tserkov'*. Moscow: Serebrianye niti, 1998.

Osipova, I. I. *'V iazvakh svoikh sokroi menia . . .': goneniia na Katolicheskuiu Terkov' v SSSR*. Moscow: Serebrianye niti, 1996.

Panin, Dmitri. *The Notebooks of Sologdin*. Translated by John Moore. London: Hutchinson, 1976.

Pantiukhin, I. V. *Stolitsa Kolymskogo Kraia: zapiski Magadanskogo prokurora*. Petrozavodsk: Folium, 2000.

252 BIBLIOGRAPHY

Pasat, V., ed. *Pravoslavie v Moldavii: vlast', tserkov', veruiushchie (1940–1953).* 4 vols. Moscow: ROSSPEN, 2009–2011.

"Pentecost in Prison." *Frontier,* January–March 1993, 21–24.

Perchatkin, B. G. *Ognennye tropy.* Seattle: Boris Perchatkin, 2002.

Peris, Daniel. *Storming the Heavens: The Soviet League of the Militant Godless.* Ithaca, NY: Cornell University Press, 1998.

Petkevich, Tamara. *Memoir of a Gulag Actress.* Translated by Yasha Klots and Ross Ufberg. DeKalb: Northern Illinois University Press, 2010.

Petrov, Aleksei Petrovich. "Vospominaniia izgnannika za veru." In Umniagin, *Vospominaniia,* Vol. 5: 62–113.

Petrus, K. *Uzniki kommunizma.* Moscow: Izdatel'stvo imeni sviatitelia Ignatiia Stavropol'skogo, 1996.

Plutser-Sarno, Alexei. "'All Power to the Godfathers!'" In Murray and Sorrell, *Russian Criminal Tattoo Encyclopedia,* vol. 3: 32–57.

Plutser-Sarno, Alexei. "The Language of the Body and Politics: The Symbolism of Thieves' Tattoos." In Murray and Sorrell, *Russian Criminal Tattoo Encyclopedia,* vol. 1: 26–53.

Pol'skii, Mikhail Afanas'evich. "Publikatsii o Solovkakh." In Umniagin, *Vospominaniia,* Vol. 2: 55–82.

Postovalova, V. I. "Christian Motifs and Themes in the Life and Works of Aleksei Fedorovich Losev: Fragments of a Spiritual Biography." *Russian Studies in Philosophy* 40, no. 3 (Winter 2001–2002): 83–92.

Priadilov, *Zapiski kontrrevoliutsionera.* Moscow: B. I., 1999.

"Prison Ordeals Made Public." *Frontier,* March–April 1991, 15.

"'Prisoners of Faith' in the USSR.'" *Frontier,* July–August 1988, 21–23.

Puzyrev, M. D. *I pokatilsia kolobok.* [Kotlas]: n.p., 1997.

Rabinovich, M. B. *Vospominaniia dolgoi zhizni.* St. Petersburg: Evropeiskii dom, 1996.

Ratushinskaya, Irina. *Grey Is the Colour of Hope.* Translated by Alyona Kojevnikov. London: Hodder & Stoughton, 1988.

Ratushinskaya, Irina. "Someone Is Thinking of Me Now." *Frontier* (March–April 1987): 12–14.

Rayner, O. T., trans. *The Criminal Code of the Russian Socialist Federative Soviet Republic.* London: H.M.S.O., 1925.

Rendle, Matthew. "Mercy amid Terror? The Role of Amnesties during Russia's Civil War." *Slavonic and East European Review* 92, no. 3 (July 2014): 449–478.

Reznikova, Irina. *Pravoslavie na Solovkakh: materialy po istorii Solovetskogo lageria.* Saint Petersburg: Memorial, 1994.

Robson, Roy. *Solovki: The Story of Russia Told through Its Most Remarkable Islands.* New Haven, CT: Yale University Press, 2004.

Ronkin, V. E. *Na smenu dekabriam prikhodiat ianvari.* Moscow: Zven'ia, 2003.

Roslof, Edward. *Red Priests: Renovationism, Russian Orthodoxy, and Revolution, 1905–1946.* Bloomington: Indiana University Press, 2002.

Rotfort, M. S. *Kolyma—krugi ada: vospominaniia.* Yekaterinburg: Uralskii rabochii, 1991.

Rozanov, Mikhail. *Solovetskii kontslager' v monastyre, 1922–1939 gody.* Vol. 1. N.p.: Izd. Avtora, 1979.

"Russian Orthodox Prisoners: Camp Conditions." *Religion in Communist Lands* 5, no. 4 (Winter 1977): 264–266.

Sadunaite, Nijole. *A Radiance in the Gulag: The Catholic Witness of Nijole Sadunaite.* Traslated by Casimir Pugevicius and Marian Skabeikis. Manassas, VA: Trinity Communications, 1987.

Sapiets, Marite. *True Witness: The Story of Seventh Day Adventists in the Soviet Union.* Keston, UK: Keston College, 1990.

Sapir, Boris Moiseevich. "Puteshestvie v severnye lageria." In Umniagin, *Vospominaniia,* Vol. 1: 134–148.

Sederkhol'm, Boris Leonidovich. "V razboinnom stane: tri goda v strane kontsessii i 'Cheki' (1923–1926)." In Umniagin, *Vospominaniia,* Vol. 1: 665–708.

BIBLIOGRAPHY 253

"Segodnia sovetskikh kontslagerei." *Posev*, no. 2 (February 1974): 14.
Senderov, V. A. "Bog i tiur'ma." *Novyi mir*, no. 11 (1995): 172–182.
"Seventh Day Adventists." *Frontier*, November–December 1990, 22–23.
Sgovio, Thomas. *Dear America! Why I Turned against Communism*. Kenmore, NY: Partner's Press, 1979.
Shalamov, Varlam. *Kolyma Tales*. Translated by John Glad. London: Penguin, 1994.
Shaufel'berger, Arnol'd Sergius Leonardovich. "Solovki." In Umniagin, *Vospominaniia*, Vol. 1: 639–660.
Shelley, Louise. "Soviet Criminology: Its Birth and Demise, 1917–1936." *Slavic Review* 38, no. 4 (December 1979): 614–628.
Shiriaev, B. N. *Neugasimaia lampada*. Moscow: T-vo rus. khudozh., 1991.
Shul'ts, V. A. "Taganka; V Srednei Azii." In *Dodnes' tiagoteet: zapiski vashei sovremennitsy*, Vol. 1, edited by S. S. Vilenskii, 185–221. Moscow: Sovetskaia pisatel', 1989.
Sidorov, Alexander. "The Russian Criminal Tattoo: Past and Present." In Murray and Sorrell, *Russian Criminal Tattoo Encyclopedia*, vol. 2: 16–43.
Skotnicki, Andrew. *Religion and the Development of the American Penal System*. Lanham, MD: University Press of America, 2000.
Smirnov, M. B., ed. *Sistema ispravitel'no-trudovykh lagerei v SSSR, 1923–1960: spravochnik*. Moscow: Zven'ia, 1998.
Solomon, Michael. *Magadan*. Princeton, NJ: Vertex, 1971.
Solonevich, Boris Luk'ianovich. "Molodezh' v GPU (Zhizn' i bor'ba sovetskoi molodezhi)." In Umniagin, *Vospominaniia*, Vol. 2: 356–426.
Solovetskaia muza: stikhi i pesni zakliuchennykh SLONa. Moscow: Vozvrashchenie, 1992.
Solzhenitsyn, Aleksandr Isaevich. *The Gulag Archipelago: An Experiment in Literary Investigation*. 3 vols. Translated by Thomas P. Whitney. New York: Harper & Row, 1974–1978.
Solzhenitsyn, Aleksandr Isaevich. *One Day in the Life of Ivan Denisovich*. Translated by Harry T. Willets. New York: Vintage, 2008.
Sooster, L. I. *Moi Sooster*. Tallinn: Avenarius, 2000.
Soshina, Antonina Alekseevna. *Na Solovkakh protiv voli: sud'by i sroki, 1923–1939*. Moscow: Izdatel'stvo TSM, 2014.
Sporov, B. F. "Pis'mena tiuremnykh sten: povest'." *Nash sovremennik*, no. 10 (1993): 65–91.
Strickland, John. *The Making of Holy Russia: The Orthodox Church and Russian Nationalism before the Revolution*. Jordanville, NY: Holy Trinity Publications, 2013.
Svianevich, S. S. *V teni Katyni*. Translated by V. Abramkina. London: Overseas Publications Interchange, 1989.
Szabados, Arpad. *Dvadtsat' piat' let v SSSR (1922–1947 gg.)*. Translated by Tatjana Lengyel. Budapest: Vadim Litinskii, 1958.
Tapley, Lauren. "'I Hasten to Establish a Common Language with You': Orthodox Christian Dissidents and the Human Rights Movement." In *The Dangerous God: Christianity and the Soviet Experiment*, edited by Dominic Erdozain, 138–157. DeKalb: Northern Illinois University Press, 2017.
Terelya, Josyp. *Witness to Apparitions and Persecution in the USSR*. Milford, OH: Faith Publishing, 1991.
Tikhanova, V. A., ed. *Tvorchestvo i byt GULAGa: katalog muzeinogo sobraniia Obshchestvo 'Memorial'*. Moscow: Zven'ia, 1998.
Tolstaia, A. L. *Probleski vo t'me*. Moscow: Patriot, 1991.
Ugrimov, A. A. *Iz Moskvy v Moskvu cherez Parizh i Vorkutu*. Moscow: Izdatel'stvo "RA," 2004.
Umniagin, Viacheslav. "Sviashchennomuchenik Ilarion (Troitskii) glazami souznikov." In Umniagin, *Vospominaniia solovetskikh uznikov*, Vol. 2: 332–341.
Umniagin, Viacheslav, ed. *Vospominaniia solovetskikh uznikov*. 5 vols. Solovki: Izdanie Solovetskogo monastyria, 2013–2018.
Usachev, A. "Mrakobes." *K novoi zhizni*, no. 2 (1971): 80.

254 BIBLIOGRAPHY

Usov, A. "Nedoumenie 'sviatoi' Agaf'i." *K novoi zhizni*, no. 12 (1968): 48.

Utevskii, B. S. *Sovetskaia ispravitel'no-trudovaia politika.* Moscow: Sovetskoe zakonodatel'stvo, 1930.

V. N. I. "Solovetskii kontslager' (so slov ochevidtsa)." In Umniagin, *Vospominaniia*, Vol. 3: 55–60.

"V tiurmakh i lageriakh." *Chronicle of Current Events*, no. 40 (May 20, 1976): 79–88.

Vagin, Evgenii. "Interv'iu 'vestniku RKhD." *Vestnik Russkogo Khristianskogo Dvizheniia* 122, no. 3 (1977): 252–262.

Vail', B. B. *Osobo opasnyi.* London: Overseas Publications Interchange, 1980.

Vasenko, P. G. *Boiare Romanovy i votsarenie Mikhaila.* Saint Petersburg: Gosudarstvennaia tipografiia, 1913.

Vasilenko, L. P. *Tiuremnye khramy Sankt-Peterburgskoi eparkhii.* St. Petersburg: Vozvrashchenie, 2003.

Verblovskaia, I. S. "Pis'mo byvshei uznitsy." In *Uroki gneva i liubvi: sbornik vospominanii o godakh repressii (20-e–80-e gg.)*, edited by T. V. Tigonen, 153–158. St. Petersburg: Vyborgskaia storona, 1993.

Vergel', Iu. "Po kom ne zvonit kolokol . . ." *Vospitanie i pravoporiadok*, no. 4 (1990): 38–40.

Vilenskii, S. S., ed. *Poeziia uznikov GULAGa: antologiia.* Moscow: Mezhdunarodnyi fond "Demokratiia," 2005.

Vilensky, Simeon, ed. *Till My Tale Is Told: Women's Memoirs of the Gulag.* Translated by John Crowfoot, Marjorie Farquharson, Catriona Kelly, Sally Larid, and Cathy Porter. Bloomington: Indiana University Press, 1999.

Vincent, Mark. *Criminal Subculture in the Gulag: Prisoner Society in the Stalinist Labour Camps.* London: I.B. Tauris, 2019.

Vinogradov, V., A. Litvin, and V. Khristoforov, eds. *Arkhiv VChK: Sbornik dokumentov.* Moscow: Kuchkovo pole, 2007.

Vins, Georgi. *Konshaubi—Free on the Inside.* Eastbourne, UK: Kingsway, 1988.

Viola, Lynne. *The Unknown Gulag: The Lost World of Stalin's Special Settlements.* Oxford: Oxford University Press, 2007.

V'iushina, L. "Antireligioznaia propaganda—vazhnyi uchastok ideologicheskoi raboty." *Ispravitel'no-trudovye uchrezhdeniia*, no. 3 (1959): 23–30. Located in GARF, f. R-9414, op. 4, d. 207.

"Vladimirskaia tiur'ma." *Chronicle of Current Events*, no. 39 (March 12, 1976): 21–22.

Volkov, Oleg Vasil'evich. "Pogruzhenie vo t'mu." In Umniagin, *Vospominaniia*, Vol. 3: 221–270.

Volovich, Hava. "My Past." In Vilensky, *Till My Tale Is Told*, 241–278.

Vospitanie i pravoporiadok, no. 3 (1993): front matter.

Vospitanie i pravoporiadok, no. 8 (1990): title page.

Vtorova-Iafa, Ol'ga Viktorovna. "Avgurovy ostrova." In Umniagin, *Vospominaniia*, Vol. 3: 383–495.

Vyshinskii, A. Ia. *Ot tiurem k vopitatel'nym uchrezhdeniiam.* Moscow: Gosudarstvennoe izdatel'stvo Sovetskoe zakonodatel'stvo, 1934.

Walters, Philipp. "From Community to Isolation: Alexander Ogorodnikov." *Frontier*, January–February 1987, 4–5.

"We Went to See Our Pastor—in Prison." *Frontier*, July–August 1988, 5.

"Within These Walls." *Frontier*, November–December 1990, 12–14.

Yakir, Pyotr. *A Childhood in Prison.* New York: Coward, McCann & Geoghegan, 1973.

Zaitsev, Ivan Matveevich. "Solovki (Kommunisticheskaia katorga, ili Mesto pytok i smerti)." In Umniagin, *Vospominaniia*, Vol. 2: 172–330.

Zarod, Kazimierz. *Inside Stalin's Gulag: A True Story of Survival.* Sussex, UK: Book Guild, 1990.

Zhigulin, A. V. *Chernye kamni: avtobiograficheskaia povest'.* Moscow: Kul'tura, 1996.

Index

For the benefit of digital users, indexed terms that span two pages (e.g., 52–53) may, on occasion, appear on only one of those pages.

Note: Figures are indicated by an italic *f* following the page number.

Ablamsky, Vladimir, 159
Adamova-Sliozberg, Olga, 97–98
Adventists. *See* Seventh-Day Adventists
Alexy II (Russian Orthodox patriarch), 225
All-Union Council of Evangelical Christians and Baptists, 99–100
Alyoshka the Baptist (character in *One Day in the Life of Ivan Denisovich*), vii–viii, 108, 109
Andreev, Gennady, 49–50, 55–56
Andreeva, Alla, 110, 115, 131–32
Andreyevsky, Ivan, 50, 54–55, 59–60, 63–64, 65–66, 67
Andronevsky Special-Purpose Camp, 14
Andronnikov Monastery, 15*f*, 20–21
antireligious propaganda in prison camps
    Brezhnev era and, 177, 178
    Corrective-Labor Code (1924) and, 29–31
    Islam as a target of, 79, 150–51
    Khrushchev era and, 146–47
    lectures and, 31–32, 45–46, 78, 100–1, 148–49, 150–51, 168, 178
    postwar diminution (1945-1953) of, 105–7
    prison libraries and, 32, 78
    prison publications and, 33–36, 46–47, 78–81, 95–96, 178
    Russian civil war period and, 29
    scientific explanations prioritized in, 31–32, 45–46, 79
    Stalin and, 71, 79
    World War II and, 100–1
Antony (Russian Orthodox archbishop), 67
Anzer Island camps, 44–45, 73–74
Arkady (Russian Orthodox bishop), 75–76
Armenia, 3, 9
Astrakhan Prison, 96–97
atheism
    Corrective-Labor Code (1924) and, 29–31
    Gorbachev reform era and, 214, 215, 222
    as official Communist Party doctrine, 33–34, 37–38, 52–53, 149–50, 180–81
    prison publications and, 35–36

Averbakh, Ida, 77

Baikal-Amursky Camp, 81
Balakhninsky County Prison, 23
Baptists
    All-Union Council of Evangelical Christians and Baptists and, 99–100
    Brezhnev era gulag camps and, 176–79, 180–81, 182–84, 188
    compulsory labor in gulag camps and, 49–50, 170
    Gorbachev era religious reforms and proselytization in gulag camps by, 216–18
    Kopelev's description of gulag experiences of, 109
    petitions for freedom of religion in gulag camps by, 192–93, 194
    proselytization and conversions in gulag camps and, 112–13, 132, 151, 188–89, 207–8
    proselytization in Russian Empire by, 9
    religious faith as a source of faith in gulag camps for, 176, 197–200
    religious services and celebrations in prison camps by, 56, 123–24, 136–37
    religious texts reproduced in gulag camps by, 169
    Sabbatarians' conflicts with, 137
Baran, Emily, 169
Barats, Vasily, 182, 197
Bardach, Janusz, 101–2, 133–34
Baturin, N. G., 192–93
Baturina, Valentina, 194–95
Begin, Menachem, 96
Belomor (Gorky), 77–78
Belov, Yuri, 170–73
Berezny Camp, 100–1
Berger, Joseph, 113, 114, 122
Bessarabia, 120
Bessonov, Yury, 53–54

256 INDEX

"bitches' war" (early 1950s), 138, 142
Bogdanov, Vladimir, 29
Bolshevik Revolution (1917), 3, 12, 26
Bolshoy Zayatskoy Island, 44–45
Brezhnev, Leonid
  antireligious propaganda in gulag camps
    under, 177, 178
  antireligious repression in gulag camps
    under, 177, 178–83
  Gulag reforms under, 176, 177, 201
  letters from gulag prisoners to family
    members during era of, 196
  petitioning for freedom of religion in gulag
    camps during reign of, 191
  religious life and identity in gulag camps
    under, 183
  size of religious prisoner population in gulag
    camps under, 177
Bucha Maximum-Security Prison, 211–13
Buddhists, 9–10, 144–45, 226
Bukin, V. I., 205
Bukovinsky, Vladislav, 126–27, 165, 174
Butman, G. I., 191–92
Butovo execution site, 226–28
Butyrka Prison (Moscow), 29, 220–21

Catacomb Church. *See* True Orthodox
    Church
Catholics
  antireligious propaganda directed at, 150–51
  compulsory labor in gulag camps and,
    81, 180–81
  Great Terror and, 93–94, 97, 98, 99
  overall number in Russian Empire of, 9–10
  prayer in gulag camps and, 110–11
  proselytization efforts in gulag camps by,
    132, 174
  religion as source of strength in gulag camps
    among, 197
  religious objects used in prison by, 127–28
  religious services and celebrations in prison
    camps by, 14, 21, 53, 126, 130–31
  at Solovki Camp, 42–43, 47–48, 53, 61–62,
    73–75, 94
  from western borderland territories,
    122, 123–24
  See also Ukrainian Greek Catholics (Uniates)
Cedfeldt, William, 219–20
Celmina, Helene, 159–60, 166, 168, 170–71,
    172, 173
Central Penal Department, 22–26, 37
Chekhranov, Pavel, 59, 60
Cheremukha, Stepan, 155

Chernobyl nuclear accident (1986), 203–4, 205
Chicherina, Elena, 81–82, 88–89
Christmas, 88, 130–31, 135, 153–54, 155*f*, 170,
    185, 189–90
Ciszek, Walter, 110–11, 112*f*, 126, 139–
    40, 153–54
Communist Party
  atheism and, 33–34, 37–38, 52–53, 149–
    50, 180–81
  Communist Youth League and, 120–21
  opening to religious groups after 1985 in, 204
  religious practices among members of, 121
  resistance in "western borderlands" of Soviet
    Union to cultural hegemony of, 120–21
compulsory labor in prison camps
  agricultural work and, 71–72
  clerical prisoners and, 48–49, 74, 77–78
  Corrective-Labor Code (1924) and, 29–31
  infrastructure projects and, 71–72, 77–
    78, 104–5
  mining and, 71–72, 84
  production targets and, 72
  punishment for infractions involving, 49–50,
    99, 108–9, 116, 184
  religious exemptions and, 15–16, 21, 49–50
  on religious holidays, 49–50
  resistance against, 50, 73–74, 89–91, 94–95,
    98–99, 101, 105–6, 107–8, 116, 121–22,
    134–35, 137, 148–49, 151, 152–53, 170–
    71, 174
  at Solovki, 42, 48
Constitution of the Soviet Union (1918), 14–15,
    24–25, 28, 37–38, 148, 191, 193, 196
Corrective-Labor Code (1924), 29–31, 212–13
Council of Relatives of Evangelical Christian-
    Baptist Prisoners, 176, 192–93
"cult workers," 73, 214

Dalstroy Camps, 97–98, 105–6, 108, 115
Danzas, Yulia, 61–62
Deresh, Pavel, 133
Dmitrovsky Camp, 79
Dolgikh, Ivan, 106, 148–49, 165
Dolgun, Alexander, 133
Dombkovsky, Nikolai, 206–7
Dovlatov, Sergei, 153
Dubitsky, Adam, 181–82, 197–98
Dubravny Camp (Dubravlag)
  antireligious propaganda at, 166, 168
  antireligious suppression at, 167–68
  Camp Division 1 at, 165–66, 167–68, 174–75
  Camp Division 7 at, 165–67
  Camp Division 10 at, 165–66

INDEX 257

Camp Division 17 at, 165–66, 167–68
Catholics at, 170, 174
designation as camp for religious prisoners
  of, 165, 175
Jehovah's Witnesses at, 166–68, 171–74
location of, 165–66
number of prisoners at, 165–66
re-education initiatives at, 167, 175
religious artifacts created at, 116
religious diversity among inmate population
  at, 136, 166, 174–75
True Orthodox Church members at, 170
Ukranian Greek Catholics at, 168–69
Ukranian prisoners at, 166
Dukhobor spiritualist movement, 9, 73–74
Dukhonchenko, Jacob, 216
Dzerzhinsky, Felix, 5–6
Dzhezkazgansky camp, 95–96

Easter
  cards created for, 116–19, 118f
  religious services in prison camps
    celebrating, 24, 28, 40, 52–53, 55–56, 58–
    59, 84, 88, 89–90, 97–98, 109–10, 114, 130,
    131–32, 153–54, 156f, 185, 189–90
  suppression of religious services celebrating,
    74, 182
Eikhmans, Fedor, 49, 52, 58–59
Elshtein-Gorchakov, Genrikh, 101, 130
"Epistle of the Solovetsky Bishops," 64–66
Estonia, 9, 120, 156–58
Etinger, Yakov, 132
Evgeny (Russian Orthodox archbishop), 62,
  63f, 64–65, 139–40

Fedorchenko, Ivan, 194
Fedorov, Leonid, 47–48, 61–62
Feodosy (Russian Orthodox archimandrite),
  49, 50–51, 52, 58–60, 63–64, 66–67
Filaret of Kyiv (Russian Orthodox
  metropolitan), 211–12, 213
Finland, 9, 120
Formakov, Arseny, 116–19
Frankl, Viktor, 2
French Revolution, 24
Frolovsky, Mikhail, 55
Fryazinov, Sergey, 27, 29
Fudel, Sergey, 29, 30f

Gagen-Torn, Nina, 136–38
Galovanova, Katya, 136–37
gangsters in gulag camps
  ballads sung by, 140–41

"bitches' war" and, 138
camp guards and, 138
Catholic beliefs among, 139–40
conversion to Christianity among, 160–61
corruption and theft reduced by, 122
religious imagery among, 138
religious tattoos and, 121, 138–39, 141–
  45, 143f
Russian Orthodox beliefs among, 121, 138–
  39, 161
violence against other inmates by, 138–39
Georgia, 9
Germanyuk, Stepan, 201–2
Gideons International, 210, 215–16
Ginzburg, Evgenia, 98–99
Golgotha camp hospital, 44–45
Golgotha memorial complex, 226
Golovinsky Convent, 18–19
Gorbachev, Mikhail
  antireligious repression in gulag camps
    under, 205–6
  Chernobyl nuclear accident (1986) and,
    203–4, 205
  economic reforms under, 203–4
  gulag reforms under, 204–5
  pardoning of political and religious prisoners
    by, 208
  political opening under, 203–4
  religious liberalization permitted under, 209,
    216, 222
  Reykjavik Summit (1986) and, 208
  Russian Orthodox Church's one-thousand
    year anniversary (1988) and, 209
Gorky, Maxim, 68, 77–78, 150–51, 178
Gorny Camp, 154
Great Patriotic War. See World War II
Great Terror (1937-1938)
  antireligious propaganda in gulag camps
    during, 95–96
  antireligious suppression in gulag camps
    during, 95–96
  Catholics targeted in, 93–94, 97, 98, 99
  crises of faith during, 92–93
  extrajudicial trials and, 94
  mass arrests during, 92, 93
  mass executions during, 92, 93–95, 226–28
  Operational Order No. 00447 and, 93–94
  religious faith as source of strength in gulag
    camps during, 92–93, 96–99
  secret police's role in, 93–94
  Stalin's role in, 92, 93
  worship sites closed during, 93–94
Grigory (Russian Orthodox bishop), 64

258 INDEX

Grinevich (Russian Orthodox archpriest), 63–64
Gruzdev, Pavel, 107, 115
Gulag camps
  bullying of religious prisoners in, 101–2, 108–9, 121–22, 151
  Christian ministry after 1985 in, 210
  "class enemies" as prisoners in, 7–8, 72, 73, 120
  clerical prisoners in, 73–76, 77–78, 81, 82–84, 90–91, 94, 96–97, 108, 109–11, 114–15, 120, 122, 123–24, 126–27, 129–30, 132–33, 135–36, 153–54, 155, 158–59, 170, 174, 180–81, 189–90, 191–92
  common criminals as inmates in, 114, 122, 160–61, 176, 211
  compulsory labor in, 7, 71–72, 73–74, 77–78, 80, 81, 84, 89–91, 98–99, 101, 104–6, 107–8, 116, 121–22, 148–49, 151, 152–53, 170–71, 180–81
  confiscation of religious literature in, 179–81, 205, 215–16
  conversions to Christianity in, 112–13, 132–33, 159–62, 174, 188–91, 207–8, 210–11, 222
  crises of faith in, 84–87, 92–93, 102, 103–4, 119, 132–34, 136, 159, 162–64, 188–89, 200–2, 206
  ecumenism at, 74–75, 90, 136–37, 170, 174, 184, 189–90
  establishment during late 1920s of, 4, 71, 90–91
  family member visits to, 185–86, 210
  former Russian Orthodox properties used as camp sites for, 14, 16
  guards and administrators in, 72, 81–82, 90–91, 92–93, 106–7, 123–24, 126–27, 128–30, 131–32, 137–38, 144–45, 151, 153–54, 159, 177, 180–83, 204–6, 214–15, 220–21
  informants in, 89–91, 101, 102, 109–10
  Khrushchev's reforms to, vii–viii, 146–47, 149, 153–54, 176
  letters from family members to, 196, 210
  memorial sites marking legacy of, 226
  Orthodox chapels established after 1990 in, 203
  overall death toll in, 72
  overall number of prisoners in, 7–8, 72, 104–5, 119, 146, 176, 210
  petitioning for freedom of religion during Brezhnev era in, 191
  postwar era (1945-1950) in, 104
  publications produced in, 71–72, 78–81, 95

  re-education initiatives at, 71–73, 75, 77–78, 80, 90–91, 105, 106–7, 146, 152, 159, 167, 175, 182, 195–96, 204–5
  religious dietary needs in, 81–82
  religious faith as source of strength in, 86–88, 90, 92–93, 96–99, 102–3, 108, 110, 111–13, 114–16, 119, 122–25, 128, 135, 159–60, 161–62, 163–64, 169–70, 176, 183–84, 186–87, 188–90, 197–200, 201–2, 205, 207, 210, 217
  religious tattoos in, 107–8, 121, 138–39, 141–45, 143f
  remote locations of, 6–7, 76–77
  sex and sexual assault in, 103–4
  United Nations Congress on the Prevention of Crime and the Treatment of Offenders (1955) and, 147–48
  uprisings of 1953-1954 in, 154–55
  World War II and, 92, 99
  See also specific camps
Gulag Museum (Moscow), 228

Harmon, Joe, 219
Hartfeld, Hermann, 188
Helsinki Accords (1975), 192–93
Herling, Gustaw, 134–36
Herlyuk-Kupchynsky, Petro, 129–30, 132–33
Hodiak, Olha, 129
Horchynska, Vanda, 125, 130

Ilarion (Russian Orhtodox archbishop), 58–60, 61–62, 63f, 66, 67
Iliodor (Russian Orthodox archimandrite), 96–97
Ivanov, Vaska, 46
Ivanovich, Vasily, 110
Ivanovsky Camp, 17

Jehovah's Witnesses
  antireligious suppression targeting, 168
  bullying in gulag camps against, 151
  Catholics' conflicts with, 174
  compulsory labor in gulag camps and, 170
  as conscientious objectors to religious service, 210
  crises of faith in gulag camps and, 159
  at Dubravny Camp, 166–68, 171–74
  group solidarity and discipline among, 171–73
  proselytization efforts in gulag camps by, 132, 151, 152, 171, 173–74
  proselytization in Russian Empire by, 9
  re-education initiatives and, 167

INDEX 259

religion as a source of inspiration in gulag
    camps for, 158
Russian Federation's restrictions after 1991
    against, 224–25
Ukranian nationalists' problems with, 173
The Watchtower magazine and, 166–
    68, 172–73
Jews
    antireligious policies in gulag camps
        targeting, 179
    anti-Semitism in gulag camps and, 143–45
    Mask of Sorrow monument and, 226
    overall number in Russian Empire of, 9–10
    religious tattoos in gulag camps displayed
        by, 144
    Sabbath observance in prison camps and, 21
John Chrysostom (saint), 54–55
John XXIII (pope), 146–47
Josephite clerics, 66–67

Kabo, Vladimir, 115
Kalinin, V., 214
Kappes, A. N., 94
Karagandinsky Camp, 94–95, 106–7, 116
Karpenko, Denis, 181
Kaufman, Walter, 107–8, 113
Kazansky Monastery, 17
Kennedy, John F., 146–47
Khajbulin, Varsonofy, 190
Kharchev, Konstantin, 208
Khlysts, 9
Khmara, Stepan, 209
Khorev, Mikhail, 185–86, 197–98, 201–2
Khrushchev, Nikita
    antireligious propaganda under, 146–47
    antireligious repression under, 146–47
    ascent to power of, 146
    gulag reforms under, vii–viii, 146–47, 149,
        153–54, 176
    political liberalization under, 146
    religious observance in gulag camps during
        rule of, 153
Kirill (Russian Orthodox patriarch), 224–25
Kirillo-Novoozersk Monastery, 76–77
Kirov, Sergey, 93
Kiselev-Gromov, Nikolay, 47–48
Klassen, David, 182–83
Klimanova, Lyudmila, 170–71, 173, 174
Klinger, Anton, 42–43, 49–50, 64
Kogan, Lazar, 81–82
Kolyma Tales (Shalamov), 108
Kopelev, Lev, 109–10
Koroblyov, Nikolai, 218

Kostyuchenko, G. V., 188–89
Kotsur, Anna, 125
Kotsylovsky, Yosofat, 132–33
Kovrovskaya Prison, 25
Kozlov, Vasily, 112–13, 193–94
Krakhmalnikova, Zoya, 201–2, 207
Krasnopevtsev, Lev, 169–70
Kryukovsky Corrective-Labor Colony, 148
Kuloisky Camp, 95–96
Kureishi, Said, 43–44
Kuzin, Anatoly, 158

Latvia, 9, 120
Latvian Christian Mission of Mercy, 210–11
Latvian prisoners in gulag camps, 121, 143,
    144, 185
League of Militant Atheists, 10
Lelekach, Ivan, 128
Lelyukhin (Russian Orthodox deacon), 64
Lenin, Vladimir
    antireligious policies and, 1–2, 10, 29
    death of, 3, 70
    economic socialism and, 3
    imprisonment by tsarist regime of, 5
    New Economic Policy and, 3
    tattoos in gulag camps depicting, 141, 142–43
Leonardovich, Mechislav, 51
Leshchenko-Sukhomlina, Tatyana, 130
Levitin-Krasnov, Anatoly, 111–12, 187–88, 191
Levitsky, Vladimir, 87
Likhachev, Dmitry, 1–2, 43, 54, 59–60, 61–
    62, 66–67
Lipper, Elena, 96, 108, 113, 121–22
Lithuania, 9, 120
Living Church, 11, 62, 64–65, 75–76, 88, 111–12
Losev, Aleksey, 85–87
Lugar, Richard, 208
Lutherans, 9–10, 123–24, 132, 144–45

Majoraité, Regina, 155–56
Maksim (Russian Orthodox bishop), 60–61,
    63–64, 66, 67
Marchenko, Anatoly, 166, 168, 169–70, 191
Marchenko, Zoya, 97, 122–23
Marhitych, Volodymyr, 168–69
Markus, Sergei, 206
Martsinkovsky, Vladimir, 27–28, 32
Marx, Karl, 5, 10, 27, 43–44, 142–43
Marxism-Leninism, 1, 29, 70, 137–38, 150–51,
    159–60, 190
Mashkov, Yuri, 159–60
Mask of Sorrow monument, 226, 227f
Matrosskaya Tishina prison, 27, 203

260 INDEX

Matyukhin, Sergey, 214–15
May Day holiday, 74
Men, Alexander, 206–7
Mennonites, 9, 123–24
Mikhalkov, Yuri Ivanovich, 195–96
Mitrotsky, Mikhail, 57–58
Moldova, 120–21
Moldovan prisoners in gulag camps, 121, 145, 171
Molokans, 9
Monument to the Fallen and Murdered in the East (Warsaw), 226
Moroz, Valentyn, 173
Moscow (Russia)
  1st Moscow Labor Colony and, 31
  Butyrka Prison and, 29, 220–21
  Moscow Women's Correctional House and, 31–32
  Russian Orthodox sites converted into penal facilities in, 17–19
  Taganskaya Prison and, 27, 28, 32
Mother of God icons, 88, 157f
Muslims
  antireligious propaganda directed at, 79, 150–51
  hostility in gulag camps toward, 144–45
  Mask of Sorrow monument and, 226
  mosques built in gulag sites by, 218–19
  overall number in Russian Empire of, 9–10
  Ramadan holiday and, 79
  suppression of, 11–12
Mykhailikha, Andriy, 132–33

Navalny, Alexei, 225–26
Nazi-Soviet Pact of 1939, 120
New Economic Policy, 3
New Solovki (prison camp newspaper), 47, 78–79
Nicholas II (tsar of Russia), 5, 8–9
Nikolay (archpriest in Josephite movement), 66
Nikonov-Smorodin, Mikhail, 60
Noble, John, 116, 123–24, 132
Nogtev, Aleksander, 49, 51–52
Novikov-Halikovsky, Viktor, 132–33
Novospassky Monastery, 19–20, 20f
NVKD. See secret police (NVKD)

Ogorodnikov, Aleksandr, 187–88, 200–2, 205–7
Old Believers, 9–10, 40–41, 83, 116–19, 166, 170–71
Olekhnovich, Franz, 46
One Day in the Life of Ivan Denisovich (Solzhenitsyn), vii–viii, 108, 109

Onezhsky penal camp, 95–96
"On the Freedom of Confession" (Soviet law, 1990), 212–13
Oreshin, Gennady, 220–21
Orhtodox Church. See Russian Orthodox Church
Orlov Province, 23–24
Osipov, Vladimir, 169–70, 171–73
Ozerny Camp, 158–59, 165

Panin, Dmitri, 102–3, 122
Pashnin-Speransky, E. I., 179, 183
Paul (saint), 197, 199, 201
Pavlovna, Tatyana, 92
Pelekh, Evhen, 129–30
Pentecostals
  Brezhnev era gulag camps and, 177, 178, 181, 182, 189
  bullying in gulag camps of, 101–2
  conversions in gulag camps and, 151
  Gorbachev era religious reforms and proselytization in gulag camps by, 216
  re-education initiatives and, 167
  religion as a source of strength in gulag camps among, 197
  religious services in gulag camps and, 156–58
  Soviet regime's suppression of, 146–47
  See also Baptists
Penza Provincial Correctional Home, 32, 34, 39
People's Commissariat of Justice, 6, 22–23, 38
Perchatkin, Boris, 179
Perm penal camps, 179, 191–92, 211
Petkevich, Tamara, 103, 122
Petr (Russian Orhtodox archbishop), 58–60, 62, 64
Petrov, Aleksey, 45, 56–57
Petrus, K., 89–90
Piskanovsky, Nikolay, 59–60
Pitirim, Hegumen, 58–59
Plutser-Sarno, Alexei, 141–42
Pokrovsky Convent, 18–19
Pokrovsky Monastery, 17
Poland, 9–10, 75, 120, 124
Polish prisoners in gulag camps, 121, 122, 124, 125–27, 130–31, 133, 134–35, 144, 145, 226
Polsky, Mikhail, 44, 58–59, 61, 64–65
Popov, Ivan, 64–65
Pospelov (Russian Orthodox archpriest), 64
Prokopy (Russian Orthodox archbishop), 62, 64–65
Pryadilov, Aleksey, 139
Psalm 137, 86

Pshenitsynaya, T. M., 196
punishment and discipline in prison camps
  capital punishment and, 49–50, 54, 60–61,
    68, 87, 108–9
  compulsory labor infractions and, 49–50, 99,
    108–9, 116, 184
  corporal punishment and, 50, 68, 73–74, 89–
    90, 133–34, 181, 205–6, 215–16
  counterrevolutionary activity as a cause for,
    89–90
  religious activity as a cause for, 89
Putin, Vladimir, 224–25, 226–28
Puzyrev, Mikhail, 121–22

Quakers, 4–5, 77

Rabinovich, Mikhail, 132, 139–40
Ratushinskaya, Irina
  on ecumenism in gulag camps, 189
  pardon and release from the gulag (1986) of,
    208, 209f
  on prayer in gulag camps, 186–87
  on punishment in gulag camps, 205–6
  on religious holidays in gulag camps, 184–85
  on religious objects in gulag camps, 179
Razveyev, Boris, 206–7
Rechnoy Camp, 154–55
Red Army, 23, 109, 120
religious observance in prison camps
  Bible reading and, 97, 110, 115, 214–15
  fasting and, 27
  prayer and, 27, 54–55, 60–61, 88, 95–96,
    97–98, 102–3, 108, 109, 110–11, 121–24,
    125–26, 134–35, 136–37, 155, 170–71,
    178–79, 181, 182–83, 185–88, 189–90, 200,
    207–8, 218
  religious objects and, 116, 117f, 118f, 127–30,
    128f, 149, 155–56, 157f, 179
  rules and regulations during early Soviet
    regime regarding, 22–23, 26, 51–52
  singing and, 27, 28, 88, 90–91, 96–98, 99,
    108–9, 114, 122–24, 130–32, 137–38, 156–
    58, 172, 184, 185, 207–8, 217
  See also religious services in prison camps
religious services in prison camps
  baptisms and, 59–60, 61
  Catholics and, 14, 21, 53, 126, 130–31
  Christmas and, 88, 130–31, 135, 153–54,
    155f, 170, 185, 189–90
  clerical inmates and, 27, 28, 51–53,
    57, 109–10
  communion services and, 29, 53, 59–60, 88–
    89, 123–24, 125–26, 184, 185

confessions and, 61
Easter and, 24, 28, 40, 52–53, 55–56, 58–59,
  84, 88, 89–90, 97–98, 109–10, 114, 130,
  131–32, 153–54, 156f, 185, 189–90
Epiphany and, 185
funding for, 25–26
Holy Week ceremonies and, 24–25
inmate attendance levels at, 23–25
last rites and, 38
Pentecost and, 220
permission to attend off-site religious
  services and, 26, 51–53, 107
Revelation (New Testament book), 11–12, 120
Reykjavik Summit (1986), 208
Rogalskaya, Dora, 116
Romanyuk, Vasily, 179
Ronkin, Valery, 166, 168, 169–70, 171–72, 173
Rotfort, Mikhail, 96–97
Rozhdestvenny Convent, 17
Rusak, Vladimir, 207
Russian civil war (1918-1921), 1, 3, 5–6,
  16, 17, 22
Russian Orthodox Church
  Gorbachev era religious reforms and
    proselytization in gulag camps by, 216, 220
  Great Terror and, 93–94
  Living Church and, 11, 62, 64, 65
  as official religion of Russian Empire, 8
  Old Believers schism and, 40–41
  one-thousand year anniversary (1988) of,
    209
  parish schools operated by, 8–9
  prison camps established on former
    properties of, 14, 16
  return of Soviet-appropriated properties after
    1991 to, 223
  Russian Federation's cultivation of ties after
    1991 with, 224–25
  Russian nationalism and, 8–9
  secret police efforts to discredit, 206–7
  Soviet regime's confiscation of properties of,
    23, 70–71
  Soviet regime's temporary reconciliation
    (1941-1953) with, 99–100, 105
  suppression of, 10, 11–12
Rybinsk Correctional Home, 31–32

Sabbatarians, 107–8, 136–37
Sadkovsky, Ignaty, 42–43
Sadunaite, Nijole, 180, 182–83, 184
Sakharov, Andrey, 191
Savino-Storozhevsky Monastery, 18
Scientology, 225

262 INDEX

secret police (KGB, after 1954)
   coercion of religious gulag prisoners and, 186, 194–95, 206–7
   Russian Orthodox Church infiltrated by, 146–47
secret police (NKVD, before 1954)
   Great Terror and, 93–94
   Gulag administration and, 4, 71–72, 89–90
   labor camps established by, 6–7
   Living Church and, 11
   monitoring of religious groups during World War II by, CROSS
   religious prisoners and, 10
   Russian Orthodox properties seized by, 70–71
   Soviet annexation of Baltic territories and, 120
Sederkholm, Boris, 45–46
Senderov, Valeri, 205
Senkyvskyi, Volodymyr, 128–29
Sergius (Russian Orhtodox metropolitan), 11–12, 64–66, 67, 99–100
Sergiusites (Russian Orthodox bishops), 65–66, 67
Seventh-Day Adventists
   compulsory labor in gulag camps and, 49–50, 107–8
   Gorbachev era religious reforms and proselytization in gulag camps by, 218
   proselytization in Russian Empire by, 9
   religious texts reproduced in gulag camps by, 169
Sgovio, Thomas, 110, 141
Shalamov, Varlam, 108–9, 139
Shamanism, 9–10
Shaufelberger, Arnold, 61
Shiraev, Boris, 59–60
Shnyrka, Agafya, 178
Shostenko, Nadezhda, 193
Shults, Vera, 92
Shumuk, Danylo, 166, 171, 172–73, 174–75
Siberian exile (tsarist era), 4, 5, 6–7
Sibirsky Camp, 81–82, 88
Sikorski-Mayski agreement, 134–35
Skachkov, Petr, 84
Skoptsy sect, 9
Slipy, Yosyf, 146–47, 168–69
Smirnov, Vasily, 83–84
Smith, Chris, 211
Sokolniki house of correction, 27, 203
Solomon, Michael, 115, 152–53
Solonevich, Boris, 39, 68
Solovki (Solovetsky Camp of Forced Labor of Special Significance, SLON)
   antireligious propaganda at, 45–47, 68

antireligious repression after 1927 at, 73–74, 75
Baptist prisoners at, 61–62
Catholic prisoners at, 42–43, 47–48, 53, 61–62, 73–75, 94
clerical prisoners at, 40, 42–43, 44–45, 47–49, 51–53, 57–68, 63f, 73–75, 94
common criminals as inmates at, 42, 45, 53
compulsory labor at, 42, 48
conflict among different Christian sects in, 61, 68
counterrevolutionary prisoner population at, 42–43, 44–45
decentralization and desecration of religious spaces at, 43–45
ecumenism suppressed at, 74–75
establishment (1923) of, 41–42
Great Terror (1937-1938) and, 94
guards and administrators at, 45, 49, 51, 61, 68
Jewish prisoners at, 42–43
Living Church and, 64
location of, 39
as "model camp" for domestic and international audiences, 39, 68, 71–72
monastery originally located on site of, 39, 40–44, 41f, 68–69, 76–77
as most populous prison camp of 1920s, 39, 41–42
Muslim prisoners at, 42–43
political prisoner population at, 42
prison publications at, 46–47
punishment and discipline at, 49–50, 68
re-education initiatives at, 75
religious conversions at, 53–54
religious services and celebrations at, 40, 51–53, 55–56, 57–58, 59–60, 66–67, 68–69
restoration of monasteries at former site of, 228–29
Russian Orthodox community tensions in, 62
Russian Orthodox prisoners at, 42, 43, 44–45
Solovki propaganda film and, 49–50, 52
violence at, 42, 47–48, 73–74
Solzhenitsyn, Aleksandr, vii, 104, 108, 127, 191
Sooster, Lidia, 107
Spaso-Vlakhernsky Convent, 18
Spaso-Voznesensky Monastery, 44–45
Spassky Monastery, 17
Sporov, Boris, 168–69
Stakhanovite movement, 70
Stalin, Joseph
   antireligious policies under, 70–71, 92–93
   antireligious propaganda under, 71, 79

ascent to power of, 3, 70
death of, 4, 92–93, 146, 148–49, 152, 153–54
five-year plans proclaimed by, 70
Great Terror and, 92, 93
Gulag system established (1929) by, 4, 90–91
Gulag system's massive scope and lethality under, 7, 176, 180–81, 228
Soviet hegemony in Eastern Europe and, 104
tattoos in gulag camps depicting, 142–43
World War II and, 99–100
Stasiv-Kalynets, Iryna, 185
Stepnoy Camp, 154–55
Superfin, Gabriel, 179
Svirsky Camp, 86–87
Svyanevich, Stanislav, 125–26
Syzran prison camps, 24–25

Taganskaya Prison, 27, 28, 32
Tamkevicius, Sigitas, 210
Tartinsky, Victor, 190
tattoos, 107–8, 121, 138–39, 141–45, 143*f*
Temnikovsky Camp, 116
Temple of the New Martyrs and Confessors of Russians, 226–28, 228*f*
Terelya, Josyp, 151, 156–58, 182–83, 188, 197, 206
Tikhon (Russian Orthodox patriarch), 11–12, 64–65
To Be Preserved Forever (Kopelev), 109–10
Tolstaya, Alexandra, 19, 21
Tolstoy, Leo, 150–51, 163–64, 178, 189–90
Tomsk Correctional-Labor House, 31–32, 212–13
Trinity Monastery of St. Sergius, 19, 40–41
Trotsky, Leon, 27, 43–44, 70
Trubitsyn, Vladimir, 223
True Orthodox Church
Brezhnev era gulag camps and, 184
in Dubravny camp, 170
Gorbachev era religious reforms and proselytization in gulag camps by, 216
Great Terror and, 94–95
Gulag uprisings of 1953-1954 and, 155
Josephite clerics and, 66
secret bishops in, 67
Sergiusites bishops and, 67
Tsaritsyn House of Correction, 33
Tsybran, Stepan, 158–59
Tula Province, 24

Ugrimov, Aleksandr, 113–14
Ukraine, 3, 95–96, 152

Ukrainian Greek Catholics (Uniates)
crises of faith in gulag camps and, 133
Gulag uprisings of 1953-1954 and, 155
prayer in gulag camps by, 136, 182–83, 188
proselytization in gulag camps and, 132–33
religion as source of strength in gulag camps among, 197
religious objects in gulag camps and, 128–30
religious services in gulag camps and, 156–58
Roman Catholic Church and, 9
Russian Orthodox gulag prisoners' relations with, 158–59
Soviet abolition of, 120
See also Catholics
Ukranian prisoners in gulag camps, 121–23, 125, 130, 131–32, 145, 154, 155–56, 161, 171
Union of Militant Atheists, 95–96
United Nations Congress on the Prevention of Crime and the Treatment of Offenders (1955), 147–48
United Nations' Universal Declaration of Human Rights, 191–92
Usoyeva, Nadia, 184
Ustvymsky Camp, 105–6
Utevsky, Boris, 77

Vagin, Yevgeny, 189–91
Vail, Boris, 169–70
Vasylyk, Pavlo, 132–33
Verblovskaya, Irina, 158
Viktor (Russian Orhtodox bishop), 59–60, 63–64, 66–67
Vinogradov, Nikolai, 46
Vins, Georgi, 178–79, 183–84, 185–86, 188, 194–95, 195*f*, 199–200
Vins, Lidia, 180
Vins, Nadezhda, 194–95
Viola, Lynne, 82
Vladimir (Russian prince), 8, 204
Vladimir Prison, 168, 170–71, 179, 191–92
Vlasov, Anatoly, 189
The Voice of the Prisoner newspaper, 34–37, 39
Volkov, Oleg, 52–53, 60
Volkov, Victor, 217
Volovich, Hava, 103–4, 139
Vtorova-Yafa, Olga, 44, 74–75
Vudka, Yuri, 180
Vyazma (Russia), 1
Vyshinsky, Andrey, 77

Walter, Anton, 99
White Army prisoners (Russian civil war), 5–6, 17, 42, 73

264   INDEX

Wolf, Frank, 211
World War II
    All-Union Council of Evangelical Christians
      and Baptists and, 99–100
    antireligious propaganda in gulag camps
      during, 100–1
    antireligious suppression in gulag camps
      during, 101
    bullying of religious prisoners during,
      101–2
    crises of faith during, 102, 103–4
    deportations of ethnic groups from Russia to
      Central Asia during, 99
    German occupation of Soviet territory
      during, 100
    prisoners of war in the Soviet Union during,
      125–26
    religious faith as source of strength in gulag
      camps during, 102–3, 136
    secret police monitoring of religious groups
      during, 101
    size of religious population in gulag camps
      during, 100
    Soviet annexation of territory in, 120
    Soviet death toll in, 92, 99

    Soviet regime's temporary reconciliation
      with Orthodox Church during, 99–100
    Soviet victory in, 104

Yakimenko, Yuri, 160
Yakir, Petr, 96–97
Yakunin, Gleb, 179, 209, 220–21, 221f
Yaroslavl (Russia), 17, 23–24, 32
Yarotsky, Aleksey, 84–85
Yasnopolskaya, Valentina, 82, 85
Yeltsin, Boris, 224–25
Yurkevich, Yury, 110
Yuvenaly (Russian Orthodox archbishop), 48–
    49, 81–82, 87, 211

Zaitsev, Ivan, 45, 47–49, 51–52, 54
Zalivako, Boris, 189–90, 191–92
Zarod, Kazimierz, 130–31, 133
Zdorovets, B. M., 181
Zheludkov, Sergei, 191
Zhigulin, Anatoly, 115
Zosima (saint), 43, 45
Zosimovsky Convent, 18–19
Zotov, Vladimir, 59–60
Zvenigorod (Russia), 18